RELIGION OF THE

RELIGION OF THE ROMANS

JÖRG RÜPKE

Translated and edited by Richard Gordon

polity

First published in German as *Die Religion der Römer* by Jörg Rüpke © Verlag C. H. Beck, München 2001.

This English translation © Polity Press, 2007

Polity Press
65 Bridge Street
Cambridge CB2 1UR, UK.

Polity Press
350 Main Street
Malden, MA 02148, USA

ISBN-13: 978-07456-3015-1
ISBN-13: 978-07456-3014-4 (pb)

A catalogue record for this book is available from the British Library.

Typeset in 10.5 on 12 pt Sabon
by Servis Filmsetting Ltd, Manchester
Printed and bound in India by Replika Press PVT Ltd, Kundli.

For further information on Polity, visit our website: www.polity.co.uk

The translation of this work was supported by a grant from the Goethe-Institut that is funded by the Ministry of Foreign Affairs.

For Ulrike

CONTENTS

CONTENTS

ILLUSTRATIONS

FOREWORD

For help in writing this book I am indebted to many different people in many different ways. Its completion affords me a welcome occasion to express my thanks.

I have been able to discuss individual points with Christoph Auffarth (Bremen), Ulrike Egelhaaf-Gaiser (Gießen), Christoph Markschies (Humboldt Universität, Berlin), Mareile Haase (Toronto), Kocku von Stuckrad (Amsterdam) and especially Andreas Bendlin (Erindale College, University of Toronto), and have thereby learned a great deal; the results are visible at various points in the book. I owe many fundamental insights into Roman religion – far more than is visible in the literature cited in the bibliography – to Hubert Cancik and Burkhard Gladigow (Berlin and Tübingen).

Bärbel Geyer and Silke Kamp (Potsdam) typed the original draft; Diana Püschel and Franca Fabricius (Erfurt) edited the final manuscript. I am most grateful to them all.

Thanks are also due to my editor at Beck-Verlag, Stefan von der Lahr, for having suggested the project in the first place and patiently followed its various phases of gestation in Tübingen, Constance, Potsdam and finally Erfurt. His numerous suggestions have been of great help.

I am very pleased that Polity has agreed to make this book available to an English-speaking audience. This has given me the opportunity to expand the final chapter and add fairly extensive notes and a consolidated bibliography. The process of translation has resulted in a thorough-going revision. Richard Gordon has not only made many suggestions concerning details and pointed out unclarities but in innumerable places he has also improved the argument, added references, or forced me by his objections to alter the point I was originally

xi

making. This experience has not always been pleasurable, but it has been extremely helpful in improving the book as a whole. In the end, though, I take responsibility for the factual mistakes that remain despite his efforts.

I would like to thank John Scheid and Nicole Belayche (Paris), Dorothee Elm von der Osten (Freiburg i/B), Ian Henderson (Montreal) and Katharina Waldner (Erfurt) for their ideas and suggestions regarding the final chapter. However my special thanks for many lively discussions about Roman religion over several years now go once again to Andreas Bendlin, my former colleague here in Erfurt, now in Toronto.

ABBREVIATIONS

AE	*L'Année épigraphique*
AHAW	Abhandlungen der Heidelberger Akademie der Wissenschaften
ANRW	H. Temporini and W. Haase (eds), *Aufstieg und Niedergang der römischen Welt* (Berlin: W. de Gruyter, 1972 –)
BEFAR	Bibliothèque de l'École française d'Athènes et de Rome
CIL	*Corpus Inscriptionum Latinarum* (Berlin, 1863 –)
CIMRM	M. J. Vermaseren, *Corpus inscriptionum et monumentorum religionis Mithriacae* (The Hague: Martinus Nijhoff, 1956–60)
CStipiVot	*Corpus delle stipi votive in Italia* (Rome: G. Bretschneider, 1994 –)
EPROER	Études préliminaires aux religions orientales dans l'Empire romain (Leyden: Brill, 1961–1999). Became RGRW
FGrH	F. Jacoby et al., *Die Fragmente der griechischen Historiker* (Leyden: Brill, 1923 –)
FRH	H. Beck and U. Walter (eds), *Die frühen römischen Historiker*, 2 vols. Texte zur Forschung, 76–77 (Darmstadt: Wissenschaftliche Buchgesellschaft, 2001–04)
GGR	M. P. Nilsson, *Geschichte der griechischen Religion*, I 3rd edn., II 2nd edn. Handbuch

	der Altertumswissenschaft 5.1-2 (Munich: Beck, 1967, 1961)
HABES	Heidelberger Althistorische Beiträge und Epigraphische Studien
Helbig[4] I–IV	W. Helbig, *Führer durch die öffentlichen Sammlungen der Stadt Rom*[4], ed. H. Speier (Tübingen: Wasmuth, 1963–72)
HrwG	H. Cancik, B. Gladigow and M. Laubscher (eds), *Handbuch religionswissenschaftlicher Grundbegriffe*, 5 vols (Stuttgart: Kohlhammer, 1988–2001)
IG	*Inscriptiones Graecae* (Berlin 1903 –)
IGUR	L. Moretti, *Inscriptiones Graecae Urbis Romae*. Studi pubbl. dall' Istituto italiano per la Storia, 17 (Rome, 1968–90)
ILLRP	A. Degrassi (ed.), *Inscriptiones Latinae Liberae Rei Publicae*. 2 vols. Biblioteca dei Studi Superiori, 23 and 40 (Florence: La Nuova Italia Editrice, 1957–63)
ILS	H. Dessau (ed.), *Inscriptiones Latinae Selectae*. 3 vols. in 5 (Berlin: Weidmann, 1892–1916; repr. 1954–55; Chicago: Ares, 1979)
InscrIt	*Inscriptiones Italiae* (Rome, 1931 –)
Lewis & Reinhold	N. Lewis and M. Reinhold (eds), *Roman Civilization, 1: The Republic; II: The Empire* (New York: Columbia University Press, 1951; repr. New York: Harper Torchbooks, 1966)
LTUR	M. Steinby (ed.), *Lexicon Topographiae Urbis Romae*, 6 vols (Rome: Quasar, 1993–2000)
LTUR Suburb	A. La Regina (ed.), *Lexicon Topographiae Urbis Romae: Suburbium* (Rome: Quasar, 2001 –)
MDAI(R)	*Mitteilungen des Deutschen Archäologischen Instituts, Römische Abteilung*
PAwB	Potsdamer Altertumswissenschaftliche Beiträge
PCPhS	*Proceedings of the Cambridge Philological Society*
POxy	*The Oxyrhynchus Papyri* (London: Egypt Exploration Society, 1902 –)

RfAC	*Reallexikon für Antike und Christentum* (Stuttgart: Anton Hiersemann, 1950 –)
RE	*Paulys Real-Encyclopädie der classischen Altertumswissenschaft* (Stuttgart/Weimar/Munich, 1894–1980)
RGRW	Religions in the Graeco-Roman World (Leyden: Brill, 1999 –)
RIC	H. Mattingly, E.A. Sydenham et al. (eds), *The Roman Imperial Coinage* (London: Spink and Son, 1923–81, reprinting 2001–)
RRC	M. H. Crawford, *Roman Republican Coinage* (Cambridge: Cambridge University Press, 1974)
SBAW	Sitzungsberichte der Bayerischen Akademie der Wissenschaften
Syll.	W. Dittenberger, *Sylloge Inscriptionum Graecarum* 3rd edn. (Leipzig: S. Hirzel, 1915–24; repr. Hildesheim: G. Olms, 1982)
WLS	B. Campbell (ed., tr., comm.), *The Writings of the Roman Land-Surveyors*. JRS Monographs, 9 (London: Society for the Promotion of Roman Studies, 2000)

Prolegomena

— 1 —

RELIGION IN THE ANCIENT WORLD

An Example

Take this poem by Horace:

> O Venus regina Cnidi Paphique,
> sperne dilectam Cypron et uocantis
> ture te multo Glycerae decoram
> transfer in aedem.
>
> Feruidus tecum puer et solutis
> Gratiae zonis properentque Nymphae
> et parum comis sine te Iuuentas
> Mercuriusque.
>
> Venus, queen of Cnidus and Paphos, Venus
> quit your chosen Cyprus and heed Glycera's
> call, with teeming incense, to take her pleasant
> shrine for your dwelling.
> Swiftly come with you the impetuous boy and
> Graces streaming open their robes, the Nymphs and
> Youth, so little gracious without you here,
> and Mercury also.
>
> (Horace, *Odes* 1.30, tr. S. Willett)

Such a text hardly needs commentary; but still, here goes. It is, obviously enough, a prayer; more precisely, a sung prayer: *hymnus*. The addressee is Venus. Texts of this type, that summon divinities from afar, or from high above, are called invocations. The reverent tone is unmistakable: a 'pleasant shrine'; the air perfumed with incense . . . And yet, on reflection, it can hardly in fact be the sort of hymn that might have been sung at a public ritual. For Venus, whom we know

3

to be the goddess of Love, is addressed as Queen of Cnidus and Paphos, two cities of Cyprus, the spot where Aphrodite first set foot on land.[1] 'Quit your chosen Cyprus' shows that the goddess is still there, and is to 'heed Glycera's call, with teeming incense, to take her pleasant shrine for her dwelling'. We know, of course, that this is a poem by the lyric poet Horace; and we know too, from earlier poems in Book 1 of the *Odes*, that Glycera is no goddess with a sanctuary in Rome that Venus might visit, but a friend of Horace's, with whom he is represented as having a sexual relation.[2] Her 'pleasant shrine' is thus not a religious building at all, but simply the house, or the room, where she happens now to be.

The rest of the poem tallies with this. Amor, 'the impetuous boy', is to attend Venus, as are the Graces, those three cadgy divinities rendered still more alluring by the fact that their robes, skimpy at the best of times, hint at joys inexpressible. The Nymphs are divine beings who are likewise regularly portrayed dancing, but, unlike the Graces, entirely nude. Then comes Iuventas, Youth, a divinity representing Greek Hebe, who replenishes the goblets of the gods on Olympus: she is responsible for the wine. Lastly comes Mercury. This must be the punch-line; but quite what the point is remains uncertain. Assuming that this Mercury is, as often at Rome, the god of gain, of commercial profit, the suggestion might be that Glycera is in fact a prostitute, so that her passion, being purchased, is not quite all it purports to be. On the other hand, Mercury here may be, as he generally is elsewhere in Horace, the god of cultivated conversation. In that case, the speaker, after evoking an entire erotic scenario through the prayer-form, says in effect: I really do appreciate all your effort, Glycera, but let's first talk, and listen to some music (Rüpke 1998a).

A text such as this vividly illustrates the problems faced by anyone working and writing on ancient religion, in our case, on Roman religion. We reconstruct meanings from texts written in a language and tone that are sometimes elusive, or at least indeterminate (the situation may in fact not have been very much different for contemporaries). We reconstruct the culture of an entire period from statements or claims made by individuals; we treat as 'sources' voices that have come down to us in often devious ways, to whom it would never occur to state simply and directly what they meant; for they were of their time, of particular times and particular places, skilled in the art of innuendo. This must give us pause, but has too its own special value: for, at the outset of the twenty-first century, it is no longer convincing to think of 'culture' in a normative fashion, in terms, say, of middle-class behavioural norms that hold society together. Instead, we think of culture anthropologically, as a chaotic system whose structures are context-bound shards – often, to be sure, astonishingly effective shards – a system in which individual exaggerations, alternatives and misunderstandings constitute the rule rather than the exception; a system, finally, whose functions are clear only to the Cassandras of crisis, ever-ready to bewail the failure of those functions in their own day.[3]

Horace's hymn is not an official liturgical text. It is nevertheless perfectly in order to start looking at Roman religion from a private, albeit published, text of this kind: it is not a parody, nor is there the slightest hint that any member of Horace's audience, or his readers, male or female, would have disapproved of it, or found anything in it objectionable from a religious point of view. An individual text such as this can thus safely be used as a basis for some preliminary observations about Roman religion and its differences from what we ordinarily understand nowadays by the notion 'religion'.

Horace's text is notable for the number of gods invoked within the space of a few lines. Religious symbols are being used for an end that is not itself sacral. Localization is also important here: the aim is not so much to universalize the gods as to concretize them. Similarly, the ritual here is conceived quite concretely. The invocation works by way of aesthetic – material – inducements: the room has been tastefully arranged, and there is incense aplenty. Above all, the divinities are invoked in deliberate combinations, some of them, such as the pairing of Venus and Amor, familiar, others, such as Iuventas and Mercury, unusual, indeed unique. In such contexts, the speaker (or the poet) is evidently free to make his or her own decisions (cf. Griffin 1997). He or she knows, or claims to know, how to match deities in particular ways for particular ends, and thus bring them to bear on this situation now.

Religion Taken for Granted

Would we call that religion? Or mis-use of religion? Either answer presupposes that one knows what religion, perhaps even 'true' religion, is. These are theological issues, however. To describe religion, say, as an 'active response by human beings to the call of the sacred', as 'experience of the numinous', or of 'power', or whatever, is, from the historian's point of view, merely to substitute a less specific term, albeit quasi-Christian or para-Christian, for the Christian God. It certainly is an interesting fact about the history of European religion that

Christian theology has cast about for a term like 'religion', by means of which it could describe itself as a special form of a much wider phenomenon (Smith 1998). But Religious Studies as a discipline is at least as indebted to Social or Cultural Anthropology and Classics as it is to Theology. It cannot therefore avoid being aware of the ideological freight of the terms it employs. 'Religion' is not an objective entity that can be established empirically. It is a term that is itself inescapably part of the history of religion (Tenbruck 1993). This does not oblige scholars to confine themselves to phenomena that themselves claim to be religious. If that were the case, there would be very few non-Christian phenomena left to study, and certainly not 'Roman religion'. We may quite properly ask whether other cultures have something comparable in form and function to our Christianized notion of 'religion'. It is the historian's business to discover whether this comparable Something is a unified whole; or has its own, different, boundaries; fulfils more or fewer functions; and then to develop the appropriate terminology. For the historian, the issue of the legitimacy or otherwise of a particular form of religion arises solely in the form of claims or judgements made by contemporaries. For the theologian, by contrast, the issue of legitimacy is central.

To be sure, religion in antiquity was familiar with all the things that are nowadays ordinarily taken to characterize religions. It knew gods and their temples (*aedes deorum*, houses of the gods), it knew holy days and priests. On the other hand, it is not easy to limit ancient religion to specific persons, times and places. I am not talking here about the casual, every-day practice of religion in the home, the offerings at meal-times, which consisted of burning at the hearth either a grain of salt, or a scrap of left-overs, or a swill of wine; nor am I talking about the small house-altars, at which again small offerings, wine, say, or a pinch of incense, were burned to celebrate special occasions such as birthdays. Such rituals differ only slightly from Christian piety (cf. Angenendt 1997: 351 ff.). And anyway, we do not know how frequently they were actually performed. What I mean, rather, is that in antiquity religious action extended to areas that are nowadays not identified as religious at all, just as it would today be unthinkable to treat, say, bilateral exchange of women between exogamous moieties, or bride-price, as legitimate forms of economic action.

Religion was particularly prominent in the political realm. The Roman Senate always met in a location that had been sacrally defined, that is, in a *templum*. As he came in, each senator burned a little incense and offered a drop of wine; and all the while an official *tibicen* played his double-'flute', *tibia*.[4] This was simply a tradition, but it was

6

one that was only questioned long after the Roman upper-class had begun to convert to Christianity, and even then the dispute, the famous controversy over the altar of Victory in AD 384, was started by an outsider, Bishop Ambrose of Milan.[5] The senior magistrates in Rome, the highest officials in the provinces, and commanders in the field all regularly performed sacrifices. Every action of any importance was prefaced and then re-confirmed by sacrifices and the taking of the auspices (in the form of observation of the flight of birds). Sacrifice and the taking of the auspices were the unquestioned preliminaries to any undertaking of significance, the declaration of war, say, or engagement in battle (Rüpke 1990: 129 f.; 147–51).

People took gods along with them on their travels: you might even take a small statue of your favourite god or goddess with you, which could be worshipped *en route*. Travelling by sea was especially risky, so ships had their own patron-gods. A ship would not named at random, but after the divinity under whose protection it sailed. The idea of the figurehead, which has a fainter religious timbre, gradually evolved from that custom (Wachsmuth 1967).

In antiquity, as in the Late Mediaeval and Early Modern periods, it was also common for the different professional associations in a town to define themselves as cultic associations. An association of bakers, say, or of leather-workers would set itself up to service the cult of a particular divinity – in the case of the bakers it would be Vesta – and to celebrate the feast-day of that divinity together. Associations that served other ends, purely convivial ends, say, or to insure individuals against the risk of failing to be properly buried (one paid a fixed sum at regular intervals into a club, to finance both burial and memorial services), were also constituted as cultic associations (Hopkins 1983: 211–17; cf. chap. 10 below). In modern terms, that would be as if trades-unions and insurance-companies were thought of as religious organizations.

However, this bond between religion and many aspects of social life does not mean that more or less everything was 'religious'. It can be shown archaeologically that some houses and tenement-blocks possessed no altar for domestic cult; and we have no right to assume that every tenant must have brought a small portable altar with him when he moved in, and took it away with him again when he cancelled the contract (cf. Bakker 1994). Normally in ancient towns there was no obligation to take part in public rituals. A glance at the dimensions of the buildings where large-scale public festivities were held makes clear that the entire population cannot possibly have taken part in such celebrations. The first explicit requirement to take part in public worship, an obligation that was truly enforced and sanctioned, is to be found in Traianus Decius' Edict of autumn/winter AD 249, at the time of the first extensive and official persecution of the Christians. Until then, no one was bound either to sacrifice or to take part in public rituals.[6] Finally, there is plenty of good evidence for consciously cynical or indifferent attitudes towards the gods, and towards religious cult. Such views can be found in works by convinced atheists and the adherents of philosophies, such as Cynicism or Epicureanism, that denied the existence of the gods or questioned their ability to act in this world.[7]

Turning to language, we can find further evidence against the view that everything was somehow connected to religion. The Latin word *sacer* of course means 'holy'; but is derived from the terminology relating to ownership.[8] Something is 'holy' if it is the property of a god or a goddess.[9] Usually this would be a plot of land on which a temple was to be built, and where in addition certain items, especially votive offerings, or statues, could be consecrated (from Latin *consecro*, though the form *consacro* is also found) and thus legally conveyed into the possession of the divinity. Of course the gods themselves cannot be 'holy' in this sense, for they cannot own themselves – such a thought verges on nonsense. The antonym of *sacer* is *profanus*, composed of two words, *pro*, 'in front of, instead of' and *fanum*, 'a piece of consecrated ground, a shrine' (from which we get the now obsolete word 'fane'). *Profanum* is everything that has its place outside the temple, outwith hallowed ground.

Another term I should mention here is *sanctus*. Like the others, it is an adjective. Think of 'saint', 'sanctify', 'sanctity', 'sanctuary', all words that in English connote holiness or making holy. By contrast, Latin *sanctus* designates a certain quality of places, but also of moveable objects. It could be used to denote the special status of the city-walls and gates, which are *res sanctae* though not divine property: *sanctum murum, qui sit circum oppidum*, 'a wall that surrounds a town is *sanctus*' (Festus p. 348.35 L.). The word could also be reinforced, and then becomes *sacrosanctus* (ablative of *sacer* + *sanctus*), a term applied, for example, to the tribunes of the people and later the emperors. Places, things and people that are *sacrosanctus* are protected by the community and are therefore inviolable. The legend of the founding of Rome offers a clear example of the rule that the life of anyone who crosses the walls without using the gates shall be forfeit. When Remus, the younger brother of Romulus, the founder of Rome, jumps over the city walls – as yet barely more than footings – in order to mock his twin, he is killed by a tribune (or, in another

8

version, by Romulus himself). This was later viewed as the beginning of violent conflict over the meaning of divinatory signs (*auspicia*), and of civil war (Livy 1.7.2).[10] But far more than that, the legend tells us that city-walls are inviolable, no matter what their height.

One last term is also familiar – *religiosus*. It too however is a false friend; it too marks the difficulty of dealing with a culture that can indeed in many ways be understood as the direct antecedent of our own civilization, but is also, in many other ways, incomprehensibly other – it is not for nothing that Roman religion is largely neglected by the History of Religions school in Chicago. For *religiosus* does not mean 'religious' in the sense of pious. The term belongs in the first instance to legal language concerned with distinctions between different types of property. *Religiosus* describes a special quality of places, especially graves, that are assigned to the dead; that are considered to be 'religious' in the sense that they deserve reverence, are not generally available to be bought and sold, and are protected from abuse or misuse by the threat of sanctions. The term remains somewhat diffuse in its wider semantic range, although non-availability to general use remains the shared characteristic. The Roman antiquarian Festus for example comments on the term *dies religiosi* as follows: *quibus, nisi quod necesse est, nefas habeatur facere*, ' "reserved" days are those on which it is forbidden by law to work or conduct business except when absolutely necessary' (p. 348.24f. L.).

One can also speak of a person as *religiosus*. People so described are pre-occupied with religious concerns and duties. In modern terms, they are the sort of people who make sure they put the right foot on the ground when they get out of bed of a morning, avoid walking underneath ladders, or regularly go to church on Sundays. The adherents of certain cults refer to themselves as *religiosi*. The nub is always the *religiones*, the feelings of commitment and religious obligation, that apply only to the individual who has taken them on, and are not considered binding upon the community as a whole. Hence *religiosus* often acquires a negative connotation; the word *superstitiosus* goes that much further, denoting someone who takes the whole religious thing too far, either out of fear or from excessive enthusiasm (*super* means 'above' or 'beyond').[11]

It would thus be only a slight exaggeration to compare religion in antiquity with eating. Both are tacitly taken for granted, 'embedded' in the habitus of a culture. We eat every day, usually without thinking much about it. You only think about it if you have not eaten for quite a while. On the other hand, food can also be stylishly prepared, become sophisticated and elaborate in its combinations of tastes, as in many of the recipes handed down under the name of Apicius. In some cases, especially when a large group is involved, eating follows very precise rules – just think of the difficulty of devising seating arrangements for a party, or deciding on the sequence of courses and the appropriate wines. Cookery-books and other aids can of course help here; but it is equally obvious that you can make, say, breakfast without any such assistance. Everyone in antiquity would have agreed that what we might call the cognitive content of eating, that is, the sum total of reflections and desires connected with eating, is smaller than the cognitive content of religion (even though we aware that gourmets do exist, who, as we say, live to eat). Religion was both taken for granted and at the same time central: the cities of antiquity acquired renown not for their libraries but for their temples. The fact that ancient religion is imbricated with other aspects of the culture, that, at the level of action, it tends to manifest itself in a diffuse rather than an organized manner, has to do with the absence of systematized instruction, with the absence of an edifice of theological reflection declared binding upon the believing community.[12] Of course religious action was the focus of ideas, questions and explanations of many kinds, and religion was the subject of discursive written treatment, but there was no official institution whose function it was to oversee such discussion. Here, however, I want only to emphasize one consequence of this fact: there was no such thing as formal religious education.

People in antiquity learned their religion through participation. Children were present at religious rituals at home and in public (at least, at some public events), and that was how they picked up the proper way to stand and pray, the songs, the signs and the sequences of action. Usually daughters accompanied and copied the role of the mother, whereas sons were taken along by their fathers (Brelich 1969). There were also youth-clubs. In these organizations religious practices were taught, or rather learned by rehearsing, songs, choruses and dances that were to be performed at public festivals.[13] These institutions, however, were not explicitly intended as means of passing on religious knowledge, nor did they manage – or even try – to reach all the young people in a township. They were small, even tiny, groups, which recruited their members from the upper-class. Nor was there any religious instruction at school. Schools only started appearing in the Latin-speaking western Mediterranean area in the Late Republic; some sort of elementary teaching was on offer in most places during the Principate.[14] But school lessons did not deal with religious matters at all. The pupils never had to copy out, say, lists of deities or prayer-formulae in the writing lessons. It is moreover worth stressing that

10

even the Christians did not challenge this strict separation of religion and school (Pack 1989), though of course in Christian contexts there was formal instruction, theological study for older people, and for grown-ups – before and after baptism – the so called catechumenate and post-baptismal instruction (preserved to us in St Ambrose's tractates *On the sacraments* and *On the mysteries*), and finally higher education in the form of philosophical schools and academies (cf. Harris 1989: 285–322; Horsfall 1991: 73–5). Analogous practices existed in pagan contexts only in mystery-cults, with their initiations preceded by various degrees of instruction. But otherwise it did not exist even to train religious specialists: they learned on the job.

From the Roman world we have just one piece of evidence for some kind of religious instruction for public cult. It occurs in a poem by the poet Statius, written at the end of the first century AD.[15] Statius reports that his father gave sons of senators instruction in religion. This instruction did not take place in Rome, however, but in Neapolis (Naples). These young people had grown up in Neapolis and had to be prepared for the political, and therefore also religious, roles – above all as members of the great priestly colleges – which they were going to play in Rome. As citizens of Magna Graecia, the largely Greek-speaking southern part of Italy, where of course Greek cult was the current form of public religious practice, they could not gain the necessary competence in Roman rituals through direct participation. We must of course be careful here, since this is the only relevant evidence, but apparently they were given some sort of religious instruction. Even so, the actual lessons were given by a rhetor, a professor of rhetoric, not by some kind of religious professional. This is comparable to what Cato the Elder does: at appropriate points in his textbook *De agri cultura*, On agriculture (mid-second century BC), he tells the reader about prayers and rituals for the conduct of business on a *latifundium*, a large-scale farm worked by slave-labour.

It would be quite wrong to deduce from the virtual absence of religious instruction that religion in antiquity was simple. The same applies to customs and usages everywhere that are maintained by oral means, which are often characterized by complicated rules for marriages, funerals or festivals. What is omnipresent is not necessarily straightforward. So once again: who knew about religion in the ancient world? Who knew how things were to be done? Was everyone present in the know? Or only a few specialists? Or particular individuals with certain roles, possibly differentiated according to gender: only the old women, only the heads of families, only the slaves of a religious group, because they always attended? We can only answer such questions indirectly, just as we have no direct access to the knowledge itself. The speculative religious ideas of individuals cannot be our yardstick. In writing a text about religion it is naturally tempting to believe we can rely mainly on texts that deal directly or overtly with religion. But in the ancient world such highly articulate reflections were restricted at most to discussions within tiny circles of the socio-political élite. In the task of reconstructing the conscious rules and strategies of normal, every-day religious life (though unfortunately here too the lack of sources limit us to dealing with the upper class), such works can only be used with extreme caution (Gladigow 1988).

Religious knowledge certainly was traditional, at Rome as elsewhere, but the traditional character of social knowledge does not mean that it is particularly stable. On the contrary: since it is conveyed by word of mouth, it is constantly endangered. Parents may die early, so that relatives in particular degrees have to fill the gap; children may die early; families may remain childless. The transmission of knowledge can so very easily be interrupted.[16] Traditional orally-transmitted knowledge is a form of knowledge that can rapidly assimilate and process new items, is flexible and adaptable, because it can only be kept vital by means of rehearsal, re-performance, in constantly-changing immediate situations. Such changes are mostly not especially registered, often are not even noticed, but may for all that be highly effective. To use Claude Lévi-Strauss' old image: even oral, 'cold', societies may on occasion become 'hot', become societies where change occurs rapidly.[17] And, finally, it is characteristic of orally-transmitted knowledge that it legitimates itself by appealing to its supposed antiquity, lives off the prestige of those who transmit it: it is formed, and deformed, by their interests and their resistance. In a world of orally-transmitted knowledge, there are always several versions in circulation, there is constant conflict between them, and it is only the continual need to act that sets limits to debate (Bendlin 2002). But when the teaching itself becomes central, texts and authoritative interpretations of them are required. The early history of Christianity is to a high degree one of interpretation, which solves conflicts by dint of exclusion: the loser in the struggle becomes a heretic, is declared a separatist, who 'chooses' his own doctrine (*hairesis* = 'choice', then 'school of belief').

The Collective Character of Religion

If one understands religion as a (loose) system of signs or symbols that help to interpret, even to construct, reality and provide orientation within this reality, then religion, like other cultural 'systems', is a collective enterprise, something shared by many individuals. Religious ideas or practices shared by just a few individuals are not thereby excluded, but they are only relevant to the issue of what religion is insofar as they are illustrative of more general features, or reveal the limits of general norms in relation to notions of divinity, say, or sexual morality. The concept of religion as a collective matter applies especially in the case of ancient religion: religion consists normally, as we shall see, in ritual action that takes place in groups. Such groups might consist of the household (*familia*), the extended family (*gens*), local communities (the town or city as a whole, its quarters, residential areas, neighbourhoods), and then also, as very commonly from the Hellenistic period, i.e. from the late fourth century BC, voluntary associations.

The predominance of ritual and the absence of autobiographical evidence in antiquity have tended to focus attention exclusively upon the group. It is often thought that there was no room for individual religiosity in antiquity, that all action was dominated by tradition, whose aim was the survival of the group; that failure to observe the rules was not seen and feared as individual 'guilt', but as disgrace in the eyes of others, as 'shame'. After all, the notion of the individual developed slowly, taking form only during the Principate and not being complete until modern times.[18] This is not wholly wrong: it serves heuristically to suggest a broad contrast with the situation in modern Europe; but it is exaggerated. Even in Archaic Greece, for example, the Bacchic mysteries and the Orphics, insofar as they can be distinguished from one another, promised individual salvation after death.[19] So the general picture needs to be nuanced, as regards details at any rate (cf. Scheid 1985a).

One obvious example of individual religiosity at Rome is Scipio Africanus, the conqueror of Carthage at the end of the Second Punic war (218–201 BC). It is reported that, from the time he began to wear the *toga virilis*, i.e. became officially adult, he used to spend hours at night praying to Jupiter Optimus Maximus in his temple. The odd thing was, he did not adopt the usual attitude of prayer, standing up with boths arms half-raised, but sat down.[20] Such accounts, whose historicity is not above suspicion, would never have entered circulation had they not suggested something about Scipio's political aspirations (which allegedly extended all the way to monarchy, hated though that word was at Rome). Yet they do also indicate what was thinkable by the end of the Republic, and no doubt much earlier. The love-poet Propertius could entertain much the same thought in relation to his beloved, whom he imagines telling Jupiter all about the serious illness she has just recovered from.[21]

A second area of individual behaviour, the whole gamut of vows (*vota*) and the corresponding votive-offerings, is known to us only through archaeology and epigraphy. If a person found him- or herself in some particular need, he or she would solemnly call upon a specific deity for help, promising to make a gift if the prayer should be answered. If it was, the person who made the vow formally gave the promised gift to the deity by consecrating it (hence the term 'ex-voto'). This act is often registered in an appropriate inscription, which enables us to identify the object concerned as a votive-offering. Reasons for making such promises varied widely, but illnesses of all kinds, and childlessness, were important grounds, as were problems in getting animals to breed successfully.

I will discuss votives in greater detail later (chap. 7 below). Here it is enough to say that these are individual concerns (even if the mass-production of votive images shows that they were very widely shared); we may assume that the promises were made, and the votives given, personally. Even if the deities and the sanctuaries that were chosen were commonly acknowledged to have particular specialisms, there was a certain measure of free choice, such that the moment chosen, and, within certain customary limits, the form of the vow, and the addressee, were all matters of personal prefer- ence. Such decisions of course did not infringe the individual's affil- iation to his or her community. At the same time, we should not forget that changes of 'natural' social group did occur in antiquity – occurred indeed on a very considerable scale. The reasons were various: they include adoption (i.e. the formal transfer from one family to another), abscondence or being exiled from one's city, and migration, voluntary and involuntary – that is, emigration, or immigration, for economic reasons, or because one had fallen into slavery. Such movements usually involved the loss of local citizenship.[22]

Thirdly, religion at Rome, as elsewhere, was connected with indi- vidual behaviour and morality. It is true that, particularly in the Republic, there was no notion of sin, of a kind that would have made it possible to view a person's entire social behaviour in the light of his or her relationship to god, and thus allowing it to be made subject to examination and sanction by the community – or, contrariwise, insu- lating it totally from such examination. Indeed, as an institution, such as 'confession', or autobiographical introspection in the manner of Augustine's *Confessions*, this kind of practice only developed in

Late Antiquity, and even then only within the Christian context.[23] Morality, 'correct behaviour', was generally justified through appeal to tradition, by reference to one's ancestors or to famous people, that is, through *exempla*: do as Regulus did, as Claudia did, as your ancestors did!

Nevertheless, the gods did take an interest in the moral behaviour of the individual, especially if it was a matter of disregard for them or their property, that is, blasphemy and temple-robbing; or the infringement of oaths and contracts; or the magic Latin word *fides*, which connotes the right to protection and the assumption of trustworthiness granted the subordinate party in many formal relations (clientship, say, or *deditio*, surrender), while not in principle infringing the right of the more powerful party to act as he thought fit.[24] But beyond that, right-minded and 'pious' behaviour (involving much more than just getting the ritual rules right) are appreciated by the gods and rewarded by having one's prayers rapidly answered. Conversely, money paid as fines was used to build temples. Whether collectively as an idea, or concretely as the owner of a shrine or the addressee of a ritual, the gods, or their earthly representatives, insisted on the need for 'good' behaviour if the political community is to endure (cf. Bendlin 2002: 91).

We must therefore not fall into the trap of playing off the collective character of religion in antiquity against those areas where individual religious feeling was decisive. We must also be wary of imagining that there was no extensive division of religious labour. Sacrifice in the context of domestic cult was conducted by the head of the family, which, during the period of time covered in this book, normally meant the oldest living male member of the family, or rather, to be precise, the oldest male member in the agnatic succession (that is, in the male line) who was present when the sacrifice was performed. In addition, the children had duties to fulfil, for example, joining in the singing or as servers, and the women too (cf. Schultz 2006). In the case of larger social units, elected representatives performed the sacrifice: at the state level, the magistrates as political leaders and heads of the (admittedly rudimentary) administration; at the level of private associations, their presidents – in the ordinary run of things, no 'priests' were involved (Scheid 2003: 129–31). Religious specialists acted rather as experts in subordinate or preparatory roles, especially in Rome, with its mass of official colleges of priests together with their free or slave assistants, as temple-vergers, and as independent providers of the gamut of services that may loosely be termed religious.

15

Polytheism

By contrast with the dominant religious traditions of mediaeval and modern Europe – Christianity, Judaism, Islam – people in the towns of antiquity worshipped many gods: they were polytheists, not monotheists. Polytheism in antiquity, however, especially in the fully-developed form known to us from Classical Greece, was not just a matter of assuming that there are many gods. The number of really powerful deities was always quite modest; indeed, from the Hellenistic period, the idea that there were only twelve Olympians acquired more or less canonical status, even if the actual contents of the list varied. These 'grand' deities had a clear internal hierarchy, and conducted themselves in relation to the others in pretty standard ways. The chief means by which this notional system was communicated to an ever-wider circle of communities in Greece was Archaic poetry, above all the Homeric epics (the *Iliad* and *Odyssey*, and the 'Homeric Hymns') and Hesiod.

It was easy to integrate important local deities into this system of 'grand' gods, whether by identifying them with central figures, by modifying the latter, or simply by adding the local god to the structure. What we call a pantheon (lit. 'all the gods') was not in fact composed of the whole gamut of local gods, but was, at least in this form of polytheism, a clearly structured group of them. Of course myths, representations and symbols do give us a sense of their individual characters, but they were not so sharply individuated that they could not fulfil a wide variety of functions, functions that indeed often rather bewilderingly overlap one another. No deity enjoyed a clear monopoly of particular functions, nor were the functions of being responsible for, or protecting, a certain type of activity (such as giving birth, the conduct of war, or agriculture) so sharply defined that only a single deity could fulfil the role.[25]

Despite the standardized name-equivalents given in a mythological handbook such as *Gods and Heroes of Classical Antiquity*, where Ares and Mars, Zeus and Jupiter, Aphrodite and Venus appear as straightforward synonyms (Aghion 1996), Roman polytheism was very different from Greek. The internal structure of the pantheon, for example, was far less clearly marked: the various deities were placed on a more or less equal footing, not in a clear hierarchy. The Roman stories about gods emphasize new divinities that were introduced at various times rather than the details of the behaviour of the old ones towards one other.[26] For a long time the group of 'grand' gods at Rome was much more variable than in Greece, and their 'personalities' were less densely

16

elaborated as complex patterns of action (cf. Mora 1995b). Instead, new gods kept being introduced into the pantheon, either as imports from beyond Rome or as indigenous new creations.

The structure of the Roman pantheon is undoubtedly connected with the specific history of Rome's social evolution. Rome emerged as a city only after a long process of fusion and re-ordering of different aristocratic and other social groups. The Roman pantheon, likewise, has all the appearance of being a ruling-class endowed with a highly-developed ability to integrate new-comers, and long able successfully to resist the exorbitant ambitions of its individual members. Since a pantheon is modelled on the activities of individual human beings, especially their external contacts, their dedications of new temples for new deities, and their tales of saving interventions by gods old and new, it is hardly surprising that we can find structural similarities to the formation of human élites. At the same time, we should not ignore the importance of other factors, such as accidental encounters due to military expansion, immigration of individuals and groups, and 'internal' theological speculation (cf. Beard, North, Price 1998: 61–72).

However, the 'grand' gods are by no means the only super-human characters that stocked the Roman (and Italic) pantheons. In texts, and occasionally even in rituals, we come across a great number of 'spirits', gods with minute, highly specific areas of responsibility, that were christened *Augenblick-* or *Sondergötter* ('gods of momentary, or limited, function') by Hermann Usener in 1896.[27] In addition, we find a plethora of gods of particular locations, divinized ancestors, and then the ever-increasing number of humans promoted to heaven, parallel to the ever-increasing host of heroes in Greece. Finally there is the large group of beings intermediate between gods and humans, *daemones* (spirits), creatures that were also very much alive in the imagination of the adherents of the so-called 'monotheistic' religions of antiquity.[28] The early Christian did not say, 'The traditional gods don't exist', but rather: 'They aren't gods, for there is only one God; they are merely *daemones*, lesser spirits'. The ideological nature of the opposition 'monotheism versus polytheism' becomes clearer still if we think, say, of the theological concept of the Trinity (God as Father, Son and Holy Spirit), which is as fine an example as one could wish of having one's cake and eating it.

City Religion

In the face of this multitude of divine beings and the (rather fewer) cults that did them honour, the question arises whether it makes much sense to talk of 'polytheistic religion'. Do all these different activities performed by such very diverse groups really belong together? Do they form one single religion, or several different ones? Even today it has become tricky to classify religion in terms of 'confessions', since to do so involves the assumption that there are indeed mutually exclusive religious options (e.g. *either* Roman Catholic *or* Protestant) – tricky at any rate once we start looking not at how things are supposed to be but at how people actually behave. Anyway, in relation to ancient communities an approach based on 'confessions' is quite useless.

In antiquity personal affiliation to individual cults depended on local and social factors; anyone might join several cults, multiple adherence was not on principle forbidden.[29] A person who was a member of a religious association – and it is only in this connection that we have epigraphic evidence of actual membership – naturally also took part in public festivals, and in the family cult. The idea of a fixed membership was not of primary importance to such groups. There were indeed some that approached it, but even there the distinction between 'members' and mere sympathizers was pretty fluid. Despite the fact that the keeping of lists and registers was an established part of administrative practice in antiquity, lists of members or entry-passes were unusual in the religious area – the fifth- and fourth-century BC Orphic-Bacchic tokens, inscribed on gold leaf and laid in the grave, are quite exceptional.[30] What might appear to be creeds, such as the Isiac aretalogies, were in fact rather hymns of praise; it was only when such texts were combined with repudiation of alternatives and a claim to exclusive truth that they came to function as a means of religious separatism (Versnel 1990: 39–95).

If we try to identify the level that most clearly integrates all these sub-groups, it must be that of the individual city, or *polis* (to use the Greek term). Membership in a *polis* was for people in the ancient Mediterranean basin, and of course especially in urbanized areas, the most important focus of geo-social identity, the strongest political tie. For it was being born into a *polis* that always remained the principal means of acquiring legal status, privileges and thus appreciable social and economic life-chances. It is hardly surprising, then, that every *polis* produced its own calendar, that is, its own ordering of time on religious lines. 'Ordering' here is used in two senses: on the one hand, every city had its own festival calendar, which laid out the days appointed for the sacrifices in honour of each god for the entire year; on the other, the calendar had a civil function, was a means of making known the names of the months and the beginning of the civil year. In both functions, the calendar served to integrate and co-ordinate the

18

activities of different groups over time. However there is no surviving example of a calendar from antiquity that listed all the religious activities that took place in the city and its territory, a 'union calendar' as it were, which provided a complete, definitive list of every single festival celebrated in outlying settlements, in the different city-quarters, and in private or semi-private groups. The calendars we know are highly selective, since they concentrate on the events taking place at the level of the city as a politico-religious entity (Rüpke 1995a: 170ff.; 523ff.).

It may seem rather odd that I use the term *polis* here. This is a deliberate choice, since I wish to avoid the term 'ancient city-state'. The term 'state' suggests many features familiar from nineteenth-century concepts of the state, but which do not apply to antiquity and may therefore arouse false expectations.[31] The cities of antiquity, the *poleis*, did not have a developed administration, no large bureaucracy or police apparatus. They had just a few elected officials, assisted by a very small staff (who were often slaves). With few exceptions, they did not have the kind of written constitutions modern democratic states generally do have. The full citizens of such a *polis* were often just a tiny proportion of the population, namely the full-grown men of wealth and substance. The level of participation in political decision-making in such communities was very variable, and sometimes hardly existent. Social and political issues were often not clearly separated from one another. It was normal for the members of the old, aristocratic families at the same time to be the political leaders, on the principle that wealth correlates with influence. In other words, ancient cities, especially in the Hellenistic and Roman periods, were mainly timocracies, republics of 'honour'.

Using the term 'religion of the *polis*', or '*polis*-religion' for short, helps us avoid the clearly anachronistic term 'state religion' (which would then have to be clearly differentiated from 'private religion').[32] Within the *polis*, religion, even in the private sphere, is under public control. For example, you could not simply move your grandfather's grave to somewhere else; you had to get permission from an official priestly body. Nor could you, as a private citizen, just carry out any form of cult in a public space of your choosing; for here too, as I will explain later, there were limits and controls. Whether you took part as a private person in the junketings at the Saturnalia, or visited the races in the circus during the games of Apollo, you were at the same time taking part in celebrations of public cult. As an ordinary person you performed your acts of cult in the temples of the *polis*, themselves built and dedicated by the political élite. In *polis*-religion everything overlaps.[33]

19

But do all sets of relations within the *polis* serve to integrate it politically? Are all external contacts irrelevant? Even full citizens of Rome
had to decide between possible options, whether to go along to a
public festival or attend a meeting of a certain club that happened to
be held at the same time. From the point of view of the individual
actor, *polis*-religion is not the right term, especially if he or she
happens to be a slave, a foreigner or a non-citizen. They too 'have' a
religion. The title of this book, *Religion of the Romans*, is to be taken
as meaning 'religion at Rome', that is, in a purely local, not an ethnic
or exclusively political, sense, which is what the expressions 'Roman
religion', or 'the religion of the Romans', usually suggest. The city of
Rome here of course also implies its immediate, and indeed its distant,
surroundings (ultimately, the empire) – the local history of religion
must always also be the regional history of religion. This will
become clearer later on, in chapter 8, when I look at religious road-
and boundary-markers.

If the function of religion is not to be limited to social integration –
and one of my main aims in writing this book is to make this point –
we need to take into account the fact that in the city of Rome religions
and cults of different geographic and ethnic origins came into contact
and influenced one another. It is all very well to tot up cult-sites and
social groups in a town, but no less important is the question of how
they related to one another, how cults borrowed from one another, in
celebrating a procession, say, or in the choices made by an individual
at different times and in different circumstances during his or her
life. It is not only a matter of selecting from among pre-existing
alternatives.[34]

Just as a pantheon is a local phenomenon and the Fortuna of the
Forum Boarium is not identical with the Fortuna of Praeneste, so the
'universal' religions, such as Judaism, Christianity, or the cult of
Mithras, clearly assumed local forms. If we are considering local or
particularist religion, the abstract claims of Christianity, as a dogmatic
structure, are irrelevant: what counts is how it looks here and now, in
this place at this time. Such local variations are generally disregarded
by the (literary) sources, for, at least ordinarily, a theologian like
Augustine emphasized not the differences between, say, Christianity
in Carthage and Christianity in Rome, but what Christianity is 'in
itself'.[35] We only hear of such local variations in exceptional cases. It
is striking that, when they got to Rome, many cults quickly reduced
their hierarchy. The influence of priests with specialist religious knowledge was reduced, and in their place we find a new emphasis on structures borrowed from professional or voluntary associations, which

20

were typically directed by an executive committee elected for five years. Once they reached Rome, religions that originated in quite different areas, with different calendars, used the Roman calendar. There is not a single Jewish date on any Jewish tombstone in Rome – we only find Roman dates, and not many of them either. We might have assumed that the Jews, whose festivals were all calculated upon a completely different (lunar) system from the Roman, would have devised their own calendar, but evidently they just adapted their weekly rhythm – the Shabbat was known to non-Jews already by the end of the first century BC – , and their various festivals, to the local calendar.[36]

Public Cults

There is a Latin term that corresponds to the term *polis*-religion, namely *sacra publica*, the public cults. Like the modern term *polis*-religion, the Roman expression focuses upon the internal religious structure of the city. *Sacra* denotes the rituals that the humans owe the gods. The most important criterion for distinguishing between the sacra publica and other cults is the question of funding: who pays for these cults?[37] The costs of maintaining them were borne by the political community, whose substantial income was generated mainly from direct taxes, customs duties and the proceeds of war. If there happened to be no private funds on offer, the land for temples was purchased, and their building-costs paid for, out of this income. Sanctuaries and temples for the *sacra publica* were constructed on public ground; each site was then solemnly transformed into a *locus sacer*, a 'site reserved to the gods', by an act of consecration, thus becoming the personal property of a deity.

However cults also have running costs as it were, such as the annual expenditure on sacrificial animals and other offerings, and payments for the construction of stages, for actors, for chariot-horses. Their funding too had to be taken care of. The significance of this side of religion is clear even in the mythico-historical tradition. The legendary founder of Roman religion, Numa Pompilius, the second king of Rome, not only established numerous cults and priesthoods, but also ensured their existence in the future (cf. Dionysius of Halicarnassus, *Ant. Rom.* 2.75.3). In each case, a piece of land was allotted to the maintenance of a cult, and income normally generated from it by leasing it out on a regular basis. This money would be used to finance a cult or priesthood, such as that of the Vestal virgins. The impressive scale of the sums here involved is made clear by the report that Sulla's

21

urgent sale of lands set aside 'by Numa' to finance the public cults, in order to raise funds for the war against Mithridates, fetched 9,000 Roman lbs in gold = 36 million sesterces (Appian, *Mithr.* 22). Assuming an average price of 1,000 sesterces per *iugerum*, this sum represents an area of substantially more than 20,000 hectares (49,420 acres), without by any means exhausting such land-reserves – the *sacra publica* continued as before (Bodei Giglioni 1977).[38]

This kind of financing – today we would call it the creation of a capital-stock in the form of fixed property – was into modern times, and not merely in Europe, the typical means of defraying religious costs, and even long-term current expenses of state. Constantine I endowed his Christian basilica in the Lateran *c.* AD 320 in exactly the same way. Until the Early-Modern period, the Church only accepted the founding of a chapel, say, if it were endowed with a plot of land that could produce enough to pay for the recurrent costs, the priest's salary and the costs of repairs etc. The older colleges of Oxford and Cambridge, and Harvard and Yale, were all endowed by the same means.

Given the fact that our sources provide merely haphazard snippets of information, it is hard to calculate absolute numbers. Nevertheless a model-calculation such as the following does provide some idea of the scale involved. The best estimate of the gross domestic product (GDP) of the empire in the second century AD is about 13.7 billion sesterces.[39] Government spending in the same period, mainly on defence, amounted to three-quarters to one billion sesterces, say 6.6% of GDP.[40] The annual running costs of the Roman games and priest-hoods can thus hardly have exceeded 1% of GDP. This sum was supplemented by private funds, which in exceptional cases might far exceed normal annual state expenditure on this head: according to Pliny the Elder, the value even of the superfluous decorations of M. Aemilius Scaurus' wooden theatre (built for his aedileship in 58 BC) was said to have amounted to 30 million sesterces (Pliny, *HN* 36.115); and Pompey spent very large sums to celebrate the inauguration of his stone theatre in 55 BC.[41]

The *sacra publica* taken as a whole can be thought of as the fulfil-ment of the political community's duty towards its gods. The gods who are supposed to sustain this social order have a right to be wor-shipped. This legitimate claim was met by the regular staging of the *sacra publica* – the religious duties that the community as a whole was obliged to fulfil. It was not possible to do less; but, since this pattern of obligation had developed incrementally over the long term, it was usually unnecessary to do more. In certain situations, when a deity showed sign of displeasure by sending earth-quakes, hail-storms or

1. Detail from the external frieze of the Ara Pacis.

The ritual here depicted brings 'priests' (*sacerdotes*), magistrates, women and children together; it was participation in such events that taught the latter the practice of religion. The toga was – especially in Augustus' view – the normative wear of Roman citizens; in the case of boys, priests and magistrates it was adorned with a purple stripe (*toga praetexta*). It is really not possible to make out individuals holding particular offices: only the *flamines* (the group of three on the left) are easily recognizable from their distinctive headgear, the *galerus* (sometimes called *apex*, which is properly only the olive-wood spike). The figure in the centre-foreground, holding an axe (*securis*), is the *flamines'* lictor; he and M. Agrippa immediately behind him have already drawn the toga over their heads, *capite velato*, 'with covered head'. The woman following them has done likewise with her *stola*. Other participants wear ceremonial crowns. Three-quarters life-size.
Marble, dedicated 12 BC. 'South' frieze, Ara Pacis, Rome.

other negative signs, the political leadership, the Senate, might well consider performing additional rituals; but usually the city was confident that it fulfilled the gods' expectations. It would have been regarded as pure supererogation for a magistrate, say, to show himself over-zealous and sacrifice to Jupiter every other day instead of twice a month, on the principle 'the more the merrier'. Such behaviour was not generally acceptable, and such a magistrate would never have got extra public funding.

In addition to this top level of public cult, at which the community is represented by its highest officials and the priests merely perform specialized tasks, there was a second level of religious institutions, concerned with the regional sub-units of the city. In the case of Rome itself, these were the Seven Hills (the festival of the *Dies septimontium*), the thirty *curiae* (an old form of political of organization, that still featured in the route taken by the procession of the Argei in May) and the *vici*, the 265 sub-divisions of the city, which were themselves aggregated into the 14 regions.[42] This list is by no means complete, since it was added to constantly as the city grew. At any rate, the official cults celebrated in these sub-units had to be financed out of public funds, since, so far as we know, they had no income themselves.

Besides the two-tiered level of the *sacra publica*, we have a complementary term, the *sacra privata*, private cults. These were the cults that individuals were responsible for, such as domestic cults and the cults of the *gentes*, the extended 'clans' of those who shared the same nomen, especially characteristic of the aristocracy.

The traditional terminology thus gives us a clearly-delineated idea of the city religion of Rome: at the highest level are the *sacra publica*, supplemented by the *sacra pro montibus, pro curiis, pro vicis*; below them are the *sacra privata*, sub-divided into cults performed by individuals, households (*familiae*) and by the *gentes*.[43] However the typology of human agents and their duties constructed by the traditional terminology does not match the social groups that actually celebrated the cults (cf. chap. 10; also Rüpke 2004). The terminology represents an harmonious social ideal, beginning with the household, continuing through the *gentes*, and on up to the public level, particular to general. It has nothing to do with the reality of divergent interests, social barriers, physical mobility and individual isolation. This will become clear if we take a second, critical, look at the level of the *sacra publica*.

The Religion of the Élite

If we take a closer look at the term 'public', we soon realize that the notion underlying the Latin word *publicus* differs from the implications of the modern term, which is that we all have access – at least in a limited kind of way, for example through the media – to a public realm, 'public opinion', created not merely by political leaders but also by institutions such as the press, political associations, 'think tanks' and so on, and manifested in the right of every individual, and every minor interest-group, to express their opinion. The Roman notion of 'public', by contrast, denotes a limited space within which only the upper class may communicate among its members (Rüpke 1995a: 606ff.). There were extremely few, and then highly ritualized, ways in which the rest of the population, more precisely: the assembly of male full-citizens, could influence 'public opinion' in this sense. Until elections were abolished in the early Principate, the right to intervene consisted merely in the right to vote in certain mass assemblies. From the time of the Late Republic, and continuing into the Byzantine period, there were also theatrical performances, during which the people, or large sub-sections of it, greeted the more important magistrates (including even the emperor) with applause or booing as they made their entrance and seated themselves in their privileged places; or interpreted the lines spoken on stage as political allusions on which they might comment with impunity. Elections were organized in a highly timocratic manner. Votes in the *comitia centuriata*, the centuriate assembly, especially important because it elected the praetors and consuls, were weighted in direct proportion to one's wealth. As the wealthiest classes voted first, and the process was stopped as soon as a majority was reached, most of those entitled to vote often got no chance to cast their ballots at all. Under such circumstances it was hardly possible for the mass of the population to influence political decisions.[44]

The Roman political élite was relatively stable in composition. The consuls, the highest officials, were generally men whose fathers and grand-fathers had held similar positions before them. If a man without ancestors who had themselves been aedile, praetor or consul was voted into a curule office, he was said to be a *novus homo*, a 'new man', an upstart. This élite seems to have completed its formation by the end of the fourth century BC, emerging out of the individual *gentes*, which hitherto had operated independently, even in military undertakings. The élite that emerged from the separate *gentes*, in Latin the *nobiles*, the nobility, is historically remarkable for its skill in channelling the competition so characteristic of aristocratic societies into ends that were integrative for their order, by reaching a consensus regarding their collective interests (above all, political power and external expansion) and their shared values. It is this ever-endangered *res publica*, this common venture, this public weal requiring constant redefinition, that nineteenth-century scholars wrongly regarded as the Roman 'state' (Hölkeskamp 1987).

It was the shared interests of the élite, and a set of rules intended to create consensus and protect that fragile plant from the excesses produced by constant competition for prestige, that constructed this 'state', not a constitution created by a sovereign citizen-body. In that respect, the public comportment of the élite was always political – its internal communication was Rome's decisive 'public sphere' (cf. Brennan 2004). This had two consequences for religion, which we can think of as the two sides of the same coin: (1) the structure of 'public' religion was fundamentally inflected by the internal structure of the élite; and (2) it can hardly be separated from the 'private religion' of this same group.[45]

As a result, we know hardly anything about the *sacra gentilicia*, the cults of the *gentes*.[46] The reason for this may well be, not that they had ceased to exist, but because they were no longer important in the new Republic. Our first reliable report of the existence of gentilicial cults is owed to a conflict that broke out at the end of the fourth century BC, when the cult of Hercules, which had hitherto been in the hands of two patrician gentes, the Pinarii and the Potitii, was removed from them and turned into a *sacrum publicum*, performed by public slaves with public money. The author of this reform was the censor of 312 BC, Appius Claudius Caecus, whose office was created by the aristocracy to monitor its own code of behaviour.[47]

In view of the special structure of the Roman élite, conflicts between a gentilician cult and the public system were not conflicts between two different levels of cult, state and private, but rather conflicts within the aristocracy. When we hear of discussions – and they are especially frequent at the beginning of the second century BC – about sumptuary laws, the prohibition of excessively splendid tombs or restrictions on the amount that could be lavished on marriage-feasts and other banquets, these concern private cults. Limitations imposed upon private cults, or their transformation into *sacra publica*, or religious roles becoming 'state priesthoods', all these should be seen as alternative strategies to ensure that the common weal is put first; such strategies are indeed a characteristic feature of the religious history of Rome.

Although members of the élite during the Mid- and Late Republic were evidently more interested in founding new public cults, we again find reports of gentilician cults during the period of transition to the Principate (cf. Beard, North, Price 1998: 1, 67f.). Remarkably enough, these reports concern the gentilician cult of the Iulii, the *gens* of the dictator C. Iulius Caesar and his great-nephew and adoptive son C. Iulius *divi filius* Caesar, whom we call Octavian/Augustus, who between them put an end to the untrammelled rule of the aristocracy – the *gens* that (through adoption) provided all the emperors until the time of Nero. The Julian *gens* maintained a cult in the small Latin town of Bovillae. As we know from the discovery of an altar there, it took the form of a cult of the god Veiovis. His worship seems to have been linked with the family's defunctive cult, the cult of its ancestors. It was in the tradition of this gentilician cult that the cult of *divus Augustus* was created in Rome in AD 14 and entrusted to the care of the newly-founded fraternity of the 21 (later 28) *sodales Augustales*.[48] One the other hand, its object was not the defunct *princeps* but the divinized *princeps*, the immortal *divus Augustus*. To that extent it concerned the public realm, the *res publica*; membership of the Sodales was a public appointment.

The site of conflict between particular or private religious activities and collective interests is at the same time a locus of innovation. This starts with the restructuring or suppression of old traditions; and continues with the introduction of new cults. Of course the Senate, the representative institution of the aristocracy, could resolve that a new cult be introduced, for example the god of healing, Asklepios/ Asclepius, in Latin Aesculapius, in the year 293 BC or of the Mater Magna, the 'great Idaean (i.e. from the Phrygian Mt. Ida) Mother of the Gods' in the year 205 BC.[49] But individuals too could take the initiative, for example a commander who had won a war. From the proceeds of the booty won by his army he would build a temple in Rome – a choice that also solved the problem of how to invest the spoils in a manner at once prestigious and unobjectionable. The historical record shows that the name of the founder continued to be linked to the object for a very long time. He was not building his temple for a god who already possessed a shrine in the city, but for a new one, whose name he thus associated with himself – a symbol of grand generosity that might come in handy when canvassing for election to another office; or, since such victors, as consuls, had usually reached the end of their public career, a descendant might appeal to such a gesture by a forebear.[50] Celebrating games (*ludi*) constituted an alternative strategy that might in the short run be even more effective at boosting the prestige of the individual victor (rather than that of a deity). The wider use of the proceeds of war-booty to construct secular buildings too, such as the Basilica Sempronia built in 169 BC by Tib. Sempronius Gracchus (cos. I, 177 BC), shows that this system of distinction extended far beyond the religious sphere in the narrow sense.[51]

A glance at the procedure reveals how intimately this religious activity was connected with other élite values (the same holds good for many other areas too) (Rüpke 1995b). Once the vow had been made on the battle-field, and the commander had returned safely to

Rome, a solemn decision was made to build a temple. Then followed the leasing of the building-contract by the censors. The next step was the definition and dedication, according to the letter of the sacral law, of the plot of land that had, it seems, been selected beforehand by the donor with specialist advice so as to avoid infringing that law. The act of dedication solemnly transferred the land to the deity, and included the laying of the foundation-stone and the related sacrifices. Normally however it is not that date but the date of completion that was commemorated by the cult as the *dies natalis templi*, the 'temple's birthday'. On this occasion too the *lex templi*, the detailed regulations governing the cult, which might also include the temple's official calendar of festivals (*feriale*), was drawn up.[52]

The Republican élite's aim of distributing power as widely as possible in order to achieve consensus is exemplified in the fact that several groups, or their representatives, took part in the procedure. In order to define the sacred space (in Latin: *templum*) on which the building itself (*aedes*) was erected, one needed an Augur: he ascertained that the area was free of other possible religious claims, and provided a clear sacral definition of the piece of land. A *pontifex* was usually needed for the rite of dedication and consecration of the land (*dedicatio et consecratio*): he recited the formulae and ritually indicated the points where the building was to stand, or, alternatively, touched a door-post (*postem tenere*), in those cases in which these had already been erected. According to a law of 304 BC, if the dedicator himself no longer held public office, he was required to obtain a fresh legitimation by being elected temporarily into a special magistracy, the *duoviri aedi dedicandae*, the pair of magistrates appointed to carry out the procedure for founding a temple.[53] A famous passage of Livy, relating to the passing of this law, reveals how politically charged all this might become:

> He (Gn. Flavius, an aide of Appius Claudius Caecus, who has already been introduced as the donor of the temple) dedicated a temple of Concord in the Area Vulcani (on the Forum Romanum), greatly to the annoyance of the nobility. Cornelius Barbatus, the pontifex maximus, was forced by the unanimous demands of the people to dictate the form of the prayer for Gn. to repeat after him, even though Barbatus claimed that tradition permitted no one but a consul or other commander with *imperium* to dedicate a temple. It was this incident that prompted the Senate to present to the popular assembly a law forbidding anyone officially to dedicate a temple or an altar without the authorization of the Senate or of a majority of the tribunes of the people.[54]

28

If the donor were dead by the time of the dedication and consecration, the duovirate was usually granted to his son.[55] If no public funding were involved, which was of course administered by the Senate, the presence of further magistrates was not required.

It will thus be clear that religious innovation represented a real threat to the solidarity of the élite. For that reason, control over religion was one of the basic elements of the system. This control was exercized primarily by the Senate, and supplemented the self-control demanded of all citizens. A further implication is that the *sacra publica* should be understood not only as religious ceremonial organized by the élite so as to attach the ignorant masses to itself and ensure their loyalty through fear of the gods (a perception widespread even in antiquity), but also as that important part of the religious system as a whole that was performed by the members of the upper-class, in fact as a system of signs, as a medium of internal communication. And, at any rate in the eyes of the participants, it was at the same time an efficient means of fulfilling the gods' expectation that their gifts should be properly recognized.

Sacra Privata

The *sacra privata* too were regarded as a duty owed by the community to the gods. At any rate, that is the claim we find in Cicero's *De legibus* (On the Laws), where the author, writing in the very last years of the Republic, designs an ideal constitution that deals at great length with religious matters (the second of the three books is in fact dedicated entirely to this topic). The Romans' interest in such matters can be explored by looking at two topics, both of which happen to be connected to the law of succession.

The first is the control of adoption. Adoption was common at Rome. For the successful consul or praetor who lacked a son who had managed to survive to maturity, it was a sound move to adopt someone intelligent, adaptable and eloquent, but whose father had unfortunately never managed to rise beyond the rank of quaestor (the lowest office in the senatorial *cursus honorum*).[56] The age of the child or young man (Roman adoption was always of males, never of girls) was of little matter. Adoption involved a complete substitution of family. Of course the adopted person could still visit his biological parents, but he lost his original names and assumed the *praenomen* and *nomen* of his new father, his family of origin being noted, if at all, by a second *cognomen* (thus L. Manlius L.f. L.n. Acidinus Fulvianus, cos. 179 BC, took his *tria nomina* from his adoptive father, L. Manlius Acidinus, praetor 210, but added Fulvianus to them to show he was born a (?) C. or M. Fulvius). A radical caesura of this kind also meant that such a man could no longer be responsible for the cult of his family of origin, his own *sacra familiaria*, but had now to carry out the cult of his new family. Under these circumstances, if the designated heir(s) of a family died prematurely and the others had been adopted out, the family cult would come to an end with the death of the father, the head of the family, as happened in the case of L. Aemilius Paullus (cos 182, 168 BC). This was highly undesirable, and adoptions were therefore controlled and authorized by an ancient council, the *comitia curiata*, presided over by the *pontifex maximus*, who had wide authority especially in the legal area. Movement of males between families was thus made a public issue, and controlled.

The other area is the law of succession. In accepting an inheritance, one might also incur religious responsibilities. Besides the financial benefits (or even instead of them) there might be burdensome responsibilities to fulfil; of these the organization of the funeral was the most important. A *sine sacris hereditas*, an 'inheritance without religious strings', was one without worry, free of irksome duties (Festus p. 370, 14–20 L.). Many testators got round the reluctance or even neglect of their heirs by ensuring the continuity of their funerary-cult, either by establishing foundations, or promising money or an income to a third party, such as a freedman, on condition that they kept up the cult.[57]

In reality the situation was of course not quite as simple as the Roman jurisprudents suggest, namely an unproblematical co-operation between public and private cults, in which the public cults ensured the continuity of the private ones. Much remained uncertain. The *pontifices* were quite uninterested in ensuring the continuity of religious associations that threatened to dissolve, nor did they dream of supervising the religious activities of immigrants, of slaves and traders from Asia, Northern Europe or Africa, who had their own cults in Rome ('Syrian' merchants, for example, were active all over the Mediterranean area and often brought their cults with them). As long as these did not create any public conflicts, the guardians of the *sacra* ignored them. There was no consumer-protection organization to certify the wholesomeness of cults, and there was no Wahabite religious police to supervise the spread of Roman polytheism. But when fears of revolution or conspiracy were abroad, others' feelings of religious commitment might be considered of very little value, and sometimes none at all.

30

Tightening Control

Rome's perceived need to exercize control in the religious sphere grew as the city expanded politically. Here we should distinguish between intensification and extension. Control at the centre was intensified, while at the same time supervision was extended further and further beyond the boundaries of the city. At the very beginning of reliable historical reporting, the censorship of Appius Claudius Caecus (cos. 307, 296 BC), stands for the drive to concentrate religious control in the hands of the political community's central institution, the Senate.[58] This bid was only partly successful, but the Senate's authority in religious matters, and its powers of control, gradually increased: it was to that body that the priestly colleges presented their opinions on specific issues, and it was there that prohibitions or interdictions were decided and later reported upon. It was only during the Principate that the Senate gradually lost these powers as they were taken over by the emperor and his *consilium* (the emperor's official advisers, whose members were drawn from the Senate).

But the Senate also extended its control in space. In the course of the second century BC, the pontifices began to take Latium and certain Etruscan towns in the vicinity of Rome into account when they were considering bad omens, *prodigia*. Since they had not occurred on public land belonging to the *civitas Romana* but in independent polities, such events had traditionally had no religious significance for Rome. Moreover the *decemviri sacris faciundis*, the priestly college responsible for the Sibylline books, a highly respected collection of oracles, began to take cognizance even of omens from distant places such as Sicily.[59] Tendencies of this kind are the correlate in the religious context of the increasing integration of Italy (Gargola 1995).

Something similar happened when, during the Principate, the law applying to land in the city of Rome was extended to land in the provinces, and the Senate and the magistrates of the city of Rome, including the priestly colleges, extended their fields of action far beyond the city boundaries. The effects can clearly be seen in the late-antique law-collections (Beard, North, Price 1998: 1, 320f., 339ff.).

What religious control by Rome might actually involve is illustrated by one of the best-known events of the Republican period, the famous persecution of the Bacchanals in 186 BC.[60] The cult of the god Dionysus (in Latin: Bacchus or Liber) was widespread in the Mediterranean world, a god of the vine whose worship was connected with the consumption of wine and ecstatic possession, but also quite markedly with soteriological ideas – newly vigorous life, salvation after death. The places where his worship was conducted were called in Latin *bac(ch)analia*. Such worship had been carried on in the Greek-speaking part of Italy for centuries without any problem: there is evidence for the existence of the cult in Campania already in the sixth century BC. It also seems clear that it had been practised at Rome at least since the third century BC.[61] However the Roman élite were suspicious of it, partly because worship took place at night, but mainly because men and women celebrated together. It was assumed that people who met in secret, that is, who shunned the public sphere, must also be plotting against it. In Greece, adherents of 'mystery' cults were regarded as respectable and pious; at Rome they were regarded as potential revolutionaries (Kippenberg 1997). In this particular case, the Roman authorities thought that a large number of people were already involved, indeed that the conspiracy had advanced so far that a revolution was imminent. There were allegedly seven thousand bacchants in Rome alone. This aroused the attention of the Roman Senate. It decided on immediate police measures, the dissolution of the Bacchic associations, arrest and execution of the 'ring-leaders', and, for the longer term, strict control over Dionysiac cult. The size of associations was limited to five men, which was tantamount to prohibition. Women were forbidden to hold important positions in these groups, a bit of misogyny that wonderfully reveals the character of dominant Roman values.[62] No Roman citizen was permitted to become a priest in the cult – a rule that had already been applied recently in relation to the castrated *galli* of the Mater Magna.

The decree of the Senate (SC) relating to the Bacchanalia:

> The consuls Q. Marcius, son of L., and Sp. Postumius, son of L., consulted with the Senate on the Nones of October (7 October 186 BC) in the temple of Bellona. Present at the writing [of the decree] were M. Claudius, son of M., L. Valerius, son of P., and Q. Minucius, son of C.
>
> In the matter of Bacchic rites they passed a decree that the following proclamation be issued to those allied to the Romans by treaty:
>
> Let none of them be minded to have a place of Bacchic worship (*bacchanal*). Should there be some who say that they must needs maintain a place of Bacchic worship, they must come to the urban praetor at Rome, and our Senate, when it has heard what they have to say, shall take a decision on the matter, provided that at least one hundred senators be present when the matter is deliberated.
>
> Let no man, whether Roman citizen or Latin, or one of the allies, be minded to attend a meeting of Bacchant women without approaching the urban praetor and obtaining his authorization with the approval of

the Senate, provided that at least one hundred senators be present when the matter is deliberated. Adopted.

Let no man be a priest (*sacerdos*). Let no man or woman be *magister* (head of an association); nor let any of them be minded to keep a common fund; nor let any person be minded to make either man or woman a magister or pro-magister, or be minded henceforth to exchange oaths, vows, pledges or promises with others, or be minded to plight faith with others. Let no one be minded to perform ceremonies in secret; nor let anyone be minded to perform ceremonies, whether in public or in private or outside the city, without approaching the urban praetor and obtaining his authorization with the approval of the Senate, provided that at least one hundred senators be present when the matter is deliberated. Adopted.

Let no one be minded to hold services in a group larger than five men and women together, and let not more than two men and three women be minded to be present there, except on the authorization of the urban praetor and the Senate as recorded above.

The text concludes with some regulations relating to the publication of the decree, by public proclamation and on bronze, and the immediate dismantling of any *bacanalia* in the city's territory.[63]

This text was published and enforced not only in Rome but also all over Italy, or at least in a good many Italian towns, in the form of bronze copies, which are durable and not easy to alter. This was the method adopted to ensure the enforcement of the Senate's decree by the city authorities in Italy.[64] This is clearly an act of repression that severely affected the performance and celebration of the different cults of Bacchus, even though it did not forbid them (as is clear from later evidence). Two aspects of this interference by the political leadership are worth stressing. (1) The year 186 BC seems to have been the first occasion when the worship of a prestigious and prominent deity was perceived as a real threat to the community, although there had already been some disturbances in 213 (during the Second Punic war) which had led to the prohibition of foreign rites being celebrated in public; (2) it was obviously felt necessary to justify this first case of direct policing of a basically non-Roman cult. The main justification offered was the threat of conspiracy, not the voyeuristic phantasies of nightly orgies reported by Livy, or the pre-view of the so-called oriental cults, which have obsessed so many accounts of these events.

The treatment meted out to the Bacchanals was to repeat itself in the course of Roman history. Between the second century BC and the first century AD, there were periodic expulsions of astrologers, philosophers and even teachers of rhetoric (who until the beginning of the first century BC were considered equally dangerous to the health of the population), as well as Jews and repeatedly, until the time of Claudius, the adherents of the cult of Isis. These prohibitions however also reveal the limitations of attempts to police the Rome of the late Republic, for, although their adherents were supposed to have been banished and their temples destroyed, the decrees and destructions had to be repeated a couple of years later. The desire to control foreign influence outran the resources available to enforce the sanctions.[65]

From the time of Caesar, *collegia*, voluntary associations, were regulated by a series of ordinances.[66] Clubs or claques that might represent a political threat were forbidden (this had already been attempted in the Late Republic, but, as the tensions between optimates and populares increased, was impossible to enforce); religious associations, as long as they were active only in the religious sphere, were granted a relatively large amount of freedom. Such tolerance however could always be withdrawn. As soon as the authorities had reason to think that a *collegium* was politically or morally suspect, it could be suppressed without further ado. In the Principate, finally, there came to be organized persecutions, ending under certain circumstances in execution. In the case of the Druids in Gaul, the grounds for their suppression was the allegation that they sacrificed human beings – a topos that occurs repeatedly in exclusionary or boundary discourses.[67] There was also the rather sporadic and localized persecution of Christians. It was not until the middle of the third century, during the Decian persecution, that such razzias, sometimes ending in execution, were conducted on the basis of an explicit legal order, not indeed Empire-wide, but certainly on a large scale.[68] Even when we look very closely at the persecution of the Christians, however, it remains quite unclear what the Roman authorities intended to achieve by it: compliance, renunciation, or simply the pacification of local conflicts? Part of the problem was certainly the character of Christianity, but we need also to consider that the boundary between licit and illicit religious behaviour was always quite fluid, since a judgement that some particular behaviour was illicit had a great deal to do with subjective feelings of being threatened in particular situations, and with political considerations too – it was not a judgement based upon considered reflection about how far a cult advocating 'atheism' could be publicly tolerated (Digeser 2006).

Roman classifications of 'other' religions were poorly developed. Roman sacral vocabulary does indeed differentiate between *ritus graecus* and *ritus romanus* (or *patrius*), between Greek and traditional Roman rites. In the Greek mode, the participants wore wreaths. That was a clear difference that at first sight served to distinguish between 'our' religion and 'theirs'. The 'Greek' cults however are otherwise unexceptional: they are in fact entirely traditional (Scheid 1993; 1995). So this distinction amounts to the creation of internal differentiation, within the realm of the *sacra publica*, which has no historical justification and whose only value is its inscription of a certain complexity and exoticism into the indigenous sign-system, through the deployment of a terminological polarity incapable of sustaining any external weight. Something similar holds good in the case of the *sacra peregrina*, so-called 'foreign' cults. These too were not, as one might suppose, genuinely exotic cults, Jewish or Christian say, but cults which were officially introduced to Rome from abroad, for example the cult of Cybele, the Mater Magna, that I mentioned earlier (p. 27). Even in cases where enemy gods were 'evoked' from their temples, in time of war, with the promise of a new temple in Rome if they deserted the enemy and ceased to protect them – even in these cases one could speak of *sacra peregrina*, be the cult as Italic as ever might be.[69] This too, then, is a term whose primary role is to create spatial complexity and historical relief within the Roman system of signs.

A term such as *religio licita*, 'approved' religion(s), which the Christian writer Tertullian uses of the Jews in the Roman empire (*Apolog.* 21.1), had no official standing. There was no register of associations that listed all those that had been approved by the authorities. Decisions about what was alien and dangerous were made from case to case, triggered by a particular incident against the background of specific ideas about what constitutes a threat. It is obvious that conceptions of what might be threatening, and the belief that barriers need to be erected against the world outside (or inversely, that integration is necessary and desirable), are very much functions of historical circumstances.

The extension of citizenship during the Principate to provincials whose first language was not Latin forms part of the developments under discussion here, culminating in the *constitutio Antoniniana* of the year AD 212, which granted citizen rights to every free inhabitant of the Empire. From now on the concept of Roman citizenship functioned not as an exclusionary term but as an universal entitlement to certain rights – and the correlative obligation to perform certain duties. Religion in particular was an area where the new requirement that everyone should sacrifice to the traditional pantheon offered practical opportunities for discrimination: it is not a coincidence that the first relatively systematic persecutions of Christians occurred in the 240s.[70]

Just as cults brought to Rome not only underwent change them-selves but also influenced religions already present in the city, so the political expansion of Rome affected religions outside, in Italy and the provinces, and even led to the re-transmission of religions which had arrived in Rome some time before. This 'export' was usually not a conscious process, and involved a whole variety of different develop-ments and measures. As a whole, however, it raises the question of the sense in which Roman religion can be said to have existed in every part of the far-flung empire.[71]

An interesting, although not necessarily the most important, part of this process was played by the *coloniae* of Roman citizens (Beard, North, Price 1998: 1, 328–34). *Coloniae* are foundations of a mother-city, in this case Rome, and their constitutions were drawn up in Rome in the form of a foundation-law. Large portions of such a con-stitution, in two copies, have come to light in a *colonia* founded by Julius Caesar at Urso (Orsuna) in Hispanica Baetica, whose official name was *Colonia Iulia Genetiva Ursonensis*.[72] The text contains extraordinarily few concrete rules relating to the gods that are to be settled in the colony, mentioning specifically only the Capitoline triad (Jupiter, Juno, Minerva; see pl. 6) and Venus, as a local protective deity. By contrast the procedures necessary for the creation of certain priesthoods (*pontifices, augures*) are laid down in great detail. The principle that the *sacra publica* are to be publicly funded is also emphasized: on its formation, the new city council is to draw up a cal-endar of public festivals and arrange for them to be properly funded (cf. Rüpke 2006a).

Excerpts from the *Lex Ursonensis*

(64) All *duoviri* holding office after the establishment of the colony shall, within the ten days next following the commencement of their magis-tracy, bring before the decurions for decision, when not less than two-thirds shall be present, the question as to the dates and number of the festal days, the sacrifices to be publicly performed, and the persons to perform such sacrifices. Whatever a majority of the decurions present at such a meeting shall have decreed or determined concerning such matters shall be lawful and valid, and such sacrifices and such festal days shall be observed in the said colony.

(69) The *duoviri*, who shall be the first after the foundation of the colony, shall during their magistracy (in the case of subsequent *duoviri* of the colony, within sixty days of their assuming office) make propos-als to the decurions, when no less than 20 are present, concerning the procedure whereby a sum shall be assigned and paid, according the stip-ulations of the contract, to the contractor or contractors who has or

have been awarded the contract for maintaining the sacrifices and upkeep of religion (*quae ad sacra resq(ue) divinas opus erunt*) . . .

(70) All *duoviri*, except those first appointed under this law, shall during their magistracy at the discretion of the decurions celebrate a gladiatorial show or dramatic spectacles in honour of Jupiter, Juno and Minerva, and the gods and goddesses, as far as possible over four days, for the greater part of each day; and on the said spectacles and the said shows each of the said persons shall expend of his own money not less than 2,000 sesterces, and out of the public money it shall be lawful for each *duovir* to appropriate and expend a sum not exceeding 2,000 sesterces, and it shall be lawful for the said persons to do so without fear of penalty.[73]

Roman citizens did not emigrate merely to *coloniae*. In many cases, it was trade that took individuals to ever more distant corners of the Empire (Beard, North, Price 1998: 1, 334–339). Our sources do not suggest that such people took their entire native pantheon with them. On the contrary, we find Romans and Italians participating in local cults all over the Empire. But such emigrants and travellers did provide at least notional alternatives to the gods worshipped in their new location, and introduced as a matter of course new cults and new types of religious action. We should not forget that the inscribed or written votive, the offering of thanks for a request answered by a god, and the stone altars that formed an enduring memorial of such transactions, rank as one of the most important 'exports' of Roman religious practice.[74]

Apart from these private-enterprise emigrants, there were always larger or smaller groups of Romans underway on official business. Roman governors performed in their provinces the same rituals that they were familiar with in Rome (Eck 1997). The Roman army took its *feriale*, its calendar of official festivals, which largely matched that of the city of Rome, even to areas, such as Dura-Europos on the Euphrates, where the Roman calendar was not in use. It is true that such practices were usually restricted to the camp, but they still made some impression. Veterans – Roman citizens or (in the case of auxiliary troops) individuals who were awarded citzenship on quitting the army – settled afterwards in the areas where they had served and thereby extended Roman influence well beyond the military itself.[75]

However, Roman religion spread even where Romans themselves were not the main actors. In order to acquire new forms of distinction and legitimation, the élite in the provinces copied Roman patterns and fashions. Urbanization, sometimes compulsory, brought about extensive changes to traditional structures; and it brought, together with new forms of social organization, the Roman style of polytheism, studded with Roman details. Local and regional, even provincial, religious systems came into existence, which can be described neither as indigenous nor as Roman. In this context, Rome played an important modelling role: since religion there was embedded in every area of daily life, it was natural that the reality of political domination should also make itself felt in the religious area. The extent of this influence is one of the great unanswered questions of the religious history of the Mediterranean area in antiquity.[76]

— 2 —

FROM THE SHE-WOLF TO CAESAR: HISTORICAL FOUNDATIONS

Sources

Every historical narrative derives its legitimacy from its sources. The next question is obviously: what sources? Prior to the middle of the second century BC, there are no Roman literary sources that discuss contemporary religion, i.e. provide observations by contemporaries rather than reconstructions or speculations by later writers. It was then that a Greek hostage at Rome, Polybius, wrote his history of Rome, and dealt extensively with religious issues.[1] The surviving works of Cato the Elder, consul, censor and bigoted traditionalist, were written around the same time; in the present connection it is not so much the fragments of his speeches that are of interest, though they do contain material relevant to religion, as the *De agri cultura*, which survives complete.[2] It describes in detail the activities and economic calculations of a landowner; for Cato, these include the appropriate ritual activities, for example purifying the fields or healing illnesses. The earliest substantial first-hand document relevant to the interface between religion and politics, the bronze slab with the *Senatus consultum de Bacchanalibus*, which I have already cited (pp. 32, 36–7), is dated a little earlier, namely 186 BC.[3] But, like the snippets of Polybius and Cato, it remains an isolated text. Otherwise, the surviving Republican inscriptions provide us with very few votive inscriptions or legal documents; moreover, the latter often concern issues outside Rome.

The situation improves only in the middle of the first century BC with the works of M. Tullius Cicero. Cicero, orator, politician and philosopher, composed a number of texts that offer reflections about religion and its practice.[4] The works that directly concern the history of religion, which also contain extensive references to earlier (Greek) authors, are *De natura deorum*, On the nature of the gods, and *De divinatione*, On divination.[5] Apart from them we have the surviving speeches, which often deploy religious themes in the course of an argument, as something Cicero shares with his audience, something that will ensure him a sympathetic hearing. Then again there are speeches that deal directly with religious issues. Among the most important of these is *De domo suo*, On his own House. The tribune P. Clodius Pulcher had managed to get Cicero's private house on the Palatine partly demolished and partly turned into a temple to *Libertas* (Freedom) when he was exiled in 58 BC, and Cicero demands in this speech to the *pontifices*, after his return the following year, that it be given back to him. The speech *De haruspicum responso*, On the Answer of the Haruspices, delivered the following year, 56 BC, deals with an opinion delivered by this (informal) priestly college, again in connection with the negotiations over the restoration of his house.[6] In his correspondence (*Ad familiares*; *Ad Atticum*) Cicero also provides us with insights into daily activities connected with religious politics in the period between the late 60s and 40s BC: what kind of prodigies occurred? What events of bad omen were noted by the Augurs? What were the religious objections raised against this or that political move? In Cicero's letters we are presented with an extremely dense record of, and responses to, contemporary events, something we do not have in remotely comparable form for any other period of Roman history.

Our sources for the first century BC are uniquely rich thanks to the survival of so much Cicero, but they are not limited to him. There is also poetry that alludes to religion, for example the didactic poem *De rerum natura*, On the Nature of Things, by the Epicurean Lucretius, and the personal poems of Catullus, Tibullus, Propertius and Horace (I began this book, you remember, with a poem by Horace).[7] From the late Republic, inscriptions, mainly on stone, began to be produced in ever-larger numbers; they provide masses of evidence for individual careers within the élite, in the form of funerary and honorific inscriptions, and for religious acts, in the form of votive-inscriptions.[8] Both types of text reach an apogee between around 180–220 AD; thereafter they decline, at different rates in different provinces. The records of the meetings of the Arval Brothers, copied on stone at La Magliana outside Rome, provide us with precisely-dated evidence extending throughout the Principate for the routine activities of one priesthood.[9] Nothing comparable exists from antiquity, with the partial exception of the description of rituals recorded in the *Tabulae Iguvinae*, seven bronze tablets in the Oscan language (one actually in early Latin) found in 1444 near the Roman theatre in Gubbio and dated to the second century BC, a text likewise created by a fraternity, the Atiedii.[10] Extensive protocols of two different cycles of Saecular Games survive from the imperial period.[11] A plethora of other texts and documents: calendars and commentaries on calendars; novels, history, satire and epic, and their scholia; a handful of invaluable antiquarian texts or least extensive excerpts and summaries of them (Varro; Festus); the legal codes; philosophical texts; oracles and aretalogies; immense numbers of votive inscriptions; an array of texts by primitive Christians, canonical and pseudepigraphic, Jewish writers, adherents of Hermes Thrice Greatest, Graeco-Egyptian 'magicians', and Manicheans, as well as an extensive range of sermons and polemics by Christian authors, form the basis of our knowledge of the history of religion under the Empire.

Here however I want to concentrate upon historiography. Roman historical writing (including biography), with its marked moralizing tendency, certainly does reflect the pre-occupations of the time of composition. Nevertheless it is still possible to find in it genuine information about earlier periods. Of the massive historiographical output during the Principate just a small number of texts have survived, works by Plutarch, Tacitus, Suetonius, Cassius Dio, Herodian, the pseudonymous author(s) of the *Historia Augusta*, Ammianus Marcellinus, and then an ever larger number of texts from Late Antiquity. Together they cover roughly the entire imperial period to AD 600, though there are a number of gaps. But the most important and influential work is that composed by the Augustan historian Livy (Titus Livius).[12] His account begins with the founding of Rome (traditional date: 753 BC). The first decade (group of ten books) continues the story down to the year 293 BC. Then there is a break, as books 11 to 20 are missing, but the period from 218 to 166 BC is narrated in the next twenty-five books. Livy quickly gained such authority that the other histories of the Republic written in Latin (and Greek) ceased to be re-copied even in antiquity and so were lost apart from fragments. Our modern idea of the regal period and the Republic is largely derived from him.

We know of scarcely any reliable texts dating from the period before 300 BC that could have been drawn upon in the late first century BC.[13] The names of peoples, places and individuals are mentioned in narratives from a much later date; a few documents do exist (for example the treaty with Carthage, and the bi-lingual gold tablets from Pyrgi, both mentioned p. 52 below), but they tend to be either difficult to understand and contextualize (e.g. the Lapis Niger, see p. 51 below), or have been subjected to heavy editing over time (e.g. the Twelve Tables). Quite apart from problems of dating, archaeological

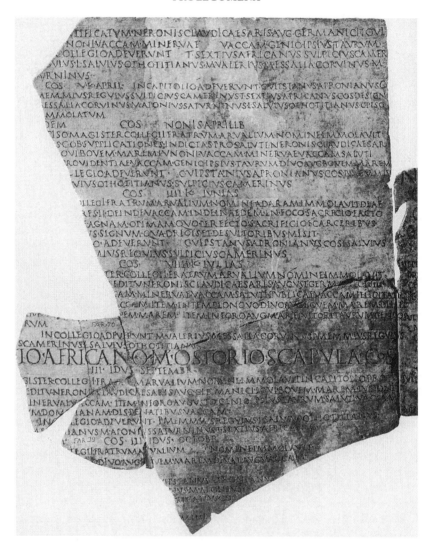

2. Fragment of the minutes of the Arval Brothers (*fratres Arvales*).

Over the period of three hundred years during which copies were inscribed on stone, the minutes of the *fratres Arvales* reveal considerable differences in content and execution. This fragment, from the reign of Nero, is organized in a comprehensible manner that makes the chronological sequence quite clear – special emphasis is laid on the change of ordinary consuls (the large capitals towards the bottom), marking the new civil year.

The centring of the dates within a given year (the consuls are denoted simply by the abbreviation *cos* without naming them each time) highlights

42

discoveries are often quite indeterminate as regards the overall nature of a site, its purpose, and the identity of those who used it. It would be methodologically quite wrong to try and integrate such sources straightforwardly into the image of early Roman history offered by the historiographical tradition – in other words, given the virtually total loss of earlier Roman historiography and the wreckage of the Greek historiography of Rome, Livy.[14] What we can extract from the texts that describe the founding of Rome, the regal period, and the early Republic, is the idea of their own history entertained by the Romans of the Late Republic and early Principate.

Every society creates an image of its own history. This image is configured by certain current or contemporary pre-occupations and interests, and is directed far more towards these than by a concern for how things really were. Even when it is quite impossible to know how things really stood, societies yearn for a pre-history. Take the example of the early Germanic tribes, who were taken up quite inappropriately by Wilhelmine Germany as the fore-fathers of the Reich, and still feature as such in some popular histories, even though large parts of what is now southern and central Germany were inhabited historically by Celtic peoples.[15] That is one unwelcome fact suppressed in this ideologically driven version of history; others are that one can only describe the Germanic peoples as an ethnic group from the pre-Roman iron age, that is from about 500 BC; and only speak of 'Germania' from about the time of Julius Caesar (Todd 1975: 15–54). But historical facts are of course quite uninteresting if a society is bent on creating a unified history stretching as far back in time as possible: the mythical ancient Germans were, so to speak, the children of the failed German revolution of 1848. In much the same way, the image of early Roman history in the work of Livy or Dionysius of Halicarnassus mirrors the interests and ideas of their time (Haehling 1989). It is only occasionally that we can find authentic details relevant to the history of the period narrated.[16]

---

2. Fragment of the minutes of the Arval Brothers (*continued*).

the further subdivisions of the text. The inscription details the performance of a number of non-routine sacrifices (performed on 5 and 28 March, 5 April, 29 May, 23 June, 11 September, 12 and 13 October), but the entries also devote a good deal of space to listing the individuals present on each occasion. Three fragments a-c: the large one was excavated at La Magliana in 1868/9; the first line of the year's entry is on the previous slab. Dimensions: *c.* 1.00m x 0.77m. Marble, AD 59/60. Museo Nazionale delle Terme. *CIL* VI 2042 = Scheid 1998a: 70–75 no. 28.

For a historian of religion there is another difficulty apart from the question of sources. Under ancient conditions religion does not really have an independent history. As I have suggested above, religion is intimately bound up with political life and to that extent is an epi-phenomenon of social, economic and political history.[17] Décalages nevertheless may occur: some trends may set in long before they become politically explosive; or changes may take place in the politi-cal or economic sphere and only later have cultural or social effects. It is not difficult to provide examples of such décalage. Grave-goods are always very important in pre-historic archaeology. In constructing a chronology of such finds, we have to take into account that they belonged to the dead person, and as such may have been manufac-tured up to fifty years earlier. There may thus be a gap of up to a half-century between the socio-historical phenomenon – the accumulation of wealth or the import of luxuries – and the religious act documented by the archaeological find.

From the kind of sources at our disposal, it is impossible to extract a narrative history of Roman religion from its beginnings to the late Republic that makes much sense. All we can do is to highlight import-ant non-religious factors that influenced the development of religious institutions. This will help to provide a context for the few known facts of religious significance. It will also help to develop the reader's awareness of the historical contingency of the topics discussed in the following thematic chapters. The book closes with a continuation of this historical sketch to include the Empire up to the late fourth century AD, which has been completely rewritten for this edition.

Periodization

The periodization of Roman political history can reasonably be based on a single criterion, its changes of constitution, and so employ head-ings such as Regal period (before 509 BC), Republic (509–27 BC), Principate (27 BC–AD 284), and Dominate (from AD 284). However such a model, when applied to religion, implies both a narrative continuity and a primacy of political development that are inappro-priate to crucial features of the religious history of antiquity. The following alternative periodization for the time before the Principate is intended to highlight processes and change, though admittedly it is not based on a single yardstick:

1. **Pre-history**: from around 1000 BC to 625 BC, with the paving of the Forum as a cut-off point (Cornell 1995: 94);

2. Urbanization and development of the social structure of Rome, from 625 BC to the late fourth century BC;

3. Politicization: from the end of the institutionalizing processes marked by the Lex Ogulnia of 300 BC. As the cut-off point between this phase and the next one might choose 196 BC, the year of the foundation of the priesthood of the *Tresviri epulonum*, the last of the city's prestigious priestly colleges to be founded prior to the third century AD.

4. Hellenization from 186 BC to 42 BC, beginning with the *SC de Bacchanalibus*, already mentioned, and ending with the deification of Julius Caesar.

Pre-history

In reconstructing pre-history we are forced to rely entirely on archaeological sources. In view of my scepticism of the literary sources, I see no point in discussing the traditions that gave rise to them. Recent excavations have found traces of settlement on the Palatine going back to the Palaeolithic (Anzidei and Gioia 1995). I begin my account, however, not with the Stone Age but at the point at which we can first speak of Latin culture. We can find evidence for such an independent culture of the Latin people only from the beginning of the first millennium BC (Smith 1996a: 24–43). For it was only at the end of the Bronze Age, at the turn of the second/first millennium, that the 'ethnogenesis' of the Latins, the process of becoming a distinct cultural entity, occurred. The culture of bronze-age Italy was strikingly uniform: it is only at the time of the transition between the Bronze Age and the Iron Age that we begin to find evidence for distinguishable peoples and ethnic groupings, in the form of regional cultures.[18]

Ethnogenesis is a very complicated process, which cannot be explained simply by appealing to the factors of immigration and the domination of peoples already settled in Italy, but has to be examined on a regional basis. Groups that had been living in a given area for a long time began to develop their own separate traditions that differentiate them both from their neighbours and from immigrant groups. The latter entered Italy from several directions: most significantly, in Lombardy and Piedmont, the 'Golasecca culture' has close links with the Hallstadt culture north of the Alps, while the Middle Adriatic (Picene) cultures of central Italy, and the Apulian culture further south, are linked, also linguistically, with different Illyrian peoples

45

across the Adriatic. In the area of Emiglia-Romana and Etruria, the dominant iron-age culture is Villanovan, characterized by a distinctive burial custom, the (bi-conical) urn placed in a deep shaft. The southernmost branch of this culture, what is now called 'Latial culture' (in Italian: *cultura laziale*), which includes the area of Rome, developed a distinctive variant of this practice: the dead were buried in hut-urns, small round urns with a roof and a little modelled door, which were themselves placed inside larger urns (Cornell 1995: 51).[19] It is also from this period, between 1000 and 900 BC, that we find the first clear traces of iron-age settlement on the site of the later city of Rome

The chronology of the Latial culture is divided into the following phases (Cornell 1995: 50; Smith 1996a: xii):

I – the first phase, 1000 to 900 BC, Final Bronze Age.
IIa – 900 to 830 BC: the early Iron Age (Villanovan): pre-urban.
IIb – 830 to 770 BC: the early Iron Age (cont'd): proto-urban.
III – 770 to 730/720 BC, the end of the early Iron Age: proto-urban.
IVa – 730/720 to 640/630 BC, the early and middle orientalizing phase: proto-urban.
IVb – 640/630 to 580 BC, the late orientalizing phase: urban (Archaic period).

Prior to phase IV, the most important sources are funerary ensembles. Burials are a first-rate source for religious history, though unfortunately only few examples survive from this early period, and indeed from the following centuries. It is a characteristic of Latial culture that graves were cared for over a long period. This is evident archaeologically from the fact that new graves are often located precisely beside old ones, even after the lapse of thirty or forty years. We can therefore conclude that the family knew exactly where a member had been buried even an entire generation earlier. Such knowledge is most easily explicable on the hypothesis that the inhabitants practised a continuous grave-cult.

From the point of view of the archaeology of religion, it is not merely the tomb itself that is of interest. What about the ground above it? If there were a cult of the grave, the deceased would have been fed there, and regular celebrations, banquets or feasts, held in his or her honour. What was eaten at these ceremonies? What was poured into the ground? The archaeologist can see from the taphonomic remains whether the people present ate pork rather than beef, or the other way round, and from pollen samples can determine the different kinds of grain used at the sacrifices. It is also possible to determine whether olive-oil was poured onto the grave. Analysis of earth-samples provides a great deal of information that we do not have from older excavations, because the relevant techniques have only been developed in recent decades. That means that archaeologists and historians of religion can rejoice at every grave that has remained undiscovered up to now, because, when found and excavated, it is sure to provide us with information that would simply have been destroyed by the process of unsophisticated digging if it had been found fifty or a hundred years ago (Morris 1992).

This problem is especially acute in the case of the early history of Rome. The most spectacular excavations relevant to this period, for example that of the Forum, were conducted already at the end of the nineteenth century and resumed only recently. Although they were carried out with a high degree of expertise and competence for the period, many questions that have arisen in the light of later knowledge were not taken into account then, and a great deal of potential information thus unknowingly destroyed (Ross Holloway 1994: 20–36). It is an increasingly oppressive truism that every excavation involves the partial or total destruction of what is uncovered.

In the early archaeology of Italy, the form of burial, whether the body was cremated or inhumated (interred in the earth), is an important criterion of difference: there is a marked boundary, roughly following the Tiber valley, between the cultures that cremated (to the north and west) and those that interred (to the south and east). It is characteristic of early Rome, set on the boundary between them, that both forms are found there. What does the tomb look like? Were the deceased placed in a squatting position? Were they buried in so-called burial-trenches, i.e. buried supine or placed on their side, with legs extended? Such things, together with osteological analysis, can provide information about the composition of a population, the deceased person's social position and age, and the probable cause of death. Such questions were already asked in the past, but the major interest then was the ensemble of grave-goods, and particularly the items of potential value to connoisseurs. Here we have another problem: tomb-raiding is a business already known in antiquity, when the Egyptian pyramids were systematically robbed, often not long after the end of the relevant dynasty. Of course, nineteenth-century archaeologists were also interested up to a point in the less valuable funerary goods, especially the pottery, but nobody would have dreamed of asking what kind of food was placed in the grave, even if it had been technically possible to provide an answer.

A question that has recently become topical concerns the relative ordering and positioning of graves in a cemetery. Especially in the early history of Latium, the precise manner in which the graves are grouped in concentric circles around a pair of ancestors, and the correlation between distance from the centre and dwindling number of grave-goods, is very relevant as an indication of the social position of the deceased. And even the size of the 'no man's land', the unused space between the groups of graves belonging to different families, can tell us a great deal about the growth of the cemetery and the social structure of the community that buried there.

As an example, I want to take the finds from near the small town of Osteria dell'Osa in the Campagna (on the road from Rome to Palestrina, near ancient Gabii). Here the Italian archaeologist Anna Maria Bietti Sestieri in the 1980s carried out one of the most interesting excavations of an early Latin cemetery. Her discoveries, on the basis of several hundred tombs, match what we know from other comparable discoveries in Latium, and can thus be used as a model of the development of many Latin sites of the early Iron Age, including Rome.[20]

A large Phase IIa (900–830 BC) necropolis at Osteria dell'Osa provides evidence for the burial practice of at least two extended families. All the tombs contain grave-goods, in the form of miniaturized versions of bronze and ceramic objects. Some were cremation burials, others, the majority, contained complete inhumations. The cremation-tombs invariably contain the remains of males, usually equipped with miniature weapons. The inhumation tombs also contained goods, though on average fewer, but no weapons. These data can be interpreted as follows: cremation-burial was reserved for leading family-members who were active as warriors, whereas everyone else was inhumated. Of course women's graves were also found; almost all, whether they contain richer or poorer grave-goods, contain a spindle as a gender-marker. Overall we can say that these are the cemeteries of fairly small villages (the population of Osteria dell'Osa may have amounted to c.100 individuals), characterized by a marked degree of family solidarity. Each person seems to have been locked into the tight solidarity of a family and, beyond that, of the whole village. Social differentiation was low, age and sex were the decisive criteria. However there were a few specialists, perhaps even a religious specialist, if we may legitimately infer this on the basis of the goods found in one tomb (no. 128), which include a terracotta figurine of a person bringing an offering, and a miniature bronze (sacrificial?) knife (Bietti Sestieri 1992: 238).

In the following period, socio-economic differentiation became more marked. Something like an upper class began to take shape. The discovery of imported goods in this phase shows that contacts with the outside world played an important role in this development. We might put it so: these people owned luxury goods because they were relatively rich; but they were rich because they had contacts to the outside world. Establishing contacts with the outside world and the accumulation of wealth seem to be two processes that are intimately related. One of the main internal functions of imported goods was as a medium of expression of claims to distinction and status (Smith 1996a: 106–25).

In Latial phase IIb (830–770 BC), we begin to find smaller settlements fusing with others to create larger ones, so that this can be considered the beginning of the proto-urban phase. This process took place in the Campagna of Latium, but not in the Alban Hills, which form the boundary of Latium to the south, and which seem to have experienced an eclipse at this time. We may assume that an analogous process took place in Rome too, where the inhabited area was now extended from the Palatine to include the Capitol and the Forum, and the Esquiline became the major necropolis. There is in fact no clear break between phases IIb and III: as the degree of general socio-economic differentation increased, so the upper class became increasingly distinct from the other social groups. This period can thus be identified as that of the creation of the *gentes*. These were stable groups, still based on kin; but whereas the older model included all members of the family on a basis of equality, we now observe a clear differentiation between a patron (and patroness) on the one hand, and their clients on the other: dependent and substantially poorer members of a *gens* at Osteria dell'Osa are in these later phases no longer buried in close proximity to the patron.[21]

The early Iron Age comes to an end with Latial IVa, the early/middle orientalizing phase (730/20 to 640/30 BC). Well-appointed burials from this period have been found at several places in Latium, for example the 'princely graves' at Praeneste, with tombs containing magnificent imported gold table-services and other objects, some with Egyptianizing motifs, which derive from the international trade-networks that criss-crossed the Mediterranean in the Archaic period.[22] Already from the beginning of Latial III, *c.* 770 BC, the Greeks had maintained a permanent presence in Italy. At around that date, the Euboeans had founded a trading post on the island of Pithecusa, today called Ischia, in the Bay of Naples. Their presence naturally had an enormous impact on the means available to the emergent élite of expressing social distinction. The Graeco-Egyptian luxury products we can identify in graves from Latial IVa were brought to Latium by Greek traders, who obtained them in turn from Phoenician or Carthaginian middle-men. The visible internal differentiation of societies, which had an immediate effect upon the religious sphere, was thus directly linked to the development of external contacts, themselves to a very large extent the result of the permanent presence of the Greeks in Italy. It did not take long before Southern Italy came to be named Magna Graecia, 'Greater Greece', a neat illustration of the density of Greek presence in Italy (Colini et al. 1977).

Urbanization and Social Development

At Rome, there are indications that suggest the fusion of the village-settlements on the Palatine/Capitol with those on the Quirinal to form a nucleated settlement (proto-urbanization) at the end of Latial phase IIb (800–770 BC). This settlement is clearly Latin; Etruscan (i.e. late Villanovan) influence is an important general factor in early Latin culture, but plays no recognizable role in the development of urbanism.[23] There is moreover no archaeological evidence for Etruscan kings at Rome. The phase of urbanization proper begins at Rome more than a century later, at the beginning of the late orientalizing period (*c.* 650/40 BC), when some wattle-and-daub huts by the (later) Via Sacra in the Forum Romanum were levelled to create a shared centre with a pavement of tamped earth. The fact that the area was paved and enlarged around 625 (or a little earlier) tends to confirm this interpretation. At around the same time, the construction of the first permanent houses, on the Velia (and, from shortly before 600 BC, an entire row of *atrium*-houses on the Palatine), built of stone and with tiled roofs, marks another aspect of the same process. They stand in sharp contrast to the informal aggregation of scattered individual house-clusters in wattle-and-daub and with thatched roofs supported by timber trusses, which had grown up over the course of the previous century or so.[24]

Archaeology therefore suggests that the city of Rome came into existence about a century after the traditional date of 753 BC. The discovery in the 1980s on the north-eastern slope of the Palatine of some remains of a wall dating from the eighth century BC and identified by the adherents of the mythico-historical school as the 'walls of Romulus' makes no difference to this conclusion (Cornell 1995: 72f.): not only are there much older remains on the Palatine, but such writers fail to enquire, as the critical historian must, how authors writing centuries later could have obtained any genuine knowledge of the remote, pre-literate past; and prefer to fall back on myth, taken to preserve nuggets of historical truth, in order to interpret archaeological data in themselves wholly inconclusive.

The crucial archaeological discoveries in the Forum are the paving of *c*. 625 BC and the inclusion of the later Comitium, an assembly-area, which was roughly circular like the sites of political assemblies we know from Greece.[25] The Forum was built up relatively quickly. Facing the Comitium, a building that can be interpreted as the first *curia*, the meeting-place of the Senate, was constructed *c*. 600 BC in stone. The first stone-built shrine in the Comitium followed shortly afterwards (*c*. 580). This is the site, facing both the Curia and the Arch of Septimius Severus, that from the early first century BC (and still today) was marked by the Lapis Niger. The 'black' (actually bluish-grey limestone) slabs were lifted in 1899 and again in 1955; among the finds beneath was a tapering *cippus* (block) of imported tufa inscribed in archaic Latin.[26] The foundation-deposit beneath this *cippus* includes a fragment of an Attic black-figure vase, dated *c*. 575–50 BC, showing Hephaestus, the Greek smith-god, riding a mule; and it is now thought that the site was a shrine (not yet a temple) for the god Vulcan, a *Volcanal*. Another early building, the *Regia*, marks the southern boundary of the Forum area (see pl. 24): this was the 'Royal Palace', and later a cult-centre reserved to the *rex sacrorum* and the *pontifex maximus*.[27]

The urbanization phase (Latial IVb) is characterized by four developments. Two I have already mentioned, namely the establishment of a central, public space; and monumentalization – the construction of stone buildings and paved areas. The third is the decline in number and quality of grave-goods. This phenomenon is very marked in the cemeteries of Latin sites outside Rome; whereas in Latial phase IVa (early-middle orientalizing phase), high-status graves were richly furnished, virtually no excavated graves can certainly be assigned to the period from *c*. 600 – 400 BC (the end of Latial late orientalizing phase, and the beginning of the Archaic period). It is generally believed that funerary expenditure during this period was lavished on 'prospective' public display, that is, on aristocratic competition in the form of banquets and entertainments, rather than on 'retrospective' treasure assigned privately to the dead (Cornell 1995: 105–8). The fourth characteristic of early urbanization is Hellenization. The black-figure vase in the foundation-deposit beneath the Lapis Niger indicates that the Roman god Volcanus (Vulcan) was already in this very early period identified with the Greek god Hephaestus. However this inference is legitimate only because this was the site of the *Volcanal*: the principle cannot be freely transferred to other cases where pottery with paintings of Greek gods has been found.[28]

Greek influence can also be discerned in the general lay-out of the city. Among the specific features of the Greek *polis* was the creation of an urban centre by dedicating a focal area to public use, and providing political institutions with their appropriate architectural expression. It is precisely this idea that is realized in Rome in the first half of the sixth century BC. Of course it had been introduced decades earlier in other parts of Italy, into both Greek and Etruscan settlements – we may think of Greek *poleis* such as Sybaris and Tarentum, where dominated Italic peoples made up part of the population; or of Etruscan cities with Greek quarters, such as Gravisca and Pyrgi (we should not ignore the presence of Greek merchants in sixth-century Rome). There are also the Phoenicians, who had been sailing the Mediterranean since the late second millennium, and, as Carthaginians, *Punici*, had had treaty-arrangements with Rome since the sixth century (Scardigli 1981). The Punic and Etruscan texts on the gold tablets from Pyrgi reveal that they maintained a cult of Astarte in that town, which is a mere 50 km (31 miles) from Rome (AA.VV. 1981).

It is unnecessary here to trace every detail of the further development of urban Rome. In general, however, we can say that the area devoted to public use grew, while the Forum itself was increasingly monumentalized. However the temple built in the form of a room to house a cult-statue, which is such a marked feature of the later city, evolved relatively late: the earliest phase of the earliest temple discovered near the church of Sant' Omobono, on the northern edge of the Forum Boarium, the 'cattle-market' (actually a later designation) near the bank of the Tiber, dates only from around 580 BC.[29] Religious monumentalization reached its first – and for long its only – climax with the construction of the temple of Jupiter on the Capitol. Completed at the end of the sixth century, it had a base measuring 61 × 55m and must have been one of the largest temples of its time in the entire Mediterranean area.[30]

This is the point at which it is advisable to expand my chronological frame so as to include later centuries that saw significant changes in Roman social structure. The expansion of cults is one important feature of the entire Archaic period up to 300 BC. It is evidenced by the increasing number of temples, the introduction of new cults from outside Latium, and the transfer of some gentilicial cults to the public sphere. In general, though, it is continuities rather than discontinuities

3. Model of mid-Republican Rome.

It was not until the building-boom of the late Republic that the topographic inconveniences of the City on the Seven Hills were gradually overcome. In this photo, which views the model from the North, from the Quirinal, you can make out, to the right, overlooking the river, the two summits of the Capitoline Hill, the rear one (*Capitolium*) dominated by the temple of Capitoline Jupiter, *Iuppiter Capitolinus*. One can also see how the Palatine (centre) overlooks the Forum (left centre), whose most imposing buildings are the temple of Castor (i.e. Castor and Pollux, the Dioscuri) and, right of it, the temple of Saturn, situated directly below the slope of the *Arx* (the nearer summit of the Capitoline). The Campus Martius is not yet built up, nor the Isola Tiberina. Moving left along from the Tiber bridge (presumably representing a wooden predecessor of the Pons Aemilius), one can pick out the valley of the Circus immediately behind and below the Palatine; beyond it is the Aventine, as yet barely inhabited. Museo della Civiltà Romana, EUR.

that characterize the period of transition from the regnal period to the Republic, that is, the late sixth and early fifth centuries BC. Apart from temple-foundations, it is difficult to isolate specifically 'religious' data. The priests seem to have been specialists, and their colleges were relatively small (Beard, North, Price 1998: 1, 18–30). On the other hand, there were a great many individual priesthoods for particular cults. Institutionalized religious specialism of this kind is intimately bound upon with social developments. The early Republic saw a growing distinction between patricians and plebeians, which only came to an end, as I have already mentioned, with the development of a unified élite at the end of the fourth century (Hölkeskamp 1987); at the same time, the compromise then arrived at involved the recognition of a continuing distinction between patricians and plebeians.[31] The annalistic tradition of assigning precise years to the passage of specific legislation here in fact conceals a highly complex process of social change that remains hard to understand. The development of the paired consulate probably belongs to this period, as does the strengthening of the agnatic principle in the family, which meant giving the *pater familias* unquestioned power over life and death in the private sphere, and reducing the influence of the clan (*gens*) in favour of the nuclear family.[32] At latest by the end of the fourth century, however, we enter a new phase, that of politicization, symbolized by the passing of the lex Ogulnia in the year 300 BC.

Politicization

The Lex Ogulnia was a law prescribing that the priestly colleges be enlarged from three, four or five members to nine in the cases of the Augurs and *pontifices*; and which established the former *duoviri sacris faciundis* – a pair of experts who, when the need arose, interpreted the oracles in the Sibylline books – as a permanent panel of ten members (*decemviri sacris faciundis*).[33] The aim of these increases was to grant wealthy plebeians places in the colleges, which up to now had been exclusively patrician. The law thus forms part of the previous period, the period of the 'Conflict of the Orders', that ended when the most important public offices, the annual magistracies and the life-long priesthoods, were opened to plebeians and were no longer the exclusive preserve of the patricians (Hölkeskamp 1987: 146f.). It hardly requires stressing that the passage of such a law presupposes that the élite, despite its difficult genesis out of the patricians and the wealthiest plebeian families, was already relatively unified. This process may be reckoned to have been completed a half-century earlier. The great expansion of Rome into Latium after the Gauls' sack of the city in 390 BC, ending with the establishment of Roman hegemony over Old Latium with the defeat of the Latin revolt in 340 BC, demonstrates that an internal consensus had been arrived at that allowed internal competition within the élite to be channelled into military aggression.

In relation to reform of the priesthoods, the Lex Ogulnia marks not an end but a beginning.[34] In the next century there were a whole series of reforms in the religious area, partly in the form of laws regulating

54

membership of the priestly colleges. The most important of these was that the creation of a special, complicated procedure for electing the *pontifex maximus*, which later became the highest priestly office, by popular vote. We can probably summarize the various developments by saying that authority in the religious area was decentralized as far as possible, quite contrary to the policy of the famous censor Appius Claudius Caecus that I mentioned in the previous chapter (p. 26 above). There grew up a set of (unwritten) rules under which, for example, a family might only be represented in a given college by one member at a time; with the result that the roster of priests at Rome already in the third century comprised more than fifty persons (Rüpke 2005a). The process of politicization is apparent here in that the social group allowed to occupy religious offices was assimilated to the one that wielded political authority. As a result religion was increasingly involved in the conflicts within the political arena: an obvious example is the reform I have just mentioned, the early third-century election of the *pontifex maximus* by seventeen of the thirty-five tribes, which replaced election by the college from among its own members.[35]

Another area where we can observe the politicization of religious rituals prior to 196 BC is that of the triumph, the ceremonious entry of the victorious army and its commander into the city of Rome after a victorious campaign (see pl. 11).[36] This ritual became ever more lavish. Indeed, an entire new genre of painting seems to have been developed in the third century for this religious context. Conquered cities and peoples were represented on placards, which were then displayed in the procession.

Another, no less important, instance is the building of temples. Large temples were paid for with war-booty, for the wars of the united élite were increasingly successful from the end of the fourth century (indeed, so successful that later historians claimed that many of the places in question had already been conquered in the fifth century or even earlier). As I have already explained, the victorious commander tried to perpetuate his name by paying for the construction of such monumental buildings. This was the chief means whereby new gods were introduced into Rome. Some of these new gods – and this is both new and characteristic of this period – reflected in their very names the ideals of an élite that both went to war and performed religious functions: in 302 BC, for example, a temple was dedicated to the goddess *Salus*, 'Safety', 'Health' or 'Welfare'; in 294, a temple to the goddess *Victoria*, 'Victory'; in 250, a temple to the goddess *Fides*, 'Loyalty to, and trust in, our social superiors'; in 233, a temple to the god *Honos*, 'Honour'. This list could easily be extended (p. 27 above).

The process of the politicization of religion can be traced further into the following period, Rome's overseas expansion after the Second Punic War. The rules dealing with *obnuntiatio*, concerning the influence that Augurs might excercise over political decision-making, above all by claiming that offences against the sacral law had taken place, were developed in the second century BC.[37] Attempts were made to extend the people's right to elect the *pontifex maximus* to the appointment of all the priests of the four main colleges. After several failures, this was achieved at the end of the second century by the passage of the lex Domitia (104 BC). The same period was full of religio-political conflicts and scandals, both forward- and backward-looking; perhaps the most spectacular is the capital trial in 114–13 BC of three Vestals for alleged unchastity, which became the occasion for a furious political confrontation and ended with the execution of all three of the unfortunate women.[38]

The rules under which the politico-religious conflicts of the late Republic were played out have their origins in this phase of politicization in the second century; despite all prophecies of doom, they were still in force right to the end of the Republic. In these conflicts, the point was not to break the religious rules oneself, but to claim that one's political opponent had done so. The one so accused would immediately try to turn the tables on his accuser. Such behaviour is not a symptom of the decline of religious belief but shows, on the contrary, how strongly the rules were in force.[39] That is the reason why I have not extended the phase of politicization right down to the end of the Republic, but have tried instead to single out yet another process and use it to designate a separate fourth phase.

Hellenization

It must already have become clear when I was discussing pre-history and urbanization that it is absurd to try to make out 'purely' Roman or Latin cultural traits, or to distinguish between them and influences from outside that might have distorted the true essence of Roman or Latin culture – the very idea is founded on a Romantic commitment to the nation and its supposed soul. As early as Latial phases III and IVa (*c.* 770–630 BC) contacts extending to North Africa and the eastern Mediterranean can be documented. However the historiography of Roman religion was influenced far into the twentieth century by an isolationist or purist approach to the subject, above all by Georg Wissowa's *Religion und Kultus der Römer* [1902[1], 1912[2]]. This is a standard work that can still be consulted today on individual points; but overall its impact has been negative, since Wissowa, in keeping with a marked trend both before and after his time, was committed to an essentialist or 'nationalist' re-construction of the early history of Roman religion, which ultimately, in the Germany of the nineteen-twenties to -forties, became explicitly racist.[40]

Non-Roman influences upon Rome are thus older than Rome itself. Thanks to her imperial expansion from the third century BC, however, such influences acquired a new intensity. During the course of the First Punic War (268–241), Rome became master of Italy, and as a consequence embarked upon a direct military confrontation, and cultural exchange, with the Greek settlements of southern Italy, most of which had however already been forced under the suzerainty of the Italic Oscans. Neapolis (Naples), the 'new city', is the only Greek city in the area that managed to survive as such into Roman times.

In the mid-third century, the first performances of literary versions of Greek dramas in the Latin language were staged at Rome. Livius Andronicus and Gn. Naevius are the two poets and 'directors' we can connect with this development. Both of them came from the south-Italian area, probably Campania, which was heavily influenced by Greek culture. Plays in the Greek language (*ludi scaenici*, stage-plays) are at least a hundred years older; Roman tradition assumes they existed already in 364 BC.[41] Since such performances took place, at least in principle, only in a sacral context, as constituent elements of religious festivals – and thus strongly influenced the wider form and content of such festivals – these are very important dates in the history of religion. Moreover Greek actors and performers were organized as Dionysiac associations (*technitai Dionysou*) and thus constituted an important extension of the range of (professional) associations in the city of Rome (Le Guen 2001). The diversity of such associations – we may think of the Bacchanals, the Jews and the adherents of Isis – is an important feature of the later history of Roman religion. The Romans themselves projected their system of associations way back into pre-history (Gabba 1984); but in fact there is no evidence for their existence before the mid-third century, nor for any organizational form other than the Hellenistic Greek type.

We can study the process of Hellenization, which I want to touch on exclusively from the point of view of the history of religion, in three further types of influence, whose main impact justifies my dating the period so late.[42]

The first is Roman appropriation of Greek sculpture and other 'art' objects. After the end of the Second Punic War (218–201 BC), thanks to the (re-)conquest of the Greek towns in Southern Italy, Sicily and elsewhere, large amounts of Greek sculpture was acquired by Romans of the élite. Though it was admired aesthetically, such sculpture was not interpreted primarily as 'art' but rather as religious artefacts, as statues of gods and heroes. They certainly were used to adorn private houses, villas and gardens, but mainly they were displayed in temples and public buildings (Pape 1975; Stewart 2003). This massive robbery of religious items from their original context heightened awareness of the supra-regional connections of local pantheons; and the fact that cult-statues, normally fixed permanently to a particular location, could be transported and re-used raised the question of the appropriate rules for handling gods, and whether one's own world-view was universally appropriate. At the same time, Greek art brought a substantial increase in complexity to the Roman system of religious signs, and thus to its expressive possibilities and its application to different aspects of reality.[43] Moreover, the mode of acquisition, forcible acquisition or plunder, clearly reveals the ambivalence of the entire process of Hellenization at Rome: an interest – in private contexts often quite an intense interest – in Greek culture co-existed with political hostility and often enough a complete disregard for the humanity of the enemy.

The influence of Greek patterns of thinking was a second, more subtle, form of import. We possess some fragments (probably the earliest extant Latin prose) of Ennius' translation or paraphrase, apparently entitled *Euhemerus*, of a Greek text, the *Sacred Record*, by Euhemerus of Messene (late fourth/early third century BC), which argued that the beings currently worshipped as gods were originally just important human beings, kings of early times.[44] Zeus/Jupiter had thus originally been a king. In contrast to the reaction of many readers, it seems that neither Euhemerus nor Ennius saw this as a criticism of religion, for nothing alters the fact that Zeus/Jupiter now has the quality of a god and is rightfully worshipped as one. Not a criticism, then, but an attempt at historicizing religion: the claim is that religion, in its present form, being product of history, was not always as it is now (Müller 1993).[45]

In the following period we repeatedly come across instances of the influence of Greek philosophy. However the earliest Latin texts of any length to reflect this influence, those of Cicero, who was philosophically an Academic (that is, a sceptic), and of the Epicurean didactic poet Lucretius, whom I have mentioned earlier, date from as late as the second third of the first century BC. The very fact that I have classified them here according to the Greek philosophical schools they represent, shows clearly enough their respective sources of inspiration.[46] Apart from such philosophical texts, however, we can also find Greek influence in the works of antiquarian writers. In the second century BC, too, the Romans started thinking systematically about the origins of their religion (and other institutions), especially their religious monuments and rituals. They did not simply take them for granted and get on with performing them, but tried to ascribe their religious institutions to specific origins: this priesthood was instituted by king Numa, that ritual was imported from Etruria or from the Sabines, and so on. This process of historicizing reflection began with Fabius Pictor, not the historian (writing history was another 'Greek' practice) but a man of the same name, possibly a *pontifex* of the second century BC, who wrote on cult-matters.[47] And it culminates in the main religious work of the polymathic M. Terentius Varro (116–27 BC), the 16 books of *Antiquitates rerum divinarum*, The Religious Antiquities, itself just part of the *Antiquitates rerum humanarum et divinarum*, The Human (Roman) and Religious Antiquities, completed in 47 BC. Varro's ambitious aim was to lay bare the historical bases of the whole of contemporary Roman religion.[48]

The structure of the *Antiquitates rerum divinarum*:

Book 1 (= Book 26 of the complete work): Introduction and plan of the work
Books 2–4:   *De hominibus*, on the priesthoods:
    2: *Pontifices*
    3: Augurs
    4: *Quindecimviri sacris faciundis*
Books 5–7:   *De locis*, on cult-sites:
    5: *Sacella* (open-air cult-sites and shrines)
    6: *Aedes sacrae* (temples in the narrower sense)
    7: *loca religiosa* (tombs etc.)
Books 8–10:   *De temporibus*, on festivals and the religious calendar:
    8: *Feriae* (festivals that 'belong' to a divinity)
    9: *Ludi circenses* (chariot-races)
    10: *Ludi scaenici* (stage performances)
Books 11–13:   *De sacris*, on rituals:
    11: Consecrations
    12: *Sacra privata*
    13: *Sacra publica*
Books 14–16:   *De dis*, about the gods, especially the etymology of their names:
    14: Gods whose names have a clear significance (*di certi*)

15: Gods whose names have no clear significance (*di incerti*)

16: Select grand deities (*di praecipui atque selecti*)

Augustine, *Civ. Dei* 6. 3 = Varro, *Antiquitates rerum divinarum* [= *RD*] frg. 4 Cardauns

A fragment from Book 1:

> The ancient Romans worshipped Summanus, who sends lightning at night, more than Jupiter, who sends lightning during the day. But once an important and lofty temple had been built in honour of Jupiter, the masses flocked to it because of its splendour, so much so that it is difficult to find anyone (nowadays) who has even read the name Summanus, let alone heard it spoken.

Varro, *RD* frg. 42 Cardauns

Varro's *Antiquitates rerum divinarum* was the standard work on Roman religion for the whole of antiquity. If a Roman wanted to find out about his religion, this is the work he would consult. If a Christian wanted to find out about Roman religion for polemical purposes, as Augustine did in the early fifth century AD, then he used this late-Republican work by Varro (by a familiar piece of irony, almost all we know of it comes from Augustine's extensive quotations). Varro himself was not a priest;[49] but he dedicated the book to Julius Caesar, in his capacity as *pontifex maximus*.

The third area of Greek influence is divine honours paid to human beings, anticipated in the title of this chapter, From the She-Wolf to Caesar. Divine honours were paid on a large scale to Romans as soon as Rome began to interfere seriously in the Greek east at the end of the third century BC (Mellor 1975). Roman generals were already worshipped as gods in Greek cities, that is, granted their own priests, festivals and festive days, at the beginning of the second century. Of course Rome itself came to be influenced by this development. It became increasingly desirable for important Roman politicians and generals to show that they stood close to divinity. Among Marius' intimates was the Syrian seer Martha (Plutarch, *Mar.* 17.1). Sulla, Pompey and Caesar all declared Venus to be their personal patron: Sulla prided himself on his special relationship to Venus/Aphrodite and assumed the *agnomen* Felix (Blessed);[50] Pompey dedicated the temple at the centre of his theatre-complex in the Campus Martius to Venus Victrix; Caesar emphasized the 'fact' that Venus was the divine ancestor of the *gens* Iulia, and accordingly consecrated the temple in the centre of his new Forum to Venus Genetrix (Venus as Parent).

60

In the end, this rubbing of shoulders between politician and god passed over into identification. Caesar was worshipped as a god in the last months of his life before his assassination. With the consecration in the year 42 BC, his apotheosis was affirmed officially.[51] This is a development that may be taken as an instance of Hellenization (despite its Roman roots, it was taken polemically by some contemporaries to be a form of Orientalization, in allusion to the behaviour of Persian kings), and at the same time forms a reasonable point at which to end a historical overview that has led us from the very beginnings of Rome to the periods from which the bulk of the evidence to be used in the following chapters derives.

Part I

Structures

— 3 —

GODS AND MEN

The Natural Philosophy of Divinity

If it makes any sense at all to speak of 'religion' in ancient Rome, we have to mean the gods. The entire apparatus of religion depends upon them. But as the Roman historian L. Cornelius Sisenna asked (*FRH* 16 fr.123): Do the gods rejoice in the worship (*cultus*) offered them by humans, or are they indifferent to human beings because they are concerned with 'higher matters'? The various Hellenistic philosophical schools, which had made it their concern to ponder what human life is about, provided a variety of answers to this question.

In Hellenistic philosophy, the nature of the gods is dealt with as part of physics. The answer to the question: what are gods? is a by-product of the answer to the question: how did the world, in all its evident complexity, come into being?[1] The Epicureans, themselves indebted to Democritus' fifth-century atomism, argued that the world came about as the result of the endless collision of atoms. Infinite swarms of these particles, in different forms, collide in their free-fall through space and create ever more complex combinations until they form entire worlds – the plural is deliberate. The gods live in the gaps or spaces between these worlds, the *metakosmia* or *intermundia*.[2] Their existence cannot be doubted, because we can see them in dreams and visions: the 'valence atoms' on the surface of their bodies impinge (as do other perceptions too) on the human retina or make an impression on the soul, which is especially receptive during sleep or in trance, though occasionally transmission is distorted.[3] Although the gods too are composed of atoms, their immortality is assured by the dynamic equilibrium between the positive and negative flow of atoms, and so their bodies never decay, as all other things do, animate and inanimate,

65

once the phase of growth is completed. The reason for their blessed-ness is that they have no worries and never will have any, since human beings are of no concern to them. This is in fact the central message of Epicurean philosophy; as Lucretius says: Shake off the fear of divine punishment in life or after-life: everything has its natural cause, the gods take no interest in us.[4]

The Stoics, whose main philosophical positions were established by Zeno of Citium (335–263 BC), Cleanthes of Assos (331–232 BC), and Chrysippus (*c.* 280–207 BC), all of whom taught at Athens in the Painted Stoa (hence the name Stoics), had a far more positive concep-tion of divinity.[5] They accepted the materialism of the Epicureans, but believed – at least some of their more important representatives did – that the universe, composed as it is of the four elements fire, air, water and earth, was subject to cyclical destruction by fire (*ekpyrosis*), fol-lowed by its identical re-creation (*apokatastasis*). Underlying these claims are two basic principles, *hylē* (matter) and *logos* (reason or God), whose interaction alone makes possible the existence of the ele-ments (which can in fact metamorphose into each other) and the for-mation of the successive universes. The four elements can come into existence only when *logos* gives form to raw matter. A special role is played by the combination of fire and air, which, in the form of *pneuma* ('living breath' → vital spirit), suffuses the universe. It can also be understood, at another level, as God (Sedley 1999: 388–90). This pure substance, or God, is concentrated especially in the human soul (*psychē*), but also, as the World-Soul, turns the entire universe into one single living being, into 'God'.

The Sun (which sometimes is called 'creative fire' as opposed to ordinary fire that burns on earth) and the stars are also formed of pure *pneuma*. Here Stoic cosmology offered opportunities for assimilation with members of local pantheons, operating, as it were, as second-class gods. Over against these gods (or in them? suffusing them? logically prior to them? – the system also derives energy from its inconsistencies) stands Logos, Order, Nature, World-reason, Fate (*heimarmenē/fatum*), Providence (*pronoia/providentia*), all of which again can be equated in some sense with God, with Zeus. Cleanthes' *Hymn to Zeus*, written in hexameters, is in fact an encomium of Logos in this sense.[6] The choice of name, and of genre, permits a juxtaposi-tion of abstract concept against the habits of Greek polytheism. Stoic theology can thus be said to combine elements of pantheism, theism and polytheism (Algra 2003: 165–70).

Neither system, Epicurean or Stoic, risked open conflict with the polytheism practised at Athens and elsewhere. Indeed, the Stoics developed a theory of what they thought of as the science of divination, the art of enquiring into the will of the gods, based on their view that there exists in nature a universal sympathy (*sympatheia*, 'co-experience'), an occult or hidden connection between apparently unconnected events, between microcosm and macrocosm. On this account, *pneuma*, which suffuses everything, generates signs that can be read as indications of future events. If we look more closely, however, we find that, committed as the Stoics were to the idea of a single, material and finite god, they have abandoned the plurality of deities, and their anthropomorphic (human) form, both essential features of polytheism. The Epicureans were happy to concede plurality after their own fashion, and permitted the practice of traditional cult up to a point (e.g. *POxy.* 215), but at the same time declared it to be unnecessary: the blessed gods have no care for humankind, so humans need have no care for gods, but should rather – freed from apprehensions – take their lives into their own hands.

What conclusions can we draw from this? To point out that a system is indifferent to self-contradiction is itself to slip into the role of the philosopher, since inconsistencies and ambivalences are inherent in any form of praxis. What we have been discussing so far in this chapter tells us something about what was thinkable in antiquity, and a little bit about what was actually thought; but otherwise, I have been doing precisely what I warned against at the outset, namely fore-grounding texts, especially discursive, argumentative or systematizing texts, as sources. Trying to regularize ancient religious practice like this, so that it can be formulated as a 'doctrine', as a system of thought, is basically to do theology. That is a legitimate undertaking, of course, but it is one that only the objects of our study, namely people in antiquity, had a right to attempt. No modern student of comparative religion can claim this right – even if Comparative Religion, being itself, among other things, a child of liberal Protestant theology, loves doing just that, constructing a new, less dogmatic (and preferably improved) theology for its objects of study.[7]

If we are interested in finding out about the gods of the ordinary man, of the average inhabitant of Rome, male or female, neither philosophically educated nor interested in philosophy,[8] we cannot expect to find answers by trying to systematize a theology that is at best merely implicit. We can only do so by describing practice, and tackling its explicit and implicit assumptions, its problems and contradictions. Practice in this sense means strategies for dealing with certain problems, means competence in using media of communication (not of

67

course unnecessary codes for something that could be expressed more easily in words; cf. Bourdieu 1977: 3–9). For that reason, I begin with people, and ask how far religious practices contributed to reflection about the limits of specifically human identity. In the case of Roman religion, two such areas come to mind: interaction with the dead, and interaction with the gods. Interaction with the animal world, which might also have been diagnostic of human limits, was not a religious issue in Rome. In Egypt, however, where a god could dwell in the body of an animal, the case was different (Dunand and Zivie-Coche 2004: 183; 331f.)

Mortality and Immortality

Ritual behaviour is stereotyped behaviour. So-called 'crisis-rituals', such as funerals, are also characterized by a marked traditionalism. In other words: people have very little choice about how properly to act at such events – one behaves *comme il faut*. Social definitions dominate organic events. This in turn means that it is hazardous to infer the ideas of the individual participants from ritual practices (Douglas 1997). Just as the custom of using wooden coffins is nowadays so ingrained that for many people the choice is not whether to have a coffin but only what kind of coffin (still less is the choice made in view of specific ideas about life after death), and people even insist on one if the deceased is to be cremated, so in Latial and later in Roman culture certain grave-goods were entirely a matter of custom or usage. The objects were often specially made in large numbers for this purpose and produced without any reference to the individual (Graepler 1997: 149–93).

One may however assume that certain symbols evoked a specific range of meanings thanks to analogous social usages, and that most people, though not all, were aware of them. The use of urns in the form of model huts is characteristic, though by no means exclusively so, of Latial culture. This suggests that the dead were expected to carry on dwelling in the locality and to continue the social structures of the living; and at the same time that an existence intimately bound to a particular locality (or rather, to a specific site or house) was regarded as normative for human-beings.[9] The fact that the dead have to be supplied with grave-goods and food-offerings shows that their continued existence to a degree lacks autonomy, that their identity is conferred, not asserted. The theme of 'shades' in later texts makes the same point.[10]

At the same time, however, we also encounter a different line of thought. Urns and sarcophagi may assume the form of temples. The evidently different existence of the dead is here being re-described with reference to the gods, more powerful beings. The fact that the dead are addressed in funerary inscriptions as *di manes*, good gods (though actually the practice only becomes normative in the Principate), is consistent with this. Nevertheless the relation of the deceased individual to the collectivity of the Manes remains unresolved. Some funeraries speak of the *manes* of so-and-so, for example: *dis manibus Publiliae Philetes*, To the Manes of Publilia Philete (*ILS* 7913, Rome); others simply juxtapose the two terms side by side, for example: *d(is) m(anibus) s(acrum). Aurelius Hermias. . .* Sacred to the Manes. Aurelius Hermias . . . (*ILS* 8094, Rome). We can also find the ambivalence expressed at the level of ritual: people deliberately sought the company of the dead at festivals, such as the Parentalia, at which they held a banquet at the grave, and shunned them on days, such as the Lemuria, when the arrival of ghosts was to be feared (Scullard 1981). Human limitation: the boundary lies not between gods and humans as such, but between between immortals (gods) and mortals (living humans). Between them is no man's land (cf. Cicero, *De legibus* 2.19; 22).

Gods of Gold and Ivory

Of course every ritual performed by humans for, or in the sight of, the gods plays a role in maintaining their mutual relation (I will discuss this more fully when we come to sacrifice). Here I want to concentrate on those situations in which Romans had immediate contact with gods, namely in front of the cult-image. Both iconic and aniconic cult were known at Rome. When they came to think about this fact, Romans like Varro – and in this they were just like the Greeks – came to the conclusion that simple aniconic cult, cult without anthropomorphic images of the gods, was earlier that the phase of anthropomorphic cult-images, which easily tends to drift into luxury and excess, and to that extent in itself implies a certain degree of decadence (Varro, *RD* frg. 18 Cardauns; cf. also frg. 15).

Now we know from the Minoan-Mycenaean finds that what the Greeks thought about their own cultic past was simply wrong: both options existed alongside one another from the earliest period for which evidence exists. What can be shown to be false in the Greek case can hardly be true for Rome either. We may allow that the grand, non-transportable cult-statue had an intimate link with its temple, and

4. Relief from the tomb of the Haterii.

This relief, which is assumed once to have adorned the tomb of a family of
building-contractors, is not just of interest because it offers the most
detailed surviving representation of a human-powered jib-crane prepared
for use (cf. Vitruvius, *De arch*. 10.2.1–10)! It also shows a funerary
monument for a woman in the form of a lavishly-decorated pro-style
temple on a high podium. The temple-form, the bust of the dead woman in

that, at the time when the forum was first paved, temples were nothing like as dominant as they were in the Late Republic. *Aedes*, the temple building itself, presupposes a certain conception of ownership that posits the deity so represented as the 'owner' of the temple in question. Thanks to this conception, the deity's connection with, and protection of, the site takes on a different character from cases in which a god is to be worshipped aniconically in a grove or at an open-air altar. In sacral law, the *templum* is not primarily a plot of land but a section of the sky observed by an Augur or magistrate; there was a secondary *templum in terris*, a 'temple' on the ground, but this referred to areas, specially marked out by a spoken formula, for observing augural signs, namely the flight of birds, or lightning.[11] But such areas are not divine 'property' in the required sense.

What distinguishes a cult-image from a representation, say a portrait-bust, in honour of a human being? The question hardly arises if we are talking about an image set up in a central position inside a temple. But even then great pains were taken to make unambiguously clear whose image it was. Statements about gods are at the same time statements about boundaries or limits, about human deficiencies vis-à-vis gods. If the statue is of super-human size, the observer is forced to gape up at it: if the cult-image of *Fortuna huiusce diei*, Today's Good Fortune, was 8m high, when the temple-columns were 11m, this was not out of a sense of fitting proportion, but because such dimensions make an

---

4. Relief from the tomb of the Haterii. (*continued*)

the tympanum, and the eagles on the architrave below it all suggest that private individuals may hope for personal deification after death. This suggestion is combined with portrait-busts of other members of the family arranged between the pilasters along the side of the temple. Busts of this kind allude to the practice of creating portrait-masks of the deceased, and thus to a form of memorialization in which the dead person lives on in the cultic memory of the family in proportion to his (or her) personal achievements. Above the temple, in 'synoptic view', is a compound image showing the dead woman on a couch (*lectus*), with her (deceased) young children playing on the floor, but also an old nurse attending (probably) to the burning of the offering to the *Manes*, spirits, of the deceased on the ninth day after the funeral. To her right is a triple *aedicula* containing a statue of a nude Venus. All this continues the theme of the heroization of the deceased due to her merits. From the Via Labicana [Via Casilina, 8.4 km out of Rome]; see *LTUR Suburb.* 3: 43f. (P. Liverani). Marble, 1.31m x 1.04m, about AD 120. Musei Vaticani , Museo Gregoriano Profano ex Laterense, inv. no. 9998.

overwhelming impression.[12] Images were bound to be beautiful too; such commissions were opportunities for top-grade artists, often brought in from outside, to give of their best; particularly impressive works would be imitated, or copied directly. Beauty could be further emphasized by the use of expensive (because 'beautiful' in the required sense) materials, in particular by the use of gold and ivory (Lapatin 2002). Finally, recognizability could be increased by the depiction of certain attributes, and any possible misunderstanding thereby avoided (see pl. 6).[13]

As far as practicable, cult-images picked up on features also found in accounts of divine epiphanies. How would you recognize a god if you met one in the street? By the features I have just mentioned: size, beauty, attributes; or by the divine scent that drifts about him (important in antiquity, a world without deodorants); or by his strangely radiant face. At any rate, cult-image and epiphany are not far apart (Gladigow 1990a).

Was the deity thought to be especially present in the cult-image? Here the man-made artefact shifts into an indeterminate zone, where one could move at will between the two opposing poles, animate and inanimate (Gordon 1979: 8–10). One might wonder whether a statue's expression had changed, be convinced it had nodded at an idea one had expressed aloud, or under one's breath – this is the typical stuff of ancient accounts. And even if such allusions are most often encountered in literary fiction rather than in the form of reports by actual witnesses, we cannot doubt that there was a widespread desire to be close to the cult-image – to see it, pray to it directly, to touch it. This is also true in negative form: anal intercourse with a statue of

---

5. Seated statue of the goddess Roma.

This colossal statue, whose trunk is made of red porphyry, not only gives an impression of what an ancient cult-statue looked like, but tells us something about how Antiquity was perceived in Late-Renaissance Rome. To create a statue of Roma, an antique white marble head of the goddess was inserted into the trunk of a late first-century AD Minerva, probably found at Cori in Etruria, and new arms and a foot added in a clearly different, modern style. The inscription testifies to the purchase of the 'image of the city of Rome' with public money in the year 1593, and its 'restoration to its former place'. The statue adorns the frontal niche, above the fountain, of Michelangelo's staircase leading up to the piano nobile of the Palazzo Senatorio in the Piazza del Campidoglio, the 'town hall' of the Commune di Roma, whose façade was rebuilt by Girolamo Rainaldi in 1592. The statue is actually much too small for the niche: Michelangelo had intended a colossal Jupiter for this position.

Aphrodite was one of the themes of *Memorabilia*, the literary genre that that collected stories from the past to offer as role models (or, in this case, anti-models); the theme would indeed be even more revealing if it never occurred in reality and were just a voyeuristic fiction (cf. Steiner 2001: 185–250; Stewart 2003: 261–99). In some rituals, the statue was treated as though it were a living person, as is clear from clothing- or washing-ceremonies, and the custom at Rome of announcing to Jupiter the names of people entering the Capitoline temple, and telling the god the time of day.[14] We cannot say for certain whether at Rome these were daily rituals or reserved to special occasions, for example at annual festivals; the latter is more likely. That however makes no difference to my point about playing on the theme of ambivalence.

By no means all images of gods possessed these special features, in the same way that many were not granted the privilege of such tender care. Large statues of gods were often dedicated as votives in temples of other gods.[15] Statuettes formed part of people's household-goods, or could be carried in their travelling luggage (e.g. Apuleius, *Apologia* 61–3). In neither case do we hear of similar accounts or practices, except in relation to the theme of being alive (the second-century BC satirist Lucilius claimed that such beliefs are simply childish: frags. 486–7 Marx). This fact shows that what we might term Roman iconolatry has nothing to do with a supposedly 'primitive' mind-set. Nor is it an item of official belief, correlated with a ritual for 'opening the mouths' of cult-statues, as in Egypt (Smith 1993). We should rather put it that certain divine statues, namely cult-statues in temples, which had a privileged role in ritual communication, *might* act as mediators between humans and gods, both by way of stories about their creation or fashioning, and through the responses of people who beheld them.[16]

There was a further reason for the success of the combination cult-image/temple at Rome (and elsewhere). The anthropomorphic cult-statue was an inherently plausible representational convention: it normally required no supplementary, miraculous legitimation, such as falling from the sky, or being discovered in circumstances that made it specially holy. It was thus freely available, and could easily be reproduced. At the same time it afforded a high degree of individualization and differentiation between deities – just imagine dozens of temples containing rows of similar tree-trunks, or even just standing empty! The relatively refined differences between Jupiter Optimus Maximus, Jupiter Stator and Jupiter Liberator – indeed the dazzling complexity of Roman polytheism *tout court* – presupposes the availability of subtly-differentiated cult-statues in human form.

Action in the Sublunar World

This differentiation was managed mainly by attributes, that is, signs (objects) that regularly accompanied the image of a deity: at Rome, say, Jupiter's thunderbolt or his eagle, Minerva's owl, the helmet of Mars or Roma, the cornucopiae of Annona or a Genius (see plates 5, 6, 13). These attributes however had another function too: they often associate the deity in question with an action. It is in this context that Greek and Roman treatments of divine images typically differ. Whereas attributes became less important in Classical Greece, where representations of the gods tended to concentrate upon idealized human figures (for example in the east-facing section of the procession on the Parthenon frieze, where the gods are hardly distinguishable from the human beings), at Rome attributes become increasingly common.

It has been suggested that this might have to do with a contrast between a Greek concern with being or state, and Roman concentration on action (Radke 1970). Such contrasts between Greece and Rome can be helpful if we are trying to chart contours and contrasts in the Mediterranean area in antiquity – such differences are easily missed nowadays because we have to look at that world from such a great temporal and cultural distance. However they are dangerous if the claim is that we are thereby saying something deeply insightful about the essential nature of both 'peoples' (a term that can anyway only be applied in quite different senses to the city of Rome and the Greek civilization of the eastern Mediterranean). One such essentialist contrast might be between the Greeks' capacity for hard thinking over against the sober, down-to-earth, practically-minded peasants of Roman Italy. Such judgements of course tell us more about the speaker than about the past, since their real function is to define a view of one's own culture by reference to ancient ones. In nineteenth-century Germany, for example, it was common to view 'the Germans', who had proved themselves in 1848 incapable of creating their own nation-state, as the pensive Greeks of the North. In the twentieth century, a similar idea continued to attract intellectuals (the study of Latin at universities still suffers from this over-valuing of the Greeks), while for others it was the Roman imperial tradition that became ever more seductive.[17]

What is the use of an opposition such as 'action' and 'state' in our context? One certainly cannot use it, for example, to explain the difference between Greek ideas about cult-statues and temples, and Roman ones. Although there are many exceptions, the Greeks often

75

placed the cult-statue somewhat away from the back-wall of the *cella* (the main central chamber), as in the case of the gold-and-ivory statue of Athena Parthenos in the Parthenon on the Acropolis at Athens, or that of Nemesis at Rhamnous in Attica. The typical Greek temple itself was erected on a stepped platform (stylobate) with between three and five stone risers; this flight of steps ran continuously along the entire perimeter of the platform, so that, although there was only one main entrance, at the east end facing sun-rise, the *pteron* (the columns running all round the temple) was accessible from all sides. Roman cult-images by contrast were normally positioned directly up against the back wall of the *cella*; the temple was built on a podium, usually two to three metres high (that of the temple of Portunus in the Forum Boarium is 2.30m; that of the temple of Castor in the Forum, however, was as much as 7m high), which often provided only enough room for the *cella* to perch on; and the sole access up to the main door at the front was a perron (a steep flight of steps), as in the Maison Carrée at Nîmes (see pl. 18; cf. pls. 13 and 24).[18]

Nevertheless, 'action' versus 'state' does help to explain some things. For example, it fits with the fact that Roman stories about gods are stories about revelation and epiphany rather than about families. It is the gods' actions that are important, not their genealogies, their family-trees, quarrels among siblings, or sexual liaisons. On the other hand, it is not the Romans' 'nature' that explains why it was these kinds of stories that were told over and over again. Just as we saw in the case of the iconographic emphasis on action in connection with cult-images, the explanation lies in social structures and social 'semantics' (habits of mind transmitted by language) developed over long periods of time.

All these features cohere once we start thinking of a discourse about gods as a discourse about power. The Roman Republic – by which I mean the polity dominated by an élite committed both to competition and to consensus – linked the bestowal of executive power to duties, the acquisition of prestige to achievement. Legitimate power was wielded only by a consul, a praetor, a dictator or legate, not by individals because they happened to be extraordinarily rich, or by the incompetent scions of ancient families. Prestige was derived from success and largesse expended for the common weal, the *res publica*, not from mere ancestry. So it is only fitting that the two gods worshipped in Greece as the Dioscuri (literally: 'sons of Zeus', a pair of brothers intimately linked to one another by their shifts of location between the world of humans and the underworld, as reported in Greek myths) at Rome did not receive a temple and cult on that account, but for riding into battle to save the Romans from the Latins

6. The Capitoline Triad.

This is the only surviving free-standing statue-group representing the three deities who were worshipped together on the Capitol and invoked above all in political contexts: in the centre, Jupiter (*Iuppiter*) with the thunderbolt, and an eagle at his feet; on the right Juno (*Iuno*) with her peacock, and on the left Minerva in a helmet, with the owl of Greek Athena. Although they are shown sitting together on a settle – quite unlike the case in the Capitoline temple, where each had a separate cult-statue – no attempt is made to suggest any family relationship. The piece was apparently found during clandestine digging in a private villa at Guidonia (territory of Tibur/Tivoli). It may have been placed in a *lararium*; at any rate, it is unlikely to be a cult-image from a temple. Its history exemplifies a standing problem of Italian archaeology: having been illegally acquired by a Swiss dealer, it was sold to a private American collector; fortunately the Italian archaeological police got wind of the affair in 1994, and managed to prevent this unique piece from disappearing into the limbo of guilty secrets. Dimensions: 1.20m long, 0.90m high. Luni marble, late Antonine (AD 160–80). Museo Archeologico Nazionale di Palestrina.

at Lake Regillus in 496 BC (Dionysius of Halicarnassus, *Ant. Rom.* 6.13.1–3; Cornell 1995: 293f.). Dionysius here speaks of two gods, but Aulus Postumius in fact only vowed a temple to Castor (Livy 2.20.13), so that, despite some muddle in our sources, it was properly known as *aedes Castoris*, the temple of Castor.[19]

In 1937, Carl Koch went still farther in his notable book on Roman Jupiter. He argued that the nobility systematically removed all genealogical features from their conception of Jupiter (who is of course politically central), thus making clear that divine ancestry was irrelevant to the political position of aristocratic Roman families. Koch took for granted that the structure of Roman polytheism was identical to that of the Greeks. This may be doubted (Mora 1995a). But his wider point, and its connection to Republican political structure, is acute. We may recall that many Roman cult-statues show the gods seated on thrones or chairs (see figs. 5 and 6). It is no accident that Roman magistrates officially received visitors, such as ambassadors, seated on the curule chair, while the visitors had to stand. In other words, the iconographic representation of the Roman gods' superiority is based on the official protocol of Roman ceremonial custom.

It would of course be wrong either to overwork such a sociological interpretation or to oversimplify it. If we look more closely, we find that political power at Rome was closely regulated in terms of time and space. The executive powers of the highest Roman magistracies were granted for one year only, and limited to a particular area, a *provincia*, province. That said, it is characteristic of the power of these magistracies that it was in principle unlimited, and only slowly came to be restricted and placed under the control (normally) of the Senate. This was a wearisome process, and even then the limitations applied only in certain cases, which had to be fully argued through. It became necessary when the basic strategy of constraining the behaviour of individual magistrates by means of the traditional virtues and values, what the Romans called *mos maiorum*, ancestral custom, failed to work.

Religion – ideas about gods, the pantheon – does not mirror exactly what is perceived as political reality. But ideas about gods can be regarded as a conceptual medium, as a language, as a set of symbols, which allow discussion about *human* behaviour, and indeed as such have a great deal of authority (Gladigow 1979). This explains why the virtues that are supposed to characterize the actions of the élite are worshipped as divinities, why cult-statues and temples are constructed for them. *Concordia, Honos, Virtus*, Concord, Honour, Manliness are just as much gods as Diana or Hercules.[20]

If we think of the invention, or rather the advent, of new gods and epithets not simply as the direct expression of political structures but as an outcome of thinking about action, we start to take note of different groups of gods. Prayers containing unusually detailed lists of gods

78

survive for some rituals. The best example is provided by the Fabius Pictor whom I mentioned earlier, the writer on pontifical law; the passage happens to be quoted by Servius, the late-antique commentator on Vergil. During the *sacrum cereale*, a ritual held on December 13th each year for the goddesses Tellus (Earth) and Ceres, who was especially concerned with grain-farming (her gifts are *cerealia*, cereals, as in corn-flakes), the priest who conducted the ritual (the *flamen Cerealis*) invoked the following twelve divinities: Vervactor, Redarator, Inporcitor, Insitor, Obarator, Occator, Sarritor, Subruncinator, Messor, Convector, Conditor, Promitor.[21] In translation the names mean: First Spring-Plougher, Second-Plougher, Ridge-Maker, Broadcaster, Seed-Coverer (or Clod-Smasher), Harrower, Manual Hoer, Manual Weed-Root-Remover, Reaper, Grain-Transporter, Granary Protector, Bringer-Forth for Use.[22] This sounds like a pretty thorough list of grain-farming pro-cedures but it could have been much longer – for example, the crucial processes of threshing and winnowing are not mentioned – and thus rep-resents a considerable simplification, even idealization, of reality.[23]

In the contexts of conception, pregnancy, birth and the child's first movements, we have reports from different sources of dozens of super-visory divinities, from Ianus, deus Consevius, Saturnus and Liber (the Liberator, who 'liberates' men in ejaculation), Fluvionia and dea Alemona (who nourish the unborn baby in the womb), Nona and Decima (responsible for ensuring birth at full-term), to Carmenta Postverta and Carmenta Prorsa (responsible for the position of the child during the birth), Intercidona, Picumnus, Pilumnus and Deverra (protection against dangers), and even Candelifera (somehow con-nected with the candle-light during childbirth) (Varro, *RD* frags. 55ff. Cardauns). This list is again of course incomplete, and a similar one could be made for the wedding, listing the *di nuptiales* or *di coniu-gales*. Where Varro found these names is unclear. Some of them may be taken from the relevant rituals, but in several cases he may himself have connected them speculatively with the issue of procreation (a number of different explanations for them survive from antiquity). This does not necessarily make him wrong. Varro cannot be treated as some older colleague in Comparative Religion, who has got things 'wrong'; his *Antiquitates RD* constitute part of our field of study, part of Roman religion.

The gods I have listed here may well sound like bad medicine or poor natural science. Ever since the Enlightenment such an interpret-ation of ancient (and not only ancient) religion has enjoyed con-siderable success. A rationalist positivist such as Auguste Comte (1798–1857), who believed in man's innate tendency towards progress, saw magic and religion as so much backsliding from the ever more effective explanation of the world along the lines of the laws of nature, that is science, leading to a progressive reduction in the scope for mystery and the unknown (cf. Preus 1987). But if one examines the areas of human endeavour addressed in this way by religious symbols, what connects them is the attempt to act in complex, high-risk situations, to act in contexts where there is a high degree of uncertainty: access to and control of power, marriage, conception and birth, travel, agriculture.[24]

Concentrating religious attention on these areas also had its downside. Roman behaviour towards the gods is characterized by the considerable distance that it posits between gods and human-beings, by its extensive 'profane' areas (Scheid 1993). Contacts between the two spheres are sporadic and limited to special situations. When they do occur, they are typically very precise: to make absolutely sure of your addressee, you addressed lesser-known gods with the formula *sive deus sive dea*, whether you be god or goddess (Alvar 1985). This is not a sign of defective individualization typical of a primitive, quasi-animist religion, as scholars of Roman religion often thought at a time when they were influenced by the evolutionary models of religion developed by Herbert Spencer (1820–96) or Edward Tylor (1832–1917). It is a true question, whose significance is only intelligible in the context of a pronounced tendency towards anthropomorphism. Such a model of the gods naturally reckons differentiation by gender to be crucial to the establishment of their identity, and thus serves to emphasize the importance of the same differentiation in Roman society (Saller 1984) But away from such points of contact, the *pax deorum* was considered to be the normal state of affairs, that is, peaceful co-existence between two parties, divine and human, who have agreed not to interfere with one another except under particular, well-defined circumstances (it is difficult to translate the nuances of the Latin phrase, hence the periphrasis).

When disturbances did occur, such as 'postulatory lightning' (*postularia fulgura*), sent to remind the Romans of sacrifices they had forgotten or vows they had left unfulfilled (Festus p. 284.9–11 L.), or other omens, it was necessary to determine again the precise identity of the deity who had taken offence. In some cases, several priestly colleges were consulted to discover the deity in question, the reason for his or her anger, and the form of ritual remedy required. This procedure too can, indeed should, be read as a distancing-strategy, as a device to ensure that each party remains in his separate sphere. If the cause were simply the misbehaviour of a single individual, the discussion took the form of enquiring how the deity could be recompensed:

a typical example is a ritual fault that has been committed unintentionally, in Latin *piaculum*, an act requiring expiation because it has interrupted the mutual *pietas* between gods and humans (Varro, *LL* 6.29; Livy 5.52.14). Such an act could be set to rights by a (reverse) *piaculum*, an expiatory sacrifice, a sacrifice to restore mutual *pietas*.[25] Otherwise, society excluded the guilty person in more or less dramatic ways, and hoped thus to escape the consequences of joint liability.[26] As for the gods, the following principle applied: those affected must help themselves; it not the responsibility of society, with its precarious internal balance of power, to do their work for them. Besides, the gods had their own means of exacting punishment, as Lactantius the Christian apologist makes all too clear in his *De mortibus persecutorum*, On the Deaths of the Persecutors (AD 317/8), where he continues Roman tradition in celebrating the vindictiveness of the Christian god against his enemies.

Polytheism Once Again

We know little about the individual, day-to-day treatment of the myriad gods of ancient polytheism. The presence of the gods in their local shrines probably was of great importance, even if that means that the number of gods available in small settlements was limited: just seven different deities are addressed in all the rites mentioned in a whole range of contexts by the elder Cato in *De agri cultura*, On Agriculture. Rome itself was a mega-city: during the Principate its population, including the extensive suburbs, is believed to have amounted to more than one million inhabitants. As such, it was by far the largest city in the entire Mediterranean area, with hundreds of public temples and several hundred, maybe thousands, of smaller shrines – we could just for a start mention the shrine of the Compitalia in each of the 265 *vici*, the city barrios or neighbourhoods. With such an array of possibilities, individual choice of worship certainly was possible; but the actual selection was surely based on pre-formed schemes learned from rituals, or customary in a family (Bendlin 2000a: 131f.).

Under these circumstances, 'choice' was perhaps more often a matter of personal rejection rather than positive selection. Augustus for example, as Suetonius, his biographer, tells us (*Aug.* 16.2), is supposed to have excluded Neptune, the traditional god of the sea, from the group of gods who were to be honoured by a procession before the races (the *pompa circensis*), because he had just previously lost a

7. Tensa Capitolina.

Images of gods and their attributes (*exuviae*), e.g. a thunderbolt for Jupiter
or a goose for Iuno, were transported in the procession to the Circus in
vehicles (*tensae*) such as these. This example, whose wooden parts have
been reconstructed, dates from the third century AD. According to Cicero
(*Respons. har.* 23), the cart was driven by a boy both of whose parents
were still living (*puer patrimus et matrimus*). Rome, Palazzo dei
Conservatori (Musei Capitolini).

great number of warships. In one of his poems, Ovid relates his reactions while looking at the images of the gods being carried on litters at another such procession, and sitting beside a woman he has not yet made into his lover:

> But here's the procession. Everybody hush.
> Give them a hand. The golden procession's here.
> First comes Victory, wings outstretched.
> Goddess, grant me victory in love!
> Neptune next. Salute him, sailors.
> Not for me the ocean – I'm a landlover.
> Soldiers, salute Mars. I'm a disarmer, all for peace and amorous plenty.
> There's Phoebus for the soothsayers, Phoebe for the hunters,
> Minerva for the master-craftsmen.
> Farmers can greet Bacchus and Ceres,
> boxers pray to Pollux and knights to Castor.
> But I salute the queen of love and the boy with the bow.
> Venus, smile on my latest venture.
> Make my new mistress willing – or weak-willed.
> A lucky sign – the goddess nodded,
> giving her promise.
>
> Ovid, *Amores* 3.2.43-58 (tr. G.M. Lee).

There are several reports of passers-by greeting shrines, or statues, with a kiss on the hand (e.g. Minucius Felix, *Octavius* 2.4, to a statue of Sarapis), but whether they did so at every shrine they passed is unknown. We should assume an entire range of individual behaviour, from abstention all the way to studied attention or even the desire to be in permanent contact with divinity. Subjective interpretation of gods too was possible, naturally within the limits of the individual's linguistic register and cultural traditions (otherwise one's meaning would not have been understood); the examples of Augustus and of Ovid just quoted, but also the poem of Horace discussed at the beginning, prove this. Such individual interpretation is the result of recombining standard items, Neptune and the sea, Venus and love, Mercury and the profession of the poet. To effect such recombinations, it was quite unnecessary to be especially educated: in the case of Horace, for example, his readers simply had to read the earlier poems in the same book.

Differing Conceptions of Divinity

Even if there are advantages in reading a religion as a way of thinking about human limits, about power and action, and at the same time as the medium by means of which this thinking can be communicated, in rituals, images and words, one can hardly expect that the products, or the course, of such reflection and communication is going to be uniform. Communication will change through time. It will function differently in different social strata. In certain contexts, the differences may be very marked, though our sources provide only meagre information about them. One example might be the fact that the founders of temples in the Republican period are very different sort of people from those who erected tombstones in the Empire: in the first case, a tiny élite, in the second, a broad segment of the population. To say more about communicatory variation, I shall have to blur still further the general picture, itself pretty vague, that I have drawn so far.

In the late Republic, cases become more frequent where we find individuals trying to escape from the model of consent, which they came to find too limiting. Individual members of the élite (whom we could also call 'politicians') began to see themselves as enjoying the special favour of certain divinities. They tried to promote these gods by selecting a special site for a new temple, by building on an especially impressive scale, by creating new religio-social hierarchies. These are all means of bolstering one's position, enhancing one's prestige.[27] The trend becomes even more marked in the Principate, though for political reasons it was rapidly limited to the current dynasty. A slowly developing absolute monarchy and a monistic world view (I mean one founded upon a unitary principle, not necessarily monotheism) are snug bed-fellows.[28] Chicken-and-egg-like, they exercize a mutual influence upon one other – sometimes, through failure to be flexible, for the worse.

At the same time, lower down the social scale, at the level of the economically successful freedmen – who formed an especially mobile element of Roman society in each locality – we find a type of ritual action generally known as personal deification (though I find the term too narrowly 'theological'). Overall there are several hundred clear examples. Such people had themselves represented on their tombstones as gods. More precisely, the person's portrait is combined with a familiar divine iconographic type, and the attributes of the god. The gods chosen are mostly Mercury and Hercules, appropriate to the freedmen's professions as merchants and craftsmen (Wrede 1981). This has nothing to do with the claim to exclusiveness asserted by upper-class genealogies, but it is a good example of how religious symbols can be used as media of communication about human actions.

Seen in the same light, the imperial cult, the deification of the emperors and the related dynastic cults, are perfectly natural developments
(Clauss 1999; Gradel 2002). The deification of human-beings, which
seems a kind of perversion to ancient Christians and modern historians of religion alike, is in fact an integral possibility of Roman polytheism, even if the aristocrats who helped rule the Empire had certain
reservations about it.

— 4 —

RELIGIOUS ACTION

At the beginning of his tract *De vera religione*, Of true religion (AD 389–91), written not long after his conversion in 386, the Christian theologian Augustine sets up a paradox within the practice of the 'nations' (he uses the word *populi* for non-Christians, not yet *pagani*, pagans). These polytheists traditionally had several different philosophical (i.e. theological) schools, but they shared the temples. They differed in their way of thinking about god and the world, but practised the same cult. One can summarize the contrast in two key-words: orthodoxy, religion as a matter of right belief (*doxa*), against orthopraxy, religion as a matter of right action.

Now, it is characteristic of this text of Augustine's, as with others of his that deal with the philosophy of religion, that, despite this initial point, it is not directed against polytheists, is not an apologetic or polemical work in which Christianity is compared with non-Christian religions. As far as Augustine is concerned, at the end of the fourth century, the decision about the true religion has long since been taken. There is no need of further argument. Rather he uses this introduction as a means of dealing with Christian heresies, that is, with theological conflicts internal to Christianity. His concern is the incompatibility between divergent belief and common worship. If that is a mark of polytheism, it must be important for Christians to make sure that those who worship together also share the same beliefs. The implication is clear: those who do not share the same beliefs (here the different must of course always be the wrong) need to be excluded from worship, from the sacramental community.

Augustine's tract makes clear why we find dealing with religion in antiquity so difficult. It is because the terms in which we think have mostly been influenced by one and a half millennia of Christian theology.

If we hear the word 'religion', we associate with it belief, a body of teachings, a clearly-delimited project with its own identity (Mol 1976). Yet it is precisely these connotations that hardly apply to a local polytheistic system, where there was no need to integrate or exclude differing interpretations. Such differences might have consequences for individual action, but did not lead to the establishment of different organizations. In the case of polytheistic religions, action, not belief, is primary.

To emphasize action is not to exclude reflection, thinking about what one is doing, thinking about the gods for whom, or with whom, one does whatever one does. But interpretation of religious action in antiquity remained amorphous, indeed desultory. Christianity, on the other hand, requires unambiguous types of interpretation for its sacraments. Thus the manner in which one celebrates the Eucharist reveals a good deal about one's religious denomination. According to Roman Catholics, the consecration of the bread and the wine at the Mass produces the enduring Real Presence of Christ, whereas for Protestants Communion has a purely symbolic significance. We can also find substantial disagreements, sometimes specially emphasized in the organization, between the different Christian religions, whether they like to call themselves churches, denominations, or sects, over the interpretation of the same sequences of action. The ritual may be virtually identical, but it is no longer shared. That is just what Augustine wanted. The opposite pole is ancient polytheism.

What is a Ritual?

I want to start with a definition offered by Walter Burkert of Zurich. Ritual, he says, 'is a form of standardized behaviour whose function is communicative, and whose pragmatic basis may be secondary, or even vanish completely' (Burkert 1984: 28; cf. 1979: 35–58). Action – Burkert speaks of behaviour – is the central issue. In Greek terminology this would be the *dromena* as opposed to the *legomena*, things done against things said. 'Ritual is standardized behaviour' means that rituals are actions (for this purpose, it does not matter whether they are entire sequences or simply brief gestures) whose repetition turns them into stereotypes, so they are available in exactly the same form for use at different times and in different situations. In his second relative clause, Burkert adds: 'whose pragmatic basis may be secondary, or even vanish completely'. Here the point is that a ritual consists of an action or actions removed from the original context, so that they have lost their pragmatic significance.

To take an example: during the course of the ritual of animal-sacrifice, there was a point at which the celebrant sprinkled salt mixed with kibbled grain (*mola salsa*) onto the animal's head.[1] The sprinkling of salt might have a role in many different contexts. Considered as a pragmatic action, it would be much more sensible to add the salt after the animal, or rather parts of it, had been put into the pot, or grilled, since there is virtually no culinary point in adding salt to hair or fur. Thus, although the use of salt might in itself have a practical purpose, in the present case the practical intention has not merely retreated into the background but seems to have vanished completely. The action thus gains a new, communicative, function. One possible interpretation is that the salted flour points forward to the cooking of the animal, in that sense destining it to be killed and eaten. The action might also be interpreted as a symbol, anticipating its transition from the human to the divine sphere: more salted flour, and wine, was sprinkled over the gods' portion of the sacrificial victim after it had been boiled or grilled and placed on the altar. There are different possibilities here, but the moment chosen for the first sprinkling with *mola salsa* surely excludes the pragmatic or culinary interpretation.

Pushing the pragmatic basis of an action into the background thus allows it to adopt a communicative function. On the other hand, every form of action has at least some communicative significance, however minute. In the case of everyday actions, which no one would call ritual, a communicative function may be combined with the pragmatic, and may even be more important than the latter (as in the case of a gift of flowers). Such issues are the subject of the branch of the social sciences called symbolic interactionism.[2] Burkert however, is interested in something completely different. His aim is to uncover the 'real' pragmatic basis from which sacrificial ritual evolved. This basis is supposed to offer a privileged explanation of the ritual, its spread and its acceptance. In other words, he offers a genetic explanation, an explanation in terms of the origin of an institution, rather than a functional one, that is, in terms of its current 'function' or value.[3]

Our knowledge of the details of ancient rituals is so small that interpretations easily become arbitrary. Such arbitrariness is unavoidable; even contemporaries had no privileged insight into the meanings of their rituals. All the more important, then, to examine the underpinning of any interpretation offered. If we cannot be bothered to do some theory, it becomes pointless to talk about ancient rituals. Burkert's historical approach to ancient religion has been very important for more than three decades. Since they are diametrically opposed to my own approach, which is to link rituals with a particular historical society, it is worth discussing his ideas a little further.

What then might the pragmatic bases of rituals be? Again, let me take an example. A ritual known to us from late-antique sources is supposed to have been performed at the Greek town of Abdera, and is also reported for other places, such as Athens and the late-antique celebration of the king of the Saturnalia (Weinstock 1964). Once a year, so the texts tell us, a person, sometimes in fact a criminal, was picked out, treated well and feasted throughout the year, at the end of which, however, he was chased through the city and driven out by violence, in some places actually stoned to death or hurled off a cliff. This person was called a *pharmakos*, 'cure' (Gebhard 1925; Bremmer 1983).

This account must remind us of the Hebrew notion of the *sha'ir la'azazel*, the scapegoat. In this case, we are dealing with a ritual on the Day of Atonement, which transferred the sins of the Israelites onto a buck-goat, which was then chased off into the desert to the demon Azazael.[4] The underlying idea is obvious, namely the ritual transfer of guilt or danger that has accumulated in a political community, or at a particular location, onto a single individual, and the demonstrative exclusion of this individual from the community – which might even involve his death.[5]

Now Burkert asked himself how this strange idea about getting rid of guilt, pollution and other such problems might have arisen. He came to the conclusion that it went back to an extremely old biological 'programme' that might be as much as one hundred thousand years old, that is, go back to the beginning of the Middle Palaeolithic. It is the situation of a group of humans, surrounded by a pack of wolves, and under constant menace from them. They say to themselves: we can solve this problem by selecting one of our number as a sacrifice. The wolves will set on him, and the rest of the group will be saved and can run for safety.[6]

Another example: in the ancient ritual of supplication, a person who wants to ask for something throws himself down in front of a statue of a god, or a powerful human-being, and, often holding a green bough or twig, clasps the addressee's knees (Gould 2001; Naiden 2006). Again, Burkert looks for the pragmatic actions that might underlie such a ritual. He finds parallels in the research on animal behaviour that shows that higher social mammals act in similar fashion. We have to do with subordination behaviour, a gesture of total self-surrender through physical contact with the potential aggressor. The animal or person does not approach the latter with a weapon, a sharpened stick say, but with a harmless green bough or twig. This then would be the basis of the ritual.

At the human level, it has no pragmatic explanation: a human-being can make his plea better if he is looking his superior in the face – but, in the animal kingdom, looking the other in the face is an act of aggression. Once again, the basis of the ritual is a biological 'programme' embedded in our genes, which thus stimulates the idea of our acting in this fashion, or at any rate, taking the point at once if someone else does so (Burkert 1996: 65–90).

Theoretically, no doubt, such an approach can explain why rather strange sequences of action come to be accepted: because they are part of our inherited set of drives and capacities, part of our biological 'programme', like other basic functions, for example laughter. What cannot be explained at all by Burkert's approach are cultural differences. Why do some people do it this way, and others that? The descent-line from hunter-gatherer cultures or pre-human hominids is the same for every extant culture: but Burkert can offer us no explanation for such differences (cf. Phillips 1998a; Csapo 2005: 161–80). Nor does his approach take into account creativity in relation to ritual. Some rituals may be ancient sequences of actions reproduced over tens of thousands of years (though, in the absence of written texts and professional priesthoods, we are entitled to be sceptical), but most have been developed over time, modified for particular reasons or purposes, adapted to new circumstances, or altered unconsciously through failing cultural memory (cf. Flaig 1995a). Rituals too have a history.

An Example

One of the most elaborate and vivid descriptions of an ancient ritual survives in a Latin novel, L. Apuleius' *Metamorphoses*, also known as *The Golden Ass*. The speaker, who is simultaneously both narrator and subject, is the novel's hero Lucius who has been transformed into an ass. He is going to be saved soon, in the course of the procession here described, by being turned back into a human being:

> (11.8) And now the prelude to the great procession gradually began to march by, everyone beautifully attired in fancy dress according to his own choice. One had strapped on a sword-belt and was playing the soldier; another, wearing a tucked-up cloak, was marked by his boots and spears as a huntsman; another, dressed in gilt slippers, a silk dress, and precious ornaments, had fastened a wig of curls to his head, and with a swirling gait was pretending to be a woman. Still another was distinguished by his greaves, shield, helmet and sword: you would think he

90

had come from a school of gladiators. There was someone playing at being a magistrate, with rods and a purple toga; and someone with a long cloak, a staff, wicker sandals and a goatee beard, pretending to be a philosopher; and a pair carrying two different kinds of rods, the one with bird-lime representing a fowler, the other with hooks a fisherman. I also saw a tame bear who was dressed like a Roman matron and carried in a sedan chair, and a monkey with a Phrygian woven cap and saffron dress, looking like the shepherd-boy Ganymede, carrying a golden cup; and an ass with wings glued on his back, walking beside a decrepit old man, so that you would call the one Bellerophon and the other Pegasus, but laugh at both.

(9) In the midst of these joyful, crowd-pleasing pageants, which wandered all over the place, the special procession of the saviour goddess was now getting under way. There were women gleaming with white vestments, rejoicing in their varied insignia, garlanded with flowers of spring; they strewed flowers in their arms along the path where the sacred company would pass. Others had shining mirrors reversed behind their backs, to show homage to the goddess as she passed; or carried ivory combs, and moving their arms and curving their fingers pretended to shape and comb the royal tresses. Still others shook out drops of delightful balsam and other ointments to sprinkle the streets. Beside these, a great throng of both sexes carried lamps, torches, candles, and other sorts of artificial light to honour the source of heavenly stars. Next a lovely orchestra of pipes and flutes played sweet melodies. They were followed by a beautiful chorus of picked youths, brightly shining in their snow-white holiday garb, repeating a charming hymn composed and set to music by a talented poet with the Muses' help; the text gave interim preludes to the 'Greater Vows'. There also came pipers dedicated to the mighty Sarapis, who, on transverse pipes held close to the right ear, repeated the traditional melody of the god and his temple; and public heralds who kept warning the people to clear the way for the holy procession.

(10) Then the crowds of those initiated into the divine mysteries came pouring in, men and women of every rank and age. They shone with the pure radiance of their linen robes; the women's hair was anointed and wrapped in a transparent covering, while the men's heads were completely shaven and their skulls gleamed brightly – earthly stars of the great religion. All together made a shrill ringing sound with their sistrums of bronze and silver, and even gold. Next came the foremost high priests of the cult, tightly garbed in white linen cinctured at the breast and reaching to their feet. They carried before them the distinctive attributes of the most powerful gods. The first held out a brightly shining lamp, not at all resembling our lamps which provide light for night banquets, but a golden boat which kindled a rather large flame in an opening at its centre. The second was similarly clad, but carried with both hands an altar, that is, *auxilia*, 'a source of help', whose special

name was derived from the helping providence of the supreme goddess. Then came the third holding aloft a palm branch made of fine gold leaves, and also a caduceus like Mercury's. The fourth showed as a symbol of justice a deformed left hand with palm extended, which, because of its natural slowness and lack of cleverness or dexterity, seemed more appropriate for justice than a right hand; he was also carrying a small golden vessel rounded like a breast, from which he poured libations with milk. The fifth carried a golden winnowing-fan woven from golden twigs; and the sixth carried an amphora.

(11) Immediately thereafter came the gods, deigning to walk with human feet. First that awesome messenger between the gods above and those below the earth, with a face now black and now gold, tall, raising high his dog's neck: Anubis, carrying a caduceus in his left hand and brandishing a green palm-branch in his right. [. . .]

(16) . . . In the meantime, amid the tumult of festive invocations, we had slowly advanced and were now approaching the seashore. We arrived at the very spot where as an ass I had been stabled the day before. There, after the images of the gods had been set in their proper places, the chief priest consecrated a ship, which was constructed with fine craftsmanship and decorated all over with marvellous Egyptian pictures. He took a lighted torch, an egg, and sulphur, uttered prayers of great solemnity with reverent lips, and purified the ship thoroughly, naming it and dedicating it to the goddess. The gleaming sail of this holy barque bore an inscription woven in letters of gold, whose text renewed the prayer for prosperous navigation during the new sailing season. Now rose the mast, a round pine, high and resplendent, visible from far off with its conspicuous masthead. The stern curved in a goose-neck and flashed light from its coating of gold-leaf, and the entire hull bloomed with highly polished, pale citron-wood. Then all the people, worshippers and uninitiated alike, outdid one another in loading the ship with baskets heaped with spices and similar offerings, and on the waves they poured libations of grain-mash made with milk. When the ship was laden with generous gifts and auspicious sacrifices, it was untied from its anchor-ropes and offered to the sea, as a mild breeze arose especially for it. After its course had taken it so far that we could no longer clearly make it out, the bearers of the sacred objects took up again what each had brought and joyfully set out on the way back to the shrine, preserving the order and fine appearance of their procession.

(17) When we arrived at the temple itself, the chief priest and those who carried the divine images and those who had already been initiated into the awesome inner sanctuary were admitted into the goddess's private chamber, where they arranged the breathing effigies in their prescribed places. Then one of this group, whom everyone called the scribe, stationed himself before the door and summoned the company of the pastophori – the name of a consecrated college – as if calling them to an assembly. Then from a lofty platform he read aloud from a book

verbatim, first pronouncing prayers for the prosperity of the great Emperor, the Senate, the knights, and the entire Roman people, for the sailors and ships under the rule of our world-wide empire. Then he proclaimed, in the Greek language and with Greek ritual, the opening of the navigation season. The crowd's acclamation which followed confirmed that his words had been auspicious to all. Then, steeped in joy, the people brought forward boughs and branches and garlands and kissed the feet of the goddess, who stood on the steps, fashioned of silver. They then dispersed to their own homes. For my part, my heart would not let me go a nail's breadth away from that spot, but I continued to concentrate on the goddess's image as I pondered my former misfortunes.

Apuleius, *Met.* 11.8-17, trans. J. Arthur Hanson

Even the abbreviated version of this description of the procession and the account of the festival of the *navigium Isidis*, The Ship (or Sailing) of Isis, that Apuleius has incorporated into it shows the complexity of the ritual here performed. Procession, prayers, lustrations and offerings succeed one another and impose a pattern as the whole moves forward in time. The crowds of participants are arranged in a graduated sequence: the internal hierarchy of the inner circle of the cult members, the priests and the initiates, is clear from the order in which they come; beyond them, we find a rather vague series of other groups containing ever fewer participants and ever more spectators. Some sections of the ritual were undoubtedly intended to allow the spectators to play an active role. In the procession (as at animal-sacrifices), it is the musicians who mark the boundary between 'inner' and 'outer' groups: the cult is differentiated by a sort of theme-tune. There are also spatial markers that create sense: the ritual has a clear symmetry: it proceeds to the sea-shore, returns to the temple. Other markers are items of clothing, which distinguish the different groups of cult-members from one another, but also the various groups of looser participants. In the next sections I want to follow up these unsystematic impressions about ritual action, and try to generalize them by citing other sources.

Marking the Non-Routine

The ritual I have just cited shows a clear *spatial* structure. It has a starting-point, an end-point, and the route is plainly marked out. The procession has been announced, and is expected. All this lends the different activities the appearance of unity. The temple is important in this connection, because the procession starts and ends there. In the

8. Depiction of a procession on the 'Nile-mosaic' of Palestrina.

The 'Nile-mosaic' once decorated the floor of a semi-circular, partly artificial grotto (nymphaeum) in a complex of public buildings below the great terraced temple of Fortuna at Palestrina, ancient Praeneste, and was intended to be seen through water. Among the fragments (section 16) is this rather heavily-restored depiction of an imaginary procession. Three, originally four, bare-chested, shaven-headed Egyptian priests (pastophori) carry a golden candelabrum on a shoulder-litter (ferculum) into a kiosk-shrine (propylum). (The candelabrum is a product of the Christian fantasy of the restorer, G.B. Calandra, in 1640; analogies suggest that the object will have been a statue of Harpocrates, perhaps inside a miniature kiosk.) Before and behind the kiosk other priests carry staves surmounted by portable images of animals, i.e. manifestations of Egyptian deities. Behind the priests are a group of six women, some of them musicians – one can see a tambourine and a double flute: a ritual must always be accompanied by music. Some of the women are turning to the right to look at something now lost – distractions and 'human interest' are also part of religion. The whole lower complex, and the mosaic, were probably constructed at the end of the second century BC. In 1939, J. Paul Getty, the American oil magnate, seriously considered buying the mosaic, then the private property of Prince Barberini, and transferring it to the USA. Upper Hall, Museo Archeologico Nazionale di Palestrina.

Apuleius passage, not much happens in the temple itself that is of interest to the public. Up to a point, at any rate, we can say that the same is generally true of the ancient world. In Roman ritual – and here it is similar to Greek – public sacrifices take place on an altar in front of the temple, but not just on any available bit of ground. They must be conducted on land adjacent to a temple, that is, on land formally consecrated to a deity. I shall discuss the internal organization of temple-areas at a later point; for the moment, I need just say that the choice of location is an important part of a ritual not only because it helps to define the action as a specifically ritual one, with the focus upon the addressee, but also because it makes clear whether the ritual in question is one that belongs to the city's political centres or at its outskirts and frontiers (Polignac 1995b).

The next aspect is the marking of the ritual context by means of *decoration of the body*, in practice mainly festive clothing. At Rome, this meant that the male citizen wore a toga, which, though traditional (cf. Verg. *Aen.* 1.282; Suetonius, *Claud.* 15.3), was not an every-day form of dress, being cumbersome to put on and hot in summer – Augustus repeatedly tried to persuade Romans to wear it more often (Suetonius, *Aug.* 40.5). In the Roman rite, the *ritus patrius*, the clearest sign of participating in a ritual, for both men and women, was pulling up part of the toga, or in the case of women, the stola, to cover the head (pl. 9). The head was then said to be 'veiled' (*caput velatum*).[7] One Roman interpretation of this custom was that it helped ensure that the ritual was not disturbed because the celebrant could only take note of what he happened to be doing.[8] The alternative to this act of covering the head was to wear a leaf-crown (cf. Blech 1982); in pl. 1, both forms can be seen together. A crown was indeed the only head-covering permitted by the rules for the *ritus graecus*, the 'Greek rite'. As I have already pointed out, this term did not refer to true Greek sacrificial ritual but to what the Romans believed to be Greek elements in their cults, for example the cult of Saturn, and the ritual at the altar of Hercules.[9]

Another marker is *music*. In my example from Apuleius, musicians lead the procession proper. In the *ritus graecus*, hymns were sung by specialists, the *cantores graeci*, Greek singers, and lyre-players, both of which were organized in *collegia* (e.g. *CIL* VI 2191f.) as were the official horn- or trumpet-players. The most widespread form of music at Roman rituals, however, was 'flute'-music played on the double-*tibia* (see pl. 14, centre scene), an instrument more nearly related to the clarinet or oboe than the flute, since it was played with a reed.[10] At least in the view of the participants, the sound was meant to guard against, or drown out, other noises (Pliny, *HN* 28.11).

Finally, *time*. Many rituals are a function of local calendars, which allocate (or restrict) certain actions to particular dates. Such calendars may take written form, but in the case of the regular *sacra publica* prior to the Principate they seem to have been oral, despite the availability of written calendars.[11] Apart from that, the timing of rituals seems to have conformed to the general Roman pattern: people began their day early in the morning, and took advantage of daylight as much as possible. Nocturnal rituals were exceptional – their problematic character can be read off from the hour at which they were celebrated.[12] Otherwise, it was considered important that the ritual should be celebrated over a specific number of days. There seems to have been a certain, though not very marked, preference for allocating celebrations to the relevant god's *feriae*, the units of time specially allocated to him or her in the calendar.

Basic Forms

Rituals can be thought of as a system of signs that, from the actor's point of view, serves to communicate with the gods, and is at the same time a medium of human communication. If we compare the system to a language, we have to ask what are the smallest significant units,

---

9. House-altar from Pompeii.

The image on this *aedicula* shows in the centre a man wearing a toga, with his head covered. With his right hand he is pouring a libation from an offering-dish (*patera*); in his left, he is holding a little box of incense-grains, thus alluding to two different moments of normal sacrifice. The human-being is framed on either side by two statues of *genii* (spirits), each of whom holds in one hand a drinking-horn (*cornu*) in the form of a capricorn (with the forequarters of a goat and the tail of a fish) and in the other a bucket for the water used in sacrifice (*situla*). Below them is a crested and bearded snake, often used to represent the *Lar familiaris*, approaching an offering of fruit on a small domestic altar. The painting is at one and the same time a cult-image, and thus itself an object of cult, and a representation of the cult performed in front of it. Sacrifices such as these did not involve the shedding of blood and were completely routinized. In the tympanum above however one can see the stylized images of blood-sacrifice: from left to right, a *bucranium* (the skulls of sacrificial oxen were often set up on temple walls as commemorations), an offering-dish, and a cooking-knife. Total height: 3.70m, aedicola: 1.30m x 0.50m; *c.* AD 62. House of the Vettii (Pompeii VI 15,1).

the phonemes as it were, from which the complex sequences of signs that compose the great rituals are built up. Catalogues of material signs, from the requisites for sacrifices to temple-architecture, from divine attributes to the varieties of votive-offerings, fill shelf after shelf in the library.[13] Much has also been written on the types of text known to have been used in ritual contexts. In Part II of this book I shall be giving some impression of them. At the moment I want to present just a brief outline of the basic actions, which are of special importance because they serve in their turn to organize the later signs. I have based my selection on the types found in the most familiar Roman rituals. However the groups so constructed have almost no counterpart in ancient thinking in this area.[14]

The simplest ritual action is *touching*. It often has an ostensive function: touching serves to specify the intention or application of indicative gestures and words. During the dedication of a temple, the magistrate who performed the consecration held a post in one hand to mark and represent the future building.[15] In the alleged ritual of creating an envoy that Livy reports (as we shall see later, it is probably fictional), the king touches the *fetialis* (priest) who is to act as ambassador with an aromatic herb that has been pulled up by the roots from the ground within the *arx*, in this case, part of the Capitoline Hill, not an augural site. Here the ostensive function passes over into a relation created by contact, in order to confirm the right of the person so touched to act as the representative of Rome.[16] Since no ancient source mentions the possibility, I am extremely sceptical of interpretations of this ritual, such as Wagenvoort's, that involve the transmission of divine energy from one person to the other, though of course such interpretations might be legitimate for Polynesian societies that believed in *mana*.[17] However, the ritual thrashing of (young) women with strips of goat-skin by the two more or less naked Luperci on February 15, which in antiquity was widely supposed to ensure fertility, does seem to imply the idea of transmission of force or power.[18] In tricky cases, touching could be replaced by ostentatious pointing: the Augurs were equipped with a curled staff, the *lituus*, with which they could delineate a space, a *templum*, beyond the reach of the arm, as they recited an appropriate formula (Cicero, *De div.* 1.30-1; Livy 1.18.3-7).

Touching can also connote close contact, a temporary negation of normal social distance that creates good-will and trust. This applies especially to the habit of touching cult-statues with the hand, or kissing some part of them. Such touching can in the long run leave its mark, as in the famous modern case of the toe of Arnulfo di Cambio's bronze statue of St Peter in St Peter's in Rome.[19] Christians of course hated such demonstrations of pagan piety: the poet Prudentius sarcastically mentions 'licking the sandals of a clay Juno' (*Apotheosis* 456). People might also kiss the threshold of a temple, perhaps when it was closed.

Touch can often be substituted by increased visibility, by promulgation, by *display* (see pl. 8). The images of gods in Apuleius' Isis-procession (§10f.) or the *pompa circensis* are typical examples: particularly during processions, the gods, who usually remain more or less unseen in their temples, are made accessible to the crowd for a while, and then restored to their places (Latin: *reponere*). At the Megalensia, the spectators cried out aloud when the statue of the Mater Magna was carried through the streets (Ovid, *Fasti* 4.185f.). In the case of the *lapis manalis*, a stone that was carried by the *pontifices* along the streets from its normal home by the Porta Capena as part of a ritual for making rain, we have an example of an aniconic object being displayed in the same manner.[20] Ceremonial revelation may also be the focus of the worship of a small circle of initiates, as at Eleusis in Attica, where ineffable secrets were revealed at the climax of the festival during worship. From here it is not far to the idea of a ritual epiphany, the actual appearance of the deity. Under certain circumstances this might even extend to a sort of dumb-show (see below). There is archaeological evidence for certain lighting-effects in the cult of Mithras, for example, that seem to have been used to suggest the god's actual presence (Clauss 2000: 125 with fig. 59).

In many cases, the *procession* is the basic element of a ritual: as we saw, the change of location produces corresponding alterations within the given set of signs (Bömer 1952; Gladigow 1992). For example, images and banners have to be taken from their usual places, the religious specialists have to be arranged in their hierarchy or proper sequence. Moreover, Apuleius' narrative illustrates how the intermingling of participants and spectators makes any sharp differentiation between them impossible; the procession includes groups who play very different roles in the more central rituals to come. The narrator Lucius, though a mere spectator, is represented as experiencing intense religious emotion: being an onlooker may be a form of active participation (cf. the spectators on the raised stands in pl. 10), as the crowds at Rhineland carnival processions can confirm (Döpp 1993).

Processions can be categorized in terms of the type of movement involved. They may proceed from one or more starting points to a central cult-site where the main ritual is to take place – Apuleius' procession belongs to this type. They may also however describe a rough circle, for example around a certain group of people or a place, thereby affirming boundaries and the differences in status that they mark, for example, inside vs outside, or clean vs unclean (Baudy 1998). This is the case with the *lustratio exercitus*, 'beating the bounds' of the army, or of the camp, or the fleet, and the *lustratio urbis*, 'beating the bounds' of the city. We could also point to the ritual of founding a colony, which involved ploughing a furrow all along the future course of the city walls (*sulcus primigenius*).[21] I dare say, however, that more attention is lavished nowadays on such patterns in space – the triumph, the route traced by the Luperci as they ran (processions do not have to proceed at walking-pace), the *lustrum missum* of the Arval Brothers, and a number of other rituals – than in antiquity.

Dance is frequently met with, and offered roles especially for the young.[22] One example of the latter is the *Salii*, who formed a college (or rather, perhaps only from the time of Augustus' reform, two colleges) of twelve young, male 'Leapers' – so the ancient etymology – that put on processions in which they danced or leaped through the city in the month of March. Until the Augustan reform, young women seem to have accompanied or assisted them.[23] But dance can also be found among the duties of priesthoods whose members were normally older. In the case of the Arval Brothers, for example, the *tripudium*, apparently a dance in triple-time, was a regular part of worship. One or two reliefs show women dancing in the cult of Isis (pl. 10).[24]

Any strenuous activity can easily become competitive (Harmon 1988), though we need hardly assume any genetic link here. A chariot-race formed part of the ancient rituals of the *Equus october*, the October Horse (15 October), and the *Equirria*, a festival held on 27 February and 14 March, both of which actually include the Latin word for horse in their name. Races of this kind were of course the central attraction of the various *ludi circenses*, held mainly in April and in the months September to November, and were an important aspect of Roman (and Byzantine) public culture to the very end of Antiquity (cf. Cameron 1973; 1976; DeVoe 1987). A special form of competition, the combat to the death of gladiators in the arena (originally in the forum: Vitruvius, *arch.* 5.1.1), was for a long time at Rome confined to the context of funerals (Ville 1981: 1–56). The usual Latin word, clearly euphemistic, is *munus*, gift. The odd link between games and funerals is very ancient, occurring already in the Homeric account of the funerary games in honour of Patroclus in *Iliad* Book 23.

With the votive *gift*, we come to a classic, perhaps even over-rated, element of ritual action. Generally speaking, gifts to the Roman gods

10. Relief from Ariccia (ancient Aricia) with scenes from the cult of Isis.

Dance was one of the basic elements of ritual 'language' at Rome, even though the occasions for such uninhibited dancing as depicted in this scene from the cult of Isis were presumably scarce. In the upper part of the relief, representing the inside of an Egyptian temple, you can make out a statue of a female divinity, perhaps Isis (l. centre), seated on her throne, and, outside the temple, one of the Apis-bull; on either side of the goddess is a statue of Bes each flanked by a pair of baboons. The dance thus takes place outside the temple. Two of the dancing women hold wooden clappers; the boomerang-like objects held by the two dancers on the left are a different sort of wooden clapper to beat the rhythm. The spectators of the dance, one holding wooden clappers, are standing on a decorated podium. Re-used in a grave; dimensions: width 1.12m (orig. 1.49m), height 0.50m. Marble, c. AD 100. Museo Nazionale Romano, Palazzo Altemps.

follow the rules for 'horizontal' gifts among humans, in particular the asymmetrical model of a person of higher social rank receiving presents from a person of lower rank. The major role of the gift to gods (who are only to a limited degree apprehensible) is definitional. On the one hand, the character of the gift defines the giver: perhaps a portrait of oneself and one's family, or the dedication of a very personal item, such as the *bulla*, the necklace-amulet that children offered to the *Lares* when they became officially adult at thirteen or fourteen. On the other, it helped define the god: the rule that female animals are

101

sacrificed to female gods is a central aspect of the gendered construction of divinity. In Roman sacrificial practice, after parts of the jointed and cooked animal had been set aside for the gods, the humans participants got back their (much larger) portion of it. This practice should be seen as part of the ritual of asymmetrical giving intended to demonstrate the generous superiority of the one side. If one concentrates only on the isolated act, it is easy to fall into mistaken generalizations (such as the over-familiar 'principle' *do ut des*, I give so that you may give, and so on). Rather, gift-giving constitutes a system of exchange, in which the (human) participants operate with a notion of generalized, or non-specific, reciprocity, just as they do in 'horizontal' transactions with one another. What they expect is a long-term gift-equilibrium, not an immediate one-to-one return.[25]

Among the various types of offering, animal-sacrifice, which combines gift and meal, was of course especially important. Of other forms of sacrifice, libation, pouring liquid (usually wine) from a *patera*, shallow dish, is the most significant, since it formed a constituent element of many rituals. To represent a human-being holding a *patera* is a straightforward way of expressing his 'piety', connoted by the act of libation, which in such cases functions as a metonym for (habitual) sacrifice (pl. 9). The fact that even gods are depicted in this way may seem strange at first sight, but was evidently meant to express the gods' integration into the system of reciprocal exchange of gifts (cf. Gordon 1990). Apart from this, we hear of offerings of incense, which were very common, because quick and easy if all that is available is an altar – perhaps portable (pl. 14, centre) – or the hearth at home;[26] of cakes or sweets, flowers, and even coins.

Gifts to the gods are not be confused with various forms of *destruction*. Dropping objects into water, for example, can be a means of transferring them to the divine world, analogous to the holocaust, the complete burning of the sacrificial animal so that nothing remains of it to eat.[27] But in the context of oath-taking, for example, analogous acts, such as throwing a stone or dismembering an animal, may be a form of self-cursing, symbolically anticipating the speaker's fate if he breaks his oath. Similar acts could be used as a form of malign magic where the animal's fate is wished on the victim.[28]

The shared *meal* has an important place in religious as in social life. Where it is consumed only by one of the two parties, it approximates to an offering. The meat from animal-sacrifice was usually eaten by the participants at a meal where other food was also served. As for food-offerings, the present of *daps*, probably some kind of porridge, for the god to consume is one of the most common private rituals mentioned by the elder Cato in *De agri cultura*. A similar offering, *epulum*, is mentioned in the context of the *sacra publica*; the *epulum Iovis*, for Jupiter, was offered him on 13 September and 13 November. Placing food in front of the statues was evidently an important part of the cult in some Roman temples (though our sources fail to tell us which). It may be that another name for these was *penetralia sacrificia*, 'sacrifices offered inside (the temple)'.[29] The *lectisternium*, which was introduced as a ritual in periods of crisis in the very early fourth century BC, is particularly interesting in this connection. It involved feeding a banquet to twelve selected gods (both the number and the identity of the twelve show Greek influence). The fact that in the course of time the female gods had to sit on chairs like Roman matrons shows that the ritual was gradually Romanized. However even the early custom was itself not wholly Greek, since in Greece free 'citizen' women were excluded from the symposium (female entertainers did not count).

In addition to feeding, we can name several other *toilet rituals* in relation to cult-statues: washing, oiling, purifying and dressing. The latter was probably carried out in connection with a ritual epiphany, to mark a special ritual situation, when the deity was deemed to be present in a more comprehensive sense than was normal. Such toilet rituals for the deity had their counterpart at the human level too: purity was a condition for participation in the ritual. Splashing water over one's face and washing one's hands was the minimum; more was required if sexual intercourse had recently taken place.[30] Critics saw their chance here: Lucian, for example, asks how rules for purity can be reconciled with the blood-stained official celebrant (*De sacrif.* 13). As so often, such criticism involves (deliberately) misunderstanding the operative rules.

Only now do I come to one of the very most important rituals, *prayer*.[31] Practically every ritual is accompanied by at least one prayer. But the reverse also seems to hold good: there are no ordained prayers without a corresponding ritual. Public prayers at Rome required silence and concentration. Ritual disturbances or interruptions had serious consequences. It is especially in this context that we learn details about normative body-posture and so on that we can surely apply to other ritual contexts. The usual posture was to stand, possibly with one's head bowed (understood as a form of humility). Kneeling was felt to communicate a higher degree of urgency, and is usually found when the person praying is very close to the cult-relief, or within the *penetralia* of the temple. Prostrating oneself on the ground betokened a higher level of urgency still. It is the hands rather than the eyes that are focussed on the deity: normally, the arms are raised and the palms opened to the sky. Alternatively, they may be lifted to the statue or altar, or even the Capitol, as the home of the gods being addressed. Clasping the hands together, as Christians do today, is known from antiquity only as an especially potent 'magical' means of hindering childbirth, or rendering religious rituals ineffectual (Pliny, *HN* 28.59). Turning to the right signalled the conclusion of the prayer.

Prayers were spoken in a raised voice. Praying in a low voice, or silently, in such a way as to prevent the intention of the prayer being overheard by others, was avoided. In matters of love such behaviour could be forgiven; but silent prayer aroused the instant suspicion that one intended to inflict harm on someone or something (Van der Horst 1994). Collective prayer normally amounted only to a final confirmatory or approbative formula spoken by everyone present after the celebrant had completed his invocation. There is however some evidence for an alternative practice, namely reciting the entire prayer together, presumably repeating the celebrant's words. In the case of public religion, the texts were usually set down in written form. Scrolls with the relevant texts were sometimes distributed to the Arval Brothers (Scheid 1990c). We cannot exclude the possibility that the hubbub of competing prayers evoked by Apuleius in his description of the festival of Isis at the harbour of Cenchreae on the Isthmus of Corinth also occurred at Rome (*Met.* 11.16). It does however seem to be at odds with other accounts that, as I have already mentioned, stress the role of the *tibicines*, 'flute'-players, in drowning out unlucky or ominous words and noises – for even a mouse-squeak might be considered a fatal disturbance (Valerius Maximus, *Mem.* 1.1.5).

Music however was also used to accompany sung prayers.[32] Hymns are a regular component of large-scale public rituals such as processions; apart from special colleges of musicians (such as the official *tibicines* and *fidicines*, lyre-players) and singers (such as the *symphoniaci*, or the *peaenistae* attached to the temple of Vespasian and Titus) for public ceremonies, which I have already mentioned, we hear of ad hoc choirs of children, or women.[33] The repeated performance of a hymn, such as Horace's *Carmen saeculare* at the Secular Games of 17 BC (which the poet himself conducted), might be used to punctuate the procedure at telling points (Cancik 1996a).

There is hardly any evidence for *readings* of texts that were not prayers or prayer-like, apart from Jewish and Christian services, where the institution of readings from canonical texts was very important. The only vague parallel in the context of the *sacra publica* might

104

be the occasion on the Nones of each month when, up to the end of the Republic, the *rex sacrorum* announced the remaining festive days before the Kalends following (Varro, *LL* 6.13; 28). However funerary orations for deceased nobles formed a very important part of such funerals, and there is evidence that, from the late third century BC, they were delivered on the basis of a written version (Kierdorf 1980).

Reading had a more important role in mystery-cults that offered some sort of salvation. In Greece, this development appears already in the fourth century BC; Orphism is characterized less by shared ritual or even organization than by texts, indeed complex theogonies (accounts of how the gods came into being), which were credited to the mythical singer Orpheus. For this movement, as the gold leaves deposited in tombs suggest, literacy was indeed fundamental (West 1983; Masaracchia 1993); the best example, however, the late fourth-century BC Derveni papyrus, only survives because it was (incompletely) burned as part of a funerary ritual. At Rome this form of religious movement is attested only by the 'discovery' in 181 BC by a *scriba pontificius* (one of the secretaries to the pontifical college) of two books supposed to have been written by the mythical second king of Rome, Numa Pompilius. They were swiftly burned by the authorities, so nothing came of the affair; but it at least shows that 'text-communities' were already familiar (Rosen 1985; Rosenberger 2006). It is hard to gauge the significance of books in the Roman versions of the cults of Isis or Dionysus (Bacchus/Liber). All we can say is that the ritual use of written texts (prayers, prophecies, miracle stories, prescriptions for the conduct of rituals, especially sacrifices) in these contexts does not amount to what Richard Reitzenstein once called 'book-mysteries' (Reitzenstein 1927: 52; Burkert 1987: 70f.).

In the ancient world, the reading of such texts might have seemed a sort of truncated *drama*. Dramatic performances were of course presented exclusively at religious festivals, and to that extent we can say that the drama represents a massive incursion of text into the field of ritual. On the other hand, the texts of the surviving plays hardly refer at all (sometimes never) to the festival at which they were presented. Moreover the plays were not revivals or 'classics', at least not until later; rather the bill was filled by impromptu performance and first productions – it was the acting, much more than the text, that connected the various genres, comedy, tragedy, Atellan farces, and mime, one to another. This was not a religious theatre, let alone a 'religion of the book'. Rather, the surviving texts thematized social values, history and Rome's international horizons, and thus encouraged communication about them. In that sense, through the drama one did, or could, learn something about the gods (Cancik 1978; Wiseman 2000).

Finally, I should at least mention one vast area of religious activity, namely *divination*, that is, attempts to discover the divine will with regard to humans. So many techniques were developed in antiquity that it makes no sense here to attempt to describe them. Its particular forms are closely linked to the areas I have already mentioned, in so far as they often occur within other rituals, for example the examination of the entrails, especially the liver, of sacrificial animals. Divination confirms the success of rituals and analyses their failures, thus representing a permanent second- or meta-level of ritual action whose importance is not to be under-estimated (Gladigow 1990b: 227f.).

Complex Rituals

This catalogue of basic forms will readily convince that Roman rituals are 'complex rituals' (Cancik 1991: 375f.). Let me here give a brief illustration of what might be meant by this – there will be opportunity enough later to look at some longer accounts.

One of the most popular, and elaborate, rituals was the triumph, the celebration of the return of a successful field commander, normally a consul, into the city of Rome. It took the form of a long procession from the Campus Martius, the Field of Mars, where the army spent the previous night, to the temple of Jupiter high up on the Capitol. The booty and prisoners were paraded on waggons and litters in front. Then came the triumphal chariot bearing the general, drawn by four horses (pl. 11), followed by the marching troops. The honorand's face was coloured red, as though he were a statue (Rüpke 2006d, contra Versuel, ibid.). A slave stood behind him, holding a heavy gold wreath above his head. The Stoic philosopher Epictetus mentions that the slave repeatedly said to him: Remember, you are but a man (*Diss.* 3.24.85), a quotation whose authenticity is confirmed by Pliny the Elder (*HN* 28.39). The phrase neatly encapsulates the core of the ritual: that the honorand has attained an exceptional, god-like, but temporary status. As I have already stressed, even such a grand procession is itself just part of a more complex ritual whole. Although the display of war-booty and prisoners became politically ever more important, the climax and finale of the triumph consisted in the sacrifice of a bull to Jupiter (Josephus, *BJ* 7.155).[34]

Meanings versus Interpretations

Any ritual action is subject to interpretation by those who are directly involved as actors; by the spectators; and finally by those who come along afterwards and and investigate it from an academic or possibly inter-cultural point of view. By contrast with the case in Christianity and religions with similar structures, interpretation of most Roman rituals had no special status. No one interpretation was officially preferred, none could claim a unique status vis-à-vis others either at the level of generalization or in detail (cf. Beard, North, Price 1998: 1, 47f.). The interpretations we know of operate primarily at the semantic level, that is, individual elements, such as the particular features of a sacrifice, are typically interpreted as such, without any reference whatever to their context or 'grammar'.

Let me take as an example a ritual that attracted lively attention already in antiquity. The *Equus october*, the October horse, which I have already mentioned, was celebrated each year on 15 October. According to the surviving sources, which allow us to reconstruct what happened at least in some degree, the ritual began with a race, put on by the priestly colleges, between *biga*-teams, that is, chariots pulled by a pair of horses. The lead- (right-hand) horse of the winning pair was then killed, apparently with a lance-thrust, by the *Flamen Martialis*, the priest of Mars. The head and tail of the dead horse were cut off. The tail was immediately taken to the Regia, the office in the Forum of the *pontifex maximus* (see pl. 24), and the blood smeared over the sacred hearth or an altar. The head was decorated with a wreath made of bread-loaves, and then given to bands of young men, one from the Subura, the other from the Sacra Via (again, pl. 24), to fight over. The Suburanenses tried to nail the head to the wall of the Regia, the Sacravienses to the *turris Mamilia*, the tower of Mamilius, a prominent land-mark in the Subura. In other words, it was a staged scrimmage or donnybrook for youths or young adult males, in which each side had to penetrate to the heart of the other's territory in order to win.[35]

This custom is unique in the entire range of Roman rituals. The ancient interpretations latch onto the exceptional features. The horse's association with Mars is sometimes understood to be due to the use of the animal in warfare. Or it is killed in order to punish it, because in battle mounted soldiers can more easily run away. On the other hand, the loaves with which the horse's head is garlanded clearly belong to the realm of agriculture: by October, the harvest has long since been gathered in, and the harvested grain is being turned into

107

bread. Some indeed have it both ways, arguing that the bread recalls harvest home, but the horse warfare, and so Mars. The earliest surviving interpretation, however, was offered in the early third century BC by the Greek historian Timaeus. According to him, the Romans, descended from the Trojans, were taking revenge for the Trojan Horse: the annual sacrifice of a horse is to avenge the ignominy of Troy having been captured by the Greeks with the help of a 'horse'.[36] In this case, the interpretation proceeds not by appeal to features of other Roman rituals, but to the Greek epic cycle. A Greek writer thus interprets a Roman ritual in terms of a mythology familiar to him.[37] M. Verrius Flaccus, the most important Roman antiquarian of the Augustan period, poured scorn on the idea; but a century later Plutarch still takes it seriously. I incline to believe that Cassius Dio 43.24.4 is a muddled account of the same ritual, implying that Julius Caesar, the *pontifex maximus*, accepted the connection with Troy.

Finding explanations is always exciting. Interpretation of Roman rituals has been pursued since antiquity, and it would be absurd to

---

11. Fragmentary relief depicting a triumphal procession.

This fragment shows the central focus of a triumphal procession. The face of the triumphator is clearly Trajan's, and the occasion depicted has been plausibly identified as the triumph for the Mesopotamian campaign posthumously celebrated in AD 117 at Selinus in Cilicia. The emperor holds a special ivory sceptre in his left hand, and wears an iron ring prominently on the index finger of his right hand. He stands, surrounded by lictors, in a high-wheeled chariot adorned with the image of Victory, and drawn by a span of four white stallions. The small figure behind him is the public slave who held the golden oak-leaf crown above a triumphator's head. The 'plebeian' style of the relief shows that it was not an official state commission; the work was probably part of an honorific monument to the dead emperor or even part of a grave monument to one of Trajan's senior associates in the war. The political message is underlined by the numerous 'mistakes', for example: the differential scales of the individuals (and animals, and objects) represented, varying in relation to their perceived significance; by the distortions (the lictors seem in fact to have preceded the chariot; here they connote both the customary crowds of spectators and the troops, who actually marched far behind, singing 'io triumphe' and obscene marching songs); and by calculated omissions (for example the actual driver of the chariot, for whom there was no room). Note how the line of gaze created by the boy in the r. foreground is picked up by the unrealistic upward gaze of the left-hand lictor in the lower row, to guide the eye to the emperor's face (which at a triumph was painted bright red). Marble, AD 120–130. Museo Archeologico Nazionale di Palestrina.

imagine that anyone could forbid the actors, the participants, from doing so. Our problem now is that we are not in a position to verify their efforts. We can acknowledge the existence of different interpretations, but there are no adequate criteria, no assured meanings, on the basis of which we can decide whether they are true or false. Roman culture itself failed to develop any rules here. On the basis of our contextual knowledge, we can sometimes judge whether contemporaries would have found a given interpretation plausible; in other cases, we can plausibly point to the interests and pre-occupations that may lie behind them. Given the nature of the Roman religious system, even a highly individual interpretation must be considered legitimate. Semantic knowledge, the actors' knowledge of the meanings of signs in the indigenous system, is necessarily uncontrolled: when verbalized, it offers us no correlations that are free of ambiguities.

'Words' versus 'Grammar'

The syntactic rules, on the other hand, the rules that state which ritual signs may be combined with one other and if so how, are very much stricter. To some extent they are explicit: for example, which animals may be sacrificed to which god. The basic principle here is that male animals are offered to male divinities, female animals to female. The age of the animals was laid down too: suckling animals were distinguished from fully-grown ones. In other respects however the rules were implicit, simply absorbed by frequent participation in rituals, just as, when you learn to speak your mother-tongue, you do not start by learning how to read and then go on to the grammar, in order finally to be able construct your own sentences; you learn your mother-tongue simply by imitating, and by trying out which syntactic combinations and words the surrounding world reacts to in a predictable way, so that certain structures emerge from the mass of possibilities. In ritual, as in language, explicit and tacit rules constantly combine: colour coding, for example, is often explicit: white animals are associated with gods up in heaven, red with gods connected to fire, black with gods of the underworld; at the same time, there is tacit knowledge of the limits of such rules, so that one is capable of finding a substitute when one kind of victim is unavailable (e.g. offering a ewe-lamb instead of a bitch), of using significantly less expensive animals such as piglets in private rituals, or generously adding an extra cow to an otherwise cheap sacrifice (*vacca honoraria*).[38]

There is some further evidence for the existence of such tacit under-standing of the semantic rules in antiquity, namely *fictive rituals* invented, so far as we can judge from the historical context, by certain groups or individuals. In some cases these rituals existed only on paper, in others they were certainly staged, but were passed off as ancient, which was essential if a ritual was to be accepted as authentic.

My example is taken from the first book of Livy's history (1.32, cf. Dion. Hal., *Ant. Rom.* 2.72.8). The alleged events took place in the early regal period; the passage concerns the ritual declaration of war. This is said to have taken place in two stages. The first is a deliberately ritualized request that booty captured in a raid be returned: in this case, the Latins had invaded Roman territory, and a Roman legate was sent to them to demand restoration of the stolen goods: *res repetere*, demanding restitution, is the technical term for this procedure. If that did not work – and in the Annalistic tradition (the traditional Roman form of hisioriography) it never worked – the Senate resolved to declare war. Sometimes – and this too is an Annalistic fiction – a full law is supposed to have been passed by the popular assembly. War was then declared in a highly ritualized manner by a special priesthood, the *fetiales*, the Fetials.

Judging by the other information we possess about this priesthood, the ritual described by Livy in the early Augustan period never really existed in this form.[39] It cannot have existed as such in his own day either, since it would have been totally impracticable. But it evidently was accepted as a genuine historical fact by his contempories, and actu-ally performed in a heavily modified version adapted to practical needs. The first occasion on which it was used was the declaration of war against Cleopatra by Augustus. This ritual however was not performed on the border to Egyptian territory, as it ought to have been, but on a fictitious piece of 'enemy territory' specially created near the temple of Bellona, the goddess of war, in the city of Rome (Servius, *Aen.* 9.52; Cassius Dio 50.4.4f.). The context of this invented tradition was a polit-ical emergency, a civil war involving Romans fighting Romans, Octavian (properly: *Caesar divi filius*, Caesar, son of the deified Caesar) versus Mark Antony. The later propaganda shows that the archaic dress was a function of the need to justify fighting a civil war, while the enemy metamorphosed from Antony into the Egyptian Queen Cleopatra.

Livy's account is as follows:

Numa had established religious observances in times of peace; Ancus provided war with an equivalent solemn ceremonial of its own. It was not enough, he thought, that wars should be fought; he believed that

111

they should also be formally declared, and for this purpose he adopted from the ancient tribe of the Aequicolae the legal formalities (now in the hands of the Fetials) by which a state demands redress for a hostile act. The procedure was as follows: when the envoy arrives at the frontier of the state from which satisfaction is sought, he covers his head with a woollen cap and says: 'Hear me, Jupiter! Hear me, land of So-and-so! Hear me, O righteousness! I am the accredited spokesman of the Roman people. I come as their envoy in the name of justice and religion, and ask credence for my work.' The particular demands follow and the envoy, calling Jupiter to witness, proceeds: 'If my demand for the restitution of those men, or those goods, be contrary to religion and justice, then never let me be a citizen of my country.' The formula, with only minor changes, is repeated when the envoy crosses the frontier, to the first man he subsequently meets, when he passes through the gate of the town, and when he enters the public square. If his demand is refused, after thirty-three days (the statutory number) war is declared in the following form: 'Hear, Jupiter; hear, Janus Quirinus; hear, all ye gods in heaven, on earth, and under the earth: I call you to witness that the people of So-and-so are unjust and refuse reparation. But concerning these things we will consult the elders of our country, how we may obtain our due.' The envoy then returns to Rome for consultation. The formula in which the king asked the opinion of the elders was approximately this: 'Of the goods, or suits, or causes, concerning which the representative of the Roman people has made demands of the representative of the Ancient Latins (*Prisci Latini*), and of the people of the Ancient Latins which goods or suits or causes they have failed to restore, or settle, or satisfy, all of them requiring restoration or settlement or satisfaction: speak, what think you?' The person thus first addressed replied: 'I hold that those things be sought by the means of just and righteous war. Thus I give my vote and my consent.' The same question was put to the others in rotation, and if a majority voted in favour, war was agreed upon. The fetial thereupon proceeded to the enemy frontier carrying a spear with a head either of iron or hardened wood, and in the presence of not less than three men of military age made the following proclamation: 'Whereas the peoples of the Ancient Latins and the men of the Ancient Latins have committed acts and offences against the Roman people, and whereas the Roman people have commanded that there be war with the Ancient Latins, and the Senate of the Roman people has ordained, consented, and voted that there be war with the Ancient Latins: I therefore and the Roman people hereby declare and make war on the peoples of the Ancient Latins and the men of the Ancient Latins.' The formal declaration made, the spear was thrown across the frontier.

Livy 1.32.5-14, transl. A. de Sélincourt (adapted).

Repetitions are common. The number three is very important: the claim is stated three times; an ultimatum of thirty-three days is set;

some invocations, e.g. Jupiter, Janus Quirinus, all the gods, have three elements. These are of course plausible details. Frontiers, and crossing frontiers, play an important part. An attempt has been made to create a series of notional audiences that can stand for Rome as a whole.

All these are features of actual Roman rituals, and for that matter of Roman law. In our case they have been used to compose a ritual that in this form, or indeed in any remotely similar form, never existed. We do not know what the ritual form of such claims was like before the Augustan period, if indeed there was one. On the other hand, we do know how wars were ritually declared: the commanding magistrate, at the head of his army, hurled a lance into enemy territory, no Fetial in sight (Varro ap. Serv. auct., *Aen.* 11.52). One might call this a 'significant action', tantamount to a ritual. Both in Livy's fiction and in the new pseudo-fetial procedure of 32 BC, the magistrate's action is re-contextualized, partly by introducing the archaic weapon and the Fetial priest, partly by relocating it away from the actual locus of war, and thereby fully ritualized. The fictive procedure thus bears out my earlier claim that rituals are composed according to certain recognized rules. In this case, indeed, the result was so convincing that Livy's readers, so far as we know, thought his account a plausible historical reconstruction.

Material Theology

The opposition between syntax and semantics, grammar and individual 'words', which I have so far discussed at the level of ritual competence, turns out to be useful in another context, the entire ritual system of a *polis*. The medium in which the whole of such a system, or at least large parts of it, can be formalized is the list of festivals, or ritual calendar. The use at Rome of a written calendar listing all the days of the year is, as far as the ancient Mediterranean area is concerned, unique (Rüpke 2003). The norm there was the list of festivals, which gave only the dates on which sacrifices or festivals were celebrated. An example might be the deme-calendars in Attica. In either case, the written calendar supplied a conspectus of festivals which had no temporal connection with one another in lived experience, but occurred only at intervals.

Given the large number of cults and rituals in a metropolis like Rome, it was and is tempting somehow to find links between them. Just as contemporaries suggested their own interpretations, modern historians of religion have speculated about possible interconnections and claimed to be able to identify underlying patterns (Dumézil 1975). Here too, I find it methodologically advisable to keep the two levels strictly separate, to distinguish clearly between the level of semantics, of interpretation, which is open-ended, and that of syntax, the ascertainable connections between rituals. There seems however to have been no such reading of the calendars in antiquity (Rüpke 1997b). Connections did nevertheless exist, in the sense that rituals, though performed at different times, were celebrated at the same spot, were conducted by the same actors (magistrates, priests), and contained identical gestures and sacrificial equipment. For want of a better name, I think of this sort of link between rituals, the significance of which usually eludes us or cannot be pursued in any specific direction, as 'material theology'.

One example would be the spring festival of Parilia, which was held on 21 April. The tradition of celebrating the 21st as Rome's birthday was probably established long before the Principate, and it was a correspondingly important occasion. We learn that Julius Caesar sent off the messenger with the news of his victory at Munda in Hispania in 45 BC – which meant the end of the civil war – just in time for him to reach Rome on the eve of the Parilia, so that he could anounce the happy news, and the birthday of Rome be celebrated the very next day. This was a very modernizing interpretation. Traditionally, the Parilia was a purification festival especially popular in rural areas. The sheeppens were decorated with branches, and then swept; the sheep themselves were then purified with sulphur. One or more fires of male olive-, pine-, juniper- and laurel-branches were lit, and offerings made to Pales, requesting protection from dangers, and agricultural prosperity. Finally the celebrants would drink milk mixed with *sapa* (mulled wine) and leap across, or through, the fire, which was the actual ritual of purification for humans. The urban version, which Ovid himself claims to have taken part in, was much simpler, though it also included leaping through or over fire.[40]

The material used for the Parilia in the city of Rome included, among other things, the ash produced by incinerating the corpses of the unborn calves cut, under the supervision of the chief Vestal and the *pontifices*, from the wombs of more than thirty pregnant cows sacrificed at the Fordicidia on 15 April. To this ash was added the blood of the October Horse, or at any rate the blood contained in the tail that, as I mentioned earlier, was taken to the sacrificial hearth of the Regia in the Forum Romanum. How much blood, has been a subject of warm debate among scholars; it has been wondered whether, if blood was the point, it would not have been more sensible to cut off the

114

pizzle and not the tail; and whether 'tail' might not mean 'pizzle'.[41] But here the determination of historians of religion to make Roman rituals 'make sense' far outruns that of their subjects.[42]

The Equus october and the Parilia were celebrated half a year apart. At Rome, the fumigation materials were handed out by priests. These priests also distributed purification-material on other days at certain points in the city. No ancient source tells us why the ashes of unborn calves from one ritual, and horse's blood from another, should have been used for a third, which happens to be a ritual of purification, nor has any modern scholar been much concerned to ask. True, the Augustan poet Propertius complains that the procedure is too elaborate (4.1.19f.). This is fine, but can hardly be thought a very exciting form of comment. The links remain uninterpreted and thus unimportant; but they clearly create 'horizontal' connections between otherwise completely unconnected rituals, and so deepen the sense in which we can speak of the different rituals, and the complicated local polytheism of Rome, as a system.

Another pervasive material connection that may be cited in the same connection is the so-called *immolationes* that were used at every Roman public sacrifice. As I have already pointed out, animals sacrificed in the *sacra publica* were all sprinkled with *mola salsa* before being slaughtered. This was a mixture of pickling-salt and kibbled wheat-meal prepared on a small number of days each year by the Vestals. As a product of one of the most important religious sites in the Forum Romanum, *mola salsa* thus creates a material connection between that central site, the labour of the priestesses of Vesta, goddess of the hearth, and every Roman public sacrifice (Servius, *Ecl.* 8.82; Porte 1989: 87).

It is important for me to emphasize this kind of syntactic connection precisely because we have no ancient interpretations of them. This is one of the few cases where 'semantics' has not obliterated the syntax. Of course, when trying to deal with the syntactical level, the problem remains that it is extremely difficult to find a point of entry if we have no access at all to the corresponding semantics.[43] Here too, however, there is a palpable difference between this type of religion and those conceptions of religion that are dominant in modern Europe, obsessed with semantics, meanings and 'discourse'.

Such devices are known in Christianity too. One example is the *fermentum*. This word denotes the practice in Rome of sending portions of the Eucharist-bread from the bishop's church to all the surrounding congregations, in order to symbolize the unity of the Church in the city. The practice, which developed in Late Antiquity

115

and spread outwards from Rome, allowed the bishop in a sense to be omnipresent, despite decentralization and the delegation of responsibility for conducting worship (Pietri 1983). In the Orthodox church, the custom is still practised, a little of the dough for the making of the bread for the Eucharist being put aside and added to the next lot, thus creating an uninterrupted tradition over the centuries back to the very beginnings of the church.

— 5 —

THINKING ABOUT RELIGION

Concepts

The expression 'thinking about religion' is more than a mere synonym for theology, God-talk. The formation of a Jewish-Christian theology is among the most momentous developments in the religious history of the ancient world. A rapid sketch of that theology will help to highlight the distinctive features of other types of discourse about religion in antiquity – and serve to remind us of the preconceptions that may be lurking when we apply the ordinary modern term theology to the ancient situation.

Christian theology as a system – to focus on that strand – was developed initially by the apologists, that is, philosophically-educated individuals who, from the second century AD, set out to defend Christianity against its critics and opponents (*apologia* = speech for the defence). The Christians they represented as an impeccably moral religious community; Christianity itself they saw in terms of categories developed within Hellenistic Greek philosophy. The message to non-Christians was this: You think we are the scum of the earth, but in fact we practise a perfectly reasonable religion, which, if you non-Christians would only consider carefully, you ought to recognize, at the very least, as an option worth respect.[1]

The apologists' systematic thinking about their own religion was at first directed towards the outside world: already in the second century AD we can name works by Justin Martyr, Aristeides and Athenagoras that are addressed to the Emperor. But what they did seems rapidly to have become important to practising Christians too, the great majority of whom were converts. The existence of Christian 'teachers', who were certainly not ordinary school-teachers, is well attested (Neymeyr 1989,

Markschies 2007). It is not at all easy to decide what position they held in their communities. They were not identical with the leaders who presided over meetings and led the religious services; on the contrary, they founded independent schools, which they ran in much the same way as philosophers did theirs – they went to a city, set up shop as teachers, received into their houses, or elsewhere, strangers who came to them to be instructed, they listened and entered into disputations. Just to take second-century Rome, we know of the philosopher Justin, his pupil Tatian, Tatian's pupil Rhodon, and the well-born martyr Apollonius; and of a similar group, the Carpocratians, brought together by a certain Marcellina. There were others too, many of them heretics, 'sectarians' from the point of view of later theology, such as the shipowner Marcion, Valentinus, Theodotus of Byzantium (who was a worker in leather), and, in the last decade of the century, Hippolytus, author of the *Refutation of all heresies*. The African jurist Q. Septimius Florens Tertullianus wrote the first apologetic works in Latin, the *Ad nationes* and the *Apologeticus*, at the end of the second century.[2]

Two processes got under way. On the one hand, thinkers such as these attempted to systematize Christians' thinking about their own religion in a comprehensive and non-parochial manner – that is, one could in principle think the same thoughts about the relation between God and man in Alexandria as in Rome. On the other, it was the administrative leaders of Christian communities, the bishops and presbyters (whose relation in the second century AD became less coordinate and increasingly hierarchical), who tended to become professionally involved with this reflection on religion, and thus manage and guide it. In other words, theologians tended increasingly to be priests, and priests theologians. When in the fourth century AD bishops and presbyters conducted disputes over the interpretation of Christian doctrine, they often did so in the context of a claim to a bishopric (e.g. Athanasius in Alexandria). It was the imbrication of political and theological issues that made such situations so very fraught.[3]

Worship, collective celebration, remained important; but the significance of theology grew by comparison with that of the correct performance of ritual. Candidates were of course admitted ritually to the Church through baptism, but this sacrament was contextualized by means of an extensive body of doctrine (Markschies 1997: 82–4); and if it ever came to the question of excluding someone from the Church, the correct performance of the rite of baptism was less important than the issue of whether his or her beliefs were orthodox, as attested by assent to individual tenets of Christian doctrine. Systematic reflection on religion might thus be employed as a test of orthodoxy.

This process has been called 'dogmatization', the process whereby specific formulations, which can notionally be fitted together into a coherent system, crystallize out of non-specific reflections. We have here to do with general assertions that give structure to the system as a whole and can constitute tests of dissentient views, but may also, when the need arises, be applied in particular cases. Such interpretation, such re-concretization of doctrinal generalizations, is the preserve of those who have oversight over the spiritual welfare of their flock, of preachers – in a word, of people who are firmly anchored in a power structure and can themselves be controlled. Historically speaking, dogmatization occurred alongside the creation of the canon, the process of declaring certain texts Holy Writ, with the result that new groups kept springing up, inspired by new texts, or by a new selection of texts, or on the basis of differences of interpretation.[4] Among them were the text-communities that were often later dismissed as 'gnostic' (Williams 1996).

Three Types of Theology

Ever since the time of Plato, the polytheistic systems of antiquity had been perfectly familiar with the word *theologia*. It may have been around the end of the second century BC that the concept of 'three types of discourse about the gods' was developed – probably in a Greek doxography, an anthology of philosophical doctrines.[5] This must be what Varro is alluding to by putting talk of the *tria genera theologiae*, the three types of theology, into the mouth of Scaevola, the *pontifex maximus*. The very term shows that it denotes not a coherent theological system but a discourse about the gods consisting of three separate facets, which makes no pretence of being a unity and has no need of doing so. In other words, it is 'theology' conceived not as a policing measure but as a meta-term for distinct types of thinking about religion (cf. Rüpke 2005c).

Some general points first. Roman thinking about religion was not a theology created by priests. Whenever we hear of people doing theology whom we also know to have been priests – the Christian colouring of that word is itself problematic – they do so wearing a different hat. Cicero was an Augur and wrote three books *De natura deorum*, On the Nature of the Gods; but he did not do so in his capacity as Augur, nor did he address them to the College of Augurs: he wrote – how shall I put it? – as an amateur of philosophy.

119

Moreover, this discursive theology is not situated in a ritual context. It is in no sense a sermon that could systematically convey teaching or interpretations of 'sacred texts' to a congregation.[6] There are really only two relevant types of texts: drama and hymns or prayers. As I have pointed out earlier, *ludi scaenici*, dramatic performances attached to certain major festivals, enjoyed a special position, being performed until the Late Republic in improvised theatres, and had no necessary thematic reference to the wider festival. The second type of text is the hymn. At any rate until the Late Empire, the known hymns intended for a cultic context are compositions commissioned for special rituals, if you like, votive offerings to the gods. Horace's *Carmen saeculare*, performed at the Saecular Games of the year 17 BC, illustrates how densely mythical and topographic allusions, and theological speculation, can be deployed:

> Phoebus and Diana, mistress of forests,
> brilliant grace of the heavens, O [you] worshipped and to be
> worshipped always, grant what we pray for at this
> holy time when the Sibyl's verses have advised that
> chosen maidens and chaste youths sing a hymn for
> the gods to whom the seven hills have given plea-
> sure.
> O nourishing Sun, who on your gleaming chariot
> 10 bring forth the day and hide it, and are reborn an-
> other and the same, may you be able to behold no-
> thing greater than the city of Rome.
> Ilithyia, gracious at fittingly bringing forth offspring
> in due season, protect our mothers, whether you
> wish to be called Lucina or Genitalis: goddess, rear
> our youth and bless the decrees of the fathers con-
> cerned with women and their need for wedlock and
> 20 on the marriage-law, fruitful of new progeny, so that
> the sure cycle of ten times eleven years may bring
> back singing and games thronged three times in
> day's brilliance and as often during the welcome of
> night.
> And you, Fates, truthful in your song, as was once
> ordained and may the steady hand of events confirm
> it, join happy destinies to those now past.
> May Earth, teeming with crops and cattle, offer
> 30 Ceres a wreath of corn; may the healthful rains and
> breezes of Jupiter nourish the harvest.
> Apollo, gentle and calm, with your weapon put
> away, hear the suppliant youths; Luna, crescent
> queen of the stars, hear the girls.

If Rome be your monument and if Ilian bands held
the Etruscan shore, a remnant ordered to change
40   their homes and city in a course that brings no harm,
for whom chaste Aeneas, survivor of his fatherland,
without harm through Troy's conflagration paved
a way for freedom, about to bestow more [good]
things than were left behind [at Troy]: gods, grant
upright ways to our educable youth, gods, [grant]
peace to [those in the] calm of old age, [grant] to the
race of Romulus both resources and offspring and
every distinction.
And what the glorious scion of Anchises and Venus
50   asks of you, with [the sacrifice of] white steers, may
he obtain, superior to his warring [foe], gentle to the
fallen enemy.
Now the Parthian fears our troops, lord of sea and
land, and the axes of Alba, now the Scythians and
the Indi, haughty until recently, seek answers [from
us]. Now Fidelity and Peace and Honour and ancient
Modesty and neglected Courage dare to return, and
blessed Plenty, with full horn, makes her appear-
60   ance.
Phoebus, prophet both graced with his gleaming
bow and dear to the nine Muses, who with his saving
art relieves the body's tired limbs, if he views with
favour the altars on the Palatine, always prolongs Roman strength and the prosperity of Latium for a further cycle and to a better age, and Diana, who holds
Aventine and Algidus, gives heed to the prayers of
70   the Fifteen and lends friendly ears to the appeals of
the youth.
That Jupiter and all the gods pay heed to these
[words] I bear home good and assumed hope, I the
chorus taught to tell the praises of Phoebus and of
Diana.

                                          tr. M. C. J. Putnam

Poets in particular enjoyed very wide freedom in their composition
of theological texts; at the same time they seem to have integrated
themselves whole-heartedly into the ritual context for which they
composed. It is not for nothing that Varro chose the 'mythical' theology of the poets as one of his three types.

The character of Varro's theology, which was set out in the first
book of *Antiquitates rerum divinarum*, is in fact known almost
entirely from Augustine's citations of it in *Civitas Dei*, The City of God

(6. 5). The following quotation shows the extent to which he drew upon a Greek framework of ideas:

> What is the significance of Varro's division of 'theology', that is, the systematic theory of the gods, into the three types, mythical, physical, and political (*genus mythicon, physicon, civile*)? . . . The name 'mythical' applies to the theology used chiefly by the poets, 'physical' to that of the philosophers, 'civil' to that of the general public.
>
> Augustine, *Civ. Dei* 6.5, tr. H. Bettensen

The philosophical component turns out in fact merely to consist in reductive naturalism: Jupiter, for example, is considered to be the equivalent of air, Ceres of grain (e.g. frag. 28 Card.), which Augustine of course finds perfectly acceptable. 'Civil theology' is more difficult to grasp. It refers to the totality of rules and practices within the sphere of public cult, in other words a normative rather than a discursive account of religious practice. And then there is 'mythical theology'. This is the category Augustine is most scathing about, but it is the one that from the modern point of view enjoyed the widest freedom and displayed the greatest theological energy; the one to which the fewest controls applied and yet, as I have stressed, in its very performability the closest of all to cult-practice.

The Philosophy of Religion

It is important to note at the outset that philosophical reflection about religion is a wholly Greek enterprise, if we mean by that the attempt systematically to think through basic questions regarding our existence as a whole, and to create coherent, discursive answers to them. Early on, among the Pre-Socratics, this effort easily led to over-generalization, extreme simplification, sometimes to counter-intuitive claims such as 'everything is fire', or 'everything is water'.[7] If we look more closely, however, we find that normal every-day assumptions are very much taken into account. These include the fact that gods exist, and that their actions are always related to human beings. As will have become clear in chapter 3, Greek philosophers in general can be described as critical of religion but not as out-and-out opponents of it. The specific excesses of religious practice, and customary beliefs, might come under fire, and the Cynics and Academics (sceptics) especially might inveigh against popular religion, but the main schools tried in one form or other to integrate the basic everyday assumptions that the gods exist into their own world-views. The two special targets are idolatry, the worship of representations (which may include aniconic representations such as stones) as though they were divine, and animal-sacrifice. Critics could however be open to compromise: Apollonius of Tyana is said to have rejected animal-sacrifice to the high or transcendent God, while allowing the formulation of rules for sacrifices to lesser deities.[8] Even for the Epicureans and Academics, the value of traditional cult in inculcating moral values and maintaining the order of society is generally beyond question.

Rome's very earliest philosophical text reveals how unlikely the shifts are here. This is the translation by Ennius of Euhemerus' *Sacred Record* that I have already mentioned (p. 58 above). As we saw, this book (perhaps an early utopian novel) argued that gods are actually human kings who after their deaths were worshipped by their subjects. At first glance, this looks as though it were criticism of religion, a tearing of the veil. The faithful imagine they are worshipping gods, who are in fact but deceased humans. Although Euhemerus was indeed frequently considered to be more or less an atheist (e.g. Cicero, *De nat. deor.* 1.119), this interpretation mistakes the intention of the work. It was written at the time of the emergence of Hellenistic ruler-cult, itself inspired by the worship of Alexander the Great, the conqueror of the Persian Empire. Euhemerus' aim was to oppose the critics of this development, by arguing that they have got hold of the wrong end of the stick: most of the gods they believe in and think real, such as Zeus, became gods in exactly the same way, for they too were great kings whose achievements caused people to start worshipping them. Euhemerus did not want to show up the 'old' gods as false but to intervene in a contemporary debate by arguing that the deification of humans is nothing new or wrong but a practice that has ancient roots (Müller 1993; Brisson 2004: 48f.).[9]

One of the most important strategies for accommodating traditional cults into philosophical schemes is by appeal to the philosophy of language. In practice this meant the systematic etymologization of cultural and religious facts. The original claim was that words do not exist purely by convention but onomatopoetically reproduce in their sound the true nature of the referent. This configuration was understood as the key to the pre-history, to the very genesis, of a concept, and might therefore provide insight into the true nature of a god.[10] In this case, Rome is more interesting than Athens, because the Romans of the Late Republic and the Augustan period, impelled by a mixture of Italian patriotic fervour, intellectual universalism, and politically-motivated pride in their own polity, were extremely interested in the different ethnic roots of their culture, in Etruscan, Sabine, Latin and Greek influences (cf. Poucet 1985).

For a long while Greek was the language of philosophy at Rome. Even if they were composed by a Roman, philosophical texts were written in Greek. The tradition continued well into the Principate: we may think of cases such as L. Annaeus Cornutus' *Epitome of the Traditions of Greek Theology* (mid-first century AD), an etymologizing and allegorizing glossary of Greek divine names and myths, or the emperor Marcus Aurelius' *Meditations*. Cicero wrote his philosophical works in Latin because he explicitly wanted to make Greek philosophical systems available more widely than to the small group of Romans willing to read long and difficult Greek texts. So he puts Greek theories into the mouths of his Roman interlocutors. The conversations are occasionally enlivened with a Roman example or two, but the theoretical approach remains wholly Greek, aiming at *to pithanon* (Gr.) or *probabile* (Lat.), the 'probable', 'what can be approved' (from *probare*, to approve of). At first sight, one might think Cicero a Stoic, because when he is comparing Stoics and Epicureans he mostly tends to prefer the former, as at the end of *De natura deorum* (3.95); but in fact, as I mentioned earlier, like Varro, he was a (New) Academic, a student of Philo of Larissa (159/8– 84/3 BC), who at Rome taught a moderately sceptical form of Platonism, which involved deciding in each case which are the most probable assumptions and, given that certain knowledge is impossible, accepting the view one finds most convincing.[11]

Now it is important to understand – and here Cicero is typical of almost all upper-class Roman philosophers – that such philosophical reflections have no implications for his understanding of his augurate, no consequences for the cults and rituals that he performed.[12] The responsibilities of an individual Augur (as opposed to the College) included the observation of adverse omens, such as bird-flight and lightning, which occurred during public business, and giving opinions on particular queries raised by others. In *De divinatione*, On divination, Cicero seems to favour a sceptical view of the entire project, adopting on this occasion an Academic not a Stoic position (which is set out, rather selectively, in Book 1 by Cicero's brother Quintus). This is neither hypocrisy nor consciously to have one's cake and eat it. Philosophical enquiry and every-day behaviour were not 'cognitively dissonant', that is, did not involve two completely different mental realms, which are not allowed to come into contact with one another.[13] Greek philosophy was not simply a kind of hobby for Cicero's social class: it was too useful in relation to many problems encountered by Rome as she expanded into the Mediterranean, and in helping the Roman élite to systematize its own traditions. But it was not used as a tool to criticize central Roman institutions such as religion: Cicero, for example, hardly touches on augury in *De divinatione* (Rüpke 2005c). One could push such theoretical knowledge too far. In the first century AD, it was commonly thought that getting too interested in the philosophy of a particular school was a mark of youthful over-enthusiasm. Before the development of Neo-Platonism in the first half of the second century AD, philosophy was not permitted to have any relevance to the practice of Roman religion. On the other hand, philosophy can be said to have been part of that religion as a 'practical discourse'. It is this possibility that makes ancient religions more complex than religions in which practical action is supposed to match the theoretical system. At any rate, if 'coherence' means that practice has to fit the theory, Roman religion, like Buddhism, Hinduism and almost all other religions, is incoherent.

But we must return to philosophy. Why did upper-class Romans bother with it at all? The answer lies in the history of the third and second centuries BC, in the confrontation, usually violent, with Hellenistic Greece, whose culture was in almost all material respects superior to that of contemporary Rome. The Romans saw themselves forced to take up a position, to set themselves in some sort of relation with the other side. In some areas this was not a problem. Roman aristocrats could easily turn the use of Greek 'art' to decorate their private houses into yet another arena of competition. Philosophy had no such immediate attraction, indeed was considered in some ways as a threat (philosophers and rhetors, teachers of rhetoric were expelled from Rome several times in the second century), and was therefore only properly received about a century later. What philosophy offered was a means of generalizing or universalizing rules and values, including Roman ones, a task quite beyond the various traditional narratives, which only made sense in the context of the history of the city.

Some did not stop there. For a number of Cicero's contemporaries, both philosophically-inspired rules about how to lead one's life and speculation about salvation after death (soteriology) became more important than acting in accordance with traditional rules of behaviour. Certain aspects of Pythagoreanism – vegetarianism, for example, and the theory of metempsychosis (the journey of the immortal soul through lives in different bodily forms) – proved especially attractive here.[14] Varro himself, second to none as a collector of information about traditional Roman cults, was buried, in accordance with Pythagorean rules, in a mixture of myrtle-, olive- and poplar-leaves

(Pliny, *HN* 35.160). Another senator of the same period, Nigidius Figulus (*c.* 100–45 BC), went in for necromancy, the use of the spirits of the dead as a means of divination.[15]

Despite that, Cicero had a positive view of Figulus' contribution to the renewal of Pythagoreanism at Rome (*Timaeus* 1). Even if more critical enquiry suggests that neither Figulus nor Varro made any recognizable theoretical contributions to the movement, Neo-Pythagoreanism is sociologically important as an 'intellectual religion', based on texts, that managed to establish itself alongside other forms of religious activity practised by the Roman élite.[16] A comparable intellectualist doctrine of individual salvation, which, being concerned only with the reading and production of texts, found no expression at the level of public cult, is Hermetism. Although the collection we possess was put together only in the Byzantine period, the Corpus Hermeticum reveals the activity, evidently quite widespread during the period AD 100–300, of reading and writing texts all of which claimed to be revelations by the ancient Egyptian-Greek god Hermes Trismegistus, the 'thrice greatest', or associated gods such as Tat (Thoth), Asclepius (Imhotep), Ammon or Agathos Daemon (Copenhaver 1992; Colpe and Holzhausen 1997). Since they make extensive use of the idiom of revelation into a mystery-cult, we may properly call them 'reading-mysteries'. It has however been argued that we should not exclude the possibility that these texts may indeed emanate from specific groups of bureaucrats and officials in the Eastern Mediterranean, or from an Egyptian temple-milieu, and thus from genuine text-communities (Fowden 1986: 186–95; Frankfurter 1998: 222f.).

Myth

Archaeologically speaking, Rome and Italy, just like the entire rest of the Mediterranean area, were full of myths (cf. Graf 1993a, 1993b). I refer here mainly to the decorations of temples – to the cult-statues or their miniatures, the figural ensembles from temple-pediments, the acroteria (terracotta decorations on the four corners of the roof of a temple, and on the gable-ends, which sometimes carry small-scale mythological scenes; later examples often take the form of statues of gods with attributes known from mythology), the antefixes (roof-tiles sometimes decorated with the faces of gods), the metopes (the reliefs decorating the entablature frieze running along the outside of a temple) – but also to the vase-paintings recovered by archaeologists. In art-historical terms, these artefacts are Greek (often Euboean), or at any rate, if they came from the eastern Mediterranean, employed motifs borrowed from Greek craftsmen or their products. We can assume that content, that is myth-variants, came with the forms thus transported, which constitute a mass of images that, especially in the minor arts, could hardly be controlled, and, given that literary evidence is rather late at Rome, provide important and exciting evidence for the early history of religion there (Wiseman 1994: 23–36; 2000).

We are hardly in a position to trace the manner in which local traditions and new interpretations were integrated. As we saw, ever since the period of Greek colonization of Magna Graecia, that is, since the eighth or seventh centuries BC, Rome had been exposed to elements of Greek culture. The most impressive early archaeological example of Greek influence at Rome is the non-peripteral Archaic temple in the Vico Iugario, just beside the church of Sant' Omobono, which I mentioned earlier (p. 52). The site is not far from the Tiber harbour (cf. Häuber and Schütz 2006: 268, fig. 4). Although full excavation has proved impracticable, the temple is generally believed to have been founded c. 580 BC. Around 530, probably following a fire, the podium was enlarged and the terracotta ornamentation of the tympanum, which shows a chariot-procession, apparently divine, renewed (Sommella Mura 1977: 68–73, esp. 72f. fig. 5). The entire site was violently destroyed c. 500 BC. Perhaps the most telling find is a two-thirds life-size group of Minerva and Heracles, now in the Capitoline Museum, which has plausibly been interpreted as the goddess introducing the new deity to the company of the other gods.[17]

So far, I have used the term myth in the sense of popular stories of gods and heroes. If we adopt a substantive definition like this, focused upon content, it is clear that there really are very few such stories of properly Roman origin. Once nineteenth-century scholarship had begun distinguishing sharply between Greek myths and Roman myths, the realization that there was a serious imbalance between them evoked radical interpretations. Georg Wissowa, for example, spoke of the Roman peasant's lack of imagination: he bothered himself with his ploughs and his harvests; he went to war if it could be fitted around his agricultural work; but he did not tell fantastic stories. That was the reason why the Romans, a nation of peasants (and) soldiers, had no myths.[18] This thesis is of course inadmissible. If we look at the economic bases of the two social formations, and use that as a gauge of their imaginative capacity, we cannot discern any significant differences between Rome and Greece. The contrast can moreover be toned down by noting the different structure of the two polytheisms, and, with Carl Koch, the political background of 'demythologization' at Rome.[19] The sheer concern to control myth is itself an indication of the importance of such legitimation for the aristocracy. Still, the gap between the two cultures remains palpable.[20] Did the Romans perhaps simply not need myth?

In place of a direct answer, we may find it preferable to alter our definition by focusing on function rather than content. In that case myths will be stories, usually set in a remote period, say the beginning of the world or remotest antiquity, that, in telling of figures, topics and events, rehearse a society's system of values, legitimate certain institutions and values, and at the same time convey a certain world-view. Examples might be tales about how the world came into being (cosmogony) or how the world functions (myths of nature); or culture-myths, that relate how, say, Prometheus brought fire down to earth from heaven, or how certain cultural traits came into being (Assmann and Assmann 1998; Segal 1999). The sequences of events and actions, and the images employed, in these stories can themselves be inspirational. To take a modern example before looking at antiquity: Max Schneckenburger's poem, *Die Wacht am Rhein*, The Watch on the Rhine, written in the furore over the Second Oriental Crisis of 1840 but only successful as a nationalist hymn when it was set to the music of Karl Wilhelm in 1854, served from that point on up to the Great War of 1914–18 to legitimate the pseudo-historical notion of an ancient feud with France.

But myths are not simply affirmative. In oral cultures the tale changes with each re-telling, is modified to fit the situation and aims of the speaker. The written form conserves and multiplies such variants, which can also take on critical functions. As a body, myths become a store of signs, which through deliberate recombination can be used as a medium in which to think alternative possibilities. Such a medium does not remain unchallenged. Philosophical criticism plays *mythos* off against *logos*, rational explanation. Myths had been criticized in Greece since the sixth century; such criticism is in fact a permanent feature of the history of religion in antiquity (Graf 1993a: 176–98; Brisson 2004). This did not however prevent myth from working. The stories remained alive, not least because of their capacity to entertain. But they did not work automatically. Ears could remain shut.

We can look at how a myth 'works' by taking the Roman claim to be descended from the Trojans. Although it had been known in Italy since the sixth century BC, the myth seems to have been first connected to Rome by Greeks during the third century BC, pretty certainly in the context of the two invasions of Italy by Pyrrhus, king of Epirus, in the first quarter of that century. The myth seems to have been given two different senses. On the one hand, it was used to stress the ancient feud between the Achaeans and the Dardanians, between the Greeks and the Trojans. Pyrrhus (who himself claimed to be descended from Achilles) invoked it in this sense when he was first invited to Italy to help the Tarentines against Rome in 280. It could also be used however to emphasize that, while the Romans were descended from the Trojans, they were culturally Greek, and had been settled on the margins of the Greek world for more than a millennium. In this version, the Trojan War was seen as a regrettable military incident which had nevertheless not ruptured the fundamental cultural identity of the Greeks and Romans. Thus the people of Segesta were the first Sicilians to support Rome against Carthage in 263 BC because they claimed likewise to be descended from Aeneas (Diodorus Siculus 23.5). Initially, then, the Trojan myth was used primarily by outsiders. In the second century, however, the Romans realized that for the Greeks myth was a means of creating a shared figurative language, and began to use the myth of being descended from Aeneas with considerable finesse. It was only in the first century BC that it was used aggressively, to legitimate Roman imperial interests in Asia Minor and justify Roman behaviour there.[21]

The second, functional understanding of myth allows us to include a second group of texts. It is characteristic of Rome that myth appears there as history, indeed as local history (Scheid 2003: 180f.). The Greeks had Hesiod's *Theogony*; the Romans had narratives of their own history: the founding of the city by Romulus; the kings: peaceful Numa, martial Tullus Hostilius, tyrannical Tarquinius Superbus; the expulsion of the overweening tyrant by L. Iunius Brutus in 245 AUC = 509 BC. Precise dating of this kind – mainly the result of calibration with the chronology of Greek historiography, but impelled too by a felt need for an intelligible structuring device – has led to misrecognition of the essentially mythical character of this narrative. The French Indo-Europeanist Georges Dumézil has done a lot of work in this area (e.g. Dumézil 1980). The situation is in fact not atypical. In the case of Rome, we have an individual city-state whose culture differs from that of Greece in that the latter was an amalgam of many different *poleis*, whose common mythical discourse had to serve a far wider range of demands – for example, supra-regional, panhellenic meanings and explanations. It was no easy matter to find a niche for the Greeks in the Roman world of myths, or rather, Roman local history. The inverse, however, was no problem: a small city in the lower Tiber valley could easily be assimilated into a mythical discourse that had anyway to cover the entire Mediterranean basin (Rüpke 2001b: 53–6).

The skilful adaptation of the genres and motifs of Greek mythology into Augustan literature considerably extended the available modalities of expression (Wallace-Hadrill 1993). Greek myths provided Romans with a language of self-representation on grave-reliefs and sarcophagi. Mythical themes in wall-paintings in private houses offered their owners new resources of articulacy about themselves, about their values, about gender-roles.[22] This ought not to blur the difference in principle between myth and other genres. It was philosophy that tried to universalize and generalize, and it was the Roman conquests of the first century BC that first made universal historical writing in Latin possible. Much later, the claims of Christian historiography were universal too; its aim however was not to search for meaning in history but to impose an external meaning upon it (Timpe 1989; Rüpke 1997c).

Theologia Civilis

Whereas language is dominant in the two types of theology I have discussed so far, namely philosophy and myth, this is not the case with Varro's 'civic theology'. This category includes everything that a political community (of course in practice the ruling class) claims to be necessary for the gods to receive proper worship, expressed at Rome by the notion of maintaining the *pax deorum*, the good-will of the gods. In short civic theology denotes the *sacra* as a whole, not merely (but crucially) the *sacra publica*. It is mostly just traditional practice, including the rules for the performance of cult, and the religious specialists. The latter area is often, especially by historians of Roman law, called *ius sacrum*, 'sacral law', but this term has no ancient currency. *Ius divinum*, divine law, at Rome is, as we have seen, the term for the gods' rights in their own property (Gaius, *Inst.* 2.1–9). The laws relating to the different cults and priesthoods, like those relating to the magistrates, formed part of the *ius publicum*, public law. Apart from these, there were other sub-categories of law, for example the *ius pontificale*, the pontifical law, or the *ius augurale*, the augural law, but they are merely handy terms for referring to the rules, and rulings, issued by the *pontifices* and the Augurs, or regulating their action, just as the *ius honorarium* referred to the body of rulings by magistrates, and *ius parietum* or *ius stillicidiorum* were terms for all the rules and rulings relating to urban servitudes involving house- and property walls, or the questions arising from rain-water being allowed to drip onto a neighbour's land.[23] Here again it is abundantly clear that in this culture there was no unified concept of religion defined by means of specific denotations. Formulations that might appear to do so (*sacra et sacerdotes*; *cura et caerimonia*; *tria genera theologiae*) are simply partial lists, each compiled from a different perspective.

The rules for the conduct of rituals are apparently legitimated by their hoary antiquity, but, as is the case with all oral traditions, they are not as unchanging as they pretend. In a society like that of Republican Rome undergoing marked internal changes 'traditions' too are likely to alter. For example, they may be adapted to fit new political situations, as when, probably in the Late Republic, the Flamen Martialis and the Flamen Quirinalis were allowed to take up governorships of a province, which of course meant that they would be absent from the city for long periods of time.[24] The inverse also occurred: there is plenty of evidence for a new rigorism, treating religious rules as an autonomous zone with interdictive authority over other spheres: for example, several Flamines Diales had to quit their office in the late third century BC because of ritual faults; and, as a member of the priesthood of the Salii, L. Cornelius Scipio Asiaticus (cos. 190 BC) interrupted his campaign before the battle of Magnesia for the thirty days during which his colleagues at Rome were performing their rituals.[25]

There was a complex reaction to the modification of tradition under the impact of irregular change, which we may summarize as documentarism. From about the First Punic War (264–41 BC) the great public priesthoods began to keep records: these took the generic form not of normative or systematic texts in the sense of Pentateuchal *Leviticus* but of minutes or protocols of the meetings of the colleges (*commentarii* or *libri pontificum*, ~ *augurum*, ~ *XVvirum sacris faciundis*).[26] Such minutes did of course include the names of new appointments and vacancies, the latter mainly through death (cf. Livy 23.21.7; 26.23.7), but they also noted ritual celebrations, detailed decisions, and individual opinions (*decreta et responsa*); as such they had a controlling and regulatory function.[27] The *commentarii* of the grand colleges are known to us only in the form of brief quotations and allusions; but the discovery at La Magliana (the shrine of the Dea Dia, on the dual-carriageway to Rome airport) of numerous marble slabs on which the *Acta* of the Arval Brothers were copied each year makes it possible for us to read quantities of similar texts covering (with large gaps) a period of almost three hundred years (Scheid 1998a).

Roman 'myths' and individual families' claims to have possessed consular ancestors in the remote past began to be systematized in a form analogous to Greek historical writing at the end of the third century BC. At first indeed they were actually written in Greek, and intended for private reading. This effort was soon extended to the creation of public lists of office-holders, and calendars with the dates of temple-dedications (the *Fasti*). Systematic, detailed descriptions or collections of the rules relating to certain offices and functions, for example *On pontifical laws, On censors, On the competences of magistracies*, followed in the second third of the second century BC. The few, almost entirely later, texts that mention them imply that they were intended not as hand-books for practical use but a means of fixing tradition; but in fact they must often have introduced interpretations and modifications (cf. Van Haeperen 2002). The authors were all senators. Much the same applies to Varro, the most important Roman antiquarian, whose aim likewise was to preserve or resurrect traditions. Despite frequent modern claims to the contrary, his *Antiquitates rerum divinarum* was not intended as a reform-programme (Jocelyn 1980; 1982; Cancik 1985–86).

That this sort of technical literature could develop its own speculative energy can be illustrated by taking the example of Rome's alleged secret tutelary deity. It is well-known that a Roman army that was besieging an enemy city might make use of a rather strange ritual (*evocare*): the commander would make a vow that, if the enemy's chief deity were to abandon its role as protector of the city and so allow the Romans to capture it, he would dedicate a temple to the god in Rome. The acceptability of the offer was inferred from the Roman success; the cult-statue would then be carried off back to Rome.[28]

The background to this ritual was that Italian cities usually had a tutelary deity (*in alicuius dei tutela*). In many places, Juno had this function, and was worshipped in an especially grand temple, on the *arx* (citadel) or somewhere similar. Macrobius, however, the learned author in the early fifth century AD of a dialogue, founded on Vergil's *Aeneid*, concerning the inheritance of classical culture, turns the whole thing round as follows (*Sat.* 3. 9.2f.):

> If every town has a tutelary deity and this tutelary deity can be evoked, then it would be better if nobody knew its name. For if we Romans were under siege, and our enemies did not know the name of our tutelary god, they could not 'evoke' it. So Rome shall never be conquered.

The sack of Rome by the Goths in AD 410 had in fact recently confuted this claim, for the first time since Brenner and the Gauls in 390

BC.[29] It is however wholly plausible in the light of ancient assumptions about names. If you know someone's name, you gain a certain power over him.[30] The most familiar example in our culture, the tale of Rumpelstiltskin, shows that such ideas were not limited to Rome. According to Macrobius, the candidates were: Jupiter, Luna, Diva Angerona, and Ops Consivia, the latter being his own personal contribution to the game.

Now Macrobius shares his interest in the idea of Rome's having a secret protector with an early fifth-century commentary on Vergil's *Aeneid*, which I have cited several times, by Servius. Servius complements Macrobius' information by saying that, according to Varro, a 'certain tribune' had been crucified for revealing the name.[31] We can add to this a claim by Pliny the Elder, also cited by Solinus 1.4–6, that one Valerius Soranus had been executed for divulging the secret name, which it was only lawful to utter at certain secret rituals, *arcanis caerimoniarum* (Pliny, *HN* 3. 65, cf. Plutarch, *QRom* 61). The learned scholar Q. Valerius Soranus (of Sora) was executed by Pompey in Sicily, where he had evidently gone with the Marian consul for the year 82 BC, Cn. Papirius Carbo (Plutarch, *Pomp.* 10; Serv. auct., *Aen.* 1.277). His death was thus the result of being proscribed (as a supporter of Marius), and has nothing to do with religious issues of any kind. At the same time, we know that Soranus wrote works of a religious-antiquarian kind, as well as verse, and was often cited by Varro.[32] This link with Varro must be the reason for associating the revelation of Rome's secret name with Soranus' violent death, for, as we saw, it is Varro whom Servius cites as his authority for linking the death with the revelation.

If we look carefully into the background of these speculations, we cannot penetrate farther back than the early Principate or late Republic, beyond Verrius Flaccus (died *c.* AD 20) and Varro (died 27 BC).[33] The idea that Rome possessed a secret name (*nomen alterum*) was created at a time when the ritual of evoking enemy gods into the city of Rome was still remembered but no longer performed. Historically speaking, all city patron-gods known to have been 'evoked' were brought to Rome under their ordinary name.[34]

There is no other evidence that Diva Angerona, apparently Verrius Flaccus' main candidate as the secret tutelary deity of Rome, had such a reputation. We do know that the statue of this deity, at the top end of the Via Nova (see pls. 21, 24), represented her either with her mouth sealed (*ore obligato obsignatoque*: Pliny, *HN* 3.65; Solinus 1.6), or with one finger raised to her lips (Macrobius, *Sat.* 3.9.4). This was – probably correctly – interpreted as an injunction to silence, and linked to ideas about a secret name: what was it the goddess was not allowed to utter? There were other speculations about this secret name, based on anagrammatic and rebus treatments of Roma: for example, it was suggested that it might be Amor (Love); Flora was another candidate, mentioned by Johannes Lydus (*De mens.* 4.73) in the sixth century AD, who produced the most elaborate scheme of the names of Rome. Sparked off by an actual cult, the educated thus gaily speculated and indulged in their fanciful reconstructions. Such speculation does fulfil certain requirements of rational coherence, but can be thought of neither as properly philosophical nor yet as mythical – the tripartite scheme is inadequate as a classification for the historian's purposes. Writing is probably a necessary pre-condition for the emergence of such a discourse, a discourse made up entirely of reading and writing antiquarian books, and which gave birth to lumberingly diverting texts such as Aulus Gellius' *Attic Nights*.

A Theory of Action?

None of this is covered by Varro's term *theologia civilis*, which is concerned with actual cult-practice, not with oral tradition or speculation. It is possible that Varro dealt with this term at such length precisely because he wanted to give ritual practice an intellectual boost, since it was under considerable pressure from intellectuals to justify itself, of course on their terms. The best means of defending cult was to include it among his 'theologies'. The Roman way, the *mos maiorum*, tradition, could thus be bolstered by appeal to the universal language of Greek philosophy, which of course had precious little to do with the actual religious praxis of Greek cities.

Part II

Religion in Action

— 6 —

SOCIAL RULES: SACRIFICE AND FEASTING

Some Examples

As soon as we come to look more closely at ritual practice, we encounter the institution of sacrifice. In its different forms, animal-sacrifice symbolizes a 'piety' that underwrites all the traditional values of Roman society, a connotation that fades only in Late Antiquity. The synecdochic value of the main actions just before and after the dispatch of the animal tends to distract attention from the obvious point that that they are only 'stills' from a much longer sequence of events.[1] I would like to offer a slightly different point of view, and start by citing a couple of the tiny number of prescriptive texts that set out how a Roman sacrifice is to be performed (by comparison with Greek sacrifice, we have almost no high-quality source-material for Rome). A special value of these examples, which are taken from the Elder Cato's *De agri cultura*, is that they refer to private cult, which most other sources ignore. Their disadvantage, however, is that they say nothing about shifts of scene, about the procession, essential to every larger public sacrifice, which takes the participants to the fixed site where the sacrifice proper is performed, be it the *area* in front of a temple, an open cult-site, or a sacred grove.[2]

As I have already pointed out, Cato does not devote a separate section of his work to religious prescriptions: he inserts them here and there without more ado into the guidance on farming. The first text refers to the *daps*, the offering of food and wine to a god, in this case on behalf of the plough-teams (*pro bubus*):

The offering is to be made in the following manner: offer to Jupiter Dapalis a cup of wine of any size you wish, observing the day as a

137

holiday for the oxen, the ox-masters, and those who make the offering. In making the (food-)offering use the following formula: 'Jupiter Dapalis, it is fitting that a cup of wine be offered to you in my house, among my family and dependants, as part of your sacred feast (*daps*). Therefore do us the honour (*macte esto*) of accepting this meal (*daps*) here.' Wash your hands, then take the (cup of) wine, and say: 'Jupiter Dapalis, do us the honour of accepting this feast (*daps*): do us the honour (of accepting this) wine that we offer you here.' You may (also) make an offering to Vesta if you wish. The food (*daps*) offered to Jupiter consists of roasted beef or mutton and an 'urn' of wine. Make the offering (*profanato*) in a state of ritual purity, in the fitting form (*sua contagione*). Once the ceremony has been performed, you may plant millet, panic grass, garlic, and lentils.

Cato, De agr. 132 (tr. Hooper/Ash, adapted)

In practice, *profanare* means to sacrifice, to make an offering. The etymology of the word however indicates that something is actually being brought from inside a sacred place (*fanum*) to the area in front (*pro*) of it – into the 'profane' world. In our case here, something is being 'profaned' within a ritual context, which means it is being rendered available for human use. The 13.13 litres of wine the 'urn' (half-amphora) contains will be drunk by the human participants, while Jupiter has to be content with the small cup of wine poured out for him onto the earth.[3]

My second example comes from the following section but one. §131 dealt with the spring ploughing, followed by the planting of millet and so on (in the last sentence of §132); §133 deals with layering and pruning fruit-trees and vines; and now we approach the harvest in autumn:

Before harvest the sacrifice of the *porca praecidanea* should be offered in the following manner: offer a sow as *porca praecidanea* to Ceres before harvesting spelt, wheat, barley, beans, and rape seed; before offering the sow, address a prayer, with incense and wine, to Janus, Jupiter and Juno. Make an offering of finger-cakes (*strues*) to Janus, with these words: 'Father Janus, in offering these cakes, I humbly beg you to be gracious and merciful to me and my children, my house and my household.' Then make an offering of cake (*fertum*) to Jupiter in these words: 'In offering this cake, Jupiter, I humbly beg that, pleased by this offering, you may be gracious and merciful to me and my children, my house and my household.' Then offer the wine to Janus saying: 'Father Janus, just as I prayed humbly in offering the cakes, so likewise do me the honour of accepting this wine offered to you.' And then pray to Jupiter thus: 'Jupiter, do me the honour of accepting the cake; do me the honour (likewise) of accepting the wine offered you.'

138

Then offer up the *porca praecidanea*. When the entrails (*exta*) have been removed, make an(other) offering of cakes (*strues*) to Janus, with a prayer as before; and an(other) offering of a cake (*fertum*) to Jupiter, with a prayer as before. In the same way, again offer wine to Janus and to Jupiter, as was previously directed for the offering of the cakes (*ob struem obmovendam*), and the consecration of the cake (*ob fertum libandum*). Afterwards offer the entrails, and wine, to Ceres.

Cato, De agr. 134 (tr. Hooper/Ash, adapted)

This is a relatively complex ritual, in which various subsidiary offerings are made not to Ceres, the main nominal object of the sacrifice, but to other gods. Janus is the god of auspicious beginnings (Varro, *LL* 6.34); Cicero's Stoic spokesman Balbus mentions that at sacrifices he was invoked first because 'beginnings (and endings) are of the greatest importance' (*De nat. deor.* 2.67). Then comes Jupiter, the highest god in a political context (and then Juno, at any rate in the pre-amble). Similarly an offering is made to Janus and Jupiter in Cato's description a few chapters later of the *lustratio agri*, the 'muster of the land' (*De agr.* 141 = Beard, North, Price 1998: 2, 152f.), which is directed primarily to Mars. In this case, where the sacrifice consists of three male animals: suckling-boar, tup-lamb and bull-calf, all still at teat and correspondingly cheap, I want to stress the rules laid down for the event that the *litatio* might fail. For if a sacrifice is to be deemed acceptable to the deity, the 'noble' entrails of the freshly-slaughtered animal must on inspection be in best condition, flawless. Cato offers two possibilities in the event of the god 'not being satisfied' (*si minus litabit*): if there is doubt in one or two cases, another of the same type of animal, say a piglet, can be offered ('*te hoc porco piaculo*'); if no positive response (*litatio*) at all is obtained, the entire ritual has to be repeated ('*te hisce suovitaurilibus piaculo*'). Here we find ritual dramatization by appeal to the possibility of 'external' disturbance: this is the function of divination, which always accompanies sacrifice.

Sacrifices can also however be quite straightforward. One example of such simplicity is the direction a couple of chapters later to the farm-overseer's wife: 'On the Kalends, the Ides and the Nones of each month, and at each religious festival, she is to hang a garland over the hearth, and on the same days she is to pray to the Lar of the family for plenty in the house (*pro copia*)' (*De agr.* 143.2). Religion can be simple too.[4]

12. Decennalia-base of Constantius I (Chlorus), Caesar AD 293–305.

One of a set of five columns with bases erected on the Rostra in AD 303 in celebration of the tenth anniversary of the First Tetrarchy (established 1 March 293) and the twentieth anniversary of Diocletian's accession (20 November, AD 284). The monument as a whole is depicted on a relief on the Arch of Constantine showing the emperor addressing the people from the Rostra: four of the columns, monoliths in Aswan granite 36 Roman feet high, carried statues, of the two Augusti and the two Caesares. Linked to it were statues of Mars, Romulus and Remus dedicated in AD 308 (*ILS* 8935). The sole surviving base, found in 1547, is decorated on all four faces. This one shows the sacrificial procession of the *suovetaurilia* (bull, ram and boar); the animals are rigged out in their sacrificial finery (esp. the *frontale* on the bull's forehead, and the *dorsuale* over his back). Note the status distinction between the supervising official, in a toga and with a staff of office, and the *victimarii* and *cultrarii*, the public slaves who did the actual killing and butchery, naked to the waist. Almost invisible on this photo is another slave behind the bull's withers, carrying fruits (which were also burned at sacrifices) on a pole-basket. Right lateral face, height: 1 m. Marble. Forum Romanum.

Sacrifice and Feasting

My examples from Cato the Elder serve to illustrate a point I made earlier: nothing works without a prayer, but prayers hardly ever occur in isolation. They are usually accompanied by a gift, which might

140

perhaps best be described as 'something to arouse the god's attention'. This can be something small, but usually consists, even when the main offering is considerable, of the heavy scent of incense, or flowers – a visual stimulus – or something to eat. The latter would be offered to the god's statue (*obmovere*, *mactare*), or poured out onto the ground, or burned on an altar. The pragmatics of divine consumption is not important: wine is poured onto the ground for Jupiter, even though he is a god of heaven. Such notions are obviously incoherent. The same point can be made in relation to the 'infrastructure' needed for performing the cult.

The main altar, usually of stone or brick, was used to burn those parts of the sacrificewhich were meant for the gods. A small transportable altar (*foculus*) was also required for the preliminary stages of sacrifice, the blood-free offerings of incense and food, which preceded the slaughter of the animal (Servius, *Aen.* 3.134). In addition to these two altars, some sort of kitchen (*culina*) was naturally required for preparing and cooking the meat.[5]

The altar itself need not have any connection with a temple: it might for example be built in a grove. If necessary, an altar could also be improvised from turf-sods (Vergil, *Aen.* 12.118; Horace, *Carm.* 3.8.4; Ovid, *Fasti* 2.645). The altar's central role in the performance of sacrifice is clear from its use as a synecdoche for the entire complex ritual. As a result, altars are a very common form of votive (Schraudolph 1993; Dräger 1994). Indeed, this function of the classical form of the altar was transposed into Christian usage.

Throughout classical antiquity we find a characteristic double sacrificial system, similar to that in the ancient Near East (Gladigow 1994). It was based on a distinction between animal-sacrifice at the altar outside the temple and the offering of food inside the temple. In the latter system, a table was set up in front of the cult-statue and offerings of food and other gifts (say, money) intended for the god were placed on it. In Greek, these offerings are called *trapezōmata*; in Latin, *mensa* or *sacrificia*.[6] In this context, communication with the deity takes a completely different form from that on the altar outside: the gifts and food-offerings are given in the same way as to a human being – the anthropomorphization of the god is very pronounced. The fate of these gifts is unclear: they were probably not burnt, but removed by the temple personnel, the priests, and eaten, or used for the maintenance of the temple.

The sacrificial ritual at the altar was not directly addressed to a cult-statue. Efforts were indeed made to align the latter with the temple-doors and the external altar, but in principle the altar did not require

141

either a temple or a cult-image. The offerings destined for the gods were burnt; the humans ate the rest. Only a select portion could be placed on the table inside the temple, thus linking the two systems of sacrifice.[7]

Humans could take their share whenever larger amounts of food were involved (remember Cato's thirteen litres of wine), as also in the case of animal-sacrifice, since the sacrifice was followed by a banquet.[8] Temple-complexes often have kitchens and dining-halls (triclinium; trichilionum) attached (Egelhaaf-Gaiser 2000: 272–329). The same is true, though more rarely, of fairly elaborate tombs or tomb-complexes, for example in the Isola Sacra necropolis near Ostia, or the tomb of C. Vibius Saturninus in the necropolis outside the Porta Ercolano at Pompeii: such tombs may be furnished with cooking-hearths and podia arranged like those in the dining-hall of a villa, from which one could eat. In a few cases there is even a brick-built table in the centre (cf. CIL VI 4710; 10315; ILS 7889).[9]

The connection between sacrifice and banquet is standard, but the one need not follow immediately upon the other. After the procession, grand or minimal, up to the altar in a temple-area (in towns this was usual even in the case of private animal-sacrifice), water was sprinkled about to effect a symbolic cleansing. After the bloodless preliminary offerings had been made, the victim was sprinkled, at any rate in public sacrifices, as I have mentioned in my earlier acount of the ritual, with mola salsa, sacred grain mixed with salt. The sacrificant, normally the person who was paying for the sacrifice, ran the knife along the animal's back. The butcher (victimarius, cultrarius or popa, which has a more general sense, 'assistant at sacrifices') asked: Agone? Shall I begin? The answer: Age! Begin! was the signal to start the slaughtering.[10] The victim was killed, bled, turned on its back and opened up. The entrails were inspected. Then it had to be jointed, and the different parts assigned to different purposes. In the case of cattle, the 'noble' entrails were boiled; of pigs and sheep, roasted on spits. Hours might thus pass before the participants could sit down and eat their share of the victim, the red meat. On certain festive days, known as dies intercisi, profane actions, lawsuits and so on, might take place during the hours that passed between the extraction of the 'noble' entrails (exta caesa) and their being burned for the gods.[11] After all this, the humans could start to eat.

There are three options here. The first was the so-called cena recta, the regular meal. That involved sitting down together, eating, drinking and celebrating. Alternatively some of the sacrificial meat and other food might not be consumed at the sacrifice itself but be put into small baskets (*sportulae*), which could be of any size, and given to the participants to take home. The third possibility (not incompatible with the first two) was for the sacrificial meat to be sold. In this case parts at least of the sacrifice would be sold off to butchers, so that the broad mass of the population could participate in the 'public sacrifices'.[12] For several reasons, this option was at Rome, as we shall see, the one normally chosen.

Such sales could cause problems. In his *First Epistle to the Corinthians*, a Christian text, the apostle Paul deals with the question of the consumption of sacrificial meat (10.25-30). His recommendation is that everything that is sold on the meat-market may be eaten, without raising any question on the grounds of conscience. If however you are invited to dinner by a non-believer and explicitly told by someone, another Christian, that the meat is sacrificial, then you should decline to eat it. Paul's basic position is stated between these two rules: everything in our world is given us by God. Even though these beasts were unlucky enough to have been subjected to a pagan ritual, they too must be counted a gift of God. Only when you might offend the conscience of another Christian should you decline the consumption of sacrificial meat.

It is noticeable that Roman sources – quite different from the case in Greece – hardly address the connection between sacrifice and the banquet. There are two ways of dealing with this situation. The first is to assume, on the basis of a few scraps of Roman evidence, that the Greek view, namely that the humans invite the gods and the two feast together, also holds true for Rome. Such a view is undoubtedly inherent in the sacrificial practice of the ancient Near East and Mediterranean Europe; and, as John Scheid showed in a brilliant article, it also corresponds to the way in which the meat was divided between gods and men at Rome.[13] Alternatively, however, we might try comparing the sacrificial banquet with other Roman banquets and once again, as in the case of the 'double sacrificial system', find interesting inconsistencies. I choose this second path (cf. Rüpke 2005b).

Who invites whom? For the Roman aristocracy, banquets are of the essence. The dining-room (*triclinium*) is the centre of the classical Roman house; the basic furnishing of three couches (Greek: *klinai*) arranged around three sides of a square, from which the room takes its name, is designed for 3 × 3 male participants, so not primarily for family-meals. Aristocrats issued mutual invitations, ate together, talked together, sang, and listened to songs in praise of their ancestors, thus strengthening their adherence to shared values (Roller 2006). The public priesthoods became proverbial for their elaborate banquets;

143

when the cult of the Mater Magna was introduced in 204 BC, the élite had nothing more pressing to do than invent a new kind of banquet, *mutitationes*, 'mutual invitations' (Ovid, *Fast.* 4.353f.; Aulus Gellius, *Att. Noct.* 18.2.11; *Fast. Praenest.* s.v. 4 April). All this encouraged communication and consensus, but by the same token also provided a new area of competition (Rüpke 1998b). High-quality dinner services are very common archaeologically already in the Latial orientalizing phase (e.g. the finds in Tomb XV in the necropolis at Ficana, Latium: Cornell 1995: 89–92); in the second century BC sumptuary-laws had to limit the excesses. So why should one not feast with the gods too?

There appears to be no unambiguous answer at Rome to one decisive issue in relation to the sacrificial banquet: who is the host, who the guest? From Plautus to Martial, from 200 BC to AD 100, a divine invitation extended to a human-being meant 'death' (Plautus, *Rudens* 362; Martial 9.91). The expression was ironical. When humans invite gods, the intention is usually that the deity should to come to 'live' in a temple that has been built (e.g. Statius, *Silv.* 3.1.138). The use of the word *lectisternium* fits this, for it is best translated not 'banquet for the gods' but 'couch-arrangement'. The word refers to the preparations for a banquet (*lectus* = couch for eating, corresponding to Gr. *klinē*); the *lectisternium* is *factum*, made or *habitum*, held, or *imperatum*, ordered (Livy 5.13.6; 8.25.1; 22.1.19f.), gods are not 'invited' to it. The banquet is given by the gods themselves (I refer to the representation, not to the actuality, which of course involved human-beings bringing out busts or statues of gods, food and so forth). Are we to suppose that the humans acted as hosts and managed the feast on holy ground with the furniture and fittings they found there? Hardly. Besides, we know that, apart from the food they brought themselves, people ate the meat that had been rendered *sacra* and then 'released' by the sacrificant's gesture of touching it, thus rendering it *profana*, profane.

The main difficulty in speaking of mutual invitation certainly lies in the fact that Romans only feasted with their social equals.[14] The equality required – again by contrast to the Greek practice – is not created by the mere possession of citizenship: the true pre-condition is not jural but social equality. That being the case, even the issue of who may eat *ex sacrificio*, of the sacrificial meat, becomes problematic. The right to consume sacrificial meat, provided and paid for by the community, without having to pay for it (*ius publice epulandi*), could not, as in Greece, be extended to all full citizens, but became a carefully protected privilege. It was accordingly confined to magistrates,

144

ex-magistrates and 'public' priests (Suetonius, *Aug.* 35.2; cf. Wissowa 1912: 419; 500). The Roman 'state-religion' that modern authors talk about, under the influence of nineteenth-century ideas, turns out once again to be in fact the 'private' religion of an élite that correlated its social prestige with its political engagement.

Hierarchies

Institutionalized ideas about Roman sacrifice are thus inconsistent. If we are concerned with the 'functions' of banqueting, historical, social, even individual, differences must move centre-stage. The example of Rome's secret patron divinity has already shown how far inter-pretations can diverge if they are not controlled by a canonical credo (p. 132–4).

The primary function of sacrifice is to define hierarchies (cf. Bourdillon and Fortes 1986). This may occur at various levels. The first and most obvious is the hierarchical distinction between gods and humans. That is made clear by two circumstances in particular. The deity or deities eat(s) first. After the cooking process (boiling or roast-ing), the gods receive their share, which is burnt with wine on the main altar, which only now, hours after the killing of the animal, becomes important. The deity eats first: even today, if one thinks of a formal or festive banquet, that is a clear sign of priority. Secondly, the god receives the most important parts of the victim, the *exta* ('noble' entrails). In Roman terminology, these are the *vitalia*, the vital parts: the liver, the gall-bladder, the lungs, and the great omentum; from the third century BC also the heart (Pliny *HN* 11.186). The remainder, in Latin the *viscera*, namely the red meat, the blood and what we call the viscera (the stomach, intestines, kidneys, womb etc), are extras the animal happens to have but does not really need. The truly important parts are these inner organs, and it is they that are given to the deity. Individual cuts or dishes, such as croquettes, called 'increments' (*aug-menta*) might be added (Varro, *LL* 5.112); individual shrines might also require 'extras' (*magmenta*).[15] What has been termed the 'topog-raphy' of sacrificial animals is admittedly a complex business.[16] For example, every fifth year at Rome the *pontifices* also offered the *caviares*, 'part of the victim right up to the tail', in a special sacrifice on behalf of the college, no doubt a reference to the usual Greek offering of the *sacrum* (Paulus, *Excerpt. Festi* p. 50, 16–18 L.). Nevertheless, although the *vitalia* do have a high cholesterol content, the whole procedure seems strange: already in Archaic Greece, where

13. Cropped shop-sign showing a probably imaginary temple.

This is perhaps the most telling surviving indication of how people actually perceived a Roman podium temple, with extensive resort to 'synoptic views'. You can only reach it by means of the flight of stairs at the front; the pro-style temple, with its Corinthian capitals, is the house (*cella*) of the gods (here, goddesses), who are represented as peeping out of it, as its owners. They are seated on a double throne; on the left is (probably) Roma, dressed as an Amazon, with one breast bare, a helmet on her lap, and a spear in her right hand; on the right is probably Annona, with a cornucopia in her left hand; she is pouring a libation of wine onto the fire alight on the small altar between the two central columns. All these are totally unrealistic details intended to suggest the cult-statues inside a temple, and the continuity of cult-service. The relief has been cropped to left and right (but is probably complete top and bottom; the frame is modern), rendering the inscription difficult to understand. It is generally thought that the key lies in the large 'dish' in front of the steps, which must be a *modius* (a measure of grain) seen schematically from above. Taken with the big storage jars on either side of it, which are otherwise never found in front of temples, the relief must be a shop-sign for a business that leased out such measures. On that basis, the reading would be: *[I]n h[is]/ [pr]aed[iis]/[Sa]bin(ii) Mat[ern(i)]/[mo]di(i) locantu[r]*, 'On these premises, belonging to Sabinius Maternus, *modius*-measures are available for hire' (the reading of *CIL* VI 29816 is to be rejected). This would also explain the joint presence of Roma and Annona (or possibly Fortuna) in a temple; it was once wrongly

146

the rules of sacrifices allocate slightly different parts of the victim to the gods, the allocation was a source of unease, hence the story of Prometheus' sacrificial 'trick' (Hesiod, *Theog.* 507–616).

It is not only gods and humans that are ranked asymmetrically, however, so are human beings. The sacrificant need not be the butcher. In this case too what we might think the climax of the sacrifice, the moment of death, fails to coincide with the social rank of the actors. The actual killing of larger animals, at least, was carried out by slave specialists, the *victimarii* and *cultrarii*. On reliefs, these men are usually wearing just a butcher's apron (*limus*) and carry either a long-handled axe (*sacena*) or a set of cooking- and skinning-knives (*cultri*). They usually wear wreaths. Other sacrificial servants (*ministri*) are often youths or even children, who are represented for example carrying, or offering to the sacrificant, the box of incense (*acerra*), and may also carry other things, the water-jug, for example, or the towel for drying one's hands; they too are recognizable by their clothing. In the Roman rite, the sacrificant and other principals, if wearing the toga (or, in the case of women, the *stola*), cover their heads.[17]

The key role played by status difference in sacrifice is hard to grasp in most other cases. One example however is the *feriae Latinae*, which involved a sacrifice at the temple of Jupiter Latiaris on the Monte Cavo (*mons Albanus*) in the Alban hills south of Rome, an old ritual in which the early Latin federal cities took part each spring, and a major obligation for all Roman consuls and magistrates (Cornell 1995: 71f.). Since membership in the Latin League depended on participation in this festival, great stress was laid on who was allowed to partake of (*particeps*, participant) of the sacrificial meat, and in what order of precedence. The Latin word *princeps*, later used for the emperor, denotes 'one who takes his share first'; the metaphor seems to be derived from this area, of sacrifice and banqueting (Scheid 1988).

An alternative to the order in which one eats is to vary the size of the individual portions. This idea can be found in many of the regulations for *collegia*. The presidents, often termed *Quinquennales*, thus indicating a five-year period of office, might receive a double portion, the lower functionaries, for example the treasurer and

---

13. Cropped shop-sign showing a probably imaginary
temple (*continued*)

thought that the temple was that of Concordia in the Forum (see pl. 24). Marble, h. 0.415m, w. 0.595m. Musei Vaticani, Galleria delle statue, inv. no. 568 = Helbig[4] 1, p. 105 no.140.

14. Antonine biographical sarcophagus.

The front of this sarcophagus shows three scenes from the career of a
military commander. In the centre is a detailed representation of the
sacrifice of a bull. High up in the background one can make out a temple-
façade. The action however is concentrated upon a *foculus*, a small altar
placed at the bottom of the temple steps, which are just visible to the right
of the front tripod-leg. Directly behind the altar, a *tibicen* is energetically
playing a double-'flute' (*tibia*). Left of him stands the sacrificant, whose
spear connotes that he holds a military command. With his right hand he is
pouring a small quantity of wine into the flames from a libation-dish
(*patera*). Still further to the left, directly behind him, is a servant carrying a
small water-jug (*gutus*, not confirmed as an ancient technical term); like the
tibicen, he is wearing a leaf-crown. To the right of the altar, the animal is
about to be killed: a muscled *popa* (also called a *victimarius*), wearing a
butcher's apron with an elaborately embroidered hem, is forcing down the
animal's head by holding its nostrils and one horn; you can see the sheath
containing several skinning- and cutting-knives (*culter*) on his belt.
The other *popa* has raised the stunning-axe (*securis*) ready to strike the
atlas-vertebra at the base of the skull. Marble. Sala di Troia, Palazzo
Ducale, Mantua, inv. g. 6727.

clerk, a portion and a half, ordinary members only one.[18] This
portion could be taken home in *sportulae*, baskets. Such practices
could be turned into a regular means of supporting functionaries, as
in early Christianity, where priests and deacons might receive a
double or at any rate privileged share of each meal.

One final hierarchy that is defined and articulated in various
myths connected to sacrifice is that of humans and animals (Sælid
Gilhus 2006: 114–37). The human has the privilege of killing;
the animal is always the victim. Ovid interprets the 'first' sacrifice of a
pig as a punishment, as a surrender of the guilty party (*deditio noxae*)
to Ceres, the deity whose crops the sow had grubbed up.[19] Ovid's
examples indicate that the difference between humans and animals was

problematized not in ritual itself but in reflection upon it – there is no equivalent at Rome of the Attic *bouphonia*, the 'ox-killing' at the festival of Dipolieia, which has been thought to attest to such anxieties in the medium of ritual (but see Parker 2005: 187–91).

Gifts

As a gift, the sacrifice creates obligations. The phrase *do ut des*, I give so that you may give, has often been used in modern analysis as a key to Roman sacrifice. The sacrificant offers something to the deity. This idea receives expression in reliefs depicting the second part of our 'double system', albeit at Rome much less commonly than in Egypt, the ancient Near East, or Greece. Human-beings approach a statue of a god holding an offering in their hands, or carrying it on a tray; or they point towards a table on which gifts for the god are laid out, all with the idea: I give the deity something, so that he or she may give me something in return. I do not of course expect to get the very same pig back that I have just slaughtered for the god – that would be absurd; but I do expect in due course as a counter-gift something like a good harvest, as we saw in the example from Cato: a successful seed-casting, a smooth birth, effective purification, consolation after a bereavement, success in business. To that extent, a sacrifice resembles a contract, it acquires a judicial component – my gift commits the god, morally at any rate, to giving me in return something I value.[20] The commitment is mutual: of course I will give thanks to the deity who has given me something by sacrificing in my turn again. There is thus a ceaseless cycle of obligation and gratitude, which the usual concentration on individual exchanges expressed by the phrase *do ut des* tends to obscure. There is a chain of actions, a reciprocity of gifts. That is the normal situation.

It may be however that the god's counter-gift fails to materialize. The reason may be that too little time has lapsed since the vow; alternatively, there may have been some kind of ritual error or fault. Quite apart from the issue of 'failure', however, the non-routine character of this divine-human exchange is neatly dramatized in the so-called *litatio*, the examination of the *exta*. This can be characterized as a ritual game that makes clear that there is nothing automatic or mechanical about the deity's acceptance of the offering, let alone his or her commitment to a return.[21]

The object of this examination is to discover whether the outwardly perfect animal is equally in order inside. Quite generally in antiquity it was believed that the gods' acceptance or rejection of the sacrifice will be manifest in the animal's entrails. There was therefore no a priori assumption that an outwardly normal animal will be equally healthy inside. At the moment the animal is consecrated and killed, when it passes from the human world to the realm of the gods, the deity makes a statement: I want the animal/I do not want the animal. This reply is figured in deformations of the *exta* due to disease or other causes; sometimes even – and these were really bad signs – the heart, or the 'head' of the liver, might be clean missing.[22] The sacrificant had to use his judgement here; occasionally specialist *haruspices*, Etruscan entrail-readers, were consulted, though the principle remained the same. If the outcome was positive, the *exta* were cooked (boiled or grilled, depending on the animal) separately, and later burned for the gods.[23] So the parts of the animal that are closest to divinity are those in which the message is encoded – there was even an ancient etymology that derived the word *exta* from the gods, the 'outstanding ones'.[24]

The reading of the *exta* dramatizes the issue of the acceptance of the gift. The *litatio*, the proof that the offering has been accepted by the god, does not have to take place at once. If it fails there are two possibilities. One is to call a halt to the entire ritual, on the grounds that the moment or occasion is evidently not opportune: the deity does not want a sacrifice at this time. Alternatively, one might continue slaughtering victims until the deity accepted the sacrifice (*usque ad litationem*). This was, or might be, an expensive business, which could therefore acquire its own expressive value. For example, the sacrificant had the opportunity of conveying how much store he set by the sacrifice, demonstratively, with an audience, or by himself, or in dialogue with participating colleagues, people of his own social level. If a general was determined to go to war, he would just kill another ox, and then another . . . ; but if he were sceptical about how keen the Senate really was to go to war, he was free to say after the first animal: Well, I'm sorry, I would have fought your war/battle, but the gods are against it, so we can pack up for today. How often that happened, we do not know. But it is worth repeating the crucial point, that, in a context where the other world is only apprehensible through signs, *litatio* dramatizes the act of communication with gods. The individuality of these deities acquires sharper contour if we reject the idea that the votive implies an automatically positive response. Above all, they acquire a degree of unpredictability, of freedom, that gives them the right to make surprising choices.

150

System

The third function of sacrifice is fairly unspecific: it creates system, of different kinds and in different areas. The social and anthropological asymmetries I have already discussed are only special cases of system in this sense. Here I want to pick up the issue of what we might call 'vertical linkages'. Different animals can be associated with particular deities. Putting it the other way round, this means the addressee is determined by the gift. To take an example from everyday life: the better one knows someone, the more personal a gift can be – including even joke-gifts, which force the recipient to assume a role that he or she may not want, or is publicly embarrassing. I have already mentioned the basic principle in my brief account of the way a gift defines a god (p. 110): particular gods are correlated with particular animals. To ward off rust, a fungal disease that could easily ruin an entire harvest, you would sacrifice a red dog.[25] A connection is established between the unnamed god (in fact *Robigo*) and the victim by means of the colour (rust-) red. A major rule I have mentioned several times already is that male animals are (in principle) sacrificed to male gods, and female to female. In addition, the character of the deity can be further specified by the size, number and age of the animals. The following text from the Acta of the Arval Brothers of the year 60 AD will clarify the point:

> During the same consulship L. Calpurnius Piso, son of L., *magister* of the college, sacrificed in the name of the Arval Brothers on the Capitol, by decree of the Senate, on the Nones of April (7th of April), in the context of the thanksgivings appointed [after the murder of Agrippina] for the well-being of Nero Claudius Caesar Augustus Germanicus: an ox (*mas bos*) to Jupiter, a cow to Juno, a cow to Minerva, a cow to the Common Well-being (*salus publica*), a cow to Providence, a bull to the emperor's Genius, an ox to the deified Augustus.
> Scheid 1998a: no. 28A-C, ll. 10–14 = *CIL* VI 2042 = *ILS* 230
> (ignoring restorations)

The list of sacrifices here contains clear correlations: Jupiter receives an ox (i.e. a castrated bull), Juno and Minerva, being goddesses, get cows, the Genius of the living Caesar is offered a bull (i.e. an uncastrated male), the deified Caesar Augustus an ox. Sacrifices of oxen are big news, providing up to 200 kg (440 lbs) of meat. In this text, nothing is said however about the age of the animals. The pre-eminent rank of the Genius of the living Caesar, Nero himself, is emphasized by his being offered a bull. This detail shows that the other 'males' (*mares boves*) are all oxen, i.e. castrated individuals, which are much easier to handle. We have here a rough hierarchization of the gods through the sex of the victims, which underscores the socio-religious priority of the Genius of the reigning emperor.

The Economics of Sacrifice

This account would be lop-sided if I said nothing about the economic aspects of sacrifice.[26] Pigs and sheep were the main private victims. Public sacrifice, however, was dominated by cattle, which were substantially more expensive and of course provided more meat. As for age, the victims in private contexts were usually young animals: they were not too expensive but could still feed a small group. There is a world of difference between having to buy a choice, fat, adult pig for sacrifice, or a small suckling-pig. The *sacra publica* fulfil a parade or ideal role, representing a 'perfect' ritual order, but even there the rules have loopholes.

Sacrifices do not fall from the sky, being performed, on the contrary, so that something else may fall from the sky. Animals have to be bred, bought and transported to the place where the sacrifice is going to take place. This presupposes an entire industry. So far we have only looked at the 'theological' side. In fact however, throughout the history of animal-sacrifice associated with festive eating, the sacrificial system had to be co-ordinated over the *longue durée* with the basics of stock-rearing. If the stock-rearing economy proves unable to provide the animals required for sacrifice, the system will collapse. Conversely, if the sacrificial system has no demand for the animals produced by that branch of the economy, there are going to be an awful lot of useless animals standing about munching. Such a situation cannot be sustained in an economy not much above the level of subsistence, and a culture that enjoined such useless production would be condemned to perish.

I want to draw attention here to just one or two implications.[27] Store animals are eaten relatively, but not extremely, young. In the case of pigs and cattle, the ratio weight-gain/feed-costs reached an optimum point somewhere between 12 and 24 months. Except in areas with very adverse conditions, if the animal is kept alive longer, the ratio progressively decreases. The sacrificial rules are therefore likely to call for animals of this optimum age.[28] Since it is omnivorous, the pig is a very attractive animal for meat-production alone. The case is more complex with cattle, which in antiquity produced meat, milk, hides and labour. In general, males were fattened and killed as young steers, unless they were castrated for farm-work; females were only killed once they became too old to carry calves to term. There was thus a very high proportion of suckler-cows to breeding-bulls.[29] Both males and females could be used as work animals, the males of course being castrated; they were slaughtered when they became too old to work (9–10 years old). Under these conditions, the ox will be the main parade sacrificial animal, and pregnant cows common.

This type of reckoning can only be confirmed by contemporary evidence to a small extent, since to do so effectively presupposes the existence of a substantial number of inventoried archaeo-zoological finds. The few archaeological facts that we have confirm that in Greece emphasis was laid on the production of (sheeps-) milk and wool, for clothing. That corresponds to the majority of Greek sacrificial rules that we know of, or at least does not contradict them: sheep were the standard sacrificial victim. Overall, the consumption of meat was low; in the case of Greece, it is calculated on the basis of the taphonomic evidence to have been less than 1 kg per person per year. If we divide the amount of meat envisaged by the Athenian calendar of official public sacrifices by the number of persons (theoretically) entitled to partake, we get a consumption of roughly 2 kg per participant per year, which is quite a lot for antiquity. Athens must have been one of the few places where more animals were sacrificed than were bred in the surrounding countryside. Such quantities imply large-scale import of sacrificial animals on the hoof. At Rome, the taphonomic finds in the Area Sacra of Sant'Omobono, by contrast, included a large quantity of pig-bones. The Athenian pattern of increased meat-consumption seems to apply to Rome as it expanded to become a great power. On the other hand, as later Roman sources confirm, the cultural dominance of sheep in Greece gives way in Rome and west-central Italy (i.e. Etruria, Latium and Campania) to that of pig. This is however not the case either in the old Greek areas of Southern Italy, where sheep maintained its dominance, nor in Northern Italy, where the availability of extensive pasture-land meant that both cattle and sheep remained important.[30]

— 7 —

MANAGING LINES OF COMMUNICATION: VOWS AND CURSES

The Archaeology of Votive Religion

When archaeologists excavate temple-areas, they often find one large, or many small pits full of complete or broken statuettes and other items, often miniaturized. At Lavinium, for example, a Latin town not very far from Rome, where according to one version of the Trojan myth Aeneas set foot in Italy and later married the Latin princess Lavinia, 15,000 miniature storage-jars were found in a complex dating from 650–600 BC but re-used in later terracing (Fenelli 1984: 331; Smith 1996a: 246). This is the first urban cult attested in Lavinium, at a time when its population must have been at least a few thousand people. The quantity of vases accumulated over a mere half-century or so is an index of the frequency with which the associated ritual was performed. If we look at other complexes, the range of votives widens considerably, for example statues, or tiny statuettes, mainly of humans, less frequently of gods. Heads and busts are usually cheaply made of clay, statues mainly of terracotta, statuettes (mostly less than 20 cm/8 ins high) often of bronze. Representations of people offering libations, bearing gifts, or praying, are common; a few plaques (*pinakes*) with sacrificial scenes are also known.[1]

Such objects were dedicated and put on show in temples and their associated areas. As numbers grew, they had to be removed from time to time by the temple servants and deposited in pits (*favissae*) (de Cazenove 1991). That is why those made of clay are often broken. Objects made of precious metal were mostly not buried but melted down to be used in the temple in a different form, for example as candelabra. We know that in Greece the priests kept records of these operations, to make sure that the labourers did not filch any of the gifts, but probably also to be able to present the deity a list of what had been donated to him or her in the past but could no longer be kept for lack of space (Aleshire 1992).

These objects were often mass-produced.[2] The heads for example seem to have been made in moulds. Their design is not individual, since basic patterns recur with few variations. Research on the diffusion of products from a single matrix, based on a number of fully-excavated deposits, reveals that the owners of the moulds were itinerant craftsmen in the sixth and fifth centuries BC who produced their wares at a given temple for a certain time before moving on. In the Mid-Republic, by contrast, local production was dominant, that is, each site produced a limited number of its own types, which differ slightly from those found elsewhere. Steady local markets emerged, enabling a craftsman settled in the vicinity of a temple to live off the sale of such votive-images, which again points to the routinization of votive-offering.

Routinization is equally evident from the choice of motifs. Many standard types can be found, irrespective of the temple-deity: full-length statues, heads and busts, miniatures of animals. The selection of types however does vary somewhat from place to place, full-length statues being more common at some sites, heads at others. Though semi-individualized images are in general pretty uncommon, sites are known where they occur in numbers.

There are however clear differences in space and time (Edlund 1987). Large numbers of bronze statuettes of people offering libation, or of deities, dating from the fourth to the first centuries BC have been found in northern Etruria up towards the Po valley, and in the Umbro-Sabellian region of central Italy; yet heads and busts in these regions are rather scarce. South of Campania, we find large numbers of statuettes and miniature terracottas – Erotes, animals, even fruit. These types of miniature terracottas occur frequently in mainland Greece, so that their occurrence here can be related to the cultural orientation of Southern Italy. Characteristic of Latium, Campania and southern Etruria is the predominance of terracottas (often almost life-size statues), including many heads and busts; and – for me an especially interesting type – anatomical votives (votives representing parts of the body). This type too was imported from Greece, where it first occurs in the fifth century BC, but only arrived in Italy about a century later. Anatomical votives are definitely characteristic of Italy, especially central Italy, being found at 130 of c. 200 excavated Etruscan and Italic sites dated between the seventh and first centuries BC. Representations of internal organs too, especially the so-called polyvisceral plaques,

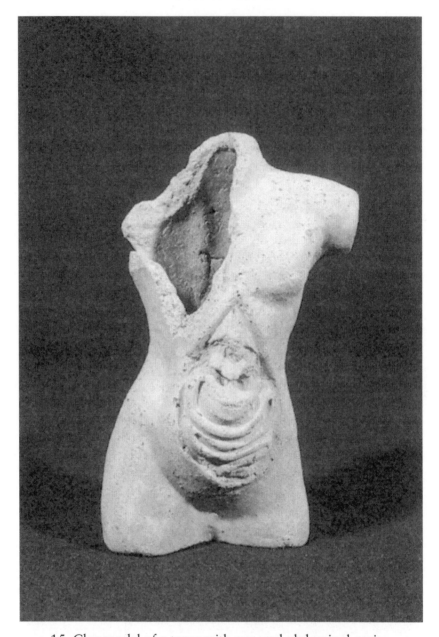

15. Clay model of a torso with exposed abdominal cavity.

Hundreds of votives representing body-parts have been found along the stretch of the Tiber that runs through Rome, to say nothing of elsewhere.

depicting a variety of organs, are much commoner here than in Greece. The parts most frequently represented are hands and feet, followed by legs, the upper arms and eyes; also genitalia (male and female) and internal organs (see pl. 15).[3]

One last observation linked to votive heads. This type, which apparently originated in sixth-century BC Etruscan Veii, spread from there, no doubt in the aftermath of the Roman conquest of the town early in the fourth century, into central Italy, and especially the area of Roman influence. At Rome itself however, a characteristic alteration took place: the heads, male and female, are veiled. This accords with the Roman practice of performing rituals *capite velato*, with covered head, and incidentally proves that the custom existed already at this early date. In the plastic recording of rituals undertaken, then, although the figures of course are not individualized, we find ritual details being noted and an imported, characteristically Etruscan, type adapted to Roman requirements.

But enough of details. We now need to turn to the question: what does all this mean?

Situations

These votive dedications are evidence for a very wide-spread religious practice hardly reflected in ancient literature.[4] Though a private act, offering a votive fell within the remit of public cult, the temples. The location itself thus ensured an audience. Moreover the desire to create a durable record of the exchange by means of a votive-gift extended the audience long past the moment of the sacrifice itself, all the more so when the circumstances of the votive were indicated in writing. Funerary inscriptions form by far the largest single group of surviving epigraphic texts; but the next-largest group are the votive-inscriptions, mainly on sizeable objects such as altars, statues, reliefs, captured

---

15. Clay model of a torso with exposed abdominal cavity (*continued*)

Many of them represent internal organs (e.g. intestines, as here, or, especially frequently, the uterus), often set in their wider somatic context. The models are not anatomically precise, but provided a 'symptomological crutch' in relation to often rather unspecifiable complaints, and were used in healing cults, such as that of Aesculapius on the Tiber Island, for purposes of clarification and communication. This example comes from the shrine of Hercules at Praeneste (Palestrina). Mid-Republican.

armour, metal plaques and so on. Perhaps years later, a reader might thus read a brief account of an illness, the intervention of a (healing-) deity and the name of the donor, male or female (quite unlike the eighteenth- to twentieth-century votive-tablets that one can see in a Roman Catholic pilgrimage church such as Altötting in Bavaria, where the name occurs at most abbreviated to the initials). Giving one's full name is a means of showing commitment and engagement in a system that lacks the concept of congregational membership (Beard 1991).

Here is a typical votive-inscription:

> Felix Asinianus, a public slave of the *pontifices*, fulfils his vow to the Bona Dea of the fields, called 'blessed' (*agrestis felicula*), (in sacrificing) a white heifer – gladly, because his eye-sight has been restored, though the doctors despaired of him. After ten months, he was cured by her thanks to our Lady's remedies (*bineficio dominaes medicinis*). [Later addition to the inscription:] Can(i)nia Fortunata has had the entire monument restored.
>
> *CIL* VI 68 = *ILS* 3513[5]

This fairly late inscription seems to have been found on the Via Ostiensis three Roman miles outside the city of Rome, beyond Trastevere, where there clearly was a healing shrine of the Bona Dea.[6] It had been damaged and, as the last line explains, restored thanks to Caninia Fortunata; she may well have been an official (e.g. priestess) of the cult who thought this evidence of the goddess's extraordinary powers of healing worth the trouble of restoring. A heifer, though appropriate in 'systemic' terms, is a relatively extravagant sacrifice for a private ritual, and suggests something of the social status, and relative wealth, of a public slave in charge of the public sacrifices held by the pontifical college.[7] The text, which rather unusually alludes not just to the fact of the cure but also to the antecedent situation ('the doctors despaired of him'), allows us a glimpse into the desperate situation – medical, psychological – of a person abandoned by the school-doctors, who will not have been cheap to consult, and has had to turn to the goddess for help.[8] Felix now claims to have been answered, whatever we are to suppose the goddess' 'remedies' consisted in.

Texts such as these lead us directly to the so-called anatomical votives I have just referred to. As these objects were mass-produced images of healthy body-parts, the affected or diseased area could be indicated with a blob of paint (which occasionally survives) and so its nature roughly specified. In some cases it is quite clear that the organ or part is diseased, implying that they were indeed dedicated by the patient involved rather than, say, merely records of a dead person's pathology. This fact dramatically reduces the value of these objects for writing medical history (Gladigow 1995). If we can assume that a woman who dedicated, say, a model of her uterus with a tumour in it was still alive when she did so, we can be sure that neither she nor her doctors had any precise idea of what was really wrong inside. Vague, unspecific symptoms produced an image that could be assimilated to traditional representations of disease or used to create imaginative personal constructions. The remains of paint are generally mere blotches that, even in retrospect, could not be correlated with any specific diagnosis.

There are two points here. First, a vow linked to an anatomical votive – remember, we do not know whether the aim of these objects was to supplement the patient's vow or to document a successful cure – is more than a brief religious act. As we saw from the case of Felix the public slave, who was treated for nearly a year, the procedure might involve extensive preparations and consultations at a healing-shrine.[9] Even without the intervention of religious specialists, we must think of the process of deciding upon the most appropriate temple or shrine, and buying or commissioning the anatomical votive, as embedded in a long process of debate and discussion with family and friends (Remus 1996).

The second point is that the production of votive-objects might constitute an important economic factor for a city (Ghinatti 1983). For example, the Roman satirist Juvenal, writing around AD 100, mentions painters who 'live off Isis' (12. 27f.), which can only mean that they received lots of orders for votives to be placed in the Isis-temples of Rome. When the apostle Paul stayed in Ephesus over the years AD 52–54/5 to spread his version of the Christian religion, the local craftsmen who lived near the great temple of Artemis, began a public protest (*Acts of the Apostles* 19. 23–36). Their annoyance had nothing to do with theology but was prompted by fear for their livelihoods. 'With your teaching and your god,' they said, 'you are ruining our businesses: we work for people who honour Artemis with their votive-offerings.'

Vows were made in many other situations than simply illness. A representation of a baby tightly wrapped in swaddling-clothes may indicate that the dedicant had just succeeded in giving birth to a child (though it might also suggest that the baby had been ill).[10] The situation is even less clear when we find a representation of keys, which could also be used to connote the desire to conceive. Such a symbol

16. Votive offering in the form of a small child.

Votive offerings, usually mass-produced by specialized craft-shops, are the
staple expression of individual religiosity. They provided a stereotyped
means of articulating an entire range of individual afflictions, and the
divine response to such appeals for aid. In this case, the shape of the skull
and the treatment of the musculature show that the model represents an
infant. Around his neck he wears a *bulla*, a protective amulet. Boys ceased
to wear these at the same time as they stopped wearing the *toga praetexta*
(a toga with a narrow purple hem-stripe), between the ages of 14 and 17,
when they were deemed to be mature and assumed the white *toga virilis*.
The *bulla* was then presented to the Lares and hung up on their shrine.
Museo Nazionale Etrusco di Villa Giulia, Rome.

shows, incidentally, that people also thought in metaphors, and did
not always have direct recourse to images of reproductive organs, such
as the uterus, common though these are.

Models of farm-animals, such as those from the temple of the Mater
Magna on the Palatine, or the temple of Aesculapius at Fregellae,
almost always indicate concern about live-stock – the fertility of a herd
or flock, protection from illness? We can hardly tell.[11] By the same
token, it is hardly ever possible to identify the relevant deity simply on
the basis of the gifts made to them. Where shrines or temples are
known solely from the archaeology, or where the material is fragmentary, the identity of the god is often quite uncertain. In the case of

a typical healing-cult, we find the same range of votives as in the case of any other goddess worshipped in the city, though the proportions will be somewhat different: anatomical votives tend to be dominant in healing-shrines, models of economically-important animals in rural temples. More we cannot say: there are virtually no votives specifically directed to Juno or Ceres, Diana or Apollo.[12]

To some extent, geographical considerations explain this non-specificity. If you wanted a baby, had a bad headache or something constantly wrong with your feet, needed protection from swine-fever and so on, you would normally go to your local shrine or temple. Healing-cults, often linked to hot-springs, are especially frequent in rural areas. For much the same reason, a rural location seems to have been preferred too for the shrines of the Greek god Asclepius. When the cult (now of Aesculapius) was brought to Rome, it was allocated an appropriate site on the as-yet unsettled island in the Tiber; many of the anatomical votives found clustered at the bridges along this stretch of the Tiber probably came from it (Pensabene et al. 1980: 17–19). The largest deposits of votives in the immediate environs of Rome have been found at the Thirteen Altars site at Lavinium (up to the early second century BC) and at Ponte di Nona, now a grim immigrant ghetto on the extreme eastern edge of the city (Via Prenestina). The apogee of the latter shrine, which was located at a road-side spring, and perhaps even boasted a bath-building, was around 250 to 150 BC; the commonest votive-type is the anatomicals (2368 feet, 971 arms/legs, 604 hands, 377 eyes, 160 male genitalia, etc). Their rather poor quality, however, and the large number of animal-votives, suggest a mainly rural clientèle (Potter and Wells 1985; Potter 1989: 97–100). Fair-sized votive-deposits have also been found at Rome itself, notably at the temple-complex of Minerva Medica, 'healing Minerva', on the Esquiline, dating from the fourth to the second centuries BC, where the largest categories were 46 feet, 39 masks, 20 hearts and the same number of hands (Gatti Lo Guzzo 1978; Cordischi 1993). By contrast, the deposit excavated near the so-called Meta Sudans, which stood at the end of the street leading down to the Colosseum from the Arch of Titus (see pl. 24), contained no anatomicals. Probably in use from as early as the sixth century, its contents are rather hum-drum, concerned mostly with family or economic problems: couples and women with children, the usual spectrum of votives, lots of food-offerings (Panella 1996). We may conclude that the expansion of the pantheon of the élite had no noticeable effects on the religious behaviour of the masses.[13]

161

Making a Ritual Vow

On the Great St Bernard, one of the most important, though difficult, passes over the Alps in antiquity, there was a temple to Jupiter Poeninus, which was linked to a *mansio* (inn) (Walser 1984; 1994: 101–07). Among the more than 50 small bronze *tabulae ansatae* (plaques) found at the site is the following text:

> To Jupiter Poeninus; L. Paccius Nonianus, son of L., of the tribe Palatina, from Fundi, centurion of the Sixth legion, Victorious, Religious and Faithful, (set up this plaque) on account of a vow he had made (*ex voto*).
>
> CIL V 6881 = *ILS* 4850c = Walser 1984: 108–10 no. 26

Nonianus does not specify what he had requested, but the location makes it evident enough: no one climbs up 2469m (more than 8000 ft) to ask a god to mend his broken leg. The worry was the road or path itself, getting up and getting down – some texts say as much.[14] Since there was no settlement worth speaking of on the pass itself, we must take it that you fulfilled your vow while still en route. No doubt you made it (*votum nuncupare* or *suscipere*) when you first approached the pass, or even when you were still at home: 'If I get over the pass and come back safely, then I will give (Jupiter) Poeninus a statuette of Hercules/a bronze pig/some money/a gold crown/a fibula'.[15] Safely over, you redeemed your vow (*votum solvere*) when you had reached the top for the second time and only had to climb down again. A vow of this kind of course need not have been redeemed right at the very end of one's journey, any more than it had to be made when you started out. Significant spots in between could be used for these purposes.

This example makes the basic structure clear: a vow is a request to a deity to perform a particular act; at the same time, the person undertakes to give the deity a particular gift if this request be fulfilled. 'Particular' here is to be taken literally: in 200 BC, for example, in the course of a debate in the Senate over whether it was permissible to make a vow without specifying a precise proportion of the booty (whose total value of course was quite unknown when the vow was made), the *pontifex maximus*, the highly experienced P. Licinius Crassus Dives, argued that bullion intended as a votive could not be used during the further course of a war and had physically to be separated from other moneys; if this were not done, the vow could not be properly redeemed.[16] From the ritual point of view, the crucial point was that if the request were fulfilled, the promised gift had to be given come what may. The person involved was *voti damnatus*, 'condemned' to pay the gift;[17] otherwise the gods might express their anger through the 'postulatory lightning' I referred to above (p. 80). Late antique commentators on Vergil actually push the legal metaphor a step further and call the person who has made a vow but not yet redeemed it *voti reus*, 'someone accused of the vow'.[18] This is an exaggeration, however. Until the god had performed what had been asked of him or her, there were no strings attached: the outcome was open. It might well happen that the request was never fulfilled, that the war dragged on, that the Princeps died. In such cases, no return gift had to be made (cf. Scheid 1990d).

This last example of the Princeps alludes to a special form of votive very common in the public realm, namely recurrent or periodic vows. At the beginning of every year (from AD 38, on 3 January), *vota publica annua*, annual public vows, were made by all magistrates and all priestly colleges for the public weal, under the Principate of course mainly *pro salute et incolumitate imperatoris*, for the well-being and physical safety of the emperor (Beard, North, Price 1998: 1, 252). At the same time, last year's vows were redeemed. The return offered, as almost always in the case of public vows, was a sacrifice. This year's request and last year's return overlap in a routine manner (e.g. *CIL* VI 2042 = Scheid 1998a: no. 28 DE, ll. 24–32), so much so that on occasions little attention can have been paid to the actual wording or content: for example, when on (probably) 3 January AD 69, the year of the Four Emperors, the Arval Brothers redeemed last year's vow *pro salute imperatoris*, for the life of the emperor, which must have been made for Nero, they fulfilled it after his death (and indeed after that of Galba, his successor); just as the new vows, this time for Otho, were redeemed under Vespasian.[19] Even so, the god is sometimes said to have failed, and the sacrifices were cancelled. This should cause no surprise: although the vow does have a certain relation to crisis, the system of annual vows was a routinized institution ill-adapted to periods of acute political confusion. From the reign of Tiberius (Cassius Dio 57.24.1; 58.24.1), perhaps already of Augustus (*Res gestae* 9.1), there were also vows for five, ten, even twenty years (*quinquennalia, decennalia, vicennalia*), which were at the same time celebrations of the emperor's regnal years.[20] As with the annual vows, the periodic ones would be renewed at the same time as the previous ones were redeemed: Severus Alexander, for example, celebrated his *vota decennalia soluta* in AD 230, at the same time as the vows for his *vicennalia* were made, *vota vicennalia suscepta* (Martin 1982: 418). These forms were routinizations of earlier usages under the Republic (e.g. Livy 22.10.2; 31.9.9).

It is worth looking more closely at the structure of the vow. Two prayers were said, the request at the outset and the concluding offering of thanks. The latter might be combined with a gift, which may still survive archaeologically today, or be attested by inscriptions such as that of Nonianus. Such permanent records are a means of reinforcing the prayer, often they are the actual gift itself. Sometimes we find representations of a sacrifice, or of a family sacrificial procession including a pig or a sheep. In these cases, the god will actually have received such an animal as a sacrifice, and not just the image.

The creation of a material or epigraphic record of a successful votive-exchange advertises to third parties who were not involved in the ritual that the god has truly answered on this occasion. The pious record is thus also a form of advertisement. Some people scoffed at this already in antiquity. One day, for example, Diagoras, the Greek 'atheist', was visiting in the company of a friend the island of Samothrake in the northern Aegean, where the shrine of the 'Great Gods' attracted pilgrims from all round the Greek (and Roman) world. Two of these gods, identified with the Dioscuri, helped sailors in distress. The friend is supposed to have said to Diagoras: 'You may claim to believe that the gods are indifferent to human concerns, but what do you say about all these votive pictures (*tabulae pictae*)? Don't they show that many, many people have escaped drowning in storms by making vows, and so reached harbour safe and sound?' Diagoras replied: 'True enough, but there are no votives here by the people who were indeed shipwrecked and drowned' (Cicero, *De nat. deor.* 3.93). Failed vows produce no votives; the system renders its failures invisible.

If we think about the psychological underpinning of the votive-system, we could say that the attraction of the vow is that, in a crisis-situation, it makes resources available that, on rational consideration, are irrelevant or inappropriate. If you are caught in a heavy storm, all the wealth in the world is of no avail. But the institution of the vow allows a person in this situation to bring the two objectively unrelated facts into some sort of connection.[21]

A further precondition for the psychological plausibility of the votive was a cultural given, namely the widespread if vague conviction that illness and crisis or danger were forms of divine punishment. Diagoras' point was particularly inappropriate on Samothrace because the mysteries there were directed precisely to annulling sin and averting divine anger, so that one could sail with a good conscience. Although divine-human communication in the votive system was coloured by contractual ideas, we almost always find too an allusion to the joy or gladness with which the vow is redeemed. One of the commonest dedicatory formulae in votive inscriptions in Latin is the acronym VSLM, the abbreviation of *votum solvit libens merito*: 'has fulfilled his vow willingly and with good reason'.[22]

Special Forms

Many large-scale public rituals at Rome consisted basically of vows and their redemption. A well known example is the triumph: on leaving Rome, the commander made a vow in the temple of Jupiter Optimus Maximus to be fulfilled in the case of victory. On his return, the procession consists of the army's festive progress through the streets to the Capitol (see pls. 11, 24). The climax of the ritual is when the commander ascends the Capitol and places his own laurel wreath on Jupiter Optimus Maximus' lap, and sacrifices oxen to him, thus fulfilling the vow he took when he left Rome (Rüpke 1990: 225). The same is true of *evocatio*, when the enemy's chief god was 'summoned away' (*evocatus*) during a siege, and a new temple subsequently founded at Rome (Bruun 1972; Rüpke 1990: 162–4).

Another typical adaptation of the votive scheme is *devotio*, a kind of self-sacrifice.[23] In this case, a Roman commander inverted the normal procedure of the vow (wish → fulfilment), declaring in effect: I sacrifice my life now, so that the Roman gods may grant us the victory. The *votum* is fulfilled first so that the god may be forced to fulfil the wish too. The self-sacrifice involved the commander charging directly into the enemy ranks, which of course usually meant he would be killed. A problem arose, however, if he did happen to survive but the Romans still won. Later, at any rate, it was thought he could then no longer be admitted into the community: a doll representing him was burned, while he himself was treated as a non-citizen (Livy 8.10.11f.). From the community's point of view, that could be construed as the fulfilment of the vow of self-sacrifice. But this is almost certainly a Late-Republican or Augustan rationalization.

Alternatives

The vow can be a very personal form of communication between humans and gods. Appearances of gods in dreams emphasize this personal component. In some votive-inscriptions we find the formula *ex visu*, literally 'from a vision', which means 'because of something I

165

saw in a dream'. The god himself ordered the person (or a proxy) in a dream to put up a statue, or revealed the cure through a dream – such experiences were induced at healing shrines by allowing sick people to sleep in the temple (for which the technical term is 'incubation').[24] One source of the second century AD gives us a fascinating example of this form of personal communication being pushed to such lengths that we can only call it a case of massive hypochondria. This is the *Hieroi logoi*, Sacred Tales, of the wealthy Greek orator P. Aelius Aristides, an account of his own illnesses and the interventions of the god Asclepius. Here we find details of the god's instructions, how they helped, then the repeated relapses (Behr 1968; Jackson 1988: 152–57). All this represents an extension, an intensification, of the relationship set up by the vow. As a result, one might even decide to take up residence near, or even in, a temple for a period of time – Aristides for example was invited to live in the house of one of the temple wardens at Pergamon for about two years, AD 145–47 – or even permanently. Temple-complexes of Asclepius had appropriate rooms at their disposal, just as they also afforded space to school-doctors; Hippocrates himself was supposed to have belonged to the guild of Asclepiads on the island of Cos.

There were however also other ways of coping with illness, involving the utterance of special formulae. This tack had no interest in the dramatization of the question: will the god do what I want or not? Instead, technical issues move to the fore: Have I spoken the correct formula? Have I followed the ritual correctly? A number of such formulae survive in technical or didactic sources, ranging from the Elder Cato's *De agri cultura* to late-antique handbooks dealing with human and animal medicine.[25]

Charms for healing:

> A dislocation may be healed by means of the following charm: Take a green reed-cane four or five foot long and split it down the centre. Let two men hold <the two pieces> to the (animal's) leg-joints. Begin the incantation: *Moetas vaeta | daries dardaries asiadarides | una pe tes* while the <two ends> come together. Brandish a knife over them. When they have come together and one half-reed has touched the other, grasp the reed with your hand and cut it at each end. Bind it onto the dislocated or broken limb, and it will heal. Each day repeat a charm as well: *huat havat huat | ista pista sista | dannabo dannaustra*.
>
> Cato, *De agric.* 160 (text from Blänsdorf 1991)

The untranslated words here are so-called 'magical words', perhaps a completely unintelligible text in Etruscan, perhaps strings of meaningless syllables. Such strings are typical of healing formulae, especially in Roman times.

Another example, this time from late antiquity:

Against tooth- or head-ache:
Turn towards the Moon and speak the following formula: New Moon, new teeth – worms that cause decay: OUT! Just as neither wolf nor dog can attack you, so can no pain touch me or my head! Then write the name on a piece of papyrus and bind it to your head.
Physica Plinii, Skt. Gallen codex 751, p.198,13ff. = Önnerfors 1985: 238 no.8[26]

Socially rather than medically speaking, healing can be defined as a process in which the ill person is given a satisfactory interpretation of his condition by an accepted authority. This step is followed by various sorts of therapy, and perhaps lasting freedom from symptoms (Rüpke 1995c). If we apply this model here (we may assume that many such 'healing events' were taken to be successful), several non-textual factors become important: the identity of the speaker, the source of the formula, how the diagnosis is arrived at (Gordon 1995: 366–70). Given the nature of our sources, this entire social dimension remains unfortunately inaccessible to us. Yet we could only hope to explore the complex relation between religion and medicine if we had access to such knowledge (the absence of divine names from the texts I have cited is purely coincidental).

Apart from protection against evil (including magical attack), the major purpose of innumerable objects used as 'amulets' (divine images and attributes, animal parts, models of powerful body-parts such as the phallus, semi-precious stones, texts inscribed on metal) was healing, or protection from illness.[27] Perhaps the most interesting group of these is the 5000 or so known 'magical amulets', which date from the second to the fifth century AD. The colour of the semi-precious stone or glass paste, the type of deity (for example Chnoubis, a snake with a lion's head, powerful against digestive problems), and the – usually but not invariably – brief text are designed to complement one another. The aims vary: to free the owner from blindness, to ensure a good digestion, to prevent a miscarriage.[28]

Curses

It would be quite mistaken to suppose that we need a term like 'magic' to characterize finds such as these. The Romans did indeed have a term *magia* (derived from *magos*, the Greek word for a Persian priest or 'magician', in Old Iranian *maguš*), and they could apply it to objects and procedures intended to afford healing and protection.[29] In this section I discuss the semantic range of Latin *magia*, but let me first make the point that the old evolutionist understanding of magic, associated with the names of Sir Edward Tylor and Sir James Frazer, that it is 'false science', a mistaken explanation of natural forces by primitive peoples, which was eventually replaced by religion (prayerful devotion to personalized forces in matters otherwise inexplicable), and finally by science (recognition of true causal relations), gets us nowhere. Such ideas about religion and science are themselves subject to the historical process.[30] The situation at Rome (as well as in Greece) clearly shows that all three systems can co-exist within the same individual and that, rather than talking of a 'magical world-view', we should be thinking in terms of particular traditional and at the same time highly specialized patterns of action. The range of actions undertaken is generally speaking very limited; the great majority of surviving texts bear a strong family resemblance to one another.

Several hundred texts dealing with the most important ritual, the *tabellae defixionum*, the curse-tablets, are now known (not all have been published).[31] To curse your enemy, you used the term *katado*, I bind you down (Greek), or *defigo*, I fix, nail you down (Latin). The surviving tablets are almost all of lead, and often have nails driven through them: the verbal formulations are reinforced by appropriate symbolic action. These are expressive actions, 'performative acts', where the speech-act itself performs the semantic content of what you say. Standard examples of performatives are: 'I greet you' (instead of 'Good morning' or 'Hi!') and 'I appoint you . . .' (rather than: 'You are now . . .'). To make doubly sure, you reinforced the performative by means of appropriate actions, such as killing a puppy, dropping the lead sheet into a well, or melting it over a fire. The most interesting thing about the *defixiones* is that these performative acts do not take place in public, but – at least in many cases – in private, even in the dark.

In the second half of the first century AD, the Elder Pliny claimed that there is no one who is not afraid of being attacked by malign magical incantation (*diris deprecationibus*) (Pliny, *HN* 28.19). Where did danger lurk? Everywhere. Your health could be attacked, you might lose your concentration when you had to think fast (fatal for lawyers, orators and teachers), things might go wrong financially, you might finding yourself falling violently in love with someone unavailable, be forced into frigidity towards someone you ought to love, and even lose the ability to make a successful sacrifice (*litatio*).[32]

A curse addressed to Seth-Typhon from Porta S. Sebastiano, Rome (late III or IV[p]) (an unknown number of lines missing, which evidently mentioned another victim, Victor, who may have been Praeseticius' father)

> .....] from this hour, from this day, from this night . . . trample, crush, smash and . . . consign to death Praeseticius the bakery-owner, son of Aselle, who lives in Regio IX, where he can be seen going about his work; and hand him over to Pluto, the King of the Dead (*praeposito mortuorum*), then if he snubs you, let him suffer from fevers, cold, torments, pallors, sweatings, shiverings morning and noon, evening and night from this hour, from this day, from this <night>; and set him to so that he has no respite, but if he does manage to get better, suffocate that Praestetius (sic), in the hot bath, in the cold bath, wherever; bind him, destroy Praeseticius the son of Aselle, and if he manages to put you off by some trick or other, and mocks you, and laughs you out, overcome him, kill him again and again, the blackguard,[33] Praesetecius (sic) the bakery-owner, son of Aselle, who lives in Regio IX, *ede ede tacy tacy* (Greek for: now now, quick, quick!)

To the lower left of the text are three roughly drawn figures, like chess-pawns, labelled: Victor – Asella the mother – Praeseticius the bakery-owner

CIL VI 33899 = ILS 8750 = Audollent 1904: 199f. no.140.

Hostility to one's enemies could thus be pushed to the point of complete physical annihilation. Actions of this type, if they could be traced to an individual and proved, might have consequences under the criminal law (Phillips 1991; Rives 2006). For that reason, such curses virtually never give the name of the *devovens* (the person on whose behalf the cursing ritual is being performed, who may be the writer, or a client).

Cases of this kind did indeed come to trial. They were initiated by people who, for example, thought that a female member of their family who acted against their wishes must have been knocked silly by a love-charm, and believed that they had thereby been done down, or by people whose fields were suddenly covered in weeds or whose harvest inexplicably failed.[34] We have further information only about a handful of cases. One of them is the complete speech in his defence on a charge of magic by Apuleius of Madaura, who wrote the novel *Metamorphoses* (also known as The Golden Ass) from which I have already quoted. Because he had married a rich widow, he was accused of sorcery by her relatives by marriage, who had been disappointed in their hope of getting her to marry one of them, and so obtaining her

169

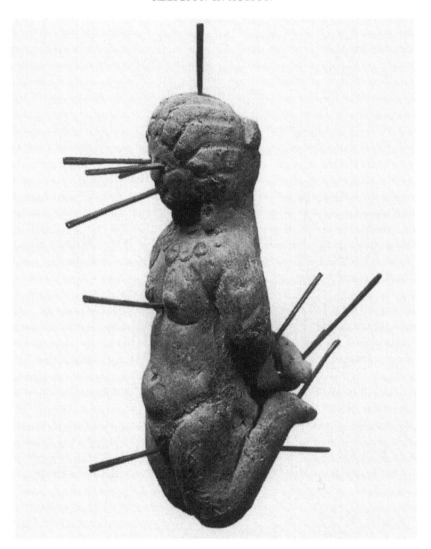

17. Female model made of unbaked clay.

This model of a naked woman (9 cm high) with arms and legs bound behind her, has been run through by pins in 13 places, the cranium, both eyes, both ears, mouth, between the breasts, in the vulva, in the anus, the soles of both feet and through each wrist or hand. The figure was part of a cursing ritual, directed at the gods of the underworld, of which it is itself the metonymic fulfilment. The curse is intended to prevent Ptolemaïs, who has evidently rejected the speaker, Sarapammon, from making love to wealth. Fortunately for lovers of Latin literature and historians of Roman religion, Apuleius happened to be a friend of the governor of the province, as well as a brilliant orator, and was able successfully to defend himself against the accusations.[35] Such trials were always tricky; malign magic was universally feared; execution routine. In Early-Modern Europe, and in modern sub-Saharan Africa too, the patterns of accusation in witch-hunts follow well-known fault-lines; to account for such explosive events, we only need to invoke the social tensions that are inevitable in times of change, and a minimum of belief in wicked spirits among the relevant groups of people.[36] Such witch-hunts may come about as the result of collective hysteria, but also, as the example of the manuals of daemonology such as Jakob Sprenger and Heinrich Kramer's *Malleus maleficarum* (1486/7) shows, become an entire speculative system, in which the possibilities of magical action are systematically thought through, and can then become the basis of accusations in concrete cases.[37]

The lawsuits however were not the reason why these texts were not recited out loud, nor to be found in books sold openly on the market. In terms of the dominant system of values, wishes such as these were asocial. Even in those cases where a prayer is directed to the gods, where one swears one's own innocence and demonstrates one's enemy's guilt, the speaker is in fact failing to follow the proper route for resolving disputes. These options are deviant; they may work (no one doubted that) but the community has expressly forbidden them. 'Cheating' is thus a better description than 'false

---

17. Female model made of unbaked clay. (*continued*)

anyone else and to be unable to eat, drink leave the house or even sleep, until she makes love to him. The figurine and the associated lead curse-tablet (*defixio*), folded up small, were found in a clay jar. The type goes back to an ancient Egyptian magical schema, the 'immobilized enemy', of which dozens of examples, from the Old Kingdom to the Ptolemaic period, survive. The model represents the enemy, often in the form of a foreigner, a Nubian or a Syro-Palestinian, as completely immobilized, i.e. subjected. The Louvre happens to own two such images, very similar to this one, though without the pins, from the Ptolemaic period (M. Étienne, *Heka* [Louvre catalogue, Paris, 2000] cat. nos. 5, 6). The pins belong to another, Graeco-Roman, type of aggressive magic; those penetrating the head and trunk are directed against Ptolemaïs' sexual orifices and her psycho-social being. No doubt 3 /4 cent. AD; probably from Antinoopolis in Middle Egypt. Département des Antiquités égyptiennes, Louvre, Paris, inv. E 27145 A.

science'. Cheating works, only you mustn't let yourself get caught. The same is true of cursing. Cheating is expensive: it costs money to provide yourself with loaded dice, marked cards, or forged notes. The same is true of cursing: if you wanted to make quite sure, you consulted a specialist, who knew the formulae, inscribed the curse-tablets, saw to their being placed in the ideal spot. This too was slightly criminal, often including breaking open graves (the curse-tablet against Praeseticius, for example, was found in a mausoleum) or trespassing. The lead tablets were sometimes buried in the graves of people who had died either 'before their time' (in Greek: *aōroi*) or by dishonourable violence, and whose spirits were therefore 'rest-less', belonging neither to this world nor to the realm of the dead (Johnston 1999: 71–81; 127–60). At Carthage, a curse-tablet against charioteers and their teams was nailed into the track near the start-line (Gager 1992: 19 fig. 4). We even hear of prepared spells being slipped under the pillow of the person to be 'caught' (Pliny, *HN* 30.143). In the context of one important type of love magic, however, the notion of 'cheating' may need to be adapted, since resort to what we might call 'female defence magic', where women attempted to prevent themselves from being abandoned by their husbands or lovers, is a response to the actual asymmetry of power in the relationship. In this case, perhaps, it is the socially dominant, the husbands, the lovers, who are 'cheated' by the women's defensive recourse to non-human agents.

The absence of an audience makes it all the more imperative to render the utterance performative.[38] Since the only witness present is the practitioner (who need not be a specialist: many shorter and less elaborate texts were clearly written by the person directly involved), the action itself has if possible to be materialized, formulated in writing. This imperative, and the growing professionalization of the practitioners in the Roman period, explain the increasing length of the texts, their embellishment with nonsensical syllables and the addition of pictures; in one famous case of compulsive love magic, the defixio was actually placed in a jar with a figurine pierced with pins – not an invention of Voodoo! (see pl. 17). Unlike curses, healing-charms were recited, often by the head of the family (Cato insists on his responsi-bility for the health of the household, including animals), sometimes by an acknowledged wise-man or -woman, in the presence of the patient, and of family and friends. By the same token, whereas in votive inscriptions the formal name of the donors is almost always given, the curse-tablets are virtually always anonymous, even though, given the sorts of places where they were deposited, their authors (or, in the case of those professionally written, clients) need hardly have feared being recognized and denounced.

Sharping gives one an edge. So does cursing. In his fine analysis of this material, John Gager suggested that part of the point was for the *defigens*, or the professional practitioner, to make hints to the intended victim, or in the neighbourhood, about what had been set in train (Gager 1992: 21). This may be so, though I think it applies, if at all, to the professional practitioner, who needed to affirm his reputation and status by such discreet advertising.[39] No, the proof that all this worked is offered not by the actual but by the potential victims, all those who thought they had to protect themselves with amulets and phylacteries, who put up a representation of a phallus against the 'evil eye' at the entrance of their houses, or in public places (street-corners, bridges, bath-houses. . .), or in their Christian cult-sites – in fact, more or less everyone.[40] Another proof is offered by those who explicitly blamed their problems and failures on malign-magical attack by their enemies (e.g. Cicero, *Brutus* 217). If they had numerous or particularly vicious enemies, such people might even have their houses searched, the wainscoting torn down (Tacitus, *Ann.* 2.69.5; Cassius Dio 57.18.9). And sometimes, if they really had been 'caught', like the fourth-century rhetor Libanius in Syrian Antioch, something incriminating might well be found – in his case, a mummified, mutilated chameleon in his lecture-theatre.[41]

— 8 —

CONTROL OF SPACE:
COMMUNICATION AND BOUNDARIES

Space and Direction

Cultural space is not mathematical space. From a certain age, people can estimate distances on the level quite well, but find it very difficult to estimate height. This is a weakness typical of our species. Other species reveal far greater deficits in connection with geometric space. Generally speaking, animals that live in the steppe or plains cannot cope at all with vertical objects that bar their way, their only technique is to run round them. By comparison, human beings are relatively well equipped for three-dimensional perception. The anatomical basis for this is, in the first place, the location of the eyes relatively close together at the front of the head, which permits proper three-dimensional vision, stereoscopy. Then there is touch: thanks to our highly discriminating hands, with their prehensile fingers and the opposed thumb, our ability to judge spatial relations is far better developed than that of other animals. In evolutionary terms, the latter development at any rate was made possible by the complete restructuring of the foot and the pelvis that produced bipedalism: it is upright posture that has allowed our hands to become so specialized.

As regards concrete orientation, the main role is played by one's own body-scheme; we do indeed measure everything by our own yardstick (Gehlen 1995). Models of space are basically subjective and topological (Hall 1966). Where my eyes are, is 'in front', where they are not, is 'behind'. The symmetry of my limbs produces 'left' and 'right'. 'Above' and 'below' are due to my upright stance. If we moved on four legs, the 'up/down' set would be less important than the others. In historical cultures, these orientations in relation to the body are fixed, and rendered communicable by agreeing on a common base-direction (cf. Hallpike 1979: 280–339). This is where religion comes in. At Rome, turning to the right signalled the conclusion of a prayer; a flash of lightning from the left or the sighting of certain birds on that side was favourable (in late-Republican augural science, *sinister*, left, seems to have had a generally positive denotation; but this was certainly not the case in Greece or in many barbarian cultures).[1] In everyday life one can find both denotations being maintained: the systematization of divinatory symbols leaves plenty of room for disagreement and interpretation.

Up there, where the gods are, is the direction in which our palms are lifted, where the smoke and steam of the sacrifice rises. There are also gods 'below', but them we address infrequently. The dead too dwell beneath the earth – people lost no time in burying their loved ones; only in the case of *sui iuris* adults, and (in particular) prominent men, the newel-posts as it were of social life, might the thing be allowed to drag out (*funus publicum*). At least in pontifical theory, a finger of the corpse, the *os resectum*, that was to be used in the rites for purifying the household, had to be cut off and concealed with earth until needed; until then, though the rest of the body had been disposed of, the household remained polluted.[2]

Many cultures lay special emphasis on the East, where the sun rises. At Rome, however, it received relatively little attention, either because, at any rate in the Republic, cults of the heavenly bodies were generally insignificant (Koch 1933), or because the complicated microtopography of the early settlement and the winding course of the Tiber did not particularly favour that (or any other) direction. Roman patterns of spatial organization were developed on the basis of points in the landscape, and encoded in regular ritual practice (Dilke 1971). One could even say that augury by bird-flight was the founding principle of Roman surveying.[3]

So much for the general point: perceptual space is not the same as (our) conceptual space. The Romans of the late Republic – and the same is probably true of all the inhabitants of Italy of the first century BC, though we hardly have enough evidence to decide – organized space not in terms of superficial area, but on the basis of roads or paths, existing boundary-markers, lines of sight, routinized religious actions, rituals. These were the things that created limits and produced clarity out of confusion (Rüpke 1990: 53–5). Yet it was material signs, often architectural structures, that in the long run fixed these, and other, non-sacral, boundaries and axes: the culturally-specific mode of perceiving space that I postulate cannot explain the Roman arch,[4] late-Hellenistic urban symmetry, the invention of concrete, or the vast domed structures it made possible (culminating in Hadrian's sacral Pantheon: de Fine Licht 1968: 203–25), all of which in their different ways are characteristic of the built-up areas of Roman towns and settlements. Isolating mentalities is always difficult.[5]

Sacred Topography: Monument and Ritual

In the city of Rome itself, the sheer number of religious buildings makes it difficult to speak of organized sacred space. From the beginning of the monumentalizing period, from the time that Rome became a true city, the Forum Romanum simply filled up (see pl. 24; compare pl. 3). Apart from the great basilicas and the Curia (which must have been technically a *templum*, since the Senate met there), it is religious buildings and sacral areas, such as the Lapis Niger (p. 51), that dominate the area. The central symbols are all there: the Regia, supposedly built by King Numa and the site of rituals conducted by the *regina sacrorum* and later the *pontifex maximus*; the temple of Vesta, with its fire that was never allowed to go out and the Palladium and other sacred objects that, at any rate from the Late Republic, were supposed to guarantee the empire; the temple of Saturn, one of the oldest temples in the city; the Lacus Curtius, a cleft into which a young aristocrat, M. Curtius, is supposed to have hurled himself in the fourth century BC to save the city; the Volcanal, an ancient shrine of Vulcan, probably on the site of the later temple to Concordia; the magnificent temple of Castor; and to them were added in the Principate grand temples in honour of the deified Caesars.[6] Since it grew over time, this sacral city-scape composed no unified or planned system of signs. And over time, equally, the significance of the individual elements inevitably shifted.[7]

Much the same occurred in the southern part of the Campus Martius. Especially from the early second century BC onwards the number of public buildings and temples here grew and grew, so that it became a city-scape of stone (later marble). Such a wealth of religious building was of course not inspired by a desire to make wall-to-wall provision for religious needs; it simply tells us something about the religiosity of an aristocracy engaged in relentless competition for prestige.[8]

In large parts of the rest of the city, except on the Palatine (which I have not yet mentioned), there were few enough temples. In their place however we find numerous open-air shrines, *sacella* and *luci*. The first were small precincts with an altar; the second, planned groves, usually also with an altar for sacrifice (the terms are occasionally used as synonyms).[9] If we can believe Juvenal, ordinary people were still making use of this religious infrastructure in the early second century AD (10.354–56; 13.232–5). The logic of the distribution of these modest shrines, few of which can even be localized, usually escapes us. Sometimes, though, they formed part of larger structures, for example the *lucus Libitinae*, the headquarters of the funeral undertakers of Rome (Plutarch, *QRom* 23, 267b), just next to a large piece of land used for cremations and inhumations (probably therefore on the Esquiline), and, near it, the grove of Juno Lucina: she was a goddess of birth, and births were somehow registered there, accompanied by a small donation.[10] Vitruvius says that shrines of Isis and Serapis ought to be placed in harbour areas, with their high proportion of immigrants and foreigners (*De arch*.1.7.1). Many new cults recruited their first members from these groups.

Shrines of a similarly modest kind (at least in their early forms) were to be found on the outskirts of the city, even well outside the inhabited area. They were often on the main exit-roads, such as the Via Appia and the Via Nomentana, which were lined as far as the eye could see with magnificent tombs. Some shrines that have been confirmed as such by excavation can be interpreted as boundary markers. Perhaps the most interesting of these, as well as the one on which, from the time of Augustus, most architectural effort was lavished, was the shrine of Dea Dia on the right bank of the Tiber at La Magliana, where, as I have mentioned (p. 40; 131), the Arval Brothers performed their cult.

Space can also be structured by lines of sight. As far as the public area of Rome is concerned, there were no grand axes created by monumental architecture, as in Baron Haussmann's Paris of the Second Empire. It was rather a matter of lines that could only be seen by specialists. Our knowledge of them is correspondingly patchy. The Augurs, the priests who specialized in observing the flight of particular species of birds and their interpretation, had *auguracula*, observation-posts, on the Capitoline (actually, the Arx, see pl. 3) and the Palatine. From these vantage-points, they may have laid sights towards particular peaks in the range of hills that surround Rome. We only hear about them when a conflict arose, for example when C. Marius decided in *c.* 100 BC to build his victory temple on the Velia to Honos and Virtus without a podium for fear that it might interfere with the taking of the public auspices (Festus p. 466.36–468.3 L.). If the *auguratorium* on the Arx is meant, this could have been the line to the highest peak of the Alban Hills, Mons Albanus, with its temple of Jupiter.

177

So far I have mentioned only immovable, mostly architectural, features. Space can also be granted significance by means of motion. As I have already pointed out (p. 99), rituals, especially in the form of processions, are an important means of connecting one place with another and so producing a new or higher-level interpretation of space. One obvious example, as we saw, is the triumph, which started in the Campus Martius and ended on the Capitol, but, at any rate in its later form, took a lengthy detour, starting from the Circus Flaminius and proceeding through the Forum Boarium (just a stone's throw from the entrance to the Capitol), along the valley of the Circus Maximus, round the south-eastern slope of the Palatine and back down the Via Sacra and the Forum Romanum (see pl. 24). The end of the procession was clearly marked by a sacrifice on the Capitol and the execution of prisoners of war below it. The symbolically-charged point of entry into the pomerium, the sacral boundary of the city, was marked by the *porta triumphalis*.[11]

Another space-marking ritual I have already referred to (p. 98) is the festival of the Lupercalia on the 15 of February, a ritual in which two sets of half-naked Roman nobles (during the Republic, at any rate; in the Principate, thanks to the Augustan sense of decorum, the ritual was performed by young *equites*) ran a good distance, clad only in a kilt.[12] The run probably started at the Lupercal, allegedly the cave where, according to the myth, a female wolf suckled Romulus and Remus (Ovid, *Fasti* 2.381–424; Livy 1.5.1f.). Since no archaeological trace of this cave has been found under the south slope of the Palatine, facing the Circus Maximus, the Lupercal may rather have been a small *lucus* with an artificial grotto.[13] It was certainly large enough to contain a statue of the wolf, and an equestrian statue of the elder Drusus (*CIL* VI 912=31200 l.9). The men ran from here to the other side of the Palatine, or even perhaps right round it, and so perhaps traced out what the Romans themselves considered to be the oldest settlement in the city. Here the past is re-constructed in space. Contempories however emphasized a quite different interpretation, claiming that the beating or lashing with leather thongs of the young girls lining the route was meant to increase fertility.[14] It is this element of popular celebration that Gelasius, bishop of Rome, found particularly offensive as late as the end of the fifth century AD (Holleman 1976; cf. Duval 1977).

An urban ritual that extended over a far wider area was the *sacra Argeorum*, held on 15 May. The Argei in this case were dolls or puppets made of rushes that were thrown into the Tiber from the Pons Sublicius at the end of the ritual. The significance of the ritual was disputed already in antiquity. In view of the old proverb *sexagenarios de ponte*, '(Throwing) sixty-year-olds from the bridge' (Cicero, *pro Rosc. Amerino* 100), the most probable interpretation is that at one time old people were actually thrown into the river from the bridge and drowned; in historical times, this practice had given way to the disposal of surrogate poppets. In the present context, however, it is the twenty-seven small *sacraria* or *sacella Argeorum* (Varro, *LL* 5.45; 48) that are of interest. These were shrines scattered round the old city, each designated by its hill and then its number within the Servian region (e.g. *Quirinalis terticeps*, 'Quirinal, no. 3'); the procession went round them one by one in a rather complicated order.[15] Perhaps the puppets were made in them out of mown rushes; they were certainly stored there and then collected and taken to the bridge.[16] In short, the procession of 15 May encompassed the hills and valleys of the old Servian 'four regions' (thus excluding the Capitoline itself) in a striking manner, and thereby gave them a certain coherence and unity.[17]

Connections in space were also forged by the processions of the Salii. At any rate from the reign of Augustus, two groups of younger aristocrats performed a special annual ritual in the month of March.[18] According to the reports, they got their equipment (archaic-looking waisted shields, swords and blunt lances) from the Regia and at least two other repositories, and roamed through the city singing and dancing (Dion. Hal., *Ant. Rom.* 2.70.1–5). At certain places they stopped to perform other rituals, in which young women sometimes played a part. They ate in temples and other public spaces. Since they were assigned to two different hills, the Palatine and the Quirinal, the two groups were called *salii palatini* and *salii quirini*. As far as contemporaries were concerned, it seemed as if armed young men in the month of Mars, the god of war, were roaming about the city to demonstrate its readiness for military service in its own defence (Bremmer 1993; Scarpi 1979). In so doing, they were taking the city seriously in all its topographical variety: not for them the routinized performance of some old ritual in the city-centre. At least some of their *curiae* or *mansiones*, lodges, that had fallen into disrepair were restored by the *pontifices* sometime after the middle of the fourth century AD.[19] We should infer that the ritual continued to be celebrated even beyond that time.

The list of rituals relating to the organization of perceptual space continues with the *Dies septimontium*, a public festival celebrated the on the 11 of December each year. The name, which probably means 'festival of the Seven Hills', implies that it brought together all the *montani*, inhabitants of the hills, as opposed to those who lived in the

179

valleys; the ritual however is frankly unknown.[20] Another important festival, which incorporated the areas outside the city boundary, was the ritual of the *Ambarvalia*, the 'Round-the-fields', which was celebrated in May at different places on the line of the boundary.[21] The spatial and temporal links with the cult of Dea Dia are striking.

There is finally the highly local cult of the *Lares compitales*, which was celebrated at small shrines at street junctions (*compita*) all over Rome (Lott 2004). These cults, now termed *Lares Augusti*, seem to have been introduced gradually into the 265 *vici*, the city *barrios* (p. 24), from the year 12 BC (*CIL* VI 452=*ILS* 3620), possibly in connection with Augustus' new role as *pontifex maximus*. Most of them however seem to have been established in 7 BC. The cult in each *vicus* was celebrated, at any rate in the early years, by (usually) four *magistri*, predominantly of freedman status, who were elected annually by the residents and received the distinction of being granted lictors and being allowed on certain festal days to wear the *toga praetexta*, with a purple hem-stripe, otherwise reserved for high officials. They were assisted by four *ministri*, servants, normally in fact slaves. In imitation of the *collegia*, the professional corporations of Rome, each magistral college created its own era, which began with the year in which it was founded (e.g. *CIL* VI 30957=*ILS* 3615). The self-importance of the early *magistri* even gave a decisive boost to the practice of setting up ornate marble altars, often with a relief of them sacrificing.[22] Quite how the *vici* were linked at the ritual level with larger units such as the fourteen Regions is unknown, though we do have evidence for *curatores regionum*, Regionary managers, and their assistants, who seem to have been responsible for the colleges in their area (*CIL* VI 975=*ILS* 6073, AD 136).

The final point is this. The city of Rome was not isolated in a sea of nothingness. Given the basically agrarian economy, in which small-scale, local exchanges predominated, Rome was intimately bound up with its Latin hinterland (Morley 1996; Parkins 1997). The point remains valid even if we allow that under the late Republic and the Empire Rome, with its population of perhaps a million, was only kept going by the political and emotional value it had for the senatorial élite, later of course increasingly the emperors, and the tradition among that élite of acquiring prestige through investing wealth in urban infrastructure and consumption. This process however was not limited to Rome. Already in the second century BC, but also after the Social War (90/89 BC), which subordinated Italy south of the Po directly to Rome and in return made Roman citizenship available to all its free inhabitants, the profits from Italian commercial expansion into the Mediterranean were invested in gigantic shrines and temples in several Etruscan and Italic cities in the neighbourhood of Rome, such as Tusculum (Hercules) and Lavinium (Juno Sospita) (Quilici and Quilici Gigli 1995). The best surviving evidence of this is the massive terrace-construction at the temple of Fortuna Primigenia at Praeneste/Palestrina (late second-century BC).[23] Apart from these private, or local, undertakings, a range of public rituals held in the centre of Rome underscored the connection between Rome and Latium, as well as Rome's claim to predominance.[24] These were rituals which, at any rate in the eyes of the actors, recalled early Roman history, and underscored the honour in which the independent city-states of Latium were held, despite the fact that it was only in these representative contexts that they enjoyed even a vestige of political existence in the form of high-sounding offices (actually held exclusively by Romans!): dictators and priests of Lanuvium, *sacerdotes Cabenses*, *sacerdotes Suciniani*, *vestales Albanae* and so on (cf. Scheid and Granino Cecere 1999). Thus it was that the Roman consuls, immediately after taking up office, hurried off to sacrifice in Lavinium;[25] and thus it was that a dictator was elected at Rome every year for no other reason than to take part in the festivities on the Mons Albanus, as one of the high delegates from thirty almost wholly fictional Latin municipalities attending the *Feriae Latinae* (Wissowa 1912: 124).

Systematization

In addition to all these rituals, which were linked to one another merely by the calendar, there were forms of boundary-marking that organized space in a more fundamental, permanent and (where possible) final manner. In this context the law of landed property worked hand-in-hand with religious forms of discrimination; sometimes this could have very considerable consequences for individual rights and duties. Please keep in mind my earlier discussion (p. 8f.; 24) of the terms *sacer* and *religiosus*, *publicus* and *privatus*, which primarily concern the law regarding landed property.

The first example is the ritual that is supposed to have been used at the foundation of Rome, but in actual fact was only ever employed when *coloniae*, Roman colonies, were founded. According to the antiquarians (and this cannot be confirmed historically) a trench (*fossa*) was dug, and in it were deposited food offerings and clods of earth from the various localities where the future inhabitants have been living. The later term for this pit was *mundus*, though there are different, and probably older, interpretations for the Mundus on the Palatine in Rome.[26] More important is the act of ploughing the *sulcus primigenius*, the 'first furrow'. Setting himself to his plough-team, which consisted of a white ox and a white cow, the officiant drove a furrow exactly along the line of the future city walls, taking care to lift the plough-share out of the ground at the points where the gates were planned. The ritual (which, to repeat, is wholly fictional in the case of Rome itself) thus drove a line around the entire projected town, a line where the furrow represented a miniature ditch and the ridge (which had to fall consistently *inwards*) a miniature wall, with a few gaps where the gates were to be.[27] Inside this line was the urban area, *domi*, 'at home', and outside it, so to speak, *militiae*, 'at war', at any rate with reference to the legal implications.[28]

In Late Republican Rome, the 'first furrow' was re-interpreted as a *pomerium*, a boundary inside the built-up area whose course was marked out at intervals by short stakes, and whose function was to distinguish the sacral area, defined as the city proper, from everything beyond it (see p. 100). This inner zone was not consecrated, but it was the area in which soldiers were not allowed openly to carry weapons (which is why in the early Principate they had to wear a toga inside the pomerium). It was also the area in which it was possible for a citizen to appeal to the tribunes and the people against the actions of a magistrate. From the same period, the pomerium was conceptually linked to the frontiers of the empire, an external border that no one bothered to define until well into the early Principate. It was established that the only person allowed to extend the pomerium in order to include areas that had long since been built up was a commander who had himself already increased the extent of empire.[29] Territorialism is actually a feature of the Early-Modern period in Europe; Roman 'frontiers', the *limites*, were more like defensible roads along which troops could be rapidly deployed, with transit points where trans-frontier movement could be controlled. Nor was there a unified set of legal rules regarding, say, ownership of land that applied to the entire empire; in the case of shrines on provincial ground, the authorities proceeded by analogy with the case in Rome.[30]

As to the question of how land at Rome was rendered sacred, the underlying point is that all land was subject to claims either by the gods or by humans, claims that had to be explicitly asserted or revoked. The latter was done by means of *liberatio*, setting free; the formal act of designating a site *res sacra* was termed *consecratio*, the transfer of property to the gods. The status of a site could not however be determined unless its boundaries were precisely defined. This was done by *effatio*, the verbal definition of a given area in full ritual form.[31]

While the act of transferring ownership fell to the responsibility of the annually- or specially-elected representatives of the community, the ritual definition and preparation of sites was the responsibility of the Augurs. The crucial word here is *templum*, a term that denotes primarily not a building but an area or a site on the ground. It might be a specific site that was then consecrated, and a house for a god (*aedes*) later constructed on it. The literary sources tells us that stars cut out of sheet-bronze were pinned up *locis inauguratis*, in properly inaugurated sites (Festus p. 476, 26–29 L.). The Senate had to meet in a *templum* (Servius, *Aen.* 7.153). That is one form.[32]

The second type of *templum*, which was created in the same way, defined a site from which omens and the flight of certain birds could be ritually observed. Such a *templum* did not in itself involve a change of ownership. The Augur, looking towards the horizon and using his curled wand (*lituus*) to give authority to his gestures, defined a rectangular section of his visual field by pointing to the four corners.[33] He then proceeded to subdivide this rectangle, again using the wand, into a left- and a right-hand side, and into a 'front' (*antica*), that is, more distant part, and a 'back' (*postica*), closer by.[34] The Augur's position on the base-line of the *templum* corresponds to the position of the god, or rather his cult-image, in his *templum* and temple; the statue stands at the rear wall of the *cella*, which is open only at the front, facing towards the perron and the area with the altar below. The analogy can be pressed even further. Temples were notionally divided into an *anticum* and a *posticum*, possibly the porch as opposed to the *cella* proper (Paulus, *Excerpt. Festi* p. 244f. L.) (see pl. 18). If there were no explicit boundary-markers to define a temple's land, it was deemed to consist simply of a strip 15 Roman feet deep directly in front of the podium. Moreover, the spot where the Augur stood to define his *templum* was termed the *templum minus* ('little *templum*') and could be screened off on the other three sides like a tent to avoid distractions (Festus p. 146, 12–17 L.).[35] This arrangement corresponds exactly to the *cella*, the central room in a temple where the statue stood (p. 76). If the *cella* were understood as the god's *templum minus* that would explain how the word *templum* could come to mean the same as *aedes*, house.

I think this helps us to understand the different ancient explanations of the word *sacellum*.[36] It is evidently a diminutive of *sacer*, 'belonging to a god' (Aulus Gellius, *Noct. Att.* 7.12.6), without however

18. Maison Carrée at Nîmes.

This temple in the Augustan colony of Nemausus gives an excellent impression of a Roman pro-style temple: the *pteron* (columnar construction) rests on a high podium (here 2.65m) only accessible by a flight of steps at the front. By contrast with a Greek peripteral temple, where the columns continue free-standing all the way round the building, with the *cella* (where the cult-statue was housed) in the centre, in Roman temples of this type the *cella* was set back to create a porch, and widened laterally, so that the rear columns of the *pteron* are only half-columns ('engaged'). For that reason such temples are technically called 'pseudo-peripteral' (see Stamper 2005). This one, measuring 26.42m × 13.54m, was dedicated to Augustus' ill-fated grandsons Gaius and Lucius Caesar, and contains several allusions to the temple of Mars Ultor in the Forum of Augustus in Rome (dedicated 2 BC). The columns are 8.96m high. Superstructure: organic limestone from the Bois de Lens quarries; date: ca. AD 1–10.

implying merely a reduction in size. Such sites did not permit the degree of discrimination that I have just described, either because there was no building on them or because it looked quite different from a normal temple. In that case it makes no difference whether Varro defines a *sacellum* in its entirety as a *cella* (*RD* frg. 62 Cardauns) or whether Verrius Flaccus in effect says the opposite ('without a roof': Festus p. 422.15–17 L.). Both are right. In this context it is irrelevant that true temples included more than a *cella* for the cult-statue: the table for the food-offerings (*mensa*), the couches for the busts or stat-uettes of gods feasting (*pulvinaria* – which actually becomes a word for a temple), firewood, water, kitchen utensils and so on. All these things were anyway kept in store-rooms, normally located in the high podium beneath (especially in Italy) or in other buildings of the complex. The *sacellum* was thus both less complex and less elabo-rately defined than a temple proper.

Theory is one thing. We often hear in the late Republic, when Rome was a mushrooming metropolis, of the disappearance of *sacella* and groves, the shrines that lacked imposing buildings (Cancik 1985–6). They were absorbed into the great villa-estates of the élite, or were built over without official priestly deconsecration, *liberatio* (e.g. Livy 40.51.8). That was of course impious. Yet the people who did such things were the same people who had their villas designed to resemble sacred buildings,[37] and indeed, as priests and magistrates, conducted religious business in them (the priestly colleges often met turn and turn about in private houses) (Rüpke 2002). In building his suburban villa, the *Horti Luculliani* (on or near the site of S. Trinità de' Monti, directly above the Spanish Steps), around 60 BC, Lucullus may have been seeking to imitate, in scale as well as manner, the great terraced temple of Fortuna Primigenia at Praeneste/Palestrina and thus tame the steep ascent up to where the lower gardens of the Villa Medici are today. The opposition between 'public' and 'private' is a Roman con-struct that turns out not to have all that much to do with the realities of their culture.

— 9 —

CO-ORDINATION: TIME AND THE CALENDAR

In this chapter, I want to use a different method, and look not so much at how Roman religion filled the calendar as at how people at Rome 'lived' time as a social phenomenon, and then analyse the role played by religion in this area.

Sources

How can we say anything worthwhile about structures of action as internalized as perceptions of time?[1] Our most important point of entry here is the calendar, the shared chronological scheme of all actions in the year. 'Year' is important: only a handful of longer cycles were recognized at Rome. The most significant of these were the Republican *lustra*, (roughly) five-year periods, and the five-, ten- and twenty-year anniversaries of the emperors (p. 163). An even longer span is represented by the *Ludi saeculares*, the 'Hundred-year Games', first celebrated (probably) in 248 BC.[2] To return to the annual cycle: such a calendar can be conceptualized as the shared pragmatic knowledge of a society; we may think of calendars as invariably written documents, but in fact writing is not essential to their existence. Indeed, Rome's written calendar is historically quite exceptional (and a blessing for historians). No other ancient society in geographical Europe produced what the Republic produced: a written list of all the regular days in the year.[3] That alone shows we need to be careful when dealing with written versions. The contents of such a calendar, just like its omissions, are a socio-historical precipitate, and not the product of such astronomical facts as that the earth turns on its axis once every twenty-four hours, or that the tropical year measures 365.242199 days.

186

In the early Principate, calendar-schedules (see pl. 19) were inscribed on large marble slabs and put on display in the public meeting-rooms of priestly colleges, *collegia* and rural towns. Several therefore survive, complete or in fragments. The most usual form, however, was probably the 'book-calendar', though we only have one example, from the fourth century AD, which was repeatedly copied into the Early Modern period.[4]

The twelve months structure the year. They in turn are structured by three recurrent dates: the Kalends at the beginning of the month, the Nones, the ninth day before the Ides (i.e. the 5th or 7th of every month), and the Ides (*eidus*) in the middle, corresponding to the 13th or 15th of our reckoning. Another recurrent element provides the basic ordering of the entire scheme: at the beginning of every entry occurs one of the letters from the recurrent sequence A–H. These are called nundinal letters and mark the eight (nameless) days of the Roman week. Like our weeks, this was a perpetual cycle that disregarded months and years, and was defined by the succession of market-days, *nundinae*, which were held every eight days (nine by Roman reckoning). The dates on which the *nundinae* fell were marked each year by a different letter, just as Sunday is marked in red in modern calendars, so that you could read off the year's market-days at a glance.

At the moment I do not want to discuss the letters that denote the legal character or status of each day, that is, C, N, F, also NP or EN. They are primarily designations to tell one whether lawsuits could be heard on that day, or *comitia* (assemblies of the people) held. They mark as it were the 'opening times' that applied to certain restricted areas of business- and (especially) political life, and tell us nothing about what was actually done.

The calendar's symbols were so complicated that even in antiquity they required exegesis. A version with annotations appeared around 170 BC, probably in the form of a fairly long heading (Rüpke 1995a: 331–68). Actual commentaries are only known from the Empire. In fact, one very early commentary does survive, unfortunately limited to the first six months of the year. This is Ovid's *Fasti* (actually: *Libri fastorum*), written in the late Augustan period at about the same time that the marble display-calendars became fashionable. It is in verse, but includes a treasure-trove of ritual details, and is at the same time one of our main sources for religious speculation at Rome (remember Varro's 'mythical' theology, p. 122).

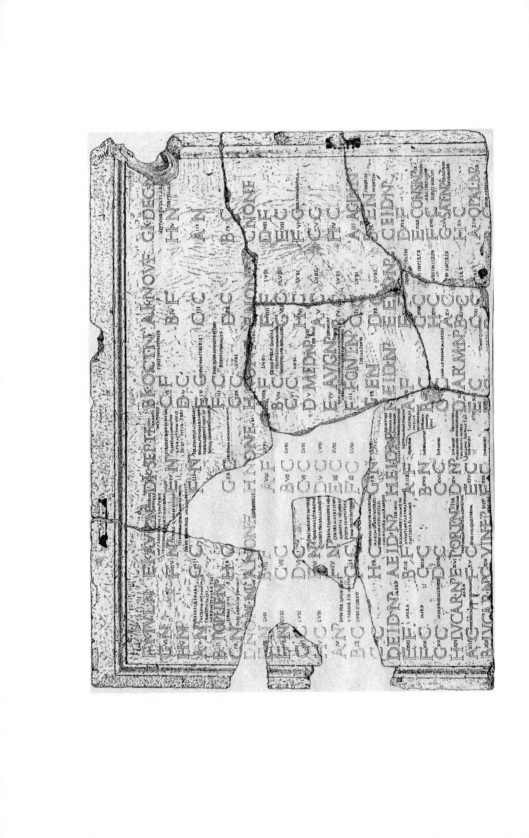

The Year

The Republican *fasti* from Antium is the only surviving calendar from the time before Julius Caesar's reform, which came into force on 1 January 45 BC. Apart from marking the Kalends, Nones and Ides,

---

19. Fasti Amiterni.

This calendar, found at Amiternum in Sabine territory (now S. Vittorino, northwest of L'Aquila), dates from the reign of Tiberius (AD 14–37). The entries in small letters indicate the large number of feriae (festive days) dedicated to the imperial house, and ludi (holidays associated with games), in the late-Augustan/early Julio-Claudian period. There were originally two marble slabs: the second one, which is shown here, features the months from July to December; breadthways it is complete, measuring 1.29m, in height it was at least 1.5m (cropped at the foot). – If we take a closer look, we see that the calendar shows the feriae to celebrate the inauguration of the Ara Pacis by Augustus on 4 July (the small writing at the top left), then comes the Poplif(ugia) in large capitals on 5 July. Right at the bottom of the same column, on the 19 and 21 of July, comes the Lucar(ia), the 'grove-festival' (lucus=[sacred] grove). On the first of August, at the top of column ii, there is a reference to the feriae to celebrate the conquest of Alexandria (30 BC), though all that it actually says is: 'because Imp(erator) Caesar, son of Divus (Iulius, i.e. Julius Caesar), saved the state from a dreadful peril'. Directly below that, you can see the entry for the holiday in honour of Caesar's victory over Pharnaces, King of the Crimea, at Zela on 2 August 47 BC, and on 9 the holiday in honour of his victory at Pharsalus in 48 BC (his opponent Pompey is not named). On the 17 is the Port(unalia), the festival of the harbour-god Portunus; after a gap of one day, as usual, there follows the next traditional celebration, the Vin(alia), a wine-festival, on the 19 of August. Moving on to column iii, we find a holiday on the Ides (eidus) of September in thanksgiving for the discovery of a conspiracy. The last imperial entry occurs in the middle of column iv on 12 October: the Aug(ustalia), to celebrate the dedication of an altar of Fortuna Redux. This new festival is marked in capitals immediately between the traditional Med(itrinalia) and the Font(inalia), respectively a wine-harvest and a sweet-water festival, ignoring the usual two-day interval. On the 19th falls the Arm(ilustrium). In November, the games (ludi) begin after the Nones, ending up with racing in the Circus from 15th to 17th. At the bottom of the last column, finally, you can see some of the December holidays: the Cons(ualia) in honour of the god Consus (15th), the Sat(urnalia) (17th) and the Opal(ia) (19th), all of them probably festivals that once were associated with the storage of grain and the resulting accumulation of wealth. The original is in the Museo Nazionale d'Abruzzo at L'Aquila.

it contains forty-eight 'main' entries (see pl. 19). All refer to religious events or festivals; in the Principate, the total increased greatly. Scholars have tried to treat these forty-eight as the Republican 'festival calendar'.[5] We may think, however, that nearly fifty festivals besides the thirty-six Kalends, Nones and Ides, to say nothing of movable and private festivals, which are not listed in the *fasti*, are just too many. What is all this information for? This in turn raises the question of the function of the written calendar. The fact that the letters F, C, N and so on are always included suggests that its main purpose was to publicize the legal or politico-legal status of each day. This was of course an extremely sensitive matter for the political community. As between Rome and the other civilizations of ancient Europe, the codification of the calendar, and its subsequent reduction to a graphic format, represent a most impressive capacity for rationalization.

The effort to systematize the calendar could not however ignore religion. The religious status of some days had more or less serious implications for the legal and political activities that could be undertaken on them. For example, popular assemblies could not be held on days allocated to the gods, *feriae*, which actually make up most of the 'main' or 'capital-letter' entries that I mentioned. This has nothing to do with a desire to encourage popular participation in the festivals. It is simply a matter of ownership. For just as a *locus sacer* consecrated to a god is his physical property, so *feriae* are his temporal property (Rüpke 1995a: 492ff.). It is indicative of the intermediate status of the emperors that, aside from one or two advanced experiments in the transition period before the Augustan system was fully established, they were not the direct recipients of *feriae*; yet the days selected for the *feriae* voted by the Senate to commemorate imperial victories, or accessions, were expressly not assigned to any other god, either then or later (Dio 47.18.6; cf. Rüpke 1995a: 515ff.).

The groups affected by ritual activities were often very small. The *Robigalia* on 25 April, for example, involved one priest at an inconspicuous shrine; the *Tubilustrium* on 23 March and 23 May involved a single college of minor priests (the *Tubicines*) in a small room in the city-centre.[6] The antiquarians suggest that there were just a handful of festivals that can be called popular.[7] Although there was no official ritual, the Kalends of January were celebrated intensively all over the Empire (Meslin 1970; Rea 1988). The run of the Luperci on 15 February pre-supposes a fairly large number of spectators; in the same month, the *Feralia* (21st), and the *Quirinalia* before it (17th), are said to have been celebrated among families or in the *curiae*, the quarters of the old city. The *Matronalia* on 1 March was a day of 'misrule', when social hierarchies were inverted: in theory at any rate female slaves were waited on by their mistresses, though in fact all it probably amounted to was just some better food and extra time off. The *Liberalia* on 17 March, the festival of the god *Liber*, was marked by food-offerings set out in the streets (Varro, *LL* 6.14). Often, but by no means always, this was the date selected by families for the bestowal of the *toga libera* (or *pura*) at a boy's coming of age. In June, women were allowed to participate in bare-foot processions to the temple of Vesta (9th–15th),[8] and to visit the temple of Mater Matuta (11th). But there is no evidence that either of these festivals, any more than the *Liberalia*, enjoyed a wide appeal. The next popular festivals seem to have been the *Poplifugia* on 5 July (*Quinctilis* until 44 BC), which was somehow linked to Romulus (Dion. Hal., *Ant. Rom.* 2.56.5; cf. Varro, *LL* 6.18), the festival of Anna Perenna on 15th, which was a day of deep drinking and merry-making on the banks of the Tiber, and then the *Neptunalia*, the feast of Neptune, on 23rd, when people constructed temporary huts or tents for themselves in the open air. Bonfires were typical for the *Volkanalia* (festival of Volcanus) on 23 August (*Sextilis* until 27 BC). The only other important popular festival was the *Saturnalia*, the festival of Saturn in the second half of December that lasted for several days, and whose great popularity is frequently attested (Döpp 1993). Authors of dialogues liked to set their literary fictions against the backdrop of such festivals, which even in town offered an occasion for legitimate enjoyment of *otium*, that is, talking to one's friends, appreciation of the fine arts, or intellectual creativity. Cicero's *De natura deorum*, On the Nature of the Gods, for example, is set at the time of the movable *feriae Latinae* (1.15). Very occasionally the names of festivals are used to date private letters and so on, so that their dates can be fixed within a day or two.

So far I have said nothing about the grand games in April/May, July, September and November. Participation in these games, whether traditional or new (when emperors decreed victory games they were often in perpetuity), came to assume a central place in what it meant subjectively to be a Roman citizen. During the Principate, because of the abolition of elections, the crucial political arena came increasingly to be the political confrontation between the side of legal privilege, that is, the magistrates, who organized and largely financed the games, and the Senate, which had the best seats, and the side of the masses, the populace, who could applaud, keep silent, hiss or yell as they pleased. The élite was under considerable social pressure to attend such events, which often took place over several consecutive days, from the second to the fifth and the seventh to the tenth hour (executions were performed during the mid-day break).[9] If we imagine a Senator's appointments diary, such occasions must have taken up a large number of pages, even if we cannot put a precise figure on it. The festivals that I listed earlier became correspondingly less important; in all likelihood, only the *Saturnalia* and the Kalends of January (New Year's day) attracted comparable numbers of people.[10]

I have here ignored all festivals that were celebrated not at Rome but in the countryside of Latium. However much they may have contributed to sweetening life there, they had little connection with the everyday life of the city itself. The same distinction seems to be implied by the list of activities that were generally forbidden on festal days, irrespective of whether the individual took part or not.[11] Virtually all of these rules concern agricultural tasks, especially work that involved disturbing the soil, such as extensive digging or ploughing; it was permitted to carry trees to a new site, for example, but not to plant them. By contrast, apart from the prohibition of lawsuits and popular assemblies marked in the calendars by N (= *nefas*, forbidden), the activities that are prohibited in the city are confined to a sort of holy air-lock that moves along with the priests, the *flamines maiores*, the *rex sacrorum* and the *pontifices* as they proceed to their sacrifice: the heralds order the people to stop working as the religious specialists pass by (Plutarch, *QRom* 25, 270d), rather as in the old days men used to stop and lift their hats to passing funerals.

Though the Roman conception of work was comparable to ours, no attempt was made to impose a general prohibition as with our bank- or national holidays. In the agricultural sector, it was left to the farmer's intelligence to decide whether to carry on with other tasks while observing the prohibitions. By contrast with Cato's all too canny list of things that may legitimately be done, Columella shows in his farming manual at the end of the first century AD that religious engagement may vary from person to person.[12] Personal predilection in such matters is thus far from being an exclusively modern phenomenon. Anyhow, the urban rules for *feriae* tended to work from analogy, which by Late Antiquity meant that more or less standardized rules were imposed on craftsmen, while the agricultural world was granted greater latitude.

One way of testing how strictly the calendar prescriptions were enforced is to look at private votives, which often give the precise date on which they were set up. They show a slight preference for imperial festivals (most of the inscriptions date from the Principate); the dates of traditional festivals were less attractive (Herz 1975). A similar conclusion is suggested by the recorded dates of the meetings and celebrations of *collegia*, which are occasionally preserved in inscriptions recording their foundation or their statutes (*lex collegii*). The festivals of the patronal deity fall on the anniversaries of the consecration of the god's temple at Rome, but the great majority of other dates are either imperial or internal to the group, corresponding mainly to the birthdays of founders and benefactors.[13]

The conclusion must be that the list of *feriae* does not represent an original festival-calendar that was gradually, as Roman society became more and more secularized, observed only by religious specialists. The definition of *feriae* in the calendar was, rather, a means of honouring a god by legally allocating to him units of time as an alternative to the conveyance of material property.

These units of time were marked primarily by prescriptions and prohibitions. The graphic was secondary, even incidental. It was only in the Principate that it became an independent medium. The new *feriae*, that commemorated the birthdays, victories and so on of the members of the dynasty, were often consciously chosen so as to link them with existing commemorative days, such as those of temple-foundations (Herz 1978: 1147f.). A classic example is the birthday of Augustus, 23 September, which the Senate decreed was also to be celebrated on the consecration-dates of the temples of Apollo, Jupiter Stator, Mars, Neptune, Juno Regina and *Felicitas*. The Princeps celebrated in select company.

The Month

The practice among *collegia* of establishing a list of annually recurring dates for meetings is surely also a consequence of the Roman laws that controlled them, which limited official meetings to one a month, and allowed monthly contributions only up to a certain sum. Tertullian, at the turn of the third century AD, alleges, probably falsely, that Christian associations – in fact churches, with their Sunday services and alms-giving – conformed to these rules (*Apol.* 39.5). We have no information about the the dates of such regular monthly meetings of any religious group, insofar as there were any in addition to the optional festivities (birthdays and so on) over the course of the year. We may however take it that they fell on one of the named days each month, the Kalends, Nones or Ides.

With respect to religion, these days involved purely routine rituals performed, at least in the historical period, more or less in private by specialists. On the Kalends, the *regina sacrorum* (the wife of the *rex sacrorum*) sacrificed a sow or an ewe to Juno in the Regia; on the Ides, the *flamen Dialis*, the priest of Jupiter, sacrificed a white ewe-lamb to Jupiter in his temple, probably the one on the Capitol.[14] At any rate before the widespread use of written calendars, the number of days until the Nones, either five or seven, was publicly announced (*kalatio*) on the Kalends by the *pontifex minor* in the Curia Calabra on the Capitol (Varro, *LL* 6.27). Originally this custom was made necessary by the use of an empirical lunar calendar prior to the end of the fifth century BC (Rüpke 2006g). On the Nones itself, as I have mentioned (p. 105), the *rex sacrorum* stood on the Arx and announced the remaining festivals of the current month. Such oral announcements must have continued until the Late Republic, thus incidentally granting *imperativae* (festivals or rituals announced short-term by a magistrate or authorized specialist) the same status as *feriae stativae*, which were fixed in the calendar. The only trace at Rome of the political significance of the Ides, known from Etruscan evidence, is the fact that the Senate met regularly on that day (Edlund-Berry 1992).

In the early history of Rome there was another fixed day in the month in addition to the Kalends, Nones and Ides, namely the Tubilustrium. This survives in the calendars as a festival on 23 March and 23 May. This is the ninth day after the Ides, and thus symmetrical to the Nones. According to Festus (p. 480.25–27 L.), an ewe-lamb was sacrificed in the *atrium sutorium* (location unknown) and the trumpets (*tubae*) sounded, possibly to strengthen the waning moon. In each case, on the following day (24th), the *rex sacrorum* offered sacrifice and the *pontifex maximus* presided over an assembly, the *comitia calata*, which in the historical period comprised just thirty lictors, the official servants of the old *curiae*.[15]

At the political level, there seem to have been no clear monthly rhythms until the Augustan period, when the Senate began to meet regularly on the Kalends and the Ides (*senatus legitimus*).[16] This explicit regulation of the Senate's meetings under the Principate, which also appears in the calendars, represents a degree of domestication of that body, which, unlike the popular assemblies, had been quite unrestricted during the Republic (Bonnefond-Coudry 1989). Even in the Republic, however, we can make out a certain concentration on the Kalends and the Ides, for example in Cicero's correspondence. This contributed significantly to the creation of a regular rhythm in the movements of the members of the Senate in and out of Rome (where the Senate generally met). Patterns in time are always in fact patterns in time *and space*. We need only think of the rush hour.

At the level of what has been called 'living interaction' (James 2003: 14), which is a little more precise than tired old 'daily life', the named days were very significant. It was customary in farms during the mid-Republic to place a garland on the hearth to mark them. In relation to financial transactions, the Kalends were the usual date for paying interest, and probably too for fixing loans. Discharge took place on the Ides (Horace, *Epod.* 2.69f.). Credit was thus granted legally for twelve and a half months.[17] It was this custom of paying interest at the beginning of the month that led to the expression 'paying on the Greek Kalends', meaning never, since the Kalends was a purely Roman institution. Vulgar though it was, the emperor Augustus often used it, causing his biographer Suetonius to wrinkle his nose (*Aug.* 87.1). Rents on houses, or on complete flats in housing-blocks (*insulae*), a privileged form of accommodation in cities, were also paid on the Kalends, usually for a year or half-year in arrears. Such rental contracts often began on the Kalends of July.[18] The day on which the tokens for the citizen grain-dole were distributed each month is unknown; at any rate Augustus failed in his attempt to limit it to three dates a year, possibly on the analogy of the three payments usual in the army (Suetonius, *Aug.* 40.2). Plautus tells us that in the mid-Republic the food allowance for slaves and their families was distributed on the Kalends (*Stichus* 60).

Sumptuary laws are another area where the named days were of use. The *lex Iulia de sumptu* of 18 BC imposed a limit on private banquets of 200 sesterces on normal days and 300 for those held on the Kalends, Nones, Ides and other festivals (Aulus Gellius, *Noct. Att.* 2.24.14). In the late first century AD, Martial suggests that ordinary men wore their best clothes, the toga, at best only on the Kalends and the Ides, which must have been the days when people took part in festivals (4.66.3, cf. Horace, *Odes* 4.11.13–20). It was obviously common to celebrate one's birthday on the Kalends of the month in which it fell rather than on the day itself.[19] Consequently Martial can make fun of someone so mad on presents that he celebrates his birthday on eight Kalends a year, thus becoming prematurely old (8.64, cf. Lucas 1938). Such 'birthdays' might continue even after death: the testament of an anonymous citizen from northern Gaul stipulates that sacrifice shall be made to his *manes* on every Kalends from April to August and in October.[20]

It is again worth taking a look at dated votive-inscriptions. *Prima facie* there seems to have been a preference in favour of the named days, but I have not checked to see whether this impression is statistically valid. However there certainly was a tendency to choose the named days for significant religious events such as consecrating temples, which would of course be kept as its *dies natalis* in perpetuity. The date of the *Tubilustrium*, which I claim was once a regular named day between the Ides and the following Kalends, was also that of several old-established festivals: the *Feralia* in February, *Parilia* in April, *Neptunalia* in July, *Consualia* in August and *Divalia* in December. The idea of linking these festivals with the days when people anyway met together was evidently to ensure, even well into the early Republic, that they came to public notice.

To confirm all this, we may just take a brief look at two groups of texts from the second half of the first century BC, Cicero's correspondence and Horace's poetry. From Cicero's correspondence it is quite clear that he thinks in terms of Kalends and Ides: not merely are these two dates often those of Senate meetings, they also structure longer journeys, eating-habits, and, to lesser degree, the dates when he writes letters. The Nones, though of minor importance, do nevertheless play a certain role. Horace's poems create dozens of situations which are of course not 'scenes from daily life' but do thematize major and minor festivals, and the every-day situations arising from them. The first thing we notice is that there are almost no references to chronology; very few poems give dates at all, and where they do occur they seem to have no special significance. But if we check them, where possible, against the calendar, they turn out, surprisingly enough, to cluster on the Kalends, Nones and Ides. Events whose dates are given indirectly also tend to take place on these days: for example, 'Diana's day' is the Ides of August (*Odes* 2.12.20); the capture of Alexandria took place on the Kalends of August 30 BC (*Odes* 4.14.34–40). The *Neptunalia* on 23 July, which seem to be alluded to at *Odes* 3.13, to the spring Bandusia, fell, like the *Terminalia* (23 February: here the matter is admittedly more complicated), on what I have called a 'Tubilustrium-date'. The glaring exception is the Shabbat, the eve of which is the temporal setting of *Satire* 1.9. But the point of this reference to a completely different calendrical scheme is finally to get rid of the Ancient Mariner figure, the poem's main character, from whom the speaker is trying to escape.

This passage actually reads: *hodie tricesima sabbata*, today is the thirtieth (and what's more), the Shabbat (*Satire* 1.9.69).[21] The 'thirtieth' (i.e. in our reckoning, 29th) must be the last day of a lunar cycle, a means of structuring time that I would classify as popular astrology, and that became increasingly important during the Principate, especially among Christians. The attribution of positive or negative value to individual days is much older however: the *dies postriduani*, the days immediately following the named days, were called *dies atri*, 'black days'. It was best to avoid taking a journey, or celebrating a marriage or any other important ritual, on these days. This belief may have originated as a means of protecting the public or collective character of the named days by prohibiting large-scale private preparations for the morrow. However that may be, the rules were effective, at any rate up to the end of the Republic. Among all the dates of temple-consecrations, not one falls on a *dies ater*. The *dies postriduani* are mostly marked *dies fasti*, but never *dies comitiales*; that is, lawsuits might be heard on them, but *comitia*, assemblies, could not be summoned.

In the middle of the second century AD, Aulus Gellius reports an extension of this type of negative marking: 'the fourth day before the Kalends, Nones and Ides is avoided by many people on the grounds that it is equally ill-omened' (*Noct. Att.* 5.17.3). The inclusively-reckoned 'fourth day before' may be the day after the middle of a nundinal 'week', that originally determined the fourfold structure Nones – Ides [– Tubilustrium] – Kalends (see below). If so, this negative marking began very early.

Most of the *dies atri* can be found under the name *dies aegyptiaci* in the calendar of Polemius Silvius from the mid-fifth century AD (*InscrIt* XIII.2: 264–75). The old 'dark days' have now been promoted to become the exotic 'Egyptian days', for nothing is older than Egyptian religion. It is precisely this denotative vacancy that ensures the survival of concepts such as this, which operate only at the level of the written calendar, and open them up for new interpretation. As for practical significance, it is worth looking at how negative marking of particular days functions in other historical and contemporary cultures. In Japan, for example, printed calendars provide detailed information about ominous or unlucky days of different kinds. The fact that they are mass-produced attests to the widespread popular awareness of such days, and people's willingness to adjust the conduct of private business, weddings and so forth to astrological schemes. In Europe, on the other hand, very few undertakings are actually put off on this account. In professional life, or at school, the pressures under which people have to work leave them little scope for such considerations. Under these circumstances, it is retrospective interpretation that becomes important: the negative marking offers a simple explanation if something goes wrong. I cannot put off the test on Friday 13th, but I am likely to be very aware of, and made anxious by, the fact that it falls on such a day.[22]

The Week

The division of the month into Nones, Ides, the residual Tubilustrium and Kalends points to an original or early pattern of three 'weeks' of eight days, which was the predecessor of the nundinal eight-day 'week' and only differed from the latter in that the weeks were not counted continuously. This sequence started afresh at the beginning of each month after the elapse of a variable number of days introduced to adjust the civil three-week 'month' to the lunar month. By contrast, from the middle Republic, as the sequence of letters A–H makes clear, the interval between one market-day (*nundinae*) and the next was always eight days. The simultaneous co-existence of both systems (the practical consequences of which are unclear) was the price that had to be paid for (1) the extraordinarily early introduction of a continuous cycle of 'weeks' that took no account of the months (the only other case is the Jewish *shabua*, introduced after the exile in Babylon) and (2) the effective imposition of an annual calendar aligned not to the cycles of the Moon but to the length of the solar year. As far as the solar year is concerned, though other nations knew the principle, the Romans were the only people of the entire Mediterranean basin to impose a working civil calendar based upon it.

Of the eight days of the nundinal week, only the *nundinae* themselves, the actual market-days, received any attention in ritual terms. On the analogy of the named days, a ram was sacrificed to Jupiter in the Regia by the *flaminica*, the wife of the *flamen Dialis* (Macrobius, *Sat.* 1.16.30).[23] As a market-day, the *nundinae* were naturally in the public eye; and equally naturally there were conflicts over whether they could be used politically. The lex Hortensia of 287 BC finally brought these to an end. The compromise was that regular *comitia* (assemblies) were not allowed, since the day was a *dies fastus*, not *comitialis*, but that *plebiscita*, resolutions of assemblies of the *plebs* duly conducted by the tribunes of the people, which were allowed to be held on such days, should have the force of laws regularly passed by the Senate and then the Populus Romanus, assembled in the *comitia tributa*. Though of great importance in the political history of the late Republic, this special position of the *concilium plebis* dwindled to unimportance already in the early Principate.[24]

At least one source tells us that another feature of the named days was also transferred to the *nundinae*: on the analogy of the 'dark' days, the day following the *nundinae* was avoided when people were planning important activites. According to Suetonius, Augustus habitually did so (*Aug.* 92.2), which tells us that even the élite was influenced by such ideas.

If we ask what ordinary people did on *nundinae*, the evidence suggests that school-children might have the day off, and adults see to their personal hygiene (for example, shaving; washing all over; cutting one's nails, beginning with the index finger). People might also arrange for a particularly elaborate meal, with a cook specially brought in; the lex Fannia, a sumptuary law of 161 BC, is supposed to have allowed a maximum of five guests instead of three on such days.[25] It should be said at once that, apart from Pliny's notice about nail-clipping, all these reports refer to the period of the Republic; later texts, down to Late Antiquity, mention only the day's current function as a market-day, which is typical of such recurrent days in many societies.[26] A possible explanation might be that the demands of Late Republican and imperial Rome rendered an eight-day market-rhythm completely obsolete. People then made their purchases daily at the city's markets, central and local (Robinson 1992: 131). The economy of the entire plain of Latium had by then been re-organized to serve the needs of the metropolis, as regards both consumption and production.

All this is, in wider historical terms, quite remarkable. The independent 'week'-cycle, though rational, failed to dominate the chronological pattern of every-day life. Indeed, as Roman society became more complex, it was the rational system that was most clearly abandoned when it came to the organization of private and public activities, while the 'soft' system of the named days survived.

In the long run perhaps, the real importance of the *nundinae* lay in preparing the ground for a different week-system, namely the seven-day planetary week. It was in this form, with its astrological colouring, that the Jewish *shabua* (week), and the Christian week that grew out of it, were absorbed into the Roman system of time-reckoning (cf. Josephus, *Contra Apionem* 2.39 §282). Now the planetary week is an astrological system of pronounced simplicity, which takes account of just seven classes of events, the individual days. It was this selectivity, together with the sheer distinctiveness of the planetary gods (Moon, Mars, Mercury, Jupiter, Venus, Saturn, Sun) and its congruence with contemporary theology and cosmology, that underlay the popularity of the system at Rome once it became known there in the second half of the first century BC.[27] Two calendars from central Italy, the *Fasti Sabini* and *Nolani*, both dating from the early or mid-Augustan period, already add a column for the letters of a seven-day, i.e. non-nundinal, week that ignores the months (*InscrIt* XIII.2: nos. 5 and 37; pls. VIIIA and LXXIII). Weekly calendars with holes for marking the days with a pin or peg (*parapegmata*) were mass-produced (e.g. *CIL* VI 32505, cf. Eriksson 1956). By AD 321, the planetary week had become so wide-spread that the emperor Constantine declared that it should become the official system of time-reckoning (*Cod. Just.* 3.12.2). Although its internal logic was quite different, the Jewish Shabbat provided a model for prohibition or avoidance of specific activities on its equivalent in the planetary week, the day of Saturn. At Rome, however, it was not widely followed. We can take it that, for the majority of the population, the point I made about the *dies atri* held good: people were aware of, took note of, particular days, but were only prepared to allow such considerations to influence their choice of action in exceptional cases, when the matter was particularly risky.

The use of the week as a device for structuring time had little wider effect. In the early Principate, the Shabbat only slowly assumed the status of a day set aside among Jews for communal religious purposes rather than for domestic worship and for rituals conducted by specialists (MacKay 1994). In the Diaspora, even such observance was often difficult (Bohak 2002). The Christians followed their lead, though few took heed of the practice of these Jewish splinter-groups. But it may be that it was precisely the unusually intense weekly rhythm of Christian worship and congregational life, prepared for as it was by the existence of the planetary week, and just about manageable for the ordinary adherent, that helped make Christianity so attractive and its organization so resistant.[28]

General Remarks

Study of the temporal rhythms of Roman society once the city became a world-metropolis enables us to re-affirm several basic features of Roman religion, such as its tight links to political institutions, the special role of the élite, the broad range of options open to the individual. The calendar set out the temporal framework within which certain legal and political actions might be performed. In the context of religion, it offered an overview of the activities of different specialists, selected on the basis of two criteria: (1) the technical character of the day (F, N, C etc.); (2) the foundation-dates of temples and festivals that were to be publicly commemorated, sometimes with the addition of relevant historical annotation. As such, it is best understood, at any rate from the period of the Late Republic, as a representative expression of élite competition and of a 'state-religion' understood, as I have repeatedly argued, as the religion of that élite rather than as the religious expression of the loyalty of the entire population.

Although it possessed some highly specialized institutions with their own temporal reference-points, Roman society was broadly speaking fissiparous, especially with regard to economic life, so that, except in relation to financial transactions, there was no need to develop generalized calendrical schemes. The system developed by the élite, with all its intricacies, was thus far in excess of the daily needs of society. The demand for still finer differentiation, when it came, was satisfied by the planetary week backed by astrological expertise, an invention whose significance for the religious history of Europe can be traced far beyond Antiquity (Stuckrad 2003).

Part III

Social Reality

—10—

RELIGION IN THE METROPOLIS

Working with a broad conception of religion, the last two chapters have described the varied types of temporal and spatial, and so also social and political, structures at Rome through the prism of terms, ideas and rituals that have some religious colouring. I propose now to complement this approach by adopting the point of view of the individual inhabitant of the city. Already when I discussed vows and curses it will have been obvious that there was more to individual religious action than the house-cult of the family and the public festivals. In addition to these three spheres, the public, the household and the individual, there is another entire spectrum of religious activities to be discussed. This is the religious practice of organized groups, which increasingly offered the individual the possibility of genuine religious choice. People were not addressed as members of a political unit, but as members of a group of slaves or freedmen, as members of a certain craft or profession, as members of a certain ethnic group, or even just as a human-being, aware that life is limited in all sorts of ways, but especially by death.

Such roles are by no means incompatible with one another. Religions of salvation, soteriological cults, namely cults mainly concerned with the 'salvation' of the individual, can also offer social contacts and provide their members with a sense of belonging. The same cult can be interpreted and practised differently by different people in different places, or even in the same place. In Greece, it was not only the Eleusinian mysteries, revealed at a sacred site some fourteen miles west of Athens, but also, at any rate from the fifth century BC, a variety of Dionysiac (Bacchic) and Orphic groups and (this is something new) texts that offered a significant extension of the religious practice of, and the range of ideas available within, public cults and their temples (Burkert 1987). The same came to be true at Rome. For, notwithstanding the repression of the Bacchanals (which incidentally gives us a good insight into the sheer range of people attracted to a cult of this kind already in the early second century BC, see p. 32), in the ordinary run of things group religiosity was legitimate at Rome: it was a natural component of the spectrum of religious options (Beard, North, Price 1998: 1, 161–66). Not but what the Roman élite was extremely sensitive when confronted with autonomous or independent associations, insisting that the sole legitimate institution for the practice of group religion at Rome should be the *collegium*, and subjecting it to a range of legal controls.[1]

The Law Relating to Voluntary Associations

The most common Latin term for an association or club is *collegium*. Other terms were *corpus*, body, and *sodalicium*, fraternity. All seem to have been synonyms in ordinary language.[2] There were also a number of Greek terms, ranging from *thiasos* and *synodos* to *synagogē*, a term that primarily denotes Jewish religious associations but could also be applied to others (Rajak 2002: 393–429; 463–78). The words rarely tell us anything about internal structure. No ancient source, for example, explains the difference between *collegium* and *sodalitas* in connection with Roman priesthoods.

The terms 'association' and 'society' are appropriate translations insofar as they connote both the requirement of formal membership and the notion of voluntarism. It is however commonly recognized that no modern English word corresponds fully to the Latin *collegium*, so that it is best to retain the term untranslated (Royden 1988: 2f.). *Collegia* were private organizations that could acquire legal personality (and so, at any rate from the reign of Marcus Aurelius, own property) by being 'registered'. The gamut of different types is very wide: the slaves owned by a large household (*familia*) might unite to form a *collegium*; independent craftsmen formed large professional organizations partly for convivial purposes but also to protect their rights and status, as the mediaeval guilds did. There were also *collegia* explicitly founded as religious associations, though it is impossible for us to distinguish in these cases between convivial aims and needs and narrowly religious ones.[3] In reading what follows, it should be remembered that *collegia*, diverse though they were, formed only one kind of association, many of which, especially religious associations, were of a much more informal and impermanent character.[4] The Christian

206

teachers I mentioned earlier afford an example of such informality (p. 118).

Under Roman law, a *collegium* had to have at least three members: *tres faciunt 'collegium'* (*Digest.* 50.16.85). A membership of between fifteen and one or two hundred members was common. The largest club on record at Rome is the *collegium fabrum tignariorum*, the association of carpenters or joiners, *fabri tignarii*, probably founded in 7 BC, with roughly 1300 members.[5] Pompeii, a town with a population of around fifteen to twenty thousand inhabitants, including children, is known to have had at least forty-five *collegia*. On the assumptions that (1) each had an average size of fifty members, and (2) that very few persons were enrolled in more than one association, we would have roughly 2,250 of a population of eight to ten thousand adults organized in *collegia* – a relatively high rate of between 28% and 22.5%.[6] From rough figures such as these we may conclude that membership in a *collegium* was an important aspect of adults' social relations.[7]

With regard to gender, the situation was highly variable. With few exceptions, only men are found as members of professional *collegia* (such women as do appear are usually given the honorific title of *mater*, mother), but women did play a role in many religious associations, for example in the cult of Isis.[8] From the epigraphic record, it seems clear that most members of professional associations in Rome or Ostia, say, were relatively well-off, owners of merchant-businesses and craft-shops, people in a position to finance the social activities of the association through their membership-fees, maintain the often elaborate club-buildings (*scholae*), and make expensive gifts to adorn it (e.g. an imperial statue, a silver bust of Concordia, a hot bath and its heating apparatus: just a few of the gifts listed in *AE* 1940: 62, from Ostia). Generally speaking, it was not the poor or the marginal who became members of an association in order to make sure they could be given a funeral (e.g. *CIL* XIV 2112 = *ILS* 7212).[9]

Even though at first sight it must seem as if there were nothing in common between a *collegium* of bakers, of merchants and of *pontifices*, their organizational structure was in fact similar. In the ancient world, aside from the differing responsibilities and prestige, people do not seem to have seen much formal difference. Of course many of the usual rules did not apply to aristocratic associations. Either exceptions were made for *collegia* that had existed from ancient times (*antiquitus constituta*: Suetonius, *Iul.* 42.3; *Aug.* 32.1), or rules were devised that only applied to *collegia tenuiorum*, associations of inferior people (the term appears in e.g. *Digest.* 47.22.1 *pr.*). Freedmen formed an important source of support, financial and other, for *collegia*, being often upwardly socially-mobile and among the more prosperous groups within the social order of the Principate.[10]

One indication that the 'public' priesthoods were thought of as *collegia* is that, in keeping with the Roman rule, they had at least three members right from the start, and were later compelled by the very important lex Ogulnia (300 BC) to have at least nine. Elsewhere we hear that between three and nine guests are the right number for banquets (Varro, *Menipp.* 333 Astbury); banqueting was of course one of the most important activities of these priestly *collegia*. Until the mid-fourth century BC the priesthood responsible for the Sibylline books, the *decemviri* (by the Late Republic *quindecimviri*) *sacris faciundis*, did not count as a proper *collegium*: we are told that originally there were only two such priests, fewer than the minimum required for a *collegium*. They only counted as a proper college after their number was increased to ten (five patricians, five plebeians), traditionally in 367 BC.[11]

To distinguish in principle between private *collegia* and 'state priesthoods' is to invoke a false conception of the ancient state (Rüpke 2002). Conversely, private *collegia* often built and supported public temples, and played a part in public rituals; we hear for example that the Roman *collegia* participated in the triumphal processions of Gallienus (AD 262) and Aurelian (AD 273), with all their banners fluttering (*HA Gall.* 8.6; *Aurel.* 34.4). A *collegium* such as the Dendrophori seems to have played a role not only on 22 March at the spring festival of the Mater Magna but also to have acted as an ordinary fire-brigade.[12] Both functions may have derived from their occupation, whatever it was; at any rate, the *collegium* continued to exist in a society dominated by Christians.[13]

Cult

The collective meal, held every month or on certain days of the year, played an important part in the life of every *collegium*. Rules governing banquets often occupy a lot of space in surviving constitutions. They lay down the frequency and dates of meetings, their financing, the basic foodstuffs required, the distribution of portions (for example of wine) among the members according to status. The hope was naturally that a rich member or external benefactor might donate so much capital that the *collegium* could exceed these minima; it was common for members to create foundations so that the members could feast in celebration of the benefactor's birthday.[14] We also hear of complaints about members who caused trouble after drinking too much at a banquet, or smashed things, or behaved improperly in public. In the Late Republic, *collegia* were heavily involved in political agitation and street violence, which prompted Julius Caesar's ban on them (between 49 and 46 BC), and Augustus' later edict in the same sense (Suetonius, *Aug.* 32.1). Though Emperor and Senate remained suspicious of *collegia* that might be turned to political purposes, already in the reign of Tiberius the rules for associations, especially professional and religious, were largely relaxed.[15]

By-laws of the *collegium* of Aesculapius and Hygia.

In memory of Flavius Apollonius, the *procurator Augusti* in charge of the imperial painting galleries, and Capito, *Augusti libertus*, his assistant, her most excellent husband, Salvia Marcellina, daughter of C., has given to the *collegium* of Aesculapius and Hygia a small shrine with a wooden porch, (containing) a marble statue of Aesculapius, and a roofed sun-terrace adjoining it, where the members of the said *collegium* may hold their banquets. It is situated on the via Appia, near the temple of Mars between milestones I and II as you leave the City, on the left hand side between the plot belonging to Vibius Calcaerus and some public land. The same Marcellina has granted and given the said *collegium* 50,000 sesterces, on the understanding that no more than sixty men shall be admitted to the said association. In the stead of deceased members, places shall be assigned in consideration of payment. The places shall be allocated to free persons. If a member wishes to leave his place to his son or brother or to a freedman, he may do so provided that he pays half of the costs of his funeral expenses into our common chest. (This gift is made) on the further understanding that the said sum shall not be converted to other uses, but that, using the interest on it, the members shall foregather at this place on the days specified below. If the membership as a whole decides to make a distribution (?) for 60 persons from the interest on the money, at a full meeting to be held in the shrine of Titus in the temple of Vespasian and Titus on 11 March [AD 153], and likewise on 19 September, the birthday of the emperor Antoninus Pius, Father of the Country, they are to make it as follows:

In the shrine of Titus in the temple of Vespasian and Titus:

To the perpetual president C. Ofilius Hermes, or whoever shall hold this position: 3 *denarii* (= 12 *sesterces*)

To Aelius Zeno, the Father of the *collegium*: 3 *denarii* (= 12 *sesterces*)

To Salvia Marcellina, the Mother of the *collegium*: 3 *denarii* (= 12 *sesterces*)

To those exempt from paying dues: 2 *denarii* (= 8 *sesterces*)

To each *curator* (financial officer): 2 *denarii* (= 8 *sesterces*)

To each ordinary member: 1 *denarius* (4 *sesterces*).

209

It has also been decided that the association shall make a distribution from the interest on 4 November, the anniversary of the foundation, in our *schola* near the temple of Mars as follows:

To the presidents present and attending: 6 *denarii* (= 24 *sesterces*)
To the Father of the *collegium*: 6 *denarii* (= 24 *sesterces*)
To the Mother of the *collegium*: 6 *denarii* (= 24 *sesterces*)
To those exempt from paying dues: 4 *denarii* (= 16 *sesterces*)
To each *curator*: 4 *denarii* (= 16 *sesterces*).
Bread to the value of 3 *asses*.[16]

Wine measures:
To each of the presidents: 9 *sextarius* measures[17]
To the Father of the *collegium*: 9 *sextarius* measures[18]
To those exempt from paying dues: 6 *sextarius* measures
To each *curator*: 6 *sextarius* measures
To each ordinary member: 3 *sextarius* measures.

On 4 January: New Year gifts are to be distributed as on 19 September.

On 22 February, the day of the *Caristia* (family feast): a distribution of bread and wine to be made at the *schola* near the temple of Mars, in the same amount as on 4 November.

On 14 March, at the same place, a dinner is to be held, which Ofilius Hermes, the president, has promised to provide each year for everyone present; alternatively a money distribution in the usual amount.

On 22 March, Violets day: in the *schola*, gifts of money, bread and wine to those present, in the amount stated above.

On 11 May, Roses day: in the *schola*, gifts of money, bread and wine to those present, in the amount stated above, on the condition, agreed at the full assembly, that the monetary gifts, bread and wine allocated to those who do not attend shall be put up for sale and given to those who do attend, except in the cases of those who happen to be abroad or who are indisposed through illness.

. . . . .

These by-laws, which apply to the entire membership (*ordo*), were agreed by a full assembly held in the shrine of Titus at the temple of Vespasian and Titus on 11 March [AD 153]. President: C. Ofilius Hermes; *curatores*: P. Aelius Onesimus, *Augusti libertus*, and C. Salvius Seleucus.

CIL VI 10234 = *ILS* 7213 = *AE* 1937: 161[19]

The range of religious ends served by *collegia* can hardly ever be deduced from such by-laws. Sometimes the name gives us a clue. In the case of primarily non-religious associations, the cults most commonly attested are those of the divine patron, and the funerary cult of deceased founders or members. Under the empire, the worship of the emperors seems to have played an important role, as in the case of the *collegium* of Aesculapius and Hygia, since that was the obvious means of demonstrating the political loyalty of the *collegium*. In the towns of Italy other than Rome, the imperial cult was largely in the hands of the *VIviri Augustales*, which functioned as a kind of *ordo* immediately beneath the decurions and usually had the same number of members (for example, one hundred at Misenum in AD 148).[20] In some places membership in such a *collegium* was highly prized by socially-mobile freedmen; elsewhere the members were mainly representatives of influential local families of the second rank.[21]

In *collegia* we might call 'priesthoods', and in soteriological associations such as Jewish synagogues, the cult of Isis, Christian house-churches, or the cult of Mithras, the group might well exercize considerable influence over the members' life-style.[22] We might here include philosophical schools (which were also a form of association), some of which required their members to become vegetarians or practise other kinds of asceticism.[23] Christians had to fulfil stiff ethical requirements. How successful such associations were in making such demands, we can hardly say. In the case of Christianity, we find complaints already in Paul's *Epistles*, in the mid-first century AD, that members were not abiding by the rules (e.g. 1 *Cor.* 7.32–35; *Rom.* 16.17–20); yet there were some radical Christian groups, such as the Montanists, whose members had to submit to even more stringent demands. Jews too might backslide: Philo of Alexandria complained that Jews were too much inclined to join non-Jewish clubs, where pagan rituals were performed.[24]

There were conflicts, then, and such cases show that they were not necessarily resolved strictly according to the rules of the association's by-laws, but that there was plenty of room for individual decisions and multiple loyalties. Of course, Christians, who in baptism underwent an elaborate initiation-process requiring special preparation, could ask: who is a (true) Christian? Under Roman law, the strongest sanction available to a *collegium* was the right to expel members. Recent investigations into how people choose their religious commitments in the modern world, working on the model of rational choice theory, have suggested that religious associations with stiff entry-conditions and high-pressure promises of salvation can be very attractive, producing the particular intimacy of marginal groups and discouraging low-intensity commitment.[25] Mild (domesticated) exoticism, in the case of Isis, and restriction of group-size, in that of Mithras, may have played a similar role in antiquity.[26] Membership itself might take very diverse forms; votive-inscriptions, bearing the donor's name and positioned permanently in the shrine, provided one important means of stating and documenting membership for third parties (Beard 1991: 46f.).

Organization

Collegia need structures, temporal, spatial and functional. As far as space is concerned, we can distinguish basically between two types of association. One type met in private houses, as was certainly the case with many of the meetings of the *sacerdotes publici* (p. 185). I have already mentioned in this connection the *collegia* of slaves belonging to a single household; we can assume that many of the early Christian groups and their 'house-churches' also belonged to this category, which presupposes that richer members placed their houses regularly at the disposal of the congregation. The second type of *collegium* built its own *schola*. We do occasionally find the terms *templum* and *aedes*, but in themselves they tell us nothing about the architectural form of the building. Relatively large meeting-rooms seem to have been common, and were used for all kinds of purposes, such as dining, assemblies and religious functions. An apse or niche might contain an image, a statue, a relief or a painting of the god, as we saw in the case of the *collegium* of Aesculapius and Hygia.[27]

Temples of Mithras, so-called mithraea, have a distinctive architectural form: they are typically long, rectangular rooms with a central aisle and raised podia running down either side of it, which served as couches for feasting. Properly termed *spelaea*, caves, they were either completely dark, or so constructed as to make a variety of lighting-effects possible that may have contributed to dramatizing the cult-relief of Mithras slaying the bull at the far end of the room.[28] Some mithraea, however, such as the one beneath S. Stefano Rotondo on the Caelian (Lissi Caronna 1986: 15), had interior decoration in keeping with contemporary domestic taste. Other cults took over the classic temple-form but adapted it to their needs by means of suitable decoration. Good examples are the exotic decorative programmes in the public areas, and subsidiary buildings, of the Serapeum at Ostia, and the temples of Isis at Pompeii, Herculaneum and Stabiae.[29]

Slaves seem to have lived in some of these buildings as *aeditui*, janitors. Some *scholae* sported a row of shops on the side facing the street, which were let out to gain income. There has recently been some discussion, in relation to Ostia, as to how far *collegia* acted as businesses, for example operating bath-houses for profit. It is probably best to be cautious here.[30] At any rate, it is hardly possible to deduce the size of

212

the *collegium* from the size of the *schola*: some associations, like that of Aesculapius and Hygia, were keen for all members to be present on certain occasions. Others met only in sub-divisions, *decuriae* or *centuriae*, terms taken from other types of organization, each with its separate funds and headed by its own *decurio*.[31]

Generally speaking, the *collegia* of the city of Rome were not sharply differentiated internally and had a broad-based, collegial leadership. Some élite priesthoods might have just a *magister* and *promagister*, who changed every year; the jobs were typically assigned to the newest, i.e. youngest, members. More usual was a broad mass of members (*plebs*, *populus* or *ordo*) and a presidency consisting of several *magistri*, who were elected for either one or five years – the latter were called (*magistri*) *quinquennales*, 'five-year-men'. Below the presidency were often a variety of special officers, scribes, treasurers (*curatores*, *quaestores*), assistants (*ministri*, usually a personal slave of the president), janitors, even a *flamen* or *sacerdos* with special religious functions. To find more of a hierarchy is unusual, except in the case of large associations with a number of *decuriae*. But, as we saw in the case of the *collegium Aesculapii et Hygiae*, quite apart from the high-status patrons of a *collegium*, there were often further honorary positions and titles, such as *quinquennales perpetui*, *magistri perpetui*, *honorati*, *immunes*, designated magistrates, Fathers of the *collegium*, Mothers of the *collegium*, occasionally *censores* and *iudices*, who were presumably responsible for serious matters such as exclusions. Sometimes, as with Salvia Marcellina and Aelius Zeno, it is unclear whether such people were proper members of the club or patrons who provided money and support from the outside.

In specifically religious contexts, such a variety of positions is unusual. Let us take the example of the cult of Mithras, which was organized, at least nominally, in seven grades: Raven, Nymphus ('male bride'), Soldier, Lion, Persian, Sun-runner and finally Father. In order to pass from one grade to the next, more or less elaborate initiations, preparations and rituals were prescribed (Claus 2000: 131–8). At Rome, however, with one exception, relating to the lowest grade, Raven, there is evidence of only two grades, Lion and Father, among around 120 Mithraic inscriptions found there. The other grades were probably not simply abolished but may have been reduced to mere brief stages. The only dated inscriptions relating to initiations, admittedly from the third quarter of the fourth century AD and deriving from the aristocratic milieu of the 'pagan reaction', may indicate as much (see p. 240 below). We may conclude that the grade-hierarchy was preserved as fiction or norm, but in reality, at least at Rome, only the lowest of the low (Ravens), Lions and Fathers were retained.[32]

Another example might be the cult of Jupiter Dolichenus, which came from Dolichē in Commagene (part of the Roman province of Syria) and arrived at Rome with a strict hierarchy, consisting of three ranks: there were the simple adherents, the 'candidates' for the office of priest, and the priests themselves. The history of one of these associations, whose temple was on the Aventine and has been partially excavated, is known from around twenty inscriptions and some fragments. Between roughly AD 160 and 300 the hierarchy of priests, with their Syrian names, was cut down and eventually replaced by a system very similar to a Roman *collegium*, with a distinguished a group of patrons, and adherents calling themselves 'brothers'. The administrative functions of the priest, who was originally responsible for all ritual activities and had to be present at every consecration, was taken over by an officer called a *notarius*, notary.[33] Religious titles and functions were thus down-played in favour of non-religious ones. Jews and Christians (at least in the early second century) seem to have created associations with similar structures.[34] One important counter-example should however be mentioned, the album (membership list) of a Dionysiac association discovered at Torrenova, between Frascati and Rome, and inscribed on the base of a statue of the priestess Pompeia Agrippinilla, which reveals a highly elaborate hierarchy of offices and named functions.[35] Two points are worth making however: the language is Greek, and it is the record of a private cult carried on within an enormous slave household.

In other words, the range of choice open to the individual did not increase simply because more (foreign) cults were represented in Rome. For theoretically it is perfectly possible that membership in such cults might often have been restricted to persons from a particular ethnic background.[36] No, the increase in choice occurred because new cults opened themselves up, adopted Roman forms of organization, so that born Romans could participate in them, relate to other members, and not be put off by completely strange customs and roles. It was this institutional assimilation that made real freedom of choice possible, enabling individuals to concentrate on the symbolic level, on ideas of god and notions of salvation. With respect to the social origins of its members, the cult of, say, Silvanus, a god by no means limited to the 'woods' his name suggests, and often the recipient of votives, hardly differs from that of Mithras.[37]

—11—

SPECIALISTS AND PROFESSIONALS

The Religious Division of Labour

Religious competence was widely distributed in Rome. You will remember from the passage of Cato that I cited earlier (p. 139) that even animal-sacrifices did not require the presence of a religious specialist. The *paterfamilias*, the head of the family, with autocratic powers, could perform a sacrifice himself in just the same way as a magistrate performed the public act. It was however characteristic of the latter that, in order to emphasize the majesty of the ritual and its model-function for the private realm, it was conducted in a grand manner. One mark of grandeur is the number of participants: children, subaltern officials and public slaves (*servi publici*) were employed as escorts, incense-carriers, water-jug-carriers, towel-carriers, musicians and assistants (*ministri*). The task of killing and disembowelling a fully-grown boar, sow, bull, ox or cow was far easier with the aid of hefty slaughterers, drawers, skinners and butchers (*victimarii, cultrarii, popae*). Only at certain moments was a functionary required whom the Romans would have called a *sacerdos*, say a *pontifex* as a prompter or a *haruspex*, Etruscan or other, to read the entrails.

This is not surprising. As we saw in the previous chapter, the members of the aristocratic priestly *collegia* had very specific duties but a very non-specific social role. They hardly differed from magistrates, whether in dress, education, political career or social origin. Even the methods of selection became increasingly similar. The most important difference was that they were usually *sacerdotes* for life (Scheid 1984; 2003: 129–43).

215

Response to a letter of congratulation on being elected Augur:

To Maturus Arrianus

Thank you for your very proper congratulations on my appointment to the office of Augur: proper because in the first place it is an honour to accept the decisions of so wise a ruler as ours even in matters less important than this, and secondly because the priesthood is an old-established religious office and has a particular sanctity in that it is held for life. There are other positions no less honourable, but they can be bestowed and taken away, whereas in this the element of chance is limited to the bestowal. I can also think of a further reason for congratulation; I have taken the place of Sex. Iulius Frontinus, one of our greatest citizens, who in recent years never failed to put up my name for the priesthood on nomination day, with the apparent intention of making me his successor; so that now, when events have approved of his choice, my election seems more than merely fortuitous. And you, as you say in your letter, are particularly pleased to see me an Augur because Cicero held the same priesthood, and are glad that I am stepping into his offices just as I am anxious to make him my model in my literary work. As I have reached the same priesthood and consulship at a much earlier age than he did, I hope I may attain to something of his genius at least in later life. But whereas everything which man can bestow has fallen to my lot as it has to many another, such genius is difficult to achieve, and almost too much to hope for; it can only be granted by the gods.

Pliny the Younger, *Epist.* 4.8, tr. B. Radice (adapted)

If we are to gain an impression of religion at Rome that goes beyond the concerns of the élite, we must also side-line their conception of *sacerdos*. I do not want to use the term 'priest', since its associations in our culture (mediator, theologian, personal sanctity) are rather misleading. I prefer the term 'religious specialist', which emphasizes rather the individuals whose expert knowledge and skills make possible an advanced degree of division of religious labour and are able to deploy and modify a whole range of symbolic systems in this area (cf. Turner and Vallier 1968; Rüpke 1996a). All the same, 'religious specialist' is a clumsy phrase, and I shall sometimes find myself slipping in the word 'priest'.

Religious Specialists at Rome

A great mass of material falls under this head. I want to deal first with the *sacerdotes publici*, the public priests. Almost all were part-time; not merely were they not paid, they actually had to expend money, and often enough a good deal of it: the cost of *honos*, honorary office. Roman politicians of the Republic were not interested in attendance-fees but in booty and provincial administration. The

216

sacerdotes therefore were not constantly occupied with their priestly tasks; indeed a given individual might be absent from Rome for years on end. Such people were in no sense pastors. Insofar as individuals did pose questions to such persons, they concerned nice issues of legal or ritual propriety. The colleges' areas of responsibility were very different from one another, and they hardly ever inter-acted. As I mentioned earlier (p. 213), the priestly colleges were not markedly hierarchical, and the chairmanship usually rotated every year. The only exception is the *pontifex maximus*, the head of the college of *pontifices*, who was elected for life. This exceptionalism was due to his unique position in the system, and naturally prompted the emperors to monopolize the office; yet in the other colleges of which they were members, the chairmanship continued to rotate every year.

Free places in the colleges were filled in the Republic by co-optation, that is, the existing members recruited other senators they considered suitable. However, at any rate in the case of the priesthoods that had political importance, the system was gradually modified in the direction of election in the patrician-plebeian *comitia tributa* (see p. 54). Already in the second half of the third century BC, the *pontifex maximus* was elected by seventeen of the thirty-five tribes chosen by lot, the election being presided over at first by a *pontifex*, later by a consul.[1] After a foiled attempt at further reform in 145 BC by the tribune L. Licinius Crassus, the lex Domitia *de sacerdotibus* of 104 BC prescribed the same method in the case of all other *pontifices*, Augurs and *Decemviri/Quindecimviri*, probably also for the *Epulones* – in short, for the four most prestigious colleges. Co-optation still played a role, since three candidates were first nominated by the relevant college. A vote of rather less than half the population then reduced the list of candidates to one; and he was in turn formally co-opted by the college (Cicero, *Leg. agr.* 2.18).

A further limiting rule was that only one member of a given family might belong to the same college at any given time. If a father who was already an Augur wanted to get his son elected to a priesthood (an excellent start to a political career, inasmuch as it showed one belonged to the inner circle of the powerful and privileged), all he could do was to try and get him co-opted by another college. In very prestigious families, the eldest son usually joined a different priesthood from his father. When the father died, this son was thus already provided for. Since he could only be a member of one college (a rule hardly ever breached until Augustus), this meant that a younger son could take his father's place as an Augur (Szemler 1972; North 1990a). Priesthoods were thus not directly inherited, but the system did provide a means of limiting significant priesthoods to a small number of families, which of course for much of the Mid- and Late Republic also provided the great majority of consuls (see p. 25).

Apart from the colleges, there were also a few individual priesthoods among the *sacerdotes publici* (Vanggaard 1988). They were called *flamines* and, like other types of votives such as days (*feriae*) or buildings (*aedes*), assigned to particular gods. We know hardly anything about the twelve so-called 'minor *flamines*', sometimes not even the name of the god to whose cult they were assigned, or the temple, though admittedly close links between *sacerdotes* and temples were uncommon at Rome. The major *flamines* (*flamines maiores*), the *flamen Dialis*, *flamen Martialis*, and *flamen Quirinalis* were subject to strict rules. This applies in particular to the first, the *flamen Dialis*, who was the special priest of Jupiter, the high political god of Rome.[2] He was not allowed to be absent from Rome for more than three nights. He had to sleep in a bed whose legs were placed directly on the earth. If he went outside into the open air, he had to wear a *galerus*, a small cap made of the skin of a sacrificial victim, with a point made of olivewood (the *apex*, often applied, slightly inaccurately, to the entire cap) to which a woollen thread was attached, the *filum* (see pl. 1). He was in fact the only *sacerdos publicus* who would have been recognizable when not actually performing a ceremony. Like magistrates, priests wore the *toga praetexta* with a wide crimson stripe; the Vestals' dress alluded to traditional bridal-wear (but see Lorsch Wildfang 2006).

If by mishap the Dialis' *galerus* fell off, he had to resign and a successor be appointed by the *pontifex maximus*. This however was a rule instituted and enforced at a time of intense competition for priesthoods, but later never used, possibly because the competitive pressure had diminished – even such apparently 'sacred' rules (*religiones*) often derive from particular socio-political circumstances (Rüpke 1996b). He also had to be married according to a specially old-fashioned rite; his wife, the *flaminica*, was responsible for conducting certain routine religious duties, such as sacrificing an ewe to Juno on the Kalends of the month (p. 194). The Dialis was also supposed to resign if his wife died; this too is a rule that oddly enough seems never actually to have been applied.[3]

What then was the specific role of these religious specialists as regards control of the system as a whole? The central point here is what the Romans called *disciplinam tenere*, 'maintaining the established discipline (i.e. the traditional rules)', that is, taking decisions on particular religio-political issues in keeping with the existing body of rules and precedents.[4] The members of the colleges, whether individually or as a group, were obliged to give advice and assistance, when consulted, in a wide variety of cases (e.g. Livy 4.31.4; 30.2.13). The Augurs only interpreted the flight of birds themselves in exceptional cases, and then only as individuals, not as a college, for that was the duty and obligation of magistrates. But a magistrate might, as he stumped off at dawn to watch for birds, take an Augur along with him and ask his advice if any problems cropped up. The same is true of the *pontifices* in relation to the religious aspects of the law relating to property. They gave advice, but the Senate took the actual decision. The *Decemviri/Quindecimviri* likewise reported to the Senate after consulting the Sibylline books (Szemler 1972: 34–46).

It is in keeping with the general character of the colleges that their members made no attempt to lay down norms in their written texts.[5] So far as we can gather from the rather wretched fragments, they made no attempt to write handbooks of religion or sacrificial ritual either for themselves or for the public at large (Rüpke 1993a). The colleges (initially, the *pontifices*) seem to have started keeping minutes of their meetings from the mid-third century BC (Rüpke 1993c, cf. Scheid 1998b). These minutes included details of religious rituals and of co-optations, and thus developed into a source for the Roman historians (Frier 1979). Decisions and accounts of rituals, however, naturally formed precedents; practice became norm. This in turn became a further reason to make a record. Futhermore, the adoption of bureaucratic literacy itself enhanced the status of the priestly colleges, and thus increased the self-confidence of its members. The brief minutes of the only *libri sacerdotium* to have come down to us on any scale, the protocols of the Arval Brothers, certainly suggest this. One of the longest citations we possess from the minutes of the *pontifices* relates to the banquet to celebrate the official induction of a *flamen* in 69 BC. It lists the names of those present, the order in which they sat, and the dishes served:

Excerpt from the fourth volume of the minutes of the Pontifical College under Q. Caecilius Metellus Pius, *pontifex maximus*:

On 22 September (probably 70 BC), when L. Cornelius Lentulus Niger was inducted as *flamen Martialis*, his house was decorated as follows: three *triclinia* of ebony were made up; on two of them were placed the *pontifices* Q. Catulus, M. Aemilius Lepidus, D. Silanus, C. Julius Caesar, the *rex sacrorum* [possibly L. Claudius], P. Mucius Scaevola in sixth place; (then) L. Cornelius,[6] P. Volumnius, P. Albinovanus (*flamines minores*) and the Augur L. Iulius Caesar, who inaugurated the *flamen*. On the third *triclinium* were the Vestals Popilia, Perpennia, Licinia, and Arruntia; and Lentulus' wife, the *flaminica* Publicia, and Sempronia, his mother-in-law.

The meal was as follows:

as *hors d'oeuvre*, sea-urchins; raw oysters, as many as the guests wished; mussels; thorny oysters, wrasse with asparagus; fattened chicken; a dish of oysters and mussels mixed; black and white sea 'acorns'; thorny oysters again; clams; sea-anemones; beccaficoes; loins of roe-deer and wild-boar; chicken in batter; beccaficoes; purple shellfish of two sorts.

The dinner itself consisted of milch-sow's udders; boar's head; a dish of fish; a dish of sow's udders; duck; boiled teal; hare; roast chicken; semolina; Picene bread.[7]

Macrobius, *Saturnalia* 3.13.10–12

Eat though they did, and heartily, the colleges were not merely inward-looking. Even outside Rome, at least in Italy, we find inscriptions mentioning pontifical rules and instructions. Their authority extended well beyond the City already in the Late Republic, under the aegis of the thinly-spread administrative structure of the empire. Indeed, they pushed ahead of it in their recognition as official prodigies of signs observed out in the towns and countryside of Italy.[8]

Sacerdotes in Urso

I have already quoted from the foundation-law of the colony of Urso (*lex coloniae Iuliae Genetivae Ursonensis*) in the Spanish province of Baetica (p. 36). It is worth coming back to it here because the information it provides about the religious institutions of the colony gives a good idea of what Roman magistrates considered to be the minimal staffing requirements of an independent community as regards public religion (Rüpke 2006b). In their view, apart from the political offices

---

20. Statue of a Vestal Virgin.

The Vestal Virgins were among the very few *sacerdotes publici* whose life was largely conditioned by their status. At the age of six, they were 'taken' by the Pontifex maximus and then obliged to serve in the *aedes Vestae* for at least thirty years. Their high standing, which was reinforced by a number of legal privileges, led to the cult and the individual Vestals becoming the focus of a whole variety of ideas, ranging from their own personal sanctity to the claim that they were the guarantors of the eternity of Rome. In the imperial period, the Vestals were honoured with statues erected in the portico of the *atrium Vestae*. The collocations of inscribed base and statues (or fragments), such as the one illustrated here, are not antique. Atrium Vestae, Forum Romanum, Rome.

221

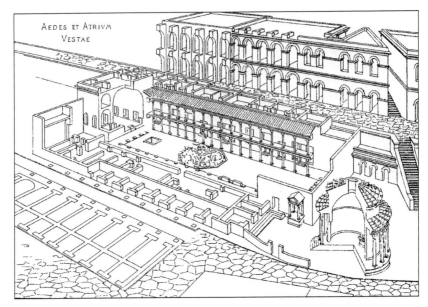

AEDES ET ATRIVM
VESTAE

21. The architecture of the cult of Vesta (reconstruction).

Cut-away isometric view of the round temple of Vesta (lower right) and of
the *atrium Vestae*, the residence of the six Vestal Virgins and the work-place
of the public slaves assigned to serve them. At the extreme right, one can
see the steps up to the Palatine from the Forum, crossing the Via Nova. The
extension of the complex probably dates from the late third century BC; the
monumentalization, on a quite different building axis, begins before the fire
of Nero (AD 64), but the whole complex was thoroughly reconstructed
under Trajan, including for example the installation of hypocaust heating.
More recent excavation has not substantially altered our knowledge of the
architecture of the Atrium itself.

and their administrative staff, a colony needed (1) a *haruspex* to read
the entrails, who counted as one of the city magistrates' subordinate
officials; (2) a *tibicen*, a double-'flute' player, to play during sacrifices;
(3) a public slave to see to the killing and butchery of the animals. That
is all the staff required. However the city government had other
responsibilities in the religious area too: a calendar of festivals and sacrifices was to be drawn up at the first meeting of the city council (the
decurions); the *IIviri*, the two magistrates in charge of the administration, had to organize the elections to the priesthoods, and were
responsible for the financing of the colony's *sacra publica*. Finally the
aediles were responsible for the stage performances, the *ludi scaenici*

222

in honour of Jupiter, Juno and Minerva, which were an important feature of the public calendar.

Of all the rich variety of *sacerdotes* in the city of Rome, only the two colleges of *pontifices* and Augurs survive in the colony's skeletal staffing. On the explicit model of the Roman colleges, they had the right of self-administration. Minimum membership was fixed at three; if their number fell below this, there had to be a further election. According to the rather general terms of §LXVI of the law, they were jointly responsible for public rituals and games. The college of Augurs had special responsibility for the auspices, but no details are given about the circumstances under which the *IIviri*, say, had to watch for bird-flights. Members of the colleges had the right to wear the *toga praetexta*, like the magistrates, and to sit among the decurions to watch the games and gladiatorial shows. Finally, it was laid down that the members of the priestly colleges, like the decurions, must reside within a Roman mile of the colony itself. Given the date of the law (during the dictatorship of Julius Caesar; the actual foundation however was carried out by Mark Antony after Caesar's murder), no mention is of course made of the imperial cult, but an inscription reveals that during the course of the first century AD a *pontifex Caesaris Augusti* was added to the list of priests.[9]

Religious specialists at Rome: a list[10]

Senatorial priesthoods

rex sacrorum (1)

regina sacrorum (1)

pontifices (from 300 BC, 9; from Sulla, 15; from Julius Caesar, 16; from Augustus, a few more; in the fourth century AD they were called *pontifices maiores* or *Vestae*)

septemviri epulones (from 196 BC, 3; from *lex Domitia*, 7; from Julius Caesar, ?10)

virgines Vestales (6; the chief Vestal was called *virgo Vestalis maxima*; the three senior ones *tres maximae*)

flamines maiores (*Dialis, Martialis, Quirinalis*, always patrician, and always listed in this order)

flaminica (*Dialis; Martialis*; there is no record of there also having been a *flaminica Quirinalis*, though her existence is probable)

flamines minores (12: the names *Carmentalis, Volcanalis, Cerealis, Portunalis, Volturnalis, Palatualis, Furrinalis, Floralis, Falacer*, and

22. Grave-monument for a married couple.

This funerary monument with the portrait-busts of the dead couple illustrates the spread of Roman (actually Hellenistic-Roman) iconography into the conquered provinces. It also illustrates how religious roles might acquire different gender-specific meanings (see Kron 1996; Schultz 2006). Whereas in the case of the wife, Licinia Flavilla, the personal priesthood of the *divae* (here *flaminic. Aug.*) represented the sole form of public responsibility available to her, the pontificate (here *pontif.*) of her husband, Sex. Adgennius Macrinus, takes its appropriate place in the (incomplete) enumeration of his civic and military career. The contrast is reinforced by

224

Pomonalis are certain; the remaining two may have been called *Virbialis* and *Lucularis*)

augures (3, then 6; from 304 BC, 9; from Sulla, 15; from Caesar, 16; from Augustus, perhaps a few more; the senior Augur in terms of age was called *augur maximus*)

quindecimviri sacris faciundis (at first 2; from 367 BC, 10; from the second century BC, 15; from Julius Caesar, 19. There were two presidents, named *magistri*)

fratres Arvales (12 members; annually rotating president, called *magister*)

sodales Titii (?12 members; supposedly founded by King Titus Tatius, and the model for the imperial *sodalitates*)

fetiales (?20 members; two named officials are known, the *pater patratus* and the *verbenarius*, who were apparently appointed at need)

salii (12 members; from Augustus, twice 12, divided into the *palatini* and *collini*. Three positions are known: *magister, praesul, vates* [whose job was to lead the singing of the hymn of the Salii]; in many cases, a short-term priesthood for *iuvenes*, young men, until another priesthood offered, or the consulate)

curio maximus (1)

pontifices Solis (created by Aurelian in AD 274, cf. Berrens 2004: 109–15; ?16 members)

---

22. Grave-monument for a married couple (*continued*)

the objects depicted on the side-frames: a double ear of grain for Flavilla, the *fasces* for Macrinus. The inscription beneath the busts reads: *D(is)* // *M(anibus)* // *Liciniae L(uci) f(iliae)* / *Flavillae* / *flaminic(ae) Aug(ustae)* // *Sex(ti) Adgennii* / *Macrini trib(uni) leg(ionis) VI* / *Vict(ricis) IIIIvir(i) iur(e) dic(undo)* / *pontif(ici) praef(ecto) fabr(um)* (CIL XII 3175). Macrinus, having held the two most important offices, religious and political, in the *colonia*, switched, like many wealthy members of the provincial élite, through his connections with the governor, or some other senator, into a (probably) military position (*praefectus fabrum*), and then, as an equestrian, into the preferred military rank for men of his class, the tribunate of a legion, the VI *victrix*, probably at Novaesium in Germania Inferior, where he could command Roman citizens rather than *peregrini*. He is shown in the full dress of that rank. The children's inscription, which is needed to complete both the sense and the visual effect of the monument, is CIL XII 3368. Limestone, 1.10m x 0.95m x 0.59m (top), 1.18m x 0.225m (bottom, inscribed field only), late first or very early second cent. AD. Lapidarium, Musée archéologique, Nîmes.

sacerdotes sacrae urbis (at least 10, attested only in AD 286: *CIL* VI 2136f.)

damiatrix (apparently the proper title of the *sacerdos Bonae Deae*: Paulus, *Exc. Festi* p. 60.1–4 L.)

Equestrian priesthoods

tubicines sacrorum p(opuli) R(omani) Quiritium (number unknown; e.g. *CIL* X 5393=*ILS* 6286)

luperci (?12 members in each of 2 groups, the *fabiani* and the *quinctiales*; a third decuria, the *luperci Iulii*, were briefly decreed in honour of Julius Caesar, cf. Suetonius, *Iul.* 76.1; originally a patrician priesthood, but by the late Republic mainly equestrian with some senators, most famously Mark Antony: Cicero, *Phil.* 3.12)

pontifices minores sacris p(opuli) R(omani) faciundis (3 members)

sacerdotes Laurentium Lavinatium (*flamines, salii, fetialis/pater patratus, pontifices, augures*; e.g. *CIL* VIII 1439=*ILS* 1430; *CIL* X 797=*ILS* 5005)[11]

sacerdotes Caeninenses (*CIL* VI 1598=ILS 1740)

(*sacerdotes*) *Albani* (*pontifices, virgines Vestales*, including a *maxima, salii*; e.g. *CIL* VI 1460 = *ILS* 887; *CIL* VI 2171=*ILS* 5010; *CIL* XIV 2410=*ILS* 6190)

sacerdotes Cabenses monti Albani (e.g. *CIL* VI 2174=*ILS* 5009), perhaps only active at the time of the celebration of the *feriae Latinae*

sacerdos confarreationum et diffareationum (known only from CIL X 6662=ILS 1455, dated AD 180–92, and perhaps a case of invented tradition, cf. Treggiari 1991: 23f.)

'Priesthoods' open to ordinary citizens

haruspices (specialist college of 60 Etruscans of good family, headed by a *magister* or an *haruspex maximus*)

curiones (30)

vicomagistri (265 × 4; also called *cultores Larum et imaginum Augusti/domini nostri/dominorum nostrorum*, e.g. *CIL* VI 307=*ILS* 3440; *CIL* VIII 17143=*ILS* 6778)

sacerdotes bidentales (at least one *decuria*, connected with the cult of Semo Sancus on the Quirinal, e.g. *CIL* VI 30994=*ILS* 3472; *CIL* XIV 188=*ILS* 4403)

harioli, magi, mathematici (all unofficial terms for diviners and astrologers)

Priesthoods of the imperial cult (held at Rome by senators)

sodales Augustales/Augustales Claudiales (21)
sodales Flaviales/Titiales
sodales Hadrianales
sodales Antoniniani, Veriani, Marciani, Commodiani, Helviani, Severiani, Antoniniani, Alexandriani . . .
flamines divorum (*Iulii/Iulialis, Augustalis, Claudialis, Neronis, Flavialis, Titialis, divi Nervae, Ulpialis, Commodianus, divi Severi*. . .)
flaminicae divarum (e.g. *Iuliae Augustae*. . .)
sacerdos divi Augusti, sacerdotes domus Augustae, sacerdos domus divinae

Subordinate personnel

kalatores/calatores (freedmen assistants of the senior colleges, responsible for day-to-day business)
publici sacerdotales (an overall term for the public slaves connected with religion, including the following:)
a commentariis (slave secretaries to the priestly colleges)
arcarii (treasurers of the colleges)
aeditui (temple janitors)
apparitores, ministri, pedisequarii (servants, bodyguards)
camilli, pueri (child-attendants)
turarii, unguentarii (attendants responsible for incense and spices)
fictores (the personnel who prepared the bread and *mola* for the *pontifices* and Vestals)
pullarii (the attendants who looked after the augural chickens)
praecones, viatores (announcers, outriders)
popae, victimarii, cultrarii (the personnel responsible for slaughter and butchery of sacrificial animals)
symphoniaci, fidicinae and other groups of musicians
vestiarii (robing assistants)
lictor Dialis (1)
lictores Vestalium (?6)
lictores curiatii (?30) (the attendants of the *curiones*)
lictores vicomagistrorum (265 × 2?)
flamines curiales (30; the men responsible under the *curiones* for the sacrifices of the *curiae*)
strufer(c)tarius (officials who made offerings at trees that had been struck by lightning: Paulus, *Excerpt. Festi* p. 377.2–3 L.)
praeficae (women who led the keening at mourning rites)

227

Independent cults (highly selective, here mainly Latin or latinized terms)

Isis: *sacerdos*; *Isiacus*; *neocorus*; *profeta*; *Anuboforus*; *aidilis lustrarius*; *melanephorus*; *pastophorus*; *hymnologus*; *aretalogus*; *cymbalistria*; *tympanistria*; *illychiniarius* (lamp-lighter); *scoparius Isidis* (floor-sweeper of Isis)

Mater Magna: *sacerdos*; *archigallus*; *sacerdos Phryx maximus*; *gallus*; *fanaticus*; *cistophorus*; *tympanistria*; *tibicen*

Jupiter Dolichenus: *notarius*; *sacerdos*; *patronus*; *princeps*; *pater candidatorum*; *candidatus*; *curator templi*; *lecticarius*

Judaei: *archisynagogus*; *archon*; *curator*; *sacerdos*; *scriba*; *patronus*

Christiani: *episcopus*; presbyter; *diaconus*; *subdiaconus*; *lector*; *ostiarius* (janitor); *fossor* (excavator of catacombs); *virgines*

Sabazius: *sacerdos*; *antistes*; *pyrphorus* (fire-bearer)

Crisis-Management

One of the main responsibilities of religious specialists involved in the public domain was divination, the technique of discovering the gods' will in present and future contingencies. Political action was embedded in that constant, intensive dialogue with the gods we term taking the auspices.[12] In the haruspication of the entrails, the sacrificial victim, itself already a medium of 'vertical' communication, was re-staged as a meta-indication of the success or failure of the initial transaction, that is, whether the offering had been acceptable. The high point of this sort of negotiation was the *augurium salutis*, a rather rare ritual performed after a state of general peace had been declared. Here the Augur had first of all to establish by means of augury whether it was proper to offer the prayer on behalf of the well-being of the Roman people at all (Cassius Dio 37.24f.).[13]

This constant checking of the acceptability of public actions routinely assumed a positive result. At the same time, through the device of *obnuntiatio*, the observation of adverse signs at critical moments, it was capable of compelling individual magistrates to act in accordance with the consensus-view of the senatorial class (cf. Cicero, *De leg.* 2.31; Rüpke 2005a: 1441–56). Parallel to this system of checks was the institution of *prodigia*, prodigies, which were seen as the gods' means of starting a process of communication, as signs that required special action if normal communicative traffic were to be restored. The recommendations made in such contexts, especially by the *Xviri/XVviri sacris faciundis*, the keepers of the Sibylline books, are among the most innovative features of the religious history of the Republic (Monaca 2005).

It would be quite wrong to see this as an open system. All those involved belonged to the political élite (the *haruspices* required for inspection of the entrails belonged to the élite of the Etruscan cities).[14] Only the highest magistrates had the right to take the auspices (*auspicium*; *auspicari ius*); if such a magistrate were compelled to resign, the phrase was *auspicia ponere* (Cicero, *De nat. deor.* 2.9). Not only did the suggestions of the *Xviri/XVviri* about ritual remedies for prodigies have to be approved by the Senate but even the admissibility of such signs was subject to decision by a magistrate (e.g. Livy 22.1.8) unless it were reported by a priestly college or some other high official (e.g. Livy 32.1.11f.; 40.19.2). The Greek verses of the Sibylline books could only be consulted by the *Xviri/XVviri* at the Senate's behest.[15] 'Illicit' Sibylline oracles were not infrequently called in, scrutinized and put to the blaze. Under the Empire, when so many emperors themselves acknowledged the power of astrology, to enquire of the demise of the reigning Princeps quickly became a temptation – and a capital offence (Fögen 1993: 89–143).

It would be equally wrong, however, to see the system as closed. My last two examples show that it was hopeless to try to limit effective divination to the political élite and its specialists. After becoming *pontifex maximus* in 12 BC, Augustus had all currently-circulating collections of oracles called in, and burned more than two thousand of them, retaining only the 'authentic' Sibylline oracles that they contained, which he added to the official copies, kept in a glass case in the temple of Apollo on the Palatine.[16] We cannot of course know whether this figure bears any relation to reality; and anyway it hardly matters, for the actual number of circulating oracles was many times larger. People needed help in taking decisions, important and trifling, and it was this market that lower-order specialists – *sortilegi, vates, harioli, coniectores, interpretes somniorum, psychomanteis, magi, astrologi, chaldaei* – enthusiastically supplied (Cicero, *De nat. deor.* 1.55f.; *De div.* 1.132). The techniques were similar as between public and private divination (we hear for example of 'private *auspicia*': Livy 4.2.5; Cicero, *De div.* 1.128), but they had a completely different social value. The Elder Cato used to joke that when two Etruscan *haruspices* pass one another in the street, they cannot help but grin at one another.[17] The Roman élite, who used Etruscan haruspicy in public cult, a complex and learned art, were perfectly capable, in a different context, of using the word *haruspex* as a synonym for the lowest sort of fortune-teller, a *vates* or a *hariolus* (Cicero, *De div.* 2.9). As competition sharpened among the political élite in the later Republic, however, they too made use of such help, just as modern politicians do: from the time of the Gracchi, more and more leading political figures counted *haruspices*, fortune-tellers and astrologers among their hangers-on.[18]

Astrology, the art of the 'Chaldaeans' or *mathematici*, seems to have spread rapidly into the eastern Mediterranean from its formation as a discourse in Hellenistic Egypt (probably Alexandria) in the early second century BC. There are indications that at least the word for an astrologer, *Chaldaeus*, 'a Babylonian', and perhaps some simple techniques of catarchic astrology (prediction of good and bad days), soon reached Rome: Cato the Elder warns that a farm-bailiff is not to be permitted to consult any *haruspicem, augurem, hariolum, Chaldaeum* (*De agr.* 5.4); and astrologers are said to have been expelled from Rome by the *praetor peregrinus* in 139 BC (Valerius Maximus, *Mem.* 1.3.3).[19] Faith in such techniques flourished in the context of ancient beliefs connected with star risings and settings, the power of the Moon-phases and the more recent authority of the week-day gods (summarized in the German word *Laienastrologie*, popular star-lore), and appears to have rapidly won ground in many areas of society, being at least faintly intelligible even to the illiterate.[20] A more sophisticated awareness of the more complex features of astrology, however, arrived in Rome only in the second half of the first century BC. At this level, the system's extreme plausibility rested theologically on the planetary deities (p. 199) and philosophically on the Stoic doctrine of a correspondence between the macrocosm and the microcosm. Representations of the zodiac in synagogues (for example at Tiberias in Galilee) and the Church Fathers' perpetual but ineffectual denunciations of astrology, tell us something of its power over Jews and Christians alike (Stuckrad 2000). The reports of expulsions and executions of astrologers, and the bans imposed in Late Antiquity (Fögen 1993: 20–53), imply a sizeable number of practitioners, some of whom, such as Tib. Claudius Balbillus, the head of the museum at Alexandria, prefect of Egypt and astrological adviser to both Nero and Vespasian, were competent astronomers and capable of complex astrological calculations using tables. Both in terms of their loose organization and their circulation of knowledge (and the growing complexity of that knowledge), astrologers can be compared to magical practitioners (Gordon 1997).

230

There is very little evidence at Rome for another type of religious specialist, prophets. This absence may however be deceptive. In the late third century BC, for example, during the war against Hannibal, the *carmina* (utterances in some kind of verse-form) of two brothers named Marcius, who proclaimed themselves *vates*, prophets, enjoyed a favourable resonance among some of the nobility.[21] When Horace in his early political poems presents himself as a *vates* announcing bad news, he is probably assuming a familiar role, alive well into the Late Republic – it is we who like to think of him exclusively as an Augustan literary poet (which of course he was too, once he had been accepted into Maecenas' circle).[22] Incidental remarks by contemporaries suggest that plenty of prophets were active in the first century BC, who derived their authority directly from the gods, and made their mark by calling for a return to traditional piety, moral renewal, and appeals to 'justice' (Wiseman 1994: 58–67).

Rituals of the Life-Cycle

This survey of religious specialists at Rome may be filled out by considering the various 'experts' and 'craftsmen', whom I have not even mentioned yet, concerned with the major transition-points in life. The latter were of course mainly managed by and for the family itself: the Roman kinship system assigned differential roles to agnatic (in the male line) and cognatic (all other relatives, e.g. sister, brother, aunts, uncles) kin, whom we may assume took part in the religious aspects of such transition-points (Bettini 1991).

Birth was the focus of all manner of protective or apotropaic rituals: people walked around the house, blocked the windows with thorns, made a noise; the new-born child was laid on the ground, and was accepted into the family by the father's action of lifting it up – there are no historical accounts of rejection, for no one cares to talk of infanticide, common though it may have been. Up to the day, the *dies lustricus*, when the child was purified and received its name, a table, *mensa*, not an altar, was erected in honour of Juno Lucina. Boys received their names on the ninth, girls already on the eighth, day (Paulus, *Exc. Festi* p. 107.28–108.2 L.). Given that practically all the elements of the classical Roman naming system were inherited either from the father or the mother (Salway 1994: 127–31), this cannot be considered a moment of real individualization, but it was crucial for socialization into the family system. The round of rituals in connection with birth was brought to a close by offering a coin at the grove of Juno Lucina (p. 177). Dionysius of Halicarnassus read this as an ingenious device by King Servius Tullius to record the birth statistics (*Ant. Rom.* 4.15.5), but it was certainly nothing of the kind.

It is quite unclear what sort of personnel ran the shrine of Juno Lucina, but the discovery at Puteoli (Pozzuoli) of the lengthy text of a law relating to the management of funerals has provided us with a good deal of information about the staff of the twin 'grove', that of Libitina. The scrappy epigraphic indications at Rome had suggested that the official funeral services were probably located in or at a 'grove', as we saw (p. 177), near the vast necropolis on the Esquiline. The inscription, which dates from the late first century BC or the Julio-Claudian period, has revealed that they were in fact a public utility, as usual leased out to a contractor, which enjoyed a supervised monopoly. The regulations we now possess, the *lex Libitinae Puteolana*, relate to Puteoli, but they may be taken as a simplified version of the rules obtaining at Rome. One of the most surprising features of the regulations is that the public funeral utility was also responsible for executions.

Law relating to the public contract 'of Libitina' (i.e. for funerals) [23]

... if any one dispose of a corpse without burial, he shall be required to pay 60 sesterces per corpse on each occasion to the contractor (*manceps*) or his associate (*socius*). In such an event, the *IIviri* shall institute a special enquiry by the recuperatorial assessors in accordance with the law of the colony.

The (slave) workers must be engaged before the start of the contract. They may not remain, or wash, in the building where the 'grove of Libitina' is situated after the first hour of the night.[24] They may not enter the city except to pick up a corpse for burial, or to inflict a punishment. On these occasions, whether en route or in the city, they are required to wear a hat of many colours. They are to be aged between 20 and 50 years of age. None of them may be knock-kneed, have a lazy eye, be mutilated, lame, blind, or bear tatoos inflicted as a punishment. The *manceps* shall retain a minimum staff (*operae*) of 32.

If a private client wishes on his own account to inflict physical punishment on a slave, male or female, the *manceps* shall carry out the punishment according to the manner requested by the client who has ordered the punishment; if he wishes an execution by the 'cross and fork', it shall be the responsibility of the contractor (*redemptor*) to provide the pole, the cross-bars, the lashings, and the whips for the men who carry out the whipping ...

If the *IIviri* conduct a public execution, they shall give the corresponding orders. Each time this occurs, the contractor shall be obliged

232

to be in attendance, ready to perform the punishment, put up the cross, and provide the nails, pitch, wax, candles and all the other equipment needed, at his own expense.[25] When he receives the order to remove the victim with the hook, his men, dressed in red, must remove the corpse to where they are piled, ringing a bell while they do so.

When a client wishes to make use of the services required in each circumstance under this regulation, he must notify, or cause to be notified, the *manceps* of the service or his associate or the person responsible for the relevant department, or, if they are away, the office he has rented or set up for the funeral-service (*libitinae exsercendae gratia*), of the day, the place and the service he wishes to take advantage of. Once this notification has duly taken place, the said *manceps*, or his associate, or the person responsible for that department, shall be obliged to provide everything required under these regulations, and furnish the client who has given such notice first with all requisite services, and then all the others in the order of their notification, unless the notification concerns the funeral of a decurion, or of a young person (*funus acervum*, lit. a bitter funeral), who must be given priority. In such cases, the order of the other notifications must be respected.

In cases of a reported suicide by hanging, the *manceps* must at once see to the body being cut down and removed; in the case of a slave, male or female, if the message comes before the 10th hour of the day, the body is to be removed the same day; if later, before the second hour of the following day.

(Most of the remainder, where it can be read, concerns delays, complaints and litigation arising.)

Lex Libitinae Puteolana cols. I.32–II.23[26]

The contractor (elsewhere called *libitinarius*) has thus to provide a team of at least thirty-two able-bodied and physically whole men, who had to be on call all day.[27] They were only permitted to enter the town of Puteoli when performing their professional duties, the collection of the corpses of the dead in the order in which they had been notified, and then had to wear party-coloured head-gear. The only exceptions permitted to the rule of first come, first served are the removal of the corpses of decurions, i.e. members of the city council, young people and children, and suicides, among whom free persons are to be given preference to slaves. The contractor's monopoly is protected by heavy fines imposed upon anyone who attempts to set up, or make use of, an alternative funeral service, or dispense with the bother and expense of a funeral by dumping the body. At the same time, his clients are protected by the clause that stipulates a fine of one hundred sesterces if the lessee contravenes the regulations, to be paid into the public treasury (III.22–4).

The inscription, admittedly fragmentary, says nothing about 'offerings' to Libitina when someone died. Rather, the community let out the monopoly rights to collect the dead and to supply funerals for a stipulated sum to private contractors, who made their living by charging clients fixed fees for various kinds of services.[28] Such a system had evidently existed in much the same form since the early second century BC (Livy 40.19.3). The 'grove' of Libitina at Rome was the seat of a *collegium* of *dissignatores*, funeral directors, where they stored their equipment (Horace, *Epist.* 1.7.6f.; Seneca, *De benef.* 6.38.4).[29] That is a far cry from the four grand colleges, but remains part of the infrastructure of public religion. It is also a far cry from the soteriological cults that promised a joyful existence after death, yet at the same time their pre-condition. Without proper burial the dead cannot live, and the living can enjoy no peace.

---

23. Grave-marker for a fourteen-month old baby girl.

There is a great variety of different ideas about what happens to us after death. In antiquity, such ideas ranged from the salvation (heroization) promised by the fifth- and fourth-century BC gold-leaf Orphic-Dionysiac 'passports for the dead' (texts that describe the dead person's journey into the Underworld) all the way to flat claims that after death there is simply nothing. Cult practice seems to have been surprisingly immune to such variation. Funerary feasts at the grave continued to be widely celebrated into the Christian Empire, as did means of supplying the dead with sustenance through openings in the grave-stone (as here) or even by means of tubes let down into the grave. The inscription, which unusually enough omits all reference to the mother, reads: *Dis M[a]nibus // Iunia[e] Musae / vixit a[n]no uno / et mensi[b]us duob(us) / M. Iunius Dius / pat[e]r / filiae pie[n]tissimae / fec[i]t* (CIL VI 35634). Found in 1888 beneath the mausoleum of Constantina, the elder daughter of the emperor Constantine I (mistakenly known as the mausoleum 'di S. Constanza'). First half of second cent. AD; now walled into the staircase on the S. side of S. Agnese fuori le mura, Via Nomentana, Rome.

—12—

FROM CAESAR TO THE LAMB: HISTORICAL PERSPECTIVES

History?

There is no history of Roman religion during the Empire. The most obvious sense of such a claim is that there exists no modern account that takes the story from Augustus, whom we think of as the first Princeps (in Suetonius, Late Antiquity and the mediaeval period, the sequence started with Julius Caesar, who was, after all, deified) to the sack of Rome by Alaric's Goths in AD 410, which forms a suitable point to mark the end of the political significance of Rome and her local élite, since it shattered belief in the eternity of Rome, and made plain for all to see that effective power had long since moved elsewhere, following the itinerant court.[1] That absence is itself however due to a factual circumstance: much of what we have surveyed in the previous chapters did not change under the Empire. Vows were made and redeemed; sacrifices, blood- and other, were performed, sometimes more lavishly, sometimes less; temples were built and restored; imperial celebrations introduced and later dropped to make space for new ones. Even in the fifth century AD the great popular festivals were still celebrated; traces of them can be found well into the mediaeval period, and even later. Emperors of course changed, perhaps some divine names too. But did such things make much difference?

History or Histories?

It would also be possible to take the opposite tack – people have – and pile on the change. This would be the story of fusty-dusty old Roman Republican religion, the invasion of 'oriental cults', the rise of

Christianity, persecution of the Christians, the toleration of the Church thanks to Constantine 'the Great' (the edict of Milan, AD 313), Christianity as religion of state, the hiccough under Julian (AD 360–363), the final victory of Christianity and the suppression of pagan sacrifice by Theodosius I in AD 391–2. In this version, that is where the story stops.[2] It is also possible to take sides with the pagans, and speak of 'the persecution of the pagans' (Noethlichs 1986) or the 'survival of Hellenism' (Trombley 1995), which makes the matter clearer but does not alter the overall line.

To speak of the 'struggle between paganism and Christianity' in the late fourth century, that is, the demonstrative paganism of a group of blue-blooded aristocrats, and the conflict between Symmachus and St Ambrose over the altar of Victory in the Senate-house, adds a touch of drama to the story. But it is hard to see any specifically tragic elements in a conflict that supposedly features an enlightened, yet in many ways ridiculous, traditionalism in confrontation with a brilliant intellectual such as Ambrose of Milan and his conception of monotheism. However much we strive for historical objectivity, and however much we try to apply contemporary standards of judgement, there seems simply to be no alternative between Christian theology in its platonizing form, and the smoky dimness of a mithraeum, or the bits and pieces of the body of Osiris, husband and brother of Isis. History itself confirmed that judgement with astonishing speed. The attractive power of Christianity and its extremely rapid growth-rate, sustained over several centuries, are among the most remarkable phenomena in the religious history of the Roman Empire. There have been endless attempts to explain it: Christian miracle, the attraction of Christian teachings to the underprivileged, the organizational strength of the episcopal system, the enhanced survival-chances of patients fortunate enough to be cared for in Christian communities at a time of widespread plague (Stark 1996). Individually, none of these really hits the mark, even if they do all point to non-negligible factors. I do not think we are yet anywhere near being able to draw up a final balance-sheet. Yet it is surely worth observing that individual factors such as these cannot possibly be considered central to the history of a highly composite and inflected religious system dependent on a political structure that, at any rate by comparison with that of the Republican period, cannot be considered at all religious.

Anyway, I would also point out that some of the underlying assumptions here are inappropriate. Polytheism and monotheism are not inherently or necessarily antithetical. In the context of an open polytheistic system there is room for many different cults, and it is *prima facie* of no great importance whether they worship one or more gods. Claims in favour of single worship were part of a widespread rhetoric of piety, and incapable of damaging the system as a whole so long as they were not enforced at the point of a sword, and did not try to throw the entire political system into question. Neither occurred on a large scale before the fourth century. As we saw already in chapter 4, ideas about god are not the sole, and usually not even the main, springs of religious action. Even to see the antithesis between polytheism and monotheism as a conflict is the product of a monotheistic habit of mind formed by a tightly-organized intellectual system (e.g. Philo of Alexandria). Such a move is hardly conducive to understanding the ways that other kinds of cults conceived of themselves.[3]

If we start thinking about the religious changes under the Principate by comparison with the Republic, the most important single consideration must be the expanding and shifting geographical context, the underlying cause of the increasingly intense interaction between Rome and the subject territories ('provinces') stretching out to an ever-receding periphery. The administrative and military élite operated over the entire empire, the emperors came from Spain, Africa, Syria, Illyricum. Slaves (in decreasing numbers), merchants, 'economic refugees' and 'intellectuals' all came to Rome, to the centre. To that centre came also Egyptian cults (Isis and Sarapis), Syrian cults (Jupiter Dolichenus, Jupiter Heliopolitanus, Sol Elagabalus . . .), an allegedly Persian cult (Mithras), Palestinian cults (Jews, Christians); and Rome was anyway the residence of the *deus praesens*, the ever-present god, that is, the ruling Princeps himself. Although other traditional centres continued to flourish, by the second century AD the city was itself also a centre for philosophy.[4] The need to justify Roman actions to the world, which individual late-Republican thinkers such as Cicero had grasped through their encounter with Greek culture, became increasingly concrete (Zetzel 2003). To write a history of religion in the city of Rome under the Empire increasingly means trying to isolate what is special about it, given the continuing cultural distinctiveness of individual cults and the fact of their interaction once they were forced to confront one another. In what follows, I offer some examples of what this effort might involve.

New Cults

Let me first take the cult of Mithras, which, originating somewhere in the eastern Empire, spread in Rome and then from Rome in the late first century AD.[5] Sociologically it offers an example of religious group-formation, bringing together men (and only men) of relatively high social status, particularly army centurions and other privileged ranks, and members of the administrative grades of the *familia Caesaris*, the imperial administrative class, but also many ordinary freedmen and their descendants. As we have seen (p. 212), they met in purpose-built rooms, consisting essentially of a central aisle with raised podia on either side that served as extra-long *triclinia* for common meals, and a cult-relief at the far end, opposite the entrance, with votive altars in front. Such mithraea provided room for only a couple of dozen people; even the largest could have held rather fewer than one hundred.[6]

One special feature was the absence of sources of natural light (see p. 99). At Rome (actually much more is known of the mithraea in Ostia), these temples were set up in cellars, or in ground-floor rooms in existing buildings; where a community could afford an independent building, it was often built in such a way that the floor was well below ground-level. It is thus not surprising that adherents spoke of these temples as 'caves' (*spelaeum*). However, we should not allow our fancy to run away with us here: city mithraea are decidedly human, not natural, constructions; in the provinces the sober word *templum* replaces *spelaeum*; and most mithraea were painted in current domestic styles of interior decoration.

This brings us to the question of the character of the cult. There is absolutely no doubt that the deity, and the stories told about him, hark back to the Indo-Iranian god Mithra and thus possessed an exotic allure. There is equally no doubt that these stories, and the probable use of light-effects, opened the door to astrological speculation, and thus gained additional authority through their congruence with patterns in the heavens; after all, in western Asia, Mithra was identified with the sun already in the mid-Parthian period (Strabo 15.3.13, 732C).[7] There has recently been a great deal of speculation in this sense about the nature of *the* cult of Mithras. Yet the imaginative associations of individual craftsmen (or rather their patrons), of philosophers (Pallas and Euboulus, cited by Porphyry) and of Christian apologists (such as Justin Martyr and Tertullian) tell us nothing about our mithraeum in the city of Rome and the adherents who were initiated there and celebrated their feasts. Admittedly one or two prayer- or ritual-texts are known, but there is no evidence that such texts were widely circulated or read out; the cult does not seem to have been a component of the 'religion of the intellectuals' until the second half of the third century. Thereafter it seems that philosophical (Neo-platonist) glossing and the increasingly prominent public role of the Sun (*Sol*) encouraged its reception by the élite, so that by the mid-fourth century we find several members of the Roman aristocracy including senior positions within the cult among the lists of their religious offices. Indeed, one of them, the senator Aurelius Victor Augentius, claimed in AD 376 that he had been a follower of Mithras for thirty years (*CIL* VI 751b = *ILS* 4268).

This élite interest went along with physical building and repair of mithraea and the epigraphic recording of information about initiation ceremonies of a kind hitherto almost unknown in Rome (but common in the mithraeum at Dura Europos in Syria).[8] A case in point is the same Aurelius Victor Augentius, who, together with his brother or brother-in-law Nonius Victor Olympius, likewise a senator, documented a series of initiations that they performed over the years between AD 357 and 362 in the temple founded by Olympius just off the present Piazza S. Silvestro in Capite, in the northern Campus Martius.[9] These can best be represented in a table:

10 August 357	Lions (*leontica*)
15 September 357	Lions
after 15 March 358	Lions
4 April 358	Persians (*persica*)
16 April 358	Sun-runner (*heliaca*)
19 April 358	Fathers (*patrica*)
23 April 358	?'Bridegrooms' (*cryfii*)
11 March 359	Lions
1 April 362	Lions
8 April 362	Lions
8 April 362	?'Bridegrooms' (*cryfii*)

Here I am not so much interested in careers (p. 213) as in time. The dates recorded give us a glimpse into the ordering of the calendar in this mithraeum. It is obvious that a large number of initiations took place in April. Beyond that, there is no positive indication for the use either of the seven-day week (whether Judaeo-Christian or planetary) or the eight-day (nundinal) week. The initiations fall on five of the seven week-days (Thursday to Monday), or on seven of the eight nundinal days, without noticeable preferences. The only discernible pattern is the avoidance of all days the Romans thought of as *atri* or *religiosi*, unlucky or inauspicious, that is, the days following each of the Kalends, Nones and Ides, and the three days *mundus patet*, 24 August, 5 October, 8 November. The same could be true in relation to the nundinal week: the day avoided might be the day after the *nundinae* that Augustus, as we saw (p. 198), avoided for important business, as he did the Nones. Such patterns show how deeply the cult of Mithras was embedded into the calendrical patterns of Roman polytheism, which is also clear from the way in which Mithras could be directly identified with the *Sol Invictus* of public cult: he did not have to skulk alone in his cave, but could share it with 'divine colleagues' (in Greek: *synnaoi theoi*), other deities worshipped with him in his temple, a very widespread practice in antiquity.[10]

One phenomenon not clearly attested for the cult of Mithras but manifest in the case of other cults is the marked centripetal movement upon the city of Rome from the provinces, and the permanent presence there of individuals and groups of different cultural backgrounds from all over the Mediterranean basin (Noy 2000). This influx is characteristic of the history of religion at Rome, which was anyway untypical on account of its gigantic size (equalled at the time only by a few cities in China). It is possible that imported cults long remained confined to the ethnic groups that had introduced them, and thus had no impact on the religious choices realistically open to the existing inhabitants.[11] How far this was indeed the case is difficult to decide. I have already made the crucial point, which is that exotic cults relatively rapidly adapted their organizations to accommodate themselves to their new home (p. 213).

Christianity, socially heterogeneous as it was, must obviously be included as one of the cults of the city of Rome. However sharply the Christians moved in the direction of exclusivity, the majority perspective was that devoting oneself to the worship of a single god was perfectly acceptable in the context of what, seen critically from outside but not from within, can be called polytheism. To repeat the point, the latter category is not available to a religious mentality that might – theoretically – distinguish between cults on the basis of the number of gods worshipped. It is only once you have defined yourself as a monotheist, as we can see in the case of the Jewish philosopher Philo of Alexandria, that you have a reason to start ticking the 'many gods' off on your fingers.

We can follow the same attitude into the third and fourth centuries AD. Although we only have indirect evidence of Traianus Decius' edict late in AD 249, in the form of certificates issued to those who had sacrificed acceptably, and later reports, so that we cannot be sure, it seems to have required subjects simply to offer sacrifice to the usual group of local deities, or even as one wished (see p. 8). The certificate issued in effect provided official confirmation that its possessor had also acted correctly all through the past, and to that degree can be described as measure to encourage peaceful co-existence rather than religious confrontation. Indeed Pionius' *Life of Polycarp*, which is set in the context of the Decian perscution, suggests that for Christians, at least in Asia Minor, the easiest solution, and perhaps the one most frequently adopted, was to perform a ritual in a Jewish synagogue.[12] The sometimes fanatical determination to stress the exclusive nature of Christianity, even to the point of martyrdom, likewise created a distorted view of the imperial cult: sacrifice to the emperor was not at all the ultimate insult imposed by a régime hostile to Christians that it is made to appear in the later Christian tradition, but a perfectly ordinary practice without any special theological significance that was still a feature of public life in the fifth century AD, when the military oath was sworn by God, Jesus, the Holy Ghost, and the majesty of the Emperor (Vegetius, *De re militari* 2.5).

The sources for the history of Christianity at Rome are poor; given that fact, the first point to emphasize is the movement's heterogeneity (Lampe 1989: 301–34; Scholtissek 2000). I have already mentioned (p. 118) that there were many philosophical or theological differences between the Christian groups in the city. Quite apart from such doctrinal differences, even in the second century no attempt was made to build churches, nor was there a centralized leadership: the 'Church' continued to consist of separate groups each organized in its own way. Meetings must have been held mainly in private houses. It is only in the third century that we find the first tentative evidence of a desire to set certain spaces aside for services, and furnish them in such a manner that the most important rituals, above all baptism by immersion and the eucharist, could be performed there.[13] This process probably differed considerably from group to group: as in the case of other cults, the patronage of wealthy individuals gave at least some groups the means of furnishing their meeting-places and celebrating their festivals in the proper manner (White 1990: 53–8). Patrons might however demand something in return. In the mid-second century, we know of the ship-owner Marcion of Sinope, whose gifts were given along with clearly-articulated ideas about the traditions to be followed, which soon led to open conflicts.[14] Two other contemporaries of Marcion are worth mentioning here, in further illustration of the point about diversity: Hermas, who expressed the demands of the Christian life from the point of view of a successful member of the middle-class, and whose book of literary 'visions', the *Shepherd*, soon acquired almost canonical status; and the highly-gifted intellectual Valentinus, who was later, like Marcion, classified as a 'gnostic heretic'.[15] All three spoke and wrote in Greek; all three gathered their own Christian groups around them, which in turn developed their ideas in a variety

of directions – Marcion's student Apelles founded his own independent group, and the views ascribed to later Valentinians, for example,
bear very little relation to Valentinus' own ideas.

Initially, the Christians' organization resembled that of the Jews,
who were still, in the third and fourth centuries, grouped in a variety
of synagogues, without any overall leadership (Rutgers 1995).
However, from the early third century, the 'majority Christians' began
to develop an increasingly complex central organization, headed by a
single *episkopos*, a Greek word meaning 'overseer' or 'inspector', over
whose appointment there were of course frequent conflicts. This is
part of a wider process whereby an emergent élite of *episkopoi*,
bishops, developed into an estate or rank with empire-wide connections. The bishop of Rome indeed soon became a spokesman able to
represent the interests of Christians to the imperial court, and in the
long run even to challenge its authority (Pietri 1976).

This organizational development did not mean that Christians and
Romans were continually at loggerheads. I want here to emphasize
that Christians were at the same time also Romans. Common education and values meant that the mental universe they inhabited was just
the same as that of other contemporary Romans; only then, and often
only just recently, were they Christians. Christianity became the
majority religion at Rome at best in the fifth century; but this very
achievement must have served to intensify awareness of the gap
between the standards and views of the religious élite, ascetics and
monks, and those of this large majority.

A text such as the *Consultationes Zacchaei et Apollonii*, an anonymous dialogue between the philosopher Apollonius and his Christian
friend Zacchaeus, perhaps written at Rome in the late fourth century,
suggests the development of a Christian way of life that required little
or no break with the traditions and values of the Roman social élite.[16]
In the middle of the fifth century a calligrapher, Furius Dionysius
Filocalus, produced a handsome calendar in codex-form combining
the traditional almanac of imperial festivals and holidays celebrated
in honour of the old gods with time-lines from Roman history, and the
burial-dates of the bishops of Rome and martyrs. The addressee was
certainly a Christian.[17]

The iconography of eschatological hopes to be found on Christian
sarcophagi and in the chambers of the Via Latina catacomb (via Dino
Compagni), which was decorated in the mid-fourth century, is characterized by an unself-conscious mixture of traditional mythological
motifs and a(n initially rather limited) repertoire of biblical motifs.
Jonah and the whale in one chamber, Hercules in the next.[18]

243

The educated élite had no desire to give up their treasured canons of literature, the fine arts, or architecture, for all of these were an index both of their sense of political worth and of their social superiority. Nor could they dream of accepting in their place the inept early translations into Latin. Probably after 384, Faltonia Betitia Proba, the aristocratic wife of the *Praefectus Urbi* Adelphius, put together a Vergilian *cento* entitled *De laudibus Christi*, In praise of Christ, which enjoyed enormous success despite the criticisms of form and content by Jerome, who made it his business to take care of aristocratic Christian women in Rome.[19] This same Jerome successfully aimed to give his biography of the coenobite Paul of Thebes (*Vita Pauli*) a fine fictional gloss, which brought him a wide readership; and while in Rome during the years 382–85, at the request of his patron, bishop Damasus (366–84), translated the New Testament and the Psalms afresh into Latin.[20] It was also Damasus who induced Furius Dionysius Filocalus to compose and inscribe epitaphs for all the bishops and martyrs of Rome whose graves could be identified. It was this project that set in train the extension of the catacombs, which, even more than the building of the great Constantinian basilicas, helped create a religious infrastructure that made Rome into a cynosure for pilgrims.[21]

The Built Environment

My emphasis on the contacts between different cults and the parallels between them has already suggested that it was not the new deities, numerous though they were, that dominated Roman religion in the Empire (cf. MacMullen 1981). Immigration, including soldiers posted from the provinces to Rome, of course meant new cults; but, unlike the old-established ones, with few exceptions, such as the Iseum Campense built by Gaius and re-built by Domitian, they did not call attention to themselves by means of conspicuously self-important new buildings. There were, for example, no Christian basilicas at Rome until Constantine's foundations in the first third of the fourth century.

If we look at the buildings that dominated the city-scape of Rome, what must strike us is the amount of restoration that went on (see pl. 24). After the ever more grandiose new constructions of the Late Republic, such as the Theatre of Pompey, the Forum of Caesar or the Crypta Balbi (built after 19 BC), it was Augustus who made it respectable to invest large sums in the restoration of older or fire-damaged buildings, such as the basilica of Aemilius. The habit of marking the completion of such projects by means of fresh entries in the calendars contributed greatly to the process of creating a genuinely grand set of temples and other public buildings, built in marble and with intricately-sculptured ornamentation picked out in gold-leaf.[22] New buildings, whether traditional temples or innovative forms, had to fit into this densely built-up city-scape.

The Empire did indeed produce a great diversity of new architectural forms.[23] Apart from the series of imperial forums (that of Augustus was dominated by the highly innovative ensemble that included the temple of Mars Ultor, honoured both as the avenger of Caesar's murder and as the agent of the restoration of the legionary standards lost by Crassus to the Parthians at Carrhae in 53 BC), we may think of Nero's *Domus aurea* (the Golden House),[24] Domitian's great Palatine palace or his circular temple of the Gens Flavia on the Quirinal, Hadrian's radical reconstruction of Agrippa's 'Pantheon' in the Campus Martius,[25] the three great Baths, of Trajan, Caracalla, and Diocletian, or Maxentius' innovative basilica in the Forum Romanum, completed by Constantine. As far as religious buildings are concerned, apart from the new temples required for the successive *divi*, such as Claudius, Vespasian and Titus, Nerva, Trajan, Hadrian, or Antoninus Pius and Faustina, it was mainly a matter of qualitative improvement rather than addition to the basic stock: deities already present in Rome were honoured by the construction of larger temples. Hadrian, for example, built the truly vast double-temple to Venus and Rome at the southern end of the Via Sacra, facing the Colosseum (consecrated AD 121) (see pl. 24).[26] This changed when the emperors began to patronize Christianity. The great fourth-century Christian churches, which were adaptations of a secular building-type, the basilica, were built in prominent locations so as to call attention to themselves, for example, that in the wealthy residential Lateran quarter, or the one on the established cult-area of the Vatican hill, with the tomb of St Peter, or S. Sebastiano out on the Via Appia, near the unfinished mausoleum of Maxentius (Curran 2000). There was no longer room on the Palatine to continue the practice, pursued from Augustus to the Severans, of building major cult-buildings as near as possible to the imperial palaces.[27]

Once a temple existed, and a god had been included in ritual practice and iconographic programmes, he or she could enter the political realm. The process that began in the Republic with Scipio Africanus' relation to Jupiter, Sulla's with Fortuna, and above all Pompey and Caesar's with Venus, that is, the selection of a personal protective deity (Sauron 1994), was continued with gusto by the emperors. Augustus dressed to recall Apollo; Nero had a colossal statue of the Sun built

in front of the *Domus aurea*; Commodus identified himself with Hercules; a whole series of emperors starting with Commodus, but mainly in the second half of the third century, saw themselves under the direct protection of Sol, often with the epithet Invictus, never-vanquished (Berrens 2004: 31–169); the Tetrarchs called themselves *Iovii* (the two Augusti) and *Herculii* (the two Caesares) in an

---

24. Model of the sacral centre of Rome in the Middle Principate.

Working from the bottom, you see the Flavian amphitheatre (Colosseum) and above it the largest and most splendid temple in the City, the double temple of Roma Aeterna and Venus Felix begun by Hadrian in AD 121.
Half-hidden behind the Colosseum is Domitian's fountain, the Meta Sudans, standing at the end of the street that leads up to the Arch of Titus.
Above that is the narrow triangle of the upper Via sacra (Sacred Way), bounded on the left by the *horrea*, grain-store, of Vespasian (which replaced a Republican commercial area or 'market') and the Atrium Vestae beyond it (with the Via nova running in a straight line behind them, to the foot of the Capitoline); and on the right by the Basilica nova, begun by Maxentius and completed by Constantine I, which likewise replaced commercial buildings [as with the Diocletianic monuments mentioned below, this building is incompatible with the date the model claims to depict]. The archaic Regia, and the temple of divus Julius Caesar (dedicated 29 BC) behind it, jutting out into the Via sacra, do not fit into the general building scheme. Here the Sacred Way forks. One branch goes to the left, through the Arch of Augustus (19 BC), passing the temple of Castor (i.e. Castor and Pollux) and the Basilica Iulia (ded. 46 BC, rebuilt AD 12) on the left, and the seven Diocletianic columns on the right, until it reaches the old temple of Saturn (rebuilt 42 BC). The other branch goes past the temple of Divus Antoninus and Diva Faustina and the Basilica of Aemilius Paullus (completed 34 BC, rebuilt 14 BC and AD 22), and the Curia (Senate House) beyond it. Opposite the Curia, at the far end of the 'Piazza del Foro', is the Augustan Rostra (speakers' dais), dominated by the five columns of the Tetrarchs' monument (see pl. 12); to its right is the Arch of Septimius Severus (AD 203). Immediately behind the Arch is the temple of Concordia (restored by Tiberius, AD 12), flanked by the temple of the *divi* Vespasian and Titus.
Beyond the Forum Romanum rises the Capitoline, with the temple of Iuppiter Optimus Maximus at the top left, on the lower summit, and the Arx to the right, on the higher summit, crowned by the ancient temple of Iuno Moneta (which must lie beneath the church of S. Maria in Aracoeli). Between them, directly above the temple of Concordia, is the Tabularium, where the Roman state-records were stored. In the distance beyond is the southern part of the Campus Martius, with the vast portico and theatre of Pompey (ded. 52 BC). From the model in the Museo della Civiltà Romana, EUR. See now, however, the digital images in Frischer et al. 2006.

ultimately futile attempt to bolster Diocletian's reform of the imperial system, by which the empire was divided into west and east, each half ruled by an Augustus and a Caesar. It has indeed been argued that it was the Tetrarchs' intensified identification with divine charisma that unleashed the Great Persecution of AD 303–4 (Schwarte 1994). As for Constantine I, he simply carried on the process: he chose Christ (Barceló 1999).

Monarchy and the Imperial Cult

That brings us to the question of the nature of the emperors' influence on the history of religion in the city of Rome. There are all sorts of aspects to this issue, which we should not be too quick to lump under the heading 'religious policy'. For just as there was no such thing as 'religion' at Rome, so there was no such thing as 'religious policy'. In the first place, the emperors were the grand benefactors of Rome. Without explicitly wanting to monopolize what me might call in the widest sense caritative gestures, they were very careful not to allow anyone to steal their thunder in the capital, especially in the eyes of the populace. When it came to building temples and putting on festivals and games, it was thus the emperors who took the lead.[28] Since religious images and rituals played a central role in communicating their contribution to the common welfare, their political aims and their claims to legitimacy, the imperial monopoly of minting coins and, after Tiberius, of the triumph necessarily had religious implications.

The same is true of the emperors' treatment of the priestly colleges and offices, which had played such a role in the Republican system of political management. On the one hand, the Augurs' right to interfere in political processes was drastically reduced (largely because one of the central areas of such interference, elections to magisterial office, were quickly abolished). That led to the colleges being considered all much of a muchness: as early as the funeral games in honour of Julius Caesar, the members of the different colleges were placed together as a single group of *sacerdotes*.[29] This reduced the distinctiveness of their several functions but at the same time made it necessary to think about the differences in status between them. Hitherto this had simply not been an issue, for in the Republican system the colleges had never had to act in concert. There gradually emerged a unified system of senatorial and equestrian priesthoods, the latter encompassing mainly the cults of the ancient Latin League, which now existed only in ritual contexts. Though unified, the system never became petrified: new

248

priesthoods were created; old ones, such as the Lupercals, might gain enormously in prestige; new efforts at centralization were made (cf. Rüpke 2005a: 1587–1600).

At the same time the colleges enjoyed an enormous increase in public status and self-esteem, thanks to their repeated appearance at prestigious public events, new collegial buildings, and the publication of their proceedings in the form of inscriptions – I have already mentioned this in relation to the Arval Brothers (p. 40), but it was also true of the *XVviri sacris faciundis* and the Fasti of the Augurs. Under the eye of the Princeps, who now became a member of all four main colleges, they formed an élite within the larger élite, devoted to maintaining traditional values, and conspicuously loyal to the emperor. The composition of the priestly colleges, which was recruited from the circle of senior magistrates, mainly consulars, is better understood as resulting from this co-operation than as a matter of conscious appointments by emperors.[30]

In this connection it should be pointed out that from the moment when, on the death of Lepidus, Augustus assumed the office of *pontifex maximus* in 12 BC, it became one of the core offices that constituted or defined the role of an emperor, or rather an Augustus. Nevertheless it did not bestow any extensive or clearly-defined rights, nor do emperors seem to have made much use of such competence as the office did have – on the contrary, they rather preferred to take a back-seat and refer matters to the Senate for decision, or to appeal to the decision of the lot.[31] With regard to public relations, and the impressions conveyed via coinage and incriptions, the emperors of course stressed this office rather than their membership of the other colleges. And, as I have said (p. 180), the *vicomagistri* evidently considered – no doubt correctly – that the re-organization of the subdivisions of Rome, the *vici*, and the related cult, were the result of Augustus' assumption of the role of *pontifex maximus*.

A whole variety of different imperial rituals, temple-foundations, games in celebration of victories, anniversaries of accession, and 'personal' anniversaries such as birthdays of even relatively minor members of the ruling house, were celebrated in each successive year. Quite apart from the celebrations themselves, they were noted down, at Rome and in the coloniae and muncipia, in official or public calendars, which had greatly increased in popularity with Julius Caesar's reform. Sometimes the dates of new celebrations were allowed to coincide with older ones, sometimes not; at any rate the choices of date, or their ritual character, always reveal an awareness of what was at stake in terms of the public message. When a new emperor came to the throne, and even more when a dynasty changed, such festivals might be discarded wholesale (e.g. Tacitus, *Hist.* 4.40.2).[32]

Here we come to the imperial cult proper. The process of what was perceived as Hellenization made it possible already in the Late Republic for successful politicians and commanders to be paid divine honours; contemporary intellectuals considered the divinization of persons of outstanding achievement a matter of course (see p. 60; 84).[33] What caused difficulties was the temptation to create a permanent institution out of such honours, whose effect was to elevate their recipient above the normal run of aristocratic competition. Formal divinization during the life-time of the honorand, which implied as much, was unacceptable to the aristocracy. The ritual consecration of the deceased and the resulting obligation of the community to worship him as a divinity were indeed innovations; but such resolutions were expected of the Senate from the moment it divinized Julius Caesar in 42 BC.

Resolutions to grant formal divinization usually called for the foundation of a temple to the *divus*, and the appointment of a *flamen*.[34] Except in the case of 'bad' emperors (at least in the eyes of the aristocracy), such as Tiberius, Caligula, Nero, Domitian, Commodus and Caracalla, four of whom were actually assassinated, and one of whom committed suicide, such honours were also normally decreed on the emperor's death, at least until Alexander Severus, the last of the Severan dynasty, in AD 238. In addition, a priestly college (*sodalitas*) was founded to honour the *divus*, or the dynasty as a whole. This institution began with the *sodales Augustales*, established with twenty-one places in AD 15 and manned, apart from those accorded to Augustus' relatives, by drawing lots. They were primarily responsible for maintaining the gentilician cult of the *gens Iulia* in Bovillae (p. 26); nothing is known about their possible involvement in imperial festivals and games at Rome. After AD 54 (the year Claudius died), the institution was renamed the *sodales Augustales Claudiales* and took over the gentilician cult of the *gens Claudia* in addition to that of the Iulii. The priesthood seems to have survived in this form into the early fourth century. With the change of dynasty after Nero, another priesthood, the *sodales Flaviales*, was founded on Vespasian's death in AD 79, and its name altered to *Flaviales Titiales* on Titus' unexpected death two years later. No *sodales* **Nervales* or **Traianales* are recorded, but an individual *sodalitas* was established in honour of Hadrian on his death in AD 138. All these colleges existed separately and in perpetuity.

On the death of Antoninus Pius in AD 161, a college of *sodales Antoniniani* was founded to continue his gentilician cult. Its name too was changed to *sodales Antoniniani Veriani* on the death of L. Verus in AD 169. We also find *sodales Marciani Antoniniani* in honour of the dead Marcus Aurelius (d. AD 180), but on the death of subsequent *divi* up to and including Alexander Severus in AD 238, the divine names were accumulated: we thus find references to *sodales Marciani Aureliani Commodiani Helviani Severiani* and so on (e.g. *CIL* VI 1365 = *ILS* 1160). As early as the death of Antoninus Pius, attempts were clearly made to fill most if not all of the places with the existing *sodales Hadrianales* (e.g. *CIL* XIV 3609 = *ILS* 1104), suggesting that there was palpable resistance to the unrestricted expansion of priestly offices, for of course the more of them there were, the lower the prestige attached to any. As for their actual responsibilities, there were after all other colleges doing much the same for the cult of the imperial family, for example, the Arval Brothers (p. 131).

Developments such as these had no effect upon the performance of worship independent of public cult. In particular the honours devised for the ruling emperor were related closely to the concrete local situation, and to the interests of the individual group that applied to be allowed to perform them.[35] Emperor worship was far from being, as the old stereotype had it, a mere religion of loyalty lacking all emotional input. Let us not forget that the fourth Book of Horace's Odes, written at Rome a quarter-century before Augustus' death, is an emotional evocation of this deity – and Horace was a sophisticated member of the educated class. Admittedly actual votives to Augustus are not known from Rome (though they are from elsewhere), but vows might be expressed in different language (cf. Clauss 1999: 110; 526). In addition, there developed a range of abstract ideas that were venerated as qualities of the ruling emperor by adding *Augusti*, of the emperor, such as *Aeternitas Augusti*, the emperor's eternity, *Providentia Augusti*, the emperor's wisdom, *Victoria Augusti/a*, the emperor's military prowess, or invincibility. The widespread use of such concepts, especially on coinage, tells us nothing about concrete events or experiences, but a good deal about the manner and style in which the Principate as an institution was ideally supposed to function.[36]

Further Developments

The medial presence of religion altered too. From the Late Republic, 'religion' became a subject of learning, an antiquarian good. None of the main figures here, Varro, Verrius Flaccus (who was made tutor to the princes of the imperial house late in the reign of Augustus) and Suetonius, wrote their extensive works as a religious specialist, though Suetonius was in fact a *flamen Volcanalis*. Yet they all, and especially Varro, wrote on Roman religion in such a way that educated readers could use them positively to bolster contemporary cult, or negatively, to criticize it. Such works were thus not at all in competition with, say, collections of oracles, didactic-esoteric poetry such as the second-century AD Orphic Rhapsodies, or actual cult-texts; they aimed to communicate and interpret Roman religion as a whole. This of course is quite different from what we mean by the expression 'religion of the book'; all the same, Varro and the others did in a sense turn religion into something one could read about.[37] If they were relatively even-handed, others were much more critical of particular manifestations of current religion: around AD 160 an otherwise unknown Greek philosopher Celsus wrote a devastating attack on Christianity (known to us only through the refutation by the theologian Origen a century later); and not long afterwards the satirist Lucian tried to expose the successful founder of a new oracle-cult in Asia Minor, Alexander of Abonuteichus, as a criminal charlatan. The general shift in attitude meant that, though religion as a project was not attacked, any individual form of it might come under fire and be forced to justify itself.[38]

Religion thus gradually became a type of knowledge that could be handled by antiquarians. It became aestheticized in statue, temple and iconography. As such, even non-Christian religion became acceptable to the new late-antique Christian élite. Like Macrobius in the sixth century, they might read Vergil and then write a commentary on him; like Paul the Deacon in the eighth, they might excerpt lexica, such as that of Festus; they might even, at any rate for a time, be prepared to maintain the temples of pagan deities.[39]

Religious knowledge could also be conveyed in other media. Religious motifs appeared on coins as family or personal achievements; but they might also, like Domitian's coin series on the Saecular games of AD 88, or Septimius Severus' of 202, provide detailed images of extremely complex rituals.[40] As I have already pointed out in relation to imperial festivals (p. 189), religion appeared in the calendars, and the commentaries that went along with them, as the residue of historically exemplary action (victories, temple foundations), broken up into discrete fragments, easily multiplied and as easily re-combined.

Religion, especially in the form of divination, might also however challenge legitimate power. Trials of seers, *haruspices* and astrologers were a common feature of the Principate. From the third century, and especially from the reign of Constantine I, more and more rescripts were issued to punish resort to such arts. The famously prohibited questions were: what is to happen to the ruling emperor? or even: when shall he die?, but a great many others were held to smell of treason. The practice of animal-sacrifice was declared a criminal offence. Being an adherent of certain religions or movements was declared incompatible with membership of Roman society. Such bans were a feature of the entire fifth century too.

The late-antique collections of various kinds of imperial edicts and rescripts give us some insight into the intentions and motives of the central authority, even though such rulings were normally just reactions to particular events or questions from governors. We can say nothing for certain about how such edicts were enforced, but the fact that they were often repeated after a short while suggests that they were far from being conspicuously successful.[41]

Our information about this imperial policy, which was applied unevenly, in fits and starts, and usually only in particular areas, derives mainly from Book 9 of the Theodosian Code, where we find a series of edicts *De maleficis et mathematicis et ceteris similibus*, On malign magicians, diviners, and similar sorts of people. The first is an edict of 1 February AD 319, issued at Rome by Constantine I, part of which runs as follows:

> No diviner (*haruspex*) is to approach the door of any person, not even for some purpose unrelated to divination; friendship with such persons, even if it be of long standing, is to be repudiated. (The penalty for offending against this law), in the case of the *haruspex* who goes to another's house, is to be burned alive; in the case of any person who asks him to come to his house, or offers him money or other reward, confiscation of his property and exile to an island. For those who wish to follow their superstition may attend the appropriate public rituals.
>
> Cod. Theod. 9.16.1

At this period, as another similar edict of 15 May the same year likewise makes clear (9.16.2), the public altars and temples were open for business as usual; and a distinction was still made between malign and beneficent magic: magical healing was expressly permitted (9.16.3, issued at Aquileia, AD 321). But by AD 357 the tone has become more aggressive, as this excerpt shows:

> No one is to consult a diviner (*haruspex*) or an astrologer (*mathematicus*) or a fortune-teller (*hariolus*). The wicked pronouncements of augurs and prophets must be silenced. The astrologers (*chaldaei*), magicians (*magi*) and the rest, whom ordinary people refer to as 'those who do harm' (*malefici*) because of the innumerable crimes they commit, are

forbidden to undertake any such actions. Let us have no more of this insatiable desire to know the future (*sileat omnibus perpetuo divinandi curiositas*)! For whoever refuses submission to this edict shall suffer capital punishment, laid low by the avenging sword.

Cod. Theod. 9.16.4, given at Milan, 25 January.

Those belonging to the imperial court who nevertheless practised divination were to be tortured, even if they belonged to the higher social ranks (9.16.6). The edict of 9 September 364 by Valentinian I and Valens concerning nocturnal sacrifices also relates to divination and magic:

> It is henceforth forbidden to attempt during the time of darkness to perform incantations or magical rites or necromantic sacrifices. We decree in perpetuity that anyone discovered and found guilty of such charges shall be punished with appropriate severity.
>
> *Cod. Theod.* 9.16.7 (extract)

After a temporary reduction in the sanctions against *haruspices* (*Cod. Theod.* 9.16.9), astrologers were required in 393 to burn their own books and return to the catholic faith under the supervision of their bishop; if they refused, they were to be exiled (9.16.12).

Such edicts reveal how particular religious options were officially understood as being mutually exclusive, even though that is not at all how the matter was understood among ordinary Jews and Christians, who made enthusiastic use of astrology, and magic.[42] The authorities however were determined to define a caesura between acceptable and inacceptable practice. Such normative efforts did not stem primarily from a meddling desire to distinguish between 'pagans' and 'Christians'. Their real driving force was the need to protect the emperors' claim to have a monopoly of the right to establish relations with the divine realm (Fögen 1993).

Models

The value of simple models is that they help to control the plethora of brute facts and limit the sheer variety of perceptible change. The point is not of course to write *the* history of whatever it is we are concerned with, but *different* ones. It is precisely the massive simplification of reality by means of models that reminds us that 'history' is *always* a matter of perspective, that it can *always* be written differently depending on one's point of view. The use of models also reminds us that such points of view must be consciously chosen and thought through.

254

Without explicitly making the point, I have in this book repeatedly used one particular model in tracing the main lines of the history of religion during the Republic. The model states that religious developments are to be understood as functions of changes in the composition of, and pressures upon, the political élite of a given society. As will by now be clear, we can apply the same model to the Empire. The work of Peter Brown in particular has shown that it can also be applied in the period of transition to the Late Roman period, to Late Antiquity.[43]

From this point of view, the crucial aspect of the history of religion in the Principate is the change in the nature of the system of aristocratic competition, and the consequent shifts in conceptions of legitimate power and appropriate arenas or audiences. The *cursus* through the traditional magistracies ceased to be the primary locus of competition within the élite. Public competition itself ceased to be the privileged means of establishing legitimate domination. The power of the emperor and the patrimonial bureaucracy increasingly elevated them above the other members of the élite, permanently and not, as was the case with Republican magistracies, merely for a specific, limited period. One strategy of escape from this now meaningless competition with the imperial monopoly of the means to confer 'benefits' was to retire to one's villa in the country. Yet withdrawal of this kind removed both the financial and the personal/social basis of civic religious institutions. In the city of Rome itself, however, as in other great cities, such as Antioch, the old élites carried on, maintaining their position through changing dynasties by establishing patronage networks all over the empire, insisting on their cultural superiority, and showing themselves sensitive to public needs.

In this situation, as far as the emperors were concerned, elevated as they were above aristocratic competition, the divine became an increasingly important means of legitimating imperial power: divine blessing became a dominant feature of imperial rhetoric. In the long run, however, this meant that individuals from outside the traditional élites might also be in a position to claim special access to the deity and so enjoy a divine mission. If necessary they would prove it by their asocial behaviour, for example in Egypt by *anachoresis*, retreat into the desert.

Under these circumstances, the issue of the correct god became increasingly crucial. In deciding whether claims to the throne were legitimate or illegitimate, choosing the right god came to be of decisive importance. Conversely, the idea of demons supplied a means of rejecting alternative claims. The emperor now claimed the monopoly of the right to know, and used this claim as a means of suppressing the opposition. Divine legitimation came to be a matter not simply of power but of the knowledge that gives power. Here Christian monotheism fitted snugly with Roman monarchy: Christianity provided a theory of divine legitimation and an appropriate politico-religious apparatus. The emperor became the Lord High theologian.

From the point of view of this first model, the obsessive accumulation of priestly offices by Roman aristocrats, beginning in the late third century and evident throughout the fourth, is to be understood less as the last gasp of paganism than as a strategy for recovering the political and social authority that group had lost with the removal of the centre of the Empire first to imperial palaces in the provinces and then to Constantinople. This authority had once unquestionably qualified men for priestly office; in the fourth century, they sought to turn things the other way round, as it were, and recover the authority by appealing to their accumulation of religious offices. Such a twist should be understood as a reaction to the new, distinctively religious, rules that now applied to the acquisition and maintenance of power, namely competition over the possession of the god(s) that would prove triumphant in the legitimation-stakes.

Different models provide alternative ways of looking. If we were to apply a sociological one, the religious history of the Principate could be seen as a process of emergent institutional differentiation, whereby a realm of social action, 'religion', which hitherto, because embedded, had not existed as such, gradually established its autonomy vis-à-vis other areas of social action, in particular the political. From this perspective, the process of differentiation would have been led by those cults whose significance was not exhausted by their contribution to the political community: the *sacerdotes* of the cults of Mithras, of Isis, of Jupiter Dolichenus, of Christianity too, were not *eo ipso* magistrates or officials; if they happened to hold office, that had nothing, or very little, to do with their activity as religious specialists. Moreover, the shrines of these cults were not the places where official political discussion took place or where decisions were taken. Then again, there is some scattered evidence of an increase in the specifically religious profile even of the traditional *sacerdotes publici*: for example, the *sanctitas* of the Vestals became more prominent; and the *Epulones* seem as a college to have honoured Cybele, the Mater Magna, as well as the Capitoline triad, on a pair of lead-pipes bringing water from the upper Anio into the city of Rome.[44] On this model, the Roman aristocracy appears as one of the agencies attempting to block or hinder the emergence of religion as an autonomous or quasi-autonomous institution. Even so, they could hardly evade the broader drift towards

256

differentiation. We are thus faced with a certain paradoxicality: on the one hand, the accumulation of oddly heterogeneous religious roles functioned as a means of heading off or refusing the process of differentiation; yet on the other, the act of collection itself underwrote the autonomy of religious action and the domain of religion.

The history of religion in antiquity offers plenty of scope for this sort of model-building. It was precisely during the Principate that the urban society of the Empire attained a degree of complexity not seen again in Europe until the Early-Modern period. That is what makes the models, conclusions, hypotheses and questions that arise out of an engagement with the ancient world so interesting for the present day. At the same time, these contemporary implications are bound also to call attention to the otherness of ancient society: if we want to use the ancient world in order to draw lessons for today, we must also accept that otherness. The inverse is also true: even if we are interested in the otherness of antiquity, in its exoticism, we cannot avoid seeing its contemporary relevance. We would do well not to relinquish our grasp of either term of the paradox.

NOTES

1 The identification of Venus with the Greek goddess is simply taken for granted.
2 Horace, *Odes* 1.19; cf. 1.33; 3.19.28.
3 On the problems involved in trying to apply systems-theory and Parsonian action-theory to the history of ancient religions, see Rüpke 2001c: 14–17; cf. Schluchter 1998.
4 Cf. Suetonius, *Aug.* 35.3; Cassius Dio 54.30.1.
5 On the dispute of AD 384 see Klein 1972; Wytzes 1977.
6 Participation in public cult: Beard, North, Price 1998: 1, 49–51; Decius' edict, ibid. 239; cf. Rives 1999. The deliberate, systematic character of the Decian persecution has however been called into question by Selinger 2002.
7 On atheism in antiquity, see Winiarczyk 1984, 1990, 1992; Obbink 1989; Bremmer 2006.
8 Gaius, *Inst.* 2. 3–9; Festus p. 348, 22–350, 12 Lindsay, with the correction *auspicia* for †*mysticiae* (Linderski 1986: 2186 n. 150); cf. Watson 1971: 58–60.
9 *Sacrum aedificium, consecratum deo*, 'a building is *sacer* if it has been consecrated to a god': Festus p. 348. 34f. L.
10 Cf. Krämer 1965; Cornell 1975; Miles 1995: 137–78.
11 See Macrobius, *Sat.* 1.16.18 (from Varro); on *superstitio*: Festus p. 366.2–5 L; with Beard, North, Price 1998: 1. 212–27; Martin 2004: 125–39.
12 For the concepts of 'diffuse' versus 'organized' religion, see Kehrer 1982. This corresponds to the distinction between 'common' and 'institutional' religion usual in the English-speaking sociology of religion, cf. Towler 1974: 128–62.
13 In Greece: Calame 1977/2001; Lonsdale 1993; for Rome, cf. Bremmer 1990; Ginestet 1991.
14 Harris 1989: 312 is much more pessimistic; but formal schooling was essential neither to literacy nor to religious knowledge: Horsfall 1991.
15 Statius, *Silvae* 5.3; cf. Cancik 1973.
16 Stressed by Bendlin 2000a: 130. On demographic data and its implications: Hopkins 1983: 31–200; Scheidel 2001; cf. Sullivan 1983.

17 Schott 1990; cf. Lévi-Strauss 1966: 233f. = 1962: 309f.
18 On the consequences of 'shame culture' see e.g. Mustakallio 1994: 81; cf. Bendlin 2001c. The contrast between so-called 'shame' and 'guilt' cultures is now understood to have been much exaggerated by e.g. Dodds 1951. On the development of individuality, see still Misch 1950.
19 See e.g. Graf 1991; Bernabé and Jiménez 2001.
20 Livy, 26.19.5; Aulus Gellius, *Noctes atticae* 6.1.6.
21 Propertius, 2.28b.45 f. Barber, cf. Champeaux 1989.
22 Bendlin emphasizes this for Rome in 2001b: 201; cf. Beard, North, Price 1998: 1, 245f., rightly stressing the large numbers of immigrants into Rome during the Principate (who may even have constituted the majority of the population), but rather underplaying immigration during the Republic (e.g. p. 75).
23 Cf. Misch 1950: 2, 539–667; Bendlin 2001c; Görgemanns 2003; Berschin 2003.
24 Hölkeskamp 2000; cf. Rüpke 1990: 209f.
25 Cf. Gladigow 1998; Bendlin 2000c; 2001a.
26 See Radke 1979; 1987 (though I have reservations about his methodological presuppositions); more generally, Gladigow 1979. The best example is Aius Locutius (Livy 5.32.6f.; 5.50.5).
27 Usener 1896/2000; see too Rose 1913.
28 Brenk 1986; more briefly: J. Z. Smith 1978. Judaism and Christianity alike were committed to belief in these intermediate spirits.
29 Beard, North, Price 1998: 1, 307f. are too cautious here. A cult of Zeus at Alexandria that required exclusive adherence offers an exception to the general rule that multiple membership was normal, cf. Kloppenborg 1996.
30 For lists, cf. the contributions to AA.VV. 1998. Beard 1991: 47f. suggests that recording one's name in a votive context was a means of claiming membership in a notional community of the pious.
31 Cf. Rüpke 1997a: 4ff., with particular reference to the history of religion in antiquity.
32 Brief accounts by Polignac 1995a; Scheid 1999; some criticisms of the term in Bendlin 2000a; for Greece: Cole 1995.
33 I take this to be the main message of Beard, North, Price 1998.
34 I am alluding here to Beard, North, Price's term 'elective cults' (1998: 1, 287ff.).
35 On the concept of local religion, see Kippenberg 1995.
36 Rüpke, forthcoming; on the calendar: Rüpke 1995a, 444f.
37 *Publica sacra, quae publico sumptu pro populo fiunt, quaeque pro montibus, pagis, curis, sacellis: at privata, quae pro singulis hominibus, familiis, gentibus fiunt,* 'The public cults are those which are celebrated at public expense, on behalf of the (Roman) people, and those that are celebrated in honour of the Septimontium, the *pagi* (outlying villages), *curiae* (the 30 Romulan "wards") and the "shrines" (i.e. the 27 [some claim 24] shrines of the Argei/Argea within the Servian walls). Private cults on the other hand are those that are celebrated on behalf of individuals, families and the *gentes* (the "clans" that shared the same *nomen*)': Festus p. 284, 18–21 L. The same distinction in Dionysius of Halicarnassus, *Ant. Rom.* 2.65.2.
38 20,000 ha represents 200 km^2, around 0.33% of agricultural land in Roman Italy (accepting the estimate of 20 million *iugera*).
39 Bang 2002: 12–17, who points out however that in a largely agricultural

system a very considerable proportion of the notional GDP (over 56%) has to be retained, i.e. is not available for redistribution through the tax/rent system. He reckons there was a total disposable surplus of only 6 billion HS. The value of a *sestertius* (HS) was roughly the amount of money a standard family needed to cover its daily expenses.

40 Cf. Duncan-Jones 1994: 45, arriving at an estimate of 900 million HS. On Bang's estimate, this means that 15% of the entire disposable surplus was allocated through the centre, an extremely high proportion (2002: 18f.).

41 Cicero, *Ad fam.* 7.1.2f., *Pis.* 65; *De off.* 2.57; cf. the descriptions by Cassius Dio, 39.38.1–3; Pliny, *Historia Naturalis* 8.20f., 53; Plutarch, *Pomp.* 52.54f.

42 Septimontium: Varro, *De lingua latina* 6.24; Festus p. 458, 1–5 L. and 474, 36–476, 5 L. (from Antistius Labeo); *curiae*: Festus p. 180, 32–182, 4 L; also Varro, *De lingua latina* 5. 83, cf. 5. 45ff. (Argei); *vici*: Suetonius, *Aug.* 30, 1; cf. Ovid, *Fast.*5. 145f.

43 On the *gentes*, see Smith 2006: 44–50.

44 Mouritsen 1997: 77; more subtly, Yakobson 1999.

45 This is intended to head off any interpretation (e.g. Connor 1987, on Athenian religion) that invokes the notion of 'manipulation'.

46 The material is collected in De Marchi 1903, 41–74.

47 On the Pinarii and Potiti see Livy 1.7.12–14; Dion. Hal., *Ant. Rom.* 1.40.3–5; Servius, *Aen.* 8. 269; 270. For the transfer of the cult to the *sacra publica*, see Livy 9.29.9–11; Servius, *Aen.* 8. 179.

48 Tacitus, *Ann.* 1.54.1; 3.64.3; Cassius Dio 56.46.1; on the altar to Veiovis (*ILS* 2988), cf. Weinstock 1971: 8–12. Fragments of their Acta (e.g. *CIL* VI 1984) have been discovered at Bovillae, which was evidently their official seat.

49 Livy, 10.47 (Aesculapius); 29.10f. (Cybele); cf. the brief account of Beard, North, Price 1998: 1, 69f.; 96–8.

50 Pietilä-Castrén 1967; Aberson 1994. On the resulting temple-landscape, cf. Ziolkowski 1992; and on the religious consequences, Rüpke 1990: 258ff.

51 Orlin 1997: 68–71. The basilica was built on the site of the house of Scipio Africanus at the western entrance of the Forum Romanum; it was in turn demolished to make way for the Basilica Iulia (see pl. 24).

52 For the details, see Orlin 1997: 139–89.

53 E.g. Livy 23.30.13; 31.9; 34.53.6; 35.9.6. Only one of the *IIviri* was normally involved in the dedication.

54 Livy 9.46.6f. (tr. B.O. Foster, adapted). Georg Wissowa denied the historicity of this SC, claiming that it applied only to new cults, but it is now generally accepted as authentic.

55 E.g. Livy 2.42.5; 29.11.13; cf. 40.34.5.

56 One must however not exaggerate its importance: it has been reckoned that, judging by their names, only 15 (4%) of all the consuls elected during the period 249 BC–50 BC were adopted: Hopkins and Burton 1983: 49. They conclude: 'The incidence of adoption was thus quite low.'

57 E.g. in the *Testamentum P. Dasumii Tusci* (*CIL* VI 10229 = *FIRA*[2] 3: 132–42 no.48, AD 108) lines 111–15, or the *Testamentum civis Lingonis* (*CIL* XIII 5708 = *ILS* 8379 = *FIRA*[2] 3: 142–44 no.49 = Le Bohec 2003: 353–6) I. 10–15, on which see Egelhaaf-Gaiser 2001: 226ff.

58 Cf. p. 26 n.47 above; also Palmer 1965: 320; Rüpke 1995a: 247–9 with additional literature.

59 Cf. MacBain 1982. At the same time this provided a means of deflecting pos-

sible internal problems of a religious order. An example might be the maintenance of the cult of Venus Erucina not in Rome but in Sicily (Wiseman 2000:
291).

60 Livy 39.8–19, with North 1979; Gruen 1990: 34–78; and the excellent
account of Pailler 1988.

61 This is made clear not only by the allusions in Latin comedy (Pailler 1988:
229ff.) but also by the representations of Roman or central-Italian Dionysiac
worship (mainly drawings incised on the backs of mirrors, and vase-paintings
showing Dionysiac scenes in stage performance), collected by Wiseman 2000.

62 Cf. Beard, North, Price 1998: 1, 96; Schultz 2006: 82–93. On the role of
women in Greek religion, cf. Kron 1996.

63 *CIL* I². 581 = I². 4.1 p. 907 = *ILS* 18 = *ILLRP* 511, tr. Lewis and Reinhold
1, 472f. (adapted). A photo of the bronze tablet, from Tiriolo in Calabria (*ager
Teuranus*) but now in Vienna, can be found in Pailler 1988, pl. II. Properly
speaking, the tablet contains the text of a letter from the consuls to the
Teuranians summarizing the Senate's decisions, as is commonly the case with
the texts we refer to as 'decrees of the Senate' (*senatus consulta*).

64 de Cazenove 2000 argues that the Senate imposed its decree only in those
areas of Italy where it had legal authority; the pre-amble however makes it
clear that the letter was addressed to all the allied cities. Two sites, at Musarna
nr. Viterbo, and Poggio Moscini nr. Bolsena have been claimed as examples
of destruction carried out as a result of the Senate's decree; the case for the
latter is examined again by Jolivet and Marchand 2003.

65 Astrologers: Cramer 1954: 233; Isis: Malaise 1972: 357–84; Mora 1990: 2:
72–87; Takács 1995: 56–70; Jews: Boterman 1996; cf. Egelhaaf-Gaiser 2000:
109–15.

66 Linderski 1968; Fellmeth 1987; Perry 2006; for the Principate, Cotter 1996
(not very reliable). More recently however it has been emphasized that small,
especially religious, associations were largely exempt from these restrictions:
de Ligt 2000.

67 The best discussion is Rives 1995.

68 Lane Fox 1986: 450ff.; see also Rives 1999. Beard, North, Price 1998: 1,
238–44 do not come down very clearly on either side of the fence.

69 Doren 1956; Blomart 1997; Glinister 2000: 61–4; on the Italian dimension
of the term *evocare deos*, cf. Palmer 1974; Rüpke 1990: 103–64.

70 Cf. Keresztes 1970; Beard, North, Price 1998: 1, 241; on p. 293f. they argue
that free access to citizenship brought about sharper control of religion.

71 See the prefatory remarks of H. Cancik and J. Rüpke in Belayche 2001: v–vii.

72 The best text of the five tablets found in 1870/1 and 1925, and containing
parts of §§LXI–CXXXIV, is to be found in *CIL* II²/5.1022 (with photos); a
slightly different text, with (a rather stilted) English translation and commentary in Crawford 1996: 1, 393–454 no.25; for the new tablet, found in
1990, which contains §§XIII–XIX, on the duties of magistrates, see Caballos
Rufino 2006.

73 §§64 and 70 tr. by Lewis and Reinhold 1, 421f. (adapted).

74 Bendlin 1997: 54 ff. takes this thesis further in the context of 'religious communication'; cf. already Derks 1995; 1998: 215–39.

75 Rüpke 1990: 165ff.; 250–8; Beard, North, Price 1998: 1, 324–8.

76 Cancik and Rüpke 1997; Spickermann 2001. For a sketch of a programme of
research on the topic, see Rüpke 2006c.

2 FROM THE SHE-WOLF TO CAESAR

1 On Polybius' account of Roman religion, see van Hooff 1977; Vaahtera 2000.
2 There is no full study, but note Petersmann 1973; Martin 1988; Phillips 1997.
3 See p. 31 n. 60 above; also Cancik-Lindemaier 1996.
4 Unfortunately most studies, instead of discussing the representation of religion in Cicero's work, prefer to speculate about his own personal religious feelings, e.g. Goar 1972; but cf. Leonhardt 1999.
5 The two commentaries by Pease (1920–3, 1955–8) are fundamental, if hard going. On *De natura deorum*, see Harris 1961; Brisson 2004: 41–55; on *De divinatione*, see Linderski 1982 [1983]; Beard 1986; Schofield 1986.
6 On the background, see Rawson 1975: 60–145; Mitchell 1991: 98–208. Lenaghan 1969 is a commentary on *Har. resp.*; on Cicero as a commentator on religion: Cancik 1995.
7 See the excellent account by Feeney 1998, who shows how to exploit these texts not merely as 'sources' but as elements of a discourse.
8 For the rise of epigraphic culture in the first century BC, rather than with the Augustan period, as is usually thought, see Solin 1999: 391–7.
9 Scheid 1998a; cf. 1990a; 1990b; Broise and Scheid 1987.
10 The standard text is Devoto 1962; also Morandi 1982: 75–114 no. 22; in English Poultney 1959. See further Borgeaud 1982.
11 The texts are re-printed in Pighi 1941, though there are some more recent fragments. Specifically on the Augustan games, see Schnegg-Köhler 2002.
12 See in general Luce 1977; on Livy and religion, Stübler 1941; Levene 1993; Liebeschuetz 1979: 59–62; Davies 2004: 21–142.
13 This of course also applies to the highly circumstantial narrative of Livy's contemporary, the Greek historian Dionysius of Harlicarnassos, on whom see Gabba 1991; and specifically on religion, Mora 1995a.
14 Cf. Kolb 1995: 41–8; Carandini 1997 disagrees (cf. too Carandini and Capelli 2000).
15 The northen limits of La Tène (Celtic) culture in Germany corrrespond roughly to the northern boundary of the Mittelgebirge (Sauerland and the Harz).
16 Cornell 1995: 1–30 is much less sceptical of the possibility of writing the history of early Rome.
17 This is one of the main themes of the Republican chapters of Beard, North, Price 1998.
18 See in general Moscati 1997; and, on the later period, Pallottino 1991.
19 The original objects, found by the pioneer archaeologist of the Forum, Giacomo Boni, in the years after 1898, are kept in the Antiquario del Foro (S. Francesca Romana), now the offices of the Soprintendenza Archaeologica. On Boni's achievement, see Ross Holloway 1994: 21–32.
20 Bietti Sestieri 1992; summaries in Ross Holloway 1994, 103–13; Cornell 1995: 51–3.
21 On the development of Roman family-structure, see Bettini 1991; also Linke 1995, 1998 (who makes no reference to the archaeological material).
22 Cornell 1995: 81–92; in greater detail: Meyer 1983.
23 Cornell 1995: 169–72; cf. the essays in Heurgon 1981.

24 Examples can be viewed in the basement area of the now re-opened Museo Palatino, in the former monastery of the Visitation overlooking the Circus Maximus.

25 Kolb 1981; Coarelli 1983a: 1–19.

26 *CIL* I². 1 = *ILLRP* 3, cf. Wachter 1987: 66–9; Hartmann 2005: 122–30 with fig.92; 192–7, dating to VII–VIª. Illustrated in Turcan 1988: 2, 16 no. 1 with pl. 1; there is a painted plaster-cast of the *cippus*, and model of the site, in the epigraphic section of the Museo Nazionale delle Terme. The inscription lays a curse ('sacros esed') on any violator of the site. On the Volcanal, see briefly *LTUR* 5: 209–11 (F. Coarelli).

27 Brown 1974–5; Coarelli 1983a: 56–79; *LTUR* 4: 189–92 (R. T. Scott).

28 See Cornell 1995: 162 f.; for the literary sources see Coarelli 1983a: 161–8.

29 Cf. Cristofani 1987; Ross Holloway 1994: 68–80; Bietti Sestieri 1992: 243; Cornell 1995: 147f.; Smith 1996a: 185ff.; 1996b; Forsythe 2005: 125–46.

30 Prayon 1988; cf. Cornell 1995: 96, Stamper 2005: 6–33

31 Cf. Momigliano 1967; cf. Richard 1978; Martin 1990: 227ff.; and the essays in Raaflaub 1986.

32 On the roles played by the Roman *gentes* in land-holding, warfare and the patriciate, see Smith 2006, who also stresses their role in regulating access to religious office.

33 Hölkeskamp 1987: 52 n. 3 denies that it was a true law. The main source is Livy 10.6–8.

34 At least in the long run: see Rilinger 1976: 100–2; compare Beard, North, Price 1998: 1, 68 (where they seem to be arguing two contradictory positions).

35 Rules regarding family representation: North 1990a; popular election of the *pontifex maximus*: Cicero, *De leg. agrar.* 2.16–18; for the upset at the first election: Livy 25.5.2–4. For the date and procedure: Taylor 1942; Draper 1988: 210–14.

36 Details in Rüpke 2006d; cf. Beard 2007.

37 For the details of the practice, see de Libero 1992; on the context: Burckhardt 1988.

38 See Rawson 1991; Scheid 1993; Beard, North, Price 198: 1, 108–13, 135–8.

39 Jocelyn 1976 is fundamental; cf. Scheid 1997; Beard, North, Price 1998: 1, 134; 138f.

40 For the German case, see Junginger 1999: 165ff. Altheim 1930 represents a position diametrically opposed to Wissowa's; cf. Norden 1995 [1939] with Rüpke 1993a.

41 See Livy 7.2.1–3; Valerius Maximus, *Mem.* 2.4.4; cf. Schmidt 1989; Bernstein 1998: 119–29; Goldberg 1998. Wiseman 2000 draws on archaeology to place the development in a wider context.

42 On the process of Hellenization in general, cf. Ferrary 1988; Gruen 1984, 1990, 1992.

43 Cf. Kuttner 2004; on Greek conventions affecting the design of altars, see Dräger 1994: 176f.

44 The Greek text of the fragments of Euhemerus' *Sacred Record* can be found in Winiarczyk 1991 = *FGrH* 63; on his views, and the way Ennius enthusiastically picked them up in relation to Scipio Africanus, cf. Bosworth 1999: 10. Thirteen fragments of Ennius' translation, virtually all from Lactantius, *Inst. div.* Bk. 1, can be found in the edition of J. Vahlen (1928 2nd edn) pp. 223–9, and an English trans. in Warmington 1935: 414–31; cf. Winiarczyk 1994.

45 Ennius' translation was widely read in the late Republic (Bosworth 1999: 11f.), though by then many educated people considered Euhemerus an atheist: Cicero, *De nat. deor.* 1.119; this had also been Callimachus' reaction (*Iamb.* frag. 191 Pfeiffer). The sophist Prodicus (*c.* 465–395 BC) had already argued that it was the human-beings who invented agriculture that were deified as Demeter and Dionysus (Bremmer 2006: 14f.). A number of other hostile judgements on Euhemerus are collected in *FGrH* 63 T 4 = Winiarczyck 1991 T 14–23.

46 See Jocelyn 1976; Rawson 1985; Leonhardt 1999.

47 Cf. Cicero, *Brutus* 81; he is Fabius no. 128 in *RE* 6.2 (1909) 1842–4.

48 Cf. Jocelyn 1980, 1982; critical view by Lehmann 1997. See also in brief Fantham 1996: 45f.

49 I here go against the *communis opinio* deriving from Cichorius 1922: 197–200.

50 On the eve of his march on Rome against the Marians in 84 BC, Sulla claimed to have seen a dream-vision of Ma-Enyo-Bellona, the high goddess of Comana in Cappadocia, who pressed a thunderbolt into his hand and bade him punish his enemies (Plutarch, *Sulla* 9.4; cf. Strabo 12.2.3, 535C). He thus neatly fused references to the (legitimate) power of the highest Roman political god, the blood-soaked imagery of the *bellonarii*, the ecstatic self-lacerating followers of Ma, and his exploits in Asia Minor against Mithridates.

51 Weinstock 1971 gives a full account of the pre-history of Caesar's deification (to be read with North 1975); it remains disputed whether Caesar was worshipped during his life-time as a state god, and if so in what sense: see Beard, North Price, 1998: 1, 140–9. Cf. also Wallace-Hadrill 1993 on the assimilation of Greek practices of veneration in the Republic.

3 GODS AND MEN

1 Good introductions: Hossenfelder 1995; Sharples 1996; in Rome: Erler et al. 1994.

2 Cf. Lucretius, *Nat. rer.* 3.18–24; 5.146–55. The sources for the Epicurean accounts of divinity are collected and discussed by Long and Sedley 1987: 1, 143–54; 2, 143–54.

3 On the problems connected with Epicurean views of our apprehension of the gods, see Mansfeld 1999: 472–4; for other positions, see 455–60; 469–72.

4 The Stoics too opposed irrational fear of the gods: Mansfeld 1999: 465.

5 Sources: Long and Sedley 1987: 1, 274ff.; 2, 271–7; also Algra 2003, and Gerson 1990: 142–74, who discusses the Academic criticisms.

6 The *Hymn* is preserved in Stobaeus, *Ecl.* 1.25.3–27.4 = Long and Sedley 1987: 1, 326f.; 2: 326f.; extensive commentary by Thom 2005 (translation at p. 40f.).

7 Cf. Gladigow 1988: 26f., 35f.; on theology in this sense, see Gladigow 1986.

8 Judging from Cicero's complaints, whose aim it was to make Greek philosophy at home in Rome (e.g. *De nat. deor.* 1. 7; *Tusc.* 1.3.6), the same lack of interest was widespread in the upper class too.

9 Fink 1978; Gladigow 1980; more generally, Toynbee 1971.

10 Cf. Bremmer 1994; 2002 ; Sourvinou-Inwood 1995.

11 Varro, *LL* 7.7f. with Linderski 1986: 2260–71.

12 This temple is identifed reasonably securely as the circular Temple B in the Largo di Torre Argentino, dedicated in the Campus Martius by Q. Lutatius Catulus after the battle of Vercellae in 101 BC (Plutarch, *Marius* 26.2). The dimensions given are inferences from the remains of the acrolith cult-statue (Martin 1987: 103-11 with pls.13-14), now in the Palazzo dei Conservatori, and the surviving fragments of the 18 original tufa columns; the building was twice altered, in the Late Republic and under Domitian; cf. Sauron 1994: 135-7 with pl. IX.1; *LTUR* 2: 269f. (P. Gros).

13 Gordon 1979: 11-16; Gladigow 1994; on materials used in the Republic, see Martin 1987; in the Empire: Vermeule 1987; re-use of Roman statues in the Medieval period: Wolf 1990.

14 Seneca, *De superst.* frag. 36 Haase = Augustine, *Civ. Dei* 6. 10 (translated in Beard, North, Price 1998: 2. 234f.).

15 Thus, an Aemilius Paullus (not the famous one) is said to have dedicated a statue of Athena by Pheidias in Catulus' temple of *Fortuna huiusce diei* (Pliny, *HN* 34.54).

16 Cult-statues and votive-statues are not inherently or fundamentally different, but they have different statuses in particular ritual contexts (for Greece, see Scheer 2000, 4-34, 143ff.). We need to take into account the identity of the god who 'owned' the temple. Scheer rightly argues that in Greece there was no ritual that imparted 'life' to a statue in the Classical period (111-14).

17 On Hellas in nineteenth-century Germany, see above all Marchand 1996; on Rome, Struck 2001; the Nazis and Rome: Losemann 1999. With particular reference to religion: Rüpke 2001d: 910; Scheid 1987; Durand and Scheid 1994.

18 On the typical Roman podium-temple, see Stambaugh 1978; Ziolkowski 1992; Stamper 2005. As a glance at pl. 24 will show, some especially prestigious temples at Rome, such as those of Capitoline Jupiter, Castor (as rebuilt by Tiberius), and of Venus and Rome, were built in the Greek style, i.e. fully peripteral.

19 Correctly: Cicero, *2 Verr.* 1.129; *pro Milone* 19; *Res gestae* §20; Suet. *Caes.* 10.1; Cassius Dio 37.8.2; *AE* 1974: 600 = 1980: 854; *AE* 1980: 858; *aedes Castorum*: Pliny, *HN* 10.121; *aedes Castoris et Pollucis*: Suet. *Tib.* 20; *CIL* VI 40339 = *AE* 1992: 159; *AE* 1901: 188; 1917/18: 126. The official weights and measures were kept in the temple, and epigraphic allusions to them always refer to the *(aedes) Castoris*: e.g. *CIL* V 8119.4a-h = *ILS* 8636; *AE* 1982: 818a-c.

20 Cf. Hölkeskamp 1987: 238-40. Winkler 1995 is a fine account of *Salus* (Physical and Moral Integrity).

21 Fabius Pictor, *Iur.* 6 Bremer = Serv. auct., *Georg.* 1. 21 (reading *redarator* [Salmasius] for the ms *reparator*; I retain the ms *promitor*); cf. Le Bonniec 1958: 67-77; Spaeth 1966: 35f. (faulty translation).

22 In some cases the meaning is uncertain because the words are unknown elsewhere. In order to understand the sequence, it is important to have a grasp of Roman agricultural practice, and in particular the role of the normal plough, the *ard*, which did not have a share-board, and so did not create ridges and furrows but simply disturbed the top-soil and the weeds. Ridges were only needed on heavy soils. The discussion by Spurr 1986: 23-88 is fundamental.

23 Wissowa's 'the entire cycle of agricultural work' (1912: 25) is quite mistaken. Oddly enough, Varro's six main operations or phases (*RR* 1.37.4),

which relate closely to Fabius Pictor's list, also omit threshing and winnowing.

24 A similar explanation may apply to the naming of deities that oversee the
process of removal of trees from the sacred grove of Dea Dia in the Arval Acta,
e.g. *Deferunda* (Taking down), *Coinquenda* (Chopping up), *Adolenda* (Burning
up), *Commolenda* (Pounding down): *CIL* VI 2099 = Scheid 1998a: no. 94.II.5,
13; 2107 = Scheid 1998a 105b, 12; the ritual is referred to in *CIL* VI 2065 =
32367 = Scheid 1998a: no. 55, but the deities themselves are not named.

25 E.g. Livy 1.26.12; 8.10.14; 29.8.9; *CIL* VI 1881 (for the reburial of an imperial freedman 13 years after his death); and often in the Arval Acta, e.g. *CIL*
VI 2051; 2059 = 32355; 2068; 2080 = 32375 (resp. Scheid 1998a nos. 40. II
14; 48.18, 20 etc.; 59. II 37; 69.57, 60); outside Rome: *CIL* X 8259 (reburial
after damage to tomb: Tarracina). By extension, *piaculum* can also mean the
victim offered in such a ritual: Cato, *De agr.* 139; Cicero, *De leg.* 2.57.

26 Cf. *sacer esto!* Let him be *sacer*, in the XII Tables, VIII. 21 Bruns = VIII.10a
Crawford (1996: 2, 689) (punishment for a patron who cheats his client).

27 Marius: Richard 1994; Sulla: Ramage 1991; on architecture in this context
up to the early Principate: Sauron 1994.

28 Cf. Beard, North, Price 1998: 1, 286, and, for the middle and late Empire,
Rüpke 2001c: 29f.; also Momigliano 1986.

4 RELIGIOUS ACTION

1 On the procedure at *immolatio* see Wissowa 1912: 416–20; Cancik 1991:
373–6; Scheid 2003:83–91. In the Roman rite, the entrails of cattle were
boiled, of pigs and sheep, grilled.

2 See Fischer and Marhold 1983; Mörth 1986 and 1993.

3 The most elaborate formulation is to be found in Burkert 1996; a first statement in 1983 (which appeared in German in 1972).

4 *Leviticus* 16.5–10. There are in fact two goats, one of which is sacrificed regularly (together with a bull) to the Lord as as an offering for the people.

5 Cf. Kümmel 1968; Wright 1987.

6 Burkert 1979: 71; cf. 1996: 55, taking the example of zebras and lions.

7 E.g. Cicero, *De nat. deor.* 2.10; Livy 1.18.3; 8.9.5; 10.7.10. The earliest
archaeological examples were found among the mid-Republican terracotta
statuettes dredged up from the Tiber (Pensabene et al. 1980), and in a temple
at Caere (Mengarelli 1935). Covered hands: Servius, *Aen.* 1. 292; 8. 636. Cf.
too *Tab. Iguvinae* VIb 49 (= §131 Devoto). Clothing more generally:
Bonfante Warren 1973.

8 Servius, *Aen.* 3.407; Servius Danielis (= 'Servius auctus') comments ibid. on
the exceptions.

9 Saturn: Servius, *Aen.*3.407; Dion. Hal. 6.1.4; altar of Hercules: Servius, ibid.;
Macrobius, *Sat.* 3.6.17; cf. Latte 1960: 383.

10 Sources for music: Fleischhauer 1964; Fless 1995: 79-4 (archaeology); Wille
1967: 27–9 (literary); also Quasten 1973. For the *aulos/tibia* and the *tibicines*
in particular: Cicero, *De oratore* 3. 197; Péché 2001.

11 On the *ferialia* see Rüpke 1995a: 523ff. Oral announcements by the *rex sacrorum*: Varro, *LL* 6. 13; 28; for the Principate: Rüpke ibid. 376f. on Macrobius,
Sat. 1.14.8f.

12 For the rituals at night associated with the Saecular Games, performed by Augustus himself, see Pighi 1941; cf. Paulus, *Excerpt. Festi* p. 72, 13–14 L s.v. 'Epulares'; Bravo 1997.

13 Most recently, the six volumes of Balty et al. 2004–6.

14 Wagenvoort 1947: 13ff. provides a mass of interesting material on *contactus*, unfortunately presented in an impossible framework.

15 E.g. Valerius Maximus, *Mem.* 5.10.1 = Seneca, *Consol. ad Marciam* 13.1; cf. Cancik 1991: 372.

16 Livy 1.24.5; cf. Pliny, *HN* 28.33f.; Macrobius, *Sat.* 1.12.20; 3.9.12.

17 Cf. Linderski 1986: 2290: 'Such theories normally thrive in the dim light of the Indo-European and Italic past, but dry up in the sober climate of historical Rome.'

18 Ovid, *Fasti* 2.423–28; Plutarch, *Rom.* 21.5; *Caes.* 61.2; Livy frag. 12; Servius, *Aen.* 8.343. A different tradition referring the ritual to purification can be found in Varro, *LL* 6.13; Paulus, *Excerpt. Festi* p. 75,23 -76, 5 L. s.v. 'Februarius'; cf. Dion. Hal., *Ant. Rom.* 1.83.1 = Aelius Tubero, *FRH* 18 F4. On the whole question: Wiseman 1995b: 10–15; a selection of texts is translated in Beard, North, Price 1998: 2, 119–24.

19 It has been suggested that the famous bronze Boxer, found deliberately concealed near the 'Hellenistic Ruler' bronze under soft earth (a fragmentary column had been placed under his bottom, so that he could continue to be seated) in the cellars of the Baths of Constantine on the southern Esquiline (Collis Mucialis), and now in the Palazzo Massimo at Rome (Lanciani 1892: 297ff.; Helbig[4] 3: no. 2272), was likewise the object of reverence in the later Principate: both big toes show signs of having been constantly touched.

20 Paulus, *Excerpt. Festi* p. 115, 6–12 L s.v. 'Manalem lapidem'; Serv., *Aen.* 3.175 ; cf. Wissowa 1912 : 121; Kroll 1928.

21 From the late Republic, in a classic example of invented tradition, it was believed that this was how Rome itself had been founded.

22 Petersmann 1991; for the role of young people, youths and girls: Lonsdale 1993; Calame 2001. Adams and Apostolos-Cappadona 1990 is a collection of essays on dance from the perspective of comparative religion.

23 Livy 1.20.4; Dion. Hal., *Ant. Rom.* 2.70.1–5, tr. in Beard, North, Price 1998: 2, 126f.; cf. Bloch 1958. For the dating of the reform, see Bremmer 1993.

24 The religious importance of dance is further illustrated by the numerous statuettes and frescoes of dancing Lares, the deities particular to each household (see pl. 9).

25 The classic account is Mauss 1954 (first published in 1923/4), applied to Homeric society by Finley 1962; important developments by Sahlins 1972: 185–275 and Bourdieu 1977: 4–9 (emphasizing the *deferral of expectations*), 171f. (symbolic capital); cf. Laum 1960; Schwartz 1967. The model is applied to friendship by Herman 1987.

26 On the scale of the incense-trade during Antiquity, and its importance as an economic factor, see Peacock and Williams 2006.

27 Latte 1960: 392; cf. Ziehen 1929; Burkert 1984: 63f.

28 Oath: Rüpke 1990: 111–15; malign magic: Ogden 1999: 75f.

29 On *daps*, see pp. 102 and 137 below; *epulum*: Latte 1960: 377f.; 'inside sacrifices': Paulus, *Excerpt. Festi* p. 297, 8–10 L 'Penetrale sacrificium'; for the word *penetralia* meaning the innermost part of the temple (where the cult

statue stood), see e.g. Livy 26.27.4; *Res gestae* §29; Martial 10.51.13; *penetrale sacrum*: HA *Heliog.* 6,8.

30 For the historical development of purity rules at Rome, see Cancik 1977; Liebeschuetz 1979: 48f., 99f.; in the Greek world: Chaniotis 1997; in early Christianity: Brown 1988.

31 Appel 1909 (in Latin); Weinreich 1929; Hickson 1993; Klinghardt 1999; interpretations of individual prayers in Kiley et al. 1997; for Greece: Pulleyn 1997.

32 Among the instruments used was the *hydraulus*, water organ (cf. Vitruvius, *Arch.* 10.8), which from the third century AD might be powered by a pair of bellows. It was also used in the circus. On music in the cults of the Mater Magna and Bacchus, cf. Vendries 2001; Sauron 2001.

33 For the colleges, resp. *ILS* 4965; 4966; *IG* XIV 1084; further on music and hymns: Nilsson 1945; Lattke 1991; Greek hymns in Furley and Bremer 2001.

34 Versnel 1970; Rüpke 1990: 223f.

35 Festus p. 190, 11–30 L 'October equus'; Paulus, *Excerpt. Festi* p. 71.20–2 L 'Equus'; ibid. p. 246.21–4 'Panibus'; Plutarch, *QRom.* 97; recent interpretations include Scholz 1970; Dumézil 1975: 145–56; Pascal 1981; Scullard 1981: 193f.

36 Polybius 12.4b.1; 4c.1 with Walbank 1957–79: 2, 329f.

37 There is other evidence that Timaeus advanced the Greek claim (so Erskine 2001) that the Romans were descended from the Trojans, which is clearly the starting-point for his explanation: Dion. Hal., *Ant. Rom.* 1.67.4 (Trojan pottery at Lavinium).

38 On colour coding in general, see Sahlins 1976a; 1976b: 196–204; Leach 1976: 57–60. For colour codes in the religious context at Rome: Radke 1936; Latte 1960: 209f.; Rüpke 1993b. Latte 1960: 381 cites cases in which dun or black animals were sacrificed to 'non-chthonic' deities.

39 Latte 1960: 297; Ogilvie 1965: 127–9; Rüpke 1990: 97–117; Beard, North, Price 1998: 1, 9; 26f., 111f.; 132f.; 2, 7f. (text); compare Rich 1976; Porte 1989: 96–9.

40 Ovid, *Fasti* 4.721–46; Beard 1987; Beard, North, Price 1998: 1, 174–6; 2, 116–19.

41 In German, 'Schwanz' means both 'tail' and 'penis'.

42 Cf. Scholz 1970: 126; Dumézil 1975: 185–7; Vanggaard 1979.

43 It should be admitted that it is difficult to find other good examples of this type of syntacticization.

5 THINKING ABOUT RELIGION

1 Cf. Edwards, Goodman and Price 1999; Fiedrowicz 2000.

2 See Becker 1967; Pezzella 1972.

3 E.g. Pietri and Markschies 1996: 339.

4 On the process of canon-formation, see Hengel and Deines 1994 (Septuagint); Metzger 1987 (NT); stressing the role of hermeneutic conflicts: Stroumsa 1998; Lieu 2004: 51–4. On the general problem: Assmann and Assmann 1987.

5 As argued by Lieberg 1982 (who uses the inauthentic expression *theologia tripertita*). I tend to attribute it to Varro himself.

6 Cf. p. 104f. above; Baumgarten 1998 and Rutgers et al. 1998 discuss the exceptions.

7 E.g. Kirk, Raven, Schofield 1983: frags. 144, 184 and 218.

8 Eusebius, *Praep. Evang.* 4.13; Philostratus, *Vit. Apoll.* 3.41; cf. *GGR* 2, 420f.; Attridge 1978: 63; Dzielska 1986: 136–50.

9 The fragments of his *Scipio* indicate the extent to which Ennius' activities as a translator were involved in contemporary debates (cf. p. 263 n. 44 above).

10 See Schröter 1963; Taylor 1974 [1975]; Rawson 1985: 117–31; cf. the etymologies collected in Maltby 1991.

11 See Cicero, *De nat. deor.* 1.1–12; *De div.* 2.150; *De fin.* 1.1–12; *Tusc.* 1.1–6; cf. Heilmann 1982 and Powell 1995a on Cicero's ambition to integrate philosophy socially at Rome.

12 See esp. Jocelyn 1976, 1982; Scheid 2003: 182–6; also Koch 1960.

13 'Cognitive dissonance' was a theory developed by the social psychologist Leon Festinger to explain certain aspects of apparently irrational behaviour; cf. Festinger et al. 1964: 25–30; Versnel 1990: 4–8. Paul Veyne used the expression 'balkanization of the brain': Veyne 1983: 52–68. The concept of 'differentiation' appealed to by Beard, North, Price 1998: 1,150–3, is appropriate but in itself inadequate to account for the phenomenon.

14 The historical Pythagoras was a 'philosopher' who settled in the southern Italian Greek city of Croton in the sixth century BC and founded an aristocratic ascetic 'sect'. As a result, later Greeks sometimes called it 'the Italian philosophy'. On the ramified development of Pythagoreanism in the Hellenistic period, cf. Burkert 1972; briefly Rawson 1985: 291–4.

15 Cf. Momigliano 1984; on Nigidius Figulus in this context: Dickie 2001: 169–72. I do not find the remarks of Beard, North, Price 1998: 1,152–4 of much help here.

16 Cf. Humm 1996–7; Turcan 1996: 266–90.

17 See Sommella Mura 1977; Cristofani 1987; Coarelli 1988: 205–301; cf. Richardson 1992: 35–7; Claridge 1998: 250–2.

18 Wissowa 1912: 23–7. The contrast is lifted substantially from Preller 1858: 9f., and became the dominant *communis opinio*. See e.g. Warde Fowler 1911: 14f.; 114f.; Rose 1948: 157f.; Latte 1960: 7f. Parallel to it however was a Romantic (Schelling) and post-Romantic counter-claim that a body of ancient Italo-Roman myth had indeed existed, albeit largely occluded; cf. Graf 1993b: 31–8.

19 Koch 1937 with Arcella 1986 and Montanari 1986; also Schilling 1980.

20 Beard 1993 and Beard, North, Price 1998: 1, 171–6 argue that there was in fact no significant difference.

21 Gruen 1992: 44–51; Wiseman 1995a; note also the very full account of Erskine 2001.

22 Clarke 1991: 78–265; Sauron 1994 (rather excessive); for Late Antiquity, see Muth 1998.

23 Walls: Q. Mucius Scaevola, fr. 14 Seckel/Kuebler = Cicero, *De leg.* 2. 47; rainwater: Varro, *LL* 5.27; Cicero, *De orat.* 1.173 (a fine list of analogous *iura*, bodies of law). *Ius* could also mean a collection of available actions e.g. *ius Aelianum*, the collection by Sex. Aelius Paetus Catus, cos. 198 BC.

24 *Flamines*: Tacitus, *Ann.* 3.58–59.2;71.3f. In this case, in AD 22, the decision went against Servius Maluginensis. The traditional rules are stated at Livy 24.8.10; 37.51; *Epit.* 19; Val. Max. 1.1.2; Cicero, *Phil.*11.18; Servius auct., *Aen.* 8.552 ; cf. Rüpke 1996b: 267–71.

25 *Flamines Diales*: Val. Max. 1.1.4f.; Plutarch, *Marcell.* 5; Livy 26.23.8, with Marco Simón 1996: 197f. (the rule that the *flamen Dialis* was required to wear his *galerus* at all times in the open air is stated by Aulus Gellius, *Noct. Att.* 10.15.17); Scipio: Polybius 21.13.10–14 with Walbank 1957–79: 3, 107; Livy 37.33.7.

26 E.g. Cicero, *De domo sua* 136; *Brutus* 55; *De div.* 2.42; Livy 1.60.4; 4.3.9 with Ogilvie 1965: 535; Pliny *HN* 18.14; Censorinus, *De die nat.* 17.9; Servius, *Aen.* 1.398.

27 Rüpke 1993c; Scheid 1994; Scheid 2003: 131; Scheid 1998b goes somewhat farther.

28 Cf. Blomart 1997; Gustafsson 1999; also Dumézil 1966: 412–18; Palmer 1974: 55.

29 Accepting the identification of this Macrobius with the Theodosius Macrobius who was praetorian prefect in Italy in AD 430. The traditional view fixed the date between 384 and 395.

30 Köves-Zulauf 1972; Gladigow 1981: 1206f.

31 Servius, *Aen.* 1.277; also Servius auct. ibid., and Servius, *Aen.* 2.351.

32 See frg. 2 Courtney = Augustine, *Civ. Dei* 7, 9, citing Varro's *De cultu deorum*. He also wrote an otherwise unknown *Epoptides*, which had a conspectus of contents similar to Pliny's *Natural History*, and is therefore also likely to have been encyclopaedic (*HN* praef. 33). It has been suggested that the title is the equivalent of *Tutelae*, 'Guardian Goddesses': Köves-Zulauf 1970: 322.

33 Pliny, *HN* 28.18; Serv. auct., *Aen.* 1.277.

34 List in Basanoff 1947: 43–68.

6 SOCIAL RULES

1 Van Straten 1995; Huet et al. 2004–6a; on the value of sacrifice as symbol, see Gordon 1990.

2 For the range of possible sacrificial sites, see Torelli et al. 2004–6.

3 The same goes for the meat, of course; in an earlier passage Cato says, with reference to the same offering: *ubi daps profanata comestaque erit*, 'when the *daps* has been offered and eaten . . .': *De agr.* 50.2.

4 On domestic cult, see De Marchi 1903; Orr 1978; Bakker 1994; on the Lares and Penates: Dubourdieu 1989.

5 Altars often had some protection against excessive heat: Dräger 1994: 24–8. According to Servius, *Aen.* 12.119, it might well consist simply of a piece of turf.

6 Greece: Gill 1974, 1991; Scheer 2000: 61–6; Rome: e.g. Varro, *RD* frag. 101* Cardauns; *ILS* 5050 = *AE* 2002: 192 line 115; cf. Dion. Hal. *Ant. Rom.* 2.23.5; Blanc 2004–6.

7 On the *sacrificia penetralia*, see also p. 103 above.

8 Cf. Scheid 1985b, 1988, 2005; Huet 2004–6b.

9 Isola Sacra: Pavolini 1983: 261f.; tomb of Saturninus: de Vos and de Vos 1982: 273.

10 Ovid, *Fasti* 1.319–22; Varro, *LL* 6.12; cf. Seneca, *Controv.* 2.3.19.

11 Cf. Varro, *LL* 6.31: *medio tempore inter hostiam caesam et exta porrecta*; cf. 6.16 *inter exta caesa et porrecta*.

12 The Romans themselves tended to regard this as a later custom.
13 Cf. Scheid 1988; Veyne 2000.
14 Cf. e.g. D'Arms 1984, 1990; Dunbabin 2003; Roller 2006.
15 *Magmenta:* Varro ibid.; Servius, *Aen.* 4.57; cf. Latte 1960: 389 n.2; Huet et al. 2004–5a: 1, 231f.
16 Cf. for Greece: Durand 1979; at Rome, cf. Arnobius, *Adv. nat.* 7.24 (tr. Huet et al. 2004–6a: 1, 232 no.274).
17 Scott Ryberg 1955; Turcan 1988: 2, 16–39; Fless 1995.
18 E.g. the regulations (*lex*) of the *collegium cultorum Dianae et Antinoi* in Lanuvium, AD 133: *CIL* XIV 2112 = *ILS* 7212 II, 18–20. The original is in the epigraphy section of the Museo Nazionale delle Terme in Rome.
19 Cf. Gladigow 1971 on Ovid, *Fasti* 1.335–456.
20 The classic formulation is Pernice 1885; see also Beard, North, Price 1998: 1,34, and p. 102 above.
21 Although they agree that the gods were not strictly bound by votives, Beard, North, Price 1998: 1,36 fail to see *litatio* as a ritual dramatization of this truth.
22 Cicero, *De div.*1.28; heart and head of liver missing: ibid. 119; Paulus, *Excerpt. Festi* p. 287, 7–8 L, s.v. 'pestifera auspicia'; Suetonius, *Div. Iul.* 77.
23 Separately: Livy 41.15.2; cf. Paulus, *Excerpt. Festi* p. 9, 3f. L, s.v. 'antroare'. In the case of naval sacrifices, or to marine deities, the entrails were thrown raw, but chopped up (*cruda exta caesa*) into the sea: Livy 29.27.5; Servius, *Aen.* 5.238.
24 Paulus, *Excerpt. Festi* p. 69, 9f. L, s.v. 'exta': *quod ea dis prosecuntur, quae maxime extant eminentque*, because they are cut out for the gods, who are very conspicuous and prominent (the alternative spelling of the word *exsto*, I stand out, is *exto*).
25 Festus p. 358, 27–30 L; Paulus, *Excerpt. Festi* p. 39, 13–16 L; cf. Latte 1960: 67f.; Beard, North, Price 1998: 1,47. Dog-sacrifices: Smith 1996b.
26 On the economics of incense, see p. 267 n. 26 above.
27 For Greece, cf. especially Jameson 1988; for Italy, MacKinnon 2004.
28 We also need to take feeding-régimes into account: young pigs, for example, cannot gain weight on a pure carbohydrate diet of acorns, but can do so in their second year; an 18-month-old hog can more than double its weight if fed on acorns for three autumn months (MacKinnon 2004: 156f.).
29 Varro, *RR* 2.5.12 notes the rule of having two bulls for 70 suckler-cows.
30 See Nimtz 1925; more refined figures for Italy in King 1999: 169–73 with Table A, pp. 192f.; MacKinnon 2004: 77–100 (for the pattern in N. Italy, where even so pig represents 38.6% ±11.9 of the finds; see also Alvino 1995).

7 MANAGING LINES OF COMMUNICATION

1 The materials can be found in the various volumes of *CStipiVot*; good summaries in Comella 1981; Fridh-Haneson 1987; Bouma 1996; Simon et al. 2004–6: 1, 330–59 (A. Comella); see also de Cazenove 1997.
2 For these technical details, see Comella 1981.
3 Cf. Gladigow 1995; Baggieri 1999; Simon et al. 2004–6: 1, 359–69 (A. M. Turfa); Schultz 2006: 95–120.
4 General background information in van Straten 1981.

5 Cf. Schultz 2006:101. The goddess's epithet of course recalls Felix's own name.

6 There seem to have been several minor healing shrines of Bona Dea: another inscription (*AE* 1980: 53), recording the restoration of a *fanum* and *aedes* of the same *Bona Dea agrestis felicula* by an imperial freedman, was turned up somewhere along the Viale Giulio Cesare, near St Peter's (cf. *LTURSuburb* 1: 225 [M.G. Granino Cecere]). The epithets *agrestis* and *felicula* allude to the well-known connections of the Bona dea with Ops and Ceres.

7 Felix has a second name ending in – anus to indicate that he was bought (at public expense) from another slave household, and correctly places this name after his status indication *(servus) publicus*, public slave. In this case, he evidently had belonged to one of the eminent senatorial C. or M. Asinii in the first half of the third century.

8 Other dedications *Bonae deae luciferae/oc(u)latae* record further ophthalmic interventions by the goddess (e.g. *CIL* VI 68, 73 = *ILS* 3506, 3508). Her shrine on the Minor Aventine (*subsaxana*) had its own pharmacy attached (Macrobius, *Sat.* 1.12.20–6); cf. *LTUR* 1: 200f. (L Chioffri).

9 See Behr 1968; Debord 1982: 27–40; Krug 1993: 120–87; Jackson 1988: 138–69; on dreams: Oberhelman 1987.

10 E.g. from S. Etruria and Latium: Simon et al. 2004–6: 1: 335 nos. 36–44; 359 no.294 (A. Comella). The 37 second-century BC examples found at the N. gate of Vulci had evidently been deliberately deposited some way away from an extra-mural shrine (Paglieri 1960; Pautasso 1994). In Gaul at any rate such finds occur mainly at attested healing sanctuaries.

11 Votive animals occur at about half the excavated sites (100 of 200), but in far smaller quantities than human figures, anatomical votives or pottery; cf the rapid survey in Simon et al. 2004–6: 1, 369–71 (I. Edlund-Berry).

12 There are exceptions, however, such as the important regional healing shrine of Diana at Aricia at the foot of the Alban Hills (Green 2006).

13 Inversely, however, sick members of the élite might well visit healing-shrines, e.g. the probable dedication of Sp. Postumius Albinus (cos. 110 BC) at the sulphur-water shrine of Juno Regina near Setia in Latium (*AE* 1990: 132; 1997: 282).

14 E.g. *pro itu et reditu*: *CIL* V 6873; 6875 = *ILS* 4850a. There was no proper road over the pass (cf. Walser 1984: plates 8f.) – in some places there were steps; goods were carried on mule-back. An additional worry will have been the weather. In keeping with his social status, Nonianus' is the largest (0.243 x 0.145m) and finest of the *tabulae ansatae* discovered at the site. The HQ of his legion was at this time (between AD 89 and 122) at Vetera on the lower Rhine, and he was presumably on his way to and from his home in Fundi, a famous wine-growing area 70 miles S. of Rome on the Via Appia. Since his tribe is not that of Fundi (Aemilia), his family had probably emigrated there from Rome.

15 These are some of the objects found in the excavations of the temple and the dried-up lake at Bourg-St-Pierre in the campaigns of 1890–3. Poeninus is clearly a Celtic deity, identified with Jupiter. Barocelli (1932: 38) believed that the bronze plaques, which are all slightly different, were made by craftsmen at the temple or the *mansio*.

16 Livy 31.9.7–10. Crassus (*RE* Licinius no.69) argued that vows had to be *ex certa pecunia*, of a specific amount. However, when the matter was referred

to the pontifical college, it decided that vows *ex incerta pecunia*, i.e. non-specific, were allowable, so long as the sum actually given measured up to those recently voted by the Senate for the same purpose.

17 E.g. Livy 7.28.4; *condemnare* is used of the god's putting the burden of responsibility onto the *vovens* by fulfilling the request, e.g. Titinius, *com.* 153; *ILS* 3411 lines 10-12.

18 *Reus*: Macrobius, *Sat.* 3.2.6, probably from Servius auct., *Aen.* 4.699, since Macrobius' claim is not supported by his citation from Vergil, *Aen.* 5.237.

19 *CIL* VI 2051 = Scheid 1998a: no. 40, I.10-12: *quae superio]ris anni ma [gister voverat persolvi]t et in pro | [ximum annum n]uncupavit*, 'he redeemed the vows he had made (for the emperor) as magister the previous year, and solemnly renewed them for the coming year'. Later in the same text (l.76), the name of Vitellius is suddenly substituted for that of Otho on 14 March, when vows were offered *pro salute et reditu*, for his safe return. This was in fact the date when *Otho* left Rome to meet the Vitellians before the first battle of Bedriacum (14 April), and still had a month to live (Tacitus, *Hist.* 1.90.1). The entry has thus been edited to fit the new political facts, irrespective of the words actually spoken. The minutes for the previous year were normally cut in the temple retrospectively in April or May, in this case clearly before the final victory of Vespasian was assured. It was only later, after his damnation, that Vitellius' name was systematically erased.

20 See Mattingly 1950-1; Fears 1981a: 98-100; 1981b: 814f.; for the Tetrarchy and later, cf. Heim 1991; 1992; Salama 1992.

21 Cf. Rüpke 1990: 155f. on ancient awareness of such connections.

22 *Merito* is not, as one might think, a dative of advantage 'to the deserving (god)', but an adverb, 'with good reason or cause'. In the extended formula *VSLLM*, the additional L stands for *laetens*, joyful(ly). The older form of *libens* was *lubens*, regularly found in Plautus and Terence.

23 Cf. Versnel 1976, 2004; Rüpke 1990: 156-61.

24 See p. 272 n. 9 above.

25 Collected in Heim 1892; cf. Önnerfors 1985; discussions, with numerous examples, in Önnerfors 1988, 1993; Blänsdorf 1991;Versnel 2002.

26 The first phrase sets up a relation between Moon and teeth (both are new), which is then 'cashed in' in the persuasive analogy: just as evil cannot attack the moon (natural rule: dogs and wolves cannot fly), so evil cannot attack my head (implied natural rule). From analogous efforts, it seems clear that this is a rather clumsy fusion of two originally separate self-healing charms (neither teeth nor 'worms' appear in the the analogy). The 'name' to be written on the piece of papyrus, central to the original rite, has been lost in transmission. Note how, due to its cultural prestige, writing has moved into a space that would once have been occupied by a suitable plant or animal part, with its own appropriate modes of collection and preparation.

27 On protection against evil (including exorcisms and Christian amulets): Engemann 1975, 2000; Kotansky 1991, 1995; Deschler-Erb 1998: 168-73; Gelzer et al. 1999. General on protective amulets: Bendlin 2000d.

28 Cf. M. Smith 1979, who offers a helpful contrast with the 'magical papyri'; Waegemann 1987; Fowler and Graf 2004-6: 299-301 (Á. Nagy); extensive collections of material in Bonner 1950; Michel 2001, 2004. Oddly enough, Graf 1997 has nothing to say about cures or amuletic gems; the latter are also missed by Beard, North, Price 1998.

29 Cf. Rives 2008; on Greek *magos/magia* see Graf 1997: 20–35; Bremmer 1999.

30 See Kippenberg and Luchesi 1978 on magic in general (this book consists mainly of German translations from British social anthropology of witchcraft and accusation of the 1960s, cf. Marwick 1970; Douglas 1970; Tambiah 1990); for antiquity see Phillips 1986, 1998b; Stuckrad 2002; Meyer and Mirecki 1995, 2002.

31 Graf 1997: 118–74; Beard, North, Price 1998: 1,233ff. Ogden 1999. The fundamental collection is still Audollent 1904; Gager 1992 offers a good selection of translations and images. For the present purpose I can ignore the special type of curse to regain stolen or lost property that H. Versnel has dubbed 'judicial prayers' or 'prayers for justice' (e.g. Versnel 1991, 2008; Ogden 1999: 37–44).

32 Problems that might be caused by malign magical attack: Beard, North, Price 1998: 234; inability to sacrifice: Versnel 1985.

33 The expression used here is *filius maris*, i.e. 'son of the sea', evoking a traditional usage meaning 'a cruel, hard-hearted person' (cf. Homer, *Iliad* 16.34; Catullus 64.155, Ovid, *Met*. 8.120 etc).

34 This is the interesting case of the freedman C. Furius Cresimus, who who accused (probably in the 190s BC) of 'attracting away' his neighbours' crops: Calpurnius Piso *FRH* 7 F36 = Pliny, *HN* 18.41–3; cf. Graf 1997: 62–5; Gordon 1999: 253f.; Rives 2002: 275f.

35 Graf 1997: 65–88; Hunink 1999: 1, 11–27; Gordon 1999: 199–202, 263f.

36 Cf. Thomas 1971; Levack 1987; also the anthropological work cited in n. 30 above.

37 On the *Malleus* see Anglo 1977; Clark 1997 is fundamental on European daemonology.

38 This is an important difference from the gems: Smith 1979.

39 It has however been pointed out that no practitioner of malign magic could afford to be anything but discreet, given the power of rumour and denunciation (Ogden 1999: 83f.).

40 See p. 168 above; phalloi: Varro, *LL* 7.97 with Johns 1982: 61–75; on the perspective of the potential victim, cf. Graf 1997: 153ff.

41 Libanius, *Or*. 1, 243–50; cf. Bonner 1932; Ogden 1999: 27f.

8 CONTROL OF SPACE

1 Festus p. 476, 29–35 L (from Ateius Capito) with Pease 1920–3: 482f.; Varro, *LL* 7.97. This doctrine applied fully only to signs in the NE (i.e. to the left both from the gods' point of view and from the Augur's: the gods 'faced' South, the Augur East). However there is plenty of evidence that the issue also depended on the type of sign, or the kind of bird that was seen: e.g. Plautus, *Asin*. 259–61; Cicero, *De div*. 1.12; 2.80: a crow on the left, for example, was negative.

2 Varro, *LL* 5.23; Festus p. 135.17f. L; cf. Cicero, *De leg*. 2.56. Latte's view (1960: 100f.) is contradicted by both Varro and Festus.

3 Note Hyginus' pithy phrase: *posita auspicaliter groma*, when the surveyor's cross has been positioned after taking the auspices: *Const*. <*limitum*> p. 135.3f. Thulin= *WLS* p. 136.19f. The entire tract is most instructive about the relation in Roman thinking between space, lines, limits and cosmology.

4 Debate over the origins of the Roman arch has been fierce. Basically, we must distinguish between the 'false' (corbelled) arch, and the true arch, which was most probably introduced to Italy under Hellenistic influence (cf. MacDonald 1982: 1, 4f.).

5 For my sociological understanding of space, which concentrates on composition, see Löw 2001: 131.

6 On the archaeology of the Lacus Curtius see Giuliani and Verduchi 1987: 104–15; *LTUR* 3: 166f. (C. F. Giuliani).

7 Cf. Coarelli 1983a; 1985 (rather hot-headed in places); Claridge 1998: 60–99; Hölkeskamp 2001; Frischer 2006.

8 Cf. Coarelli 1997 (again, many of his hypotheses are untenable); for a straightforward description, see *LTUR* 1: 220–4 (T. P. Wiseman); Claridge 1998: 174–226.

9 Such groves seem originally to have been numinous groups of trees or copses (Cato, *De agr.* 139) but were later often walled and domesticated. In Late Antiquity, Servius, *Aen.* 1.310 defines *lucus* as *arborum multitudo cum religione*, 'a lot of trees that have been consecrated', distinguishing it from wild nature (*silva*) and planned *arboretum* (*nemus*). This seems artificial.

10 Cf. Dion. Hal., *Ant. Rom.* 4.15.5; the grove contained an ancient 'lotus tree': Pliny, *HN* 16.235. Judging from the epigraphic finds, it must have been on the Cispian, the northern lobe of the Esquiline (the site of S. Maria Maggiore).

11 Pomerium: Rüpke 1990: 35–41; Liou-Gille 1993; *porta triumphalis*: Coarelli 1988: 363–414; also *LTUR* 3: 333f. (F. Coarelli), arguing that it was the name of one arch of the Porta Carmentalis, just below the Capitoline.

12 For images of Luperci see Wrede 1983; Estienne 2004–6: 5, 89–91 (G. Romano). The most revealing is that of Tib. Claudius Liberalis, *CIL* VI 3512.

13 The imperial 'restorations' evidently changed the appearance of the site radically: *LTUR* 3: 198f. (F. Coarelli).

14 One can get an idea of the variety of possible interpretations from Ulf 1982; Radke 1989; Wiseman 1995b. Compare the 'communication' thesis of Binder 1997.

15 The choir that sang Horace's *Carmen Saeculare* in 17 BC was composed of 27 boys and girls.

16 Festus defines *sacella* as *loc]a dis sacrata sine tecto*, 'places without a roof dedicated to the gods' (p. 422.15–17 L).

17 Varro, *LL* 5.45–54, citing an authentic third- or second-century BC pontifical document, cf. Richardson 1992: 37–9. On the meaning of the ritual, see Nagy 1985; Porte 1984; Radke 1990, none of whom has any clear methodological framework.

18 The widespread claim that the Salii also danced in October (e.g. Beard, North, Price 1998: 2, 126) has no basis in the sources.

19 *Curia*: Cicero, *De div.* 1.30; *mansio*: CIL VI 2158=*ILS* 4944.

20 Varro, *LL* 6.24; Festus p. 458, 1–5; 474, 36–476, 5 L; see also Fraschetti 1990: 134–59; Rüpke 1995a: 162f.

21 'Specifically rural festivals, outside the civic structure of the city': Beard, North, Price 1998: 1,50.

22 Rüpke 1998c; context: Zanker 1988: 129–34. Altars: Schraudolph 1993: 118; Turcan 1988: 2, 29 no.61 with pl. 30.

23 Ley and Struß 1982; Coarelli 1987; see also MacDonald 1982: 1, 7f.; Bodei Giglioni 1997; Merz 2001: 17–33.

24 See Thomas 1990; North 1995; rather briefly: Beard, North, Price 1998: 1, 323f.; rather speculative: Torelli 1984. The political history can be found in Humbert 1978; Galsterer 1976; Hantos 1983; Bleicken 1988.
25 Wissowa 1912: 164 with n.6; also 520; Lavinium: Castagnoli 1979; also Turcan 1983.
26 For the debate since Magdelain 1976, see Bendlin 2000b; on the Mundus at Rome, cf. *LTUR* 3: 288f. (F. Coarelli).
27 For the ritual, see Cato, *Origines=FRH* 3 F18a (Serv. *Aen.* 5.755); Varro, *LL* 5.143; Festus p. 514, 22–7 L; cf. Ovid, *Fasti* 4.819–36; Plutarch, *Rom.* 11.1–5. When the emperor Commodus planned to refound Rome as 'Commodiana' in AD 192, he issued an *aureus* showing himself as Hercules cutting the *sulcus primigenius* round the imaginary city: Cassius Dio 72 (73).15.2; *HA Commod.*8.9; *RIC* 3, Commodus p. 394 no. 247.
28 On *domi* and *militiae* see Rüpke 1990: 29.
29 Syme 1975–6 [1978]; Rüpke 1990: 35; Ramage 1991.
30 Pliny, *Ep.* 10.50 (Trajan); see Gaius, *Inst.* 2, 7a: *Quod in provinciis non ex auctoritate populi Romani consecratum est, proprie sacrum non est, tamen pro sacro habetur*, 'though a thing consecrated in the provinces otherwise than under the authority of the Roman people is not strictly *sacrum*, it is nevertheless considered as such' (tr. de Zulueta). However, as the Babatha archive from the province of Arabia has revealed, the Roman rules applying to landed property were in fact swiftly applied in the provinces through the medium of the governor's provincial edicts.
31 Varro, *LL* 6.53; Festus p. 146, 12–17 L; see Rüpke 1990: 32; 37.
32 Cf. Cipriano 1983; Linderski 1986: 2272; Rüpke 1990: 36f.
33 The *lituus* frequently appears on coins, particularly in the late Republic and early Principate, and occasionally on temple-friezes, denoting membership of the college of Augurs, or more vaguely the augural science: Hölscher 2004–6: 5, 394–6 (H. Schauber).
34 Varro, *LL* 7.7–9 with Norden 1995: 3–106; cf. Frontinus, <*De limitibus*> p. 10.20–11.5 Thulin=*WLS* p. 8.23–9.
35 The most complete surviving augural monument is the *templum terrestre* at Bantia (AE 1967:105; cf. Torelli 2004–6: 4, 345 no.3; Linderski 1986: 2282–5), which was used for observing the flight of birds. Although I have likened the *templum minor* to a tent, it was not covered, simply fenced off (Festus says *tabulis et linteis*, 'with boards and awnings'); rather confusingly, however, the auspicant did have a regular tent (*tabernaculum*) where he could wait around, or sleep, when not actually observing.
36 A different point of view in Fridh 1990; Torelli et al. 2004–6: 4, 313–15 (M. Menichetti).
37 Cf. Coarelli 1983b; for the case at Pompeii, see Zanker 1998: 147–52.

9 CO-ORDINATION

1 One might start with the important anthropological discussions of Bourdieu 1977 and Gell 1992.
2 See Beard, North, Price 1998: 1,71f.; 201–6; Cancik 1996a; Haase and Rüpke 2001.
3 For a survey of Greek and Roman calendars, see Hannah 2005. The first-

century BC Gaulish calendar found at Coligny (dép. Ain-Rhône Alpes), though based on lunar cycles, is clearly adapted from a Roman model (Duval and Prinot 1986). On the Egyptian calendar, highly sophisticated in other ways, see A. S. de Bomhard 1999.

4 Overview of all versions so far known in Rüpke 1995: 43–164; the Latin texts in *InscrIt* XIII.2: 237–62.

5 So Wissowa 1912: 2f., following Mommsen; likewise Michels 1967 and (basically) Beard, North, Price 1998: 1, 6.

6 *InscrIt* XIII.2 (appendix) gives the sources in chronological order day by day; the main festivals are listed by Scullard 1981. On the *Tubicines*, see Festus p.482.27–9 L; Varro, *LL* 5.117.

7 On the religious festivals during the early Principate, see Benoist 1999.

8 Ovid dates the procession to the Vestalia (9 June), but the *Fasti Filocali* enters 'Vesta aperitur' on 7th; a period of N-days begins already on 5 .

9 Laurence 1994: 124f. provides an overview.

10 Details in Bernstein 1998; instrumentalization: Flaig 1995b, cf. Toner 1995: 52; for Late Antiquity and Constantinople see Cameron 1976; Brown 1978: 81–6.

11 De Robertis 1963; Rüpke 1995a: 501–12.

12 Cato, *De agr.* 2.4; Columella, *RR* 2.21, see also Servius, *Georg.* 1.268–72; Macrobius, *Sat.* 1.16.9–12.

13 E.g *CIL* X 444=*ILS* 3546; 10234=*ILS* 7213; XIV 2112=*AE* 1983: 181.

14 Kalends: Ovid, *Fasti* 1.55; Macrobius, *Sat.* 1.15.19; Ides: Festus p.372, 8–12 L; Ovid, *Fasti* 1.56. Ovid notes that the Nones had no tutelary deity.

15 Varro, *LL* 6.31; Paulus, *Excerpt. Festi* p. 311.1–3 L with Rüpke 1995a: 214–21.

16 Suetonius, *Div. Aug.* 35.3 with Rüpke 1995a: 434f.

17 Interest rates varied widely from region to region (Gaius, ap. *Digest.* 13.4.3). A conservative rate was 4–5%, 6% was common; a rate of 1% per month (=12% p.a.) was often expected in areas with strong commerce. Cicero even mentions a man in Cilicia who hoped to make 4% per month (= 48% p.a.) (*Att.* 5.21.12). Such high rates were still common in the fourth century AD (Duncan-Jones 1982: 33 n.3; 132–6).

18 Such apartments (*cenacula*) were often sub-let by the tenant. By far the greater part of the population however had no such privilege, and was forced to pay daily, or very short-term, rent for tiny rooms in *deversoria* or *cauponae* (Frier 1977, 1980). For a realistic account of the urban poor, see Whittaker 1993.

19 E.g. Horace, *Odes* 3.8.1; Martial 9.52; 10.24; 29.3; 87.

20 *CIL* XIII 5708, II.16f. =*ILS* 8379=*FIRA* 3 no. 49.

21 The most plausible explanation is that the speaker is trying to urge his interlocutor to get off home because tomorrow is the Shabbat, which at any rate in later Jewish usage meant that it would begin already this evening. Although almost nothing is known of Jewish practices relating to the Shabbat at this period, the obvious inference is that the coincidence of the end of the (lunar) month and a Shabbat would have been considered particularly holy.

22 On ominous days in antiquity, see Grafton and Swerdlow 1988; Rüpke 1995a: 563–92; cf. Swerdlow 1999.

23 This ritual might be understood as a synthesis of the sacrifice to Juno on the Kalends, conducted in the Regia by the *regina sacrorum*, and that to Jupiter on the Ides, conducted, probably on the Capitol, by the *flamen Dialis* (see p. 194).

24 See Rüpke 1995a: 274–83; compare Hölkeskamp 1988. Because of the rule that legislation had to be published at least three *nundinae* before being resolved, these days acquired considerable importance in late-Republican politics (Lintott 1968).

25 No school, shaving: Varro, *Menipp.* 279; 186 Astbury; washing: Seneca, *Ep. mor.* 86.12 ('in the old days'); nail-trimming: Pliny, *HN* 28.28; extra cook: Plautus, *Aulularia* 324f. with Festus p.176, 27–32 L.; on the Lex Fannia: Athenaeus, *Deipn.* 6. 274c; Pliny *HN* 10.139; Aulus Gellius, *Noct. Att.* 2.24.4.

26 Mommsen in *CIL* I². p. 218 reproduces a curious schematic device for correlating the dates of the *nundinae* in a number of cities in Latium with one another and with the days of the planetary week.

27 On astrology in the imperial period, see Barton 1994; Stuckrad 2000; Beck 2007.

28 Cf. Stern 2001 on the Jewish emphasis on the 'deviant' lunar calendar against the Roman (and earlier Jewish) solar calendar.

10 RELIGION IN THE METROPOLIS

1 The most important account of the development of the late Republican legislation is Linderski 1968 (with the earlier literature cited there).

2 On *collegia* in general, see still Liebenam 1890; Ausbüttel 1982: 16ff.; Royden 1988: 3–12; Patterson 1994; terminology: Royden 1988: 2f. In Asia Minor, specifically religious associations appear long before professional *synodoi*, which developed only after the advent of Roman rule: van Nijf 1997: 7f.

3 See the various essays in Kloppenborg and Wilson 1996; Egelhaaf-Gaiser and Schäfer 2002; Harland 2003: 25–53; Bendlin 2005; also Beard, North, Price 1998: 1, 272f.

4 See White 1990: 26ff.; note also the discussion over the *collegium* of Sergia Paullina (*CIL* VI 9148 = *ILS* 7333; 9149; 10260–62; 10263 = *ILS* 7334; 10264 = *ILS* 7335): Sordi and Cavigliolo 1971; Sordi 1979; refuted by Bonfioli and Panciera 1971/2; cf. Lampe 1989: 313; White 1990: 46f.

5 The total can be calculated from the fact that there were 60 *decuriae*, and *c.* 22 members in each *decuria* (*CIL* VI 33856; 1060 = 33858 = ILS 7225); cf. Royden 1988: 127.

6 Individuals were officially only permitted to be members of one *collegium legitimum* (*Digest.* 47.22.1.2). The Ostian evidence suggests that this was broadly conformed to, except by prominent persons (Meiggs 1973: 321f.).

7 Meiggs 1973: 311–36; Van Straten 1993; for the figures, see Ausbüttel 1982: 35–7.

8 Heyob 1975; Mora 1990: 2, 1–29; Beard, North, Price 1998: 1, 296–300.

9 Cf. Ausbüttel 1982; briefly, Meiggs 1973: 312; Bollmann 1998: 28f.

10 Garnsey and Saller 1987: 114f., 120f., 200; Jongman 1988: 203–77; Schulze-Oben 1989: 169–226.

11 Cf. Dion. Hal., *Ant. Rom.* 4.62.4; Livy 6.37.12; 42.2; cf. 10.8.1–4. The full title *sacris faciundis*, 'responsible for the rites which need to be performed', makes clear that these priests were responsible for more than the Sibylline books.

12 The title *Dendrophori*, Tree-carriers, must be related to the name of the ritual on 22 March, which was *arbor intrat*: the Tree enters.

13 See Salamito 1987, by contrast with the exclusively religious interpretation offered by Beard, North, Price 1998: 1, 273; 308.

14 The importance of rich patrons for furnishing the *schola* is stressed by Meiggs 1983: 324–7; White 1990: 53–8; Bollmann 1998: 29–32; for post-Constantinian church-building, see Pietri 1978.

15 Cotter 1996 with de Ligt 2000.

16 3 *asses* are the equivalent of *HS* ¾. On these occasions, the ordinary members received no monetary *sportulae* (which ought to have amounted to 2 *den.* = *HS* 8), thus saving the fund around *HS* 280 each time. Everyone received the same amount of bread. It may seem odd to distribute such an article, but bread was a luxury; the great majority of the population subsisted on a kind of porridge (Jongman 2002: 31). The bread-ration on these occasions amounted to the entire daily wage of a labourer at Rome: Duncan-Jones 1982: 54.

17 6 *sextarii* = 1 *congius* = roughly 6 pints. The implied price of a *sextarius* of wine is *HS* 1.27–1.84.

18 Salvia Marcellina is not expected to drink wine.

19 On the financial aspects of this inscription, see Duncan-Jones 1982: 364f. The total cost of the *sportulae* was at least *HS* 1,436, implying an annual income of *HS* 2,500 at 5%, or *HS* 3,000 at 6% interest.

20 Misenum: *AE* 1993: 472f. = 1996: 424a-b = 2000: 344a-c, with the important discussion by D'Arms 2000.

21 On the *Augustales*, see Duthoy 1976; Jongman 1988, 203–77; Schulze-Oben 1989, 301–51; Abramenko 1993. Gregori 1999 is an important study of the institution at Brescia.

22 One of the most interesting inscriptions to specify ethical demands is the by-laws of a late-Hellenistic association at Philadelphia in Lydia (*Syll.* 985), discussed by Barton and Horsley 1981.

23 Cf. Seneca, *Ep. mor.* 108.17–22; among (neo-) Pythagoreans, Diogenes Laertius, *Phil.* 8.19. On the Stoic-Cynic debate on marriage/celibacy, see Deming 2004: 47–103.

24 E.g. Philo, *Inebr.* 20–26; *Leg. ad Gaium* 3.155–59; cf. Kloppenborg 1996; Mason 1996; Harland 2003: 206–10; Dunn 2007.

25 Stark 1996; the criticisms by Bruce 1999 (cf. Rüpke 2006e) affect only the issue of rational choice, not the empirical observations.

26 Beard, North, Price 1998: 1, 279; Steuernagel 1999: 167; Steuernagel 2004: 251–57. On the Isiac monuments and Egyptian monuments at Rome: Roullet 1972; on the Iseum Campense: Lembke 1994, summarized by Beard, North, Price 1998: 1, 264f. (Rome); also Egelhaaf-Gaiser 2000: 175–85. Mithras: Bakker 1994: 111–17; Clauss 2000: 42f.

27 See Bollmann 1998 with comprehensive material for Italy; also Harland 2003: 61–86. On the intermediate possibilities, see White 1990.

28 On caves and 'caves', see Egelhaaf-Gaiser and Rüpke 2000.

29 Egelhaaf-Gaiser 2000: 185–218, cf. White 1990: 126 and 137; Bricault 2001: map XXIII; on Pompeii, see also Tran tam Tinh 1964; Hoffmann 1993 (Pompeii); Herculaneum and Stabiae: Tran tam Tinh 1971.

30 See Steuernagel 2001, 2004: 186f.

31 Cf. Liebenam 1890: 191–95; Royden 1988: 12–14 (over-estimating the rarity of *centuriae*, which however occur almost exclusively in Gallia Cisalpina).

32 The main evidence relating to the normative structure is the two layers of paintings in the S. Prisca mithraeum on the Aventine, see Vermaseren and Van Essen 1965: 148–240; briefly in Beard, North, Price 1998: 2, 316f.; prosopography in Rüpke 2005a.

33 Hörig and Schwertheim 1987: 244–8 nos. 380f. = Zappata 1996: no. 18f. ; on the standing of the *notarius* at Rome, cf. Merlat 1960: 195. See further, see Rüpke 2005a: 1537–46; Rüpke (forthcoming).

34 Cf. Rajak 2002: 335–54; Harland 2003: 177–237.

35 Cf. Scheid 1986; Rüpke 2006f; on the Bacchic cult in the Principate, see Turcan 2003.

36 The low incidence of inscriptions in foreign languages that relate to foreign cults suggests that the formulation of Beard, North, Price 1998: 1, 271 is too harsh. Steuernagel 1999: 164 offers some concrete examples of exclusion from Puteoli.

37 Cf. Dorcey 1992; Clauss 1994. There are two main differences: only 14% of Silvanus dedications are by soldiers; and women, especially in Italy, Pannonia and Dacia, make up 4.1% of all dedicators to Silvanus/Silvana but are entirely (or virtually) absent from the cult of Mithras.

11 SPECIALISTS AND PROFESSIONALS

1 The date of this change is unknown; the first such election is recorded for 212 BC (Livy 25.5.1; cf. 39.46.1; 40.42.1; Cicero, *Leg. agr.* 2.18.); cf. Rüpke 2005a: 1623–5, dating to the second half of the third century.

2 The *religiones* applying to the *flamen Dialis* are given by Aulus Gellius, *Noct. Att.* 10.15.1–31; cf. Marco Simón 1996: 88–134; Beard, North, Price 1998: 1, 28f.

3 Schultz 2006: 80 even suggests that the *flamen* and the *flaminica* should be seen as a single priesthood that required the services of a married couple.

4 Linderski 1986 provides a marvellous account of these in relation to the Augural college and the individual Augurs.

5 Cf. Sini 1983; Scheid 1994; North 1998 has unfortunately little to add.

6 The text contains the name Q. Cornelius, almost certainly an error, since Q. does not occur as a *praenomen* for the Cornelii.

7 A number of the translations, especially in the *hors d'oeuvre*, are doubtful since e.g. *turdus* can mean both 'thrush' and a kind of wrasse said by Pliny to be 'noblest of rock-fish' (*HN* 32. 151). It is unclear why some items appear twice. Beccaficoes are not a species, but a general word for small birds, e.g. tits and sparrows, eaten whole. 'Picene bread' swelled like a sponge when dunked in sweet liquid (Martial 13.47).

8 Cf. McBain 1982; Rosenberger 1998: 158f.

9 *CIL* II². /5, 1033 (now lost); on this Baetican curiosity, see Étienne 1958: 231–4.

10 See briefly Scheid 2003: 134–8; with full details, Rüpke 2005a: 53–572.

11 On Laurens Lavinas see now the important Severan documents reprinted as *AE* 1998: 280–2.

12 See p. 183; also Liebeschuetz 1979: 7–29; Beard 1990: 34; North 1990b.

13 Cf. Latte 1960: 140f.; Beard, North, Price 1998: 1, 188.

14 On the *haruspices* see Cicero, *De div.* 1.92; Tacitus, *Ann.* 11.15.1; cf. Rawson 1978. Cautionary tales drew attention to the possibility that foreign

experts might play false, inasmuch as they represented non-Roman interests, but stressed that these dangers were always overcome (e.g. Livy 1.45.5f.; 55.5f.).

15 Our sources record about 50 dated consultations of the oracles between 496 and 100 BC.

16 Suetonius, *Aug.* 31.1 with Parke 1988: 141f. Tiberius did much the same in AD 19, and likewise added some of the circulating verses to the 'authentic' official copies (Cassius Dio 57.18.4).

17 Cicero, *De div.* 2.52, with Pease p. 439; *De nat. deor.* 1.71. Cato may have been intending to oppose the foreign to the Roman, but the tradition of ridiculing soothsayers goes back at least to Diogenes the Cynic (Diogenes Laertes, *Vit. philos.* 6.24).

18 I have mentioned above that Marius, for example, had a Syrian seer named Martha (see p. 60).

19 See Barton 1994: 32–41; Beck 2007; Cramer 1954: 44–69 is now rather outdated.

20 Cf. Eriksson 1956; Rüpke 1995a: 587–92.

21 Cicero, *De div.* 1.89; 2.113; Serv. *Aen.* 4.70. Livy 25.12.3 and Pliny, *HN* 7.119, however, speak of only one man; on the complex issue of the *carmina Marciana*, two of which are cited by Livy 25.12.5–10, see recently North 2000. Cicero, *De div.* 1.115 mentions another prophet, Publicius, who may have been, like the Marcii, of senatorial family. Incidentally, prophets at Rome seem not to have understood themselves as 'seers' but as mouth-pieces of a god.

22 This aspect of Horace's self-description as *vates* is neglected by Newman 1969.

23 The original inscription contained four columns of c. 80 letters width; of these only a strip of col. 2, most of col. 3 and some of col. 4 survive (named in the editions cols. I, II, III). The earlier or primary regulations are therefore all lost; what survives is mainly connected with the responsibilities of the lessee for collecting the dead and the types of litigation envisaged in case of complaint. The surviving part scarcely mentions the actual funeral (*funus, iusta*), inhumation or incineration; this topic was either dealt with in cols. 1–2, or the matter was largely left to the family of the dead person. Mention is however made of the wood for the pyre that the lessee had to keep in stock.

24 'Building': the Latin has *turris*, a tower, not necessarily part of a city-wall; 'towers' were features of many villas; Hinard and Dumont 2003: 105–8 suggest that the word could be applied to any building or cluster of buildings outside the city.

25 Public executions were evidently more terrible and shocking than private ones; this text seems to indicate that, at least at Puteoli, public malefactors were nailed to the cross after being tortured with hot pitch and scalding wax. Private ones are envisaged as using 'cross and fork', by which the condemned person was whipped through the streets on the 'fork' and then lashed to the cross.

26 The old text by L Bove, most easily available as AE 1971: 88, has been superseded by the text, translation and commentary by Hinard and Dumont 2003.

27 The number may represent a minimum of eight groups of four bier-carriers.

28 These fees were apparently termed *lucar Libitinae*; a rich decurion of Bergamum in N. Italy left a sum of money sufficient to remit them for all the citizens in perpetuity (*CIL* V 5128=*ILS* 6276).

29 It has been suggested that the 'grove' in time became entirely built over with offices and workshops, and that there was not a tree in sight (Hinard and Dumont 2003: 109).

12 FROM CAESAR TO THE LAMB

1 One exception is the account of M. P. Nilsson, *GGR* 2: 310-730, though he has relatively little to say about Rome; MacMullen 1981, on the western Empire, although a salutary critique of F. Cumont, is too one-sided; Liebeschuetz 1979 too literary; Lane Fox 1986 is hardly interested in Rome; Beard, North, Price 1998: 1: 167–388 while admirable so far as it goes, is not on the required scale; Rives 2007 is a text-book.

2 See Klein 1972; Croke and Harries 1982 (documents); Chuvin 1990; Athanassiadi and Frede 1999.

3 Ahn 1993; Bendlin 2001a; Rüpke 2001a.

4 Cf. Bowersock 1969; Reale 1990.

5 Cf. Merkelbach 1984: 146–88; Clauss 2000: 22–41; nuances in Gordon 2007. The archaeological material is collected in Vermaseren 1956-60, now rather out of date.

6 Cf. Clauss 2000: 42–8. The largest known mithraeum, at the Roman villa at Els Munts, north of Tarragona (Spain), measures 30 x 8.70m, giving a superficial area of 250m^2. The sole more or less complete album of Mithraists, from Virunum in Noricum (*AE* 1994: 1334), contains 98 names over a period of 20 years, with five recorded deaths.

7 The information probably goes back to Apollodorus of Artemita, i.e. to the first decades of the first century BC (Momigliano 1975: 139f.). The role and scope of astrology in the cult of Mithras is a heavily debated topic; for a maximal view, see Beck 2004, 2006.

8 There can however be no question that records of this kind had earlier been kept, as well as lists of members and their contributions, on wax tablets or papyrus, all naturally lost. That these ephemeral records appear now as permanent inscriptions tells us merely something about the wealth of these senators, and their determination to fix their religious commitments in stone.

9 *CIL* VI 749–51a; 752–53 = *ILS* 4267a-e = *CIMRM* 400–02, 404–05. On the late-Roman naming system see Salway 1994: 136–41.

10 *IGUR* 106 = *CIMRM* 473, with Clauss 2000: 12f.; Berrens 2004: 184–98. In this case however the *synnaoi theoi* are probably Cautes and Cautopates, the torchbearers; the most interesting feature of the inscription is that it calls the god *Zeus Helios Mithras*, attesting to Mithras' promotion in the third century AD to the rank of a cosmic, universal deity.

11 Steuernagel 2004, cf. Beard, North, Price 1998: 1, 271f.

12 §13 Musurillo. The historicity of this heavily-recensed text has been exaggerated by e.g. Lane Fox 1986: 460–8; cf. the criticisms of Grig 2004 [2005]: 24.

13 On the origins of the 15–20 pre-Constantinian titular churches in Rome, see Pietri 1978; Lampe 1989: 307–13.

14 Marcion came to Rome *c.* AD 140 and broke with the group he joined there four years later, thereupon founding his own successful movement. He was attacked as a Docetic by Irenaeus, and at great length by Tertullian, whose

surviving *Adv. Marcionem* in five books (AD 207/8) was preceded by two earlier versions.

15 On Hermas, see Rüpke 1999; on Valentinus, Markschies 1992; Quispel 1996. Valentinus too was attacked by Irenaeus and Tertullian.

16 I follow Claussen 1995 here; date and place are however very uncertain. Note also the tract [Seneca], *De superbia et idolis*, first published in 1984 under the title *Epistula Ann(a)e ad Senecam de superbia et idolis*, which is now understood to be a sort of Christian advertisement to attract pagan sympathy written at Rome in the late fourth century: cf. Cracco Ruggini 1988; Wischmeyer 1990. On the process of Christianizing the Roman élite, cf. Salzman 2002.

17 On the 'Calendar of 354' see Stern 1953; Salzman 1990; Rüpke 1995a: 90–4. The entry for April is translated in Beard, North, Price 1998: 2, 68f.

18 Kötsche-Breitenbruch 1976; Ferrua 1991; Bargebuhr 1991.

19 Jerome, *Ep.* 53.7; cf. Matthews 1992. A *cento* is a mish-mash of lines borrowed from one poem in order to make another; fortunately, 700 verses of the work has survived. Proba's epitaph can still be read: *CIL* VI 1712.

20 Cf. Rebenich 1992. Jerome translated the remainder of the OT section of the Vulgate version of the Bible from the Hebrew over the years 391–406, in Bethlehem.

21 Cf. Février 1992; Hack 1997.

22 Gros 1976; briefly, Beard, North, Price 1998: 1, 197.

23 Boethius and Ward-Perkins 1970: 245–63; Ward-Perkins 1970, 1981.

24 Cf. *LTUR* 2: 56–63 (L Fabbrini); Ball 2003.

25 Cf. Boatwright 1987: 42–6; *LTUR* 4: 54–61 (A. Ziolkowski). Agrippa's original building was probably a private shrine to Mars, paired with his 'Basilica Neptuni'. Hadrian's domed structure was modelled on the central or audience halls of secular buildings.

26 Cf. Boatwright 1987: 119–33; *LTUR* 5: 121–3 with figs. 64–7 (A. Cassatella); briefly: Beard, North, Price 1998: 1, 257f.

27 Examples might be the temple of Apollo just beside Augustus' house, Hadrian's double-temple of Venus and Roma on the Velia (which was partly dug away for the construction of the base), and the immense temple of Sol Elagabalus hurriedly built in AD 222 on a large infill-platform measuring 180 x 120m, to the l. of the clivus Palatinus as you climb up towards the domus Flaviana, the site of the later Vigna Barberini (so Broise and Thébert 1999; Cecamore 1999 disagrees). The general view at the Soprintendenza favours Broise and Thébert.

28 Cf. Flaig 1992; the point is stressed in relation to Maxentius and Constantine by Curran 2000.

29 Appian, *Civ.*2.442; Cassius Dio 44.6.2; cf. *Res gestae* §9.

30 Cf. Schumacher 1978; Scheid 1990a: 155–312; Beard, North, Price 1998: 1, 186–96.

31 Both Beard, North, Price 1998: 1, 192 and Stepper 1999 see the matter differently. My point applies mainly to the Julio-Claudians.

32 See Herz 1978; Rüpke 1995a: 396–405.

33 On the dynamic of the imperial cult, esp. in the West, see Turcan 1978; Fishwick 1987–2005; Liertz 1998; Gradel 2002; and the essays in Small 1996.

34 The same was granted to important female members of the ruling dynasty; collective honours for minor princes were the rule.

35 Cf. Price 1984; Mitchell 1993: 1, 100–17; Friesen 1993; Gradel 2002.

36 Cf. Charlesworth 1936; Étienne 1984; Heim 1991; Bergmann 1998; Smith 2000.

37 Cf. Beard, North, Price 1998: 1, 284. Elsner 1998: 207 points out that we might think in terms of image- rather than text-traditions.

38 Cf. Beard, North, Price 1998: 1, 277; also the commentary on Lucian's *Alexander* by Victor 1997.

39 Metzler 1981; Cancik 1986; Chuvin 1990: 66–81; Stroumsa 2005. Note Libanius' speech in defence of classical temples (*Or.* 30).

40 See Williams 2007 for a history of religious motifs on Roman coins.

41 The date of these edicts coincides fairly exactly with that of the malign-magical rituals, including poppets enclosed in up to three small lead canisters, and lead curse-tablets rolled up and stuffed into the wick-holes of votive lamps, that were found in the well of Anna Perenna in the Piazza Euclide, now in northern Rome, but in antiquity some way out of town, in the late 1990s (Piranomonte 2008). Some of the originals can be seen in the epigraphic section of the Museo delle Terme, Rome.

42 Cf. Aune 1980; Meyer and Smith 1994; Schäfer 1990; 1997; Betz 1997; Stuckrad 2000.

43 See e.g. Brown 1978, 1995, 1997; on what follows, see also Rüpke 2001a.

44 *CIL* XIV 3469f. Although they are not expressly named as members of the college, the list of seven names can hardly mean anything else, cf. Rüpke 2005a: nos. 2390, 2421, 2713 etc.

BIBLIOGRAPHY

FURTHER READING

Beard, M., North, J. and Price, S. *Religions of Rome. 1: A History*; *2: A Sourcebook* (Cambridge: Cambridge University Press, 1998). An excellent, wide-ranging, well-illustrated survey, written at a fairly demanding level; the second volume is arranged thematically.
Liebeschuetz, J. H. W. G. *Continuity and Change in Roman Religion* (Oxford: Clarendon Press, 1979). An historical account, with some original ideas, from the Late Republic up to the fourth century AD.
J. Rüpke (ed.) *The Blackwell Companion to Roman Religion* (Oxford: Blackwell, 2007). An extensive collection of essays by different hands, adding up to a complete historical survey.

The greatest work on Roman religion, still worth consulting on specific points though in many ways out-dated, is:
Wissowa, G. *Religion und Kultus der Römer* 2nd edn. Handbuch der Altertumswissenschaft 5,4 (Munich: Beck, 1912).

Other introductions

Scheid, J. *An Introduction to Roman Religion*. Trans. by Janet Lloyd (Edinburgh: Edinburgh University Press, 2003; original ed. 1998) 273–87.
North, J. A. *Roman Religion*. New Surveys in the Classics, 30 (Oxford: Oxford University Press, 2000).
Rives, J. B. *Religion in the Roman Empire* (Malden, MA and Oxford: Blackwell Publishing, 2007 [2006]).

Survey articles and bibliographies

Belayche, N., Bendlin, A. et al. 'Römische Religion (1990–1999)', *Archiv für Religionsgeschichte* 2 (2000) 283–345; 5 (2003) 297–371 (with extensive bibliographies).
Krause, J. -U., Mylonopoulos, J. and Chengia, R., *Bibliographie zur römischen*

285

BIBLIOGRAPHY

Sozialgeschichte, 2: Schichten, Konflikte, religiöse Gruppen, materielle Kultur, ed. G. Alföldy. HABES 26 (Stuttgart: F. Steiner, 1992).

History of scholarship

Scarsi, M. *Introduzione allo studio delle religioni del mondo classico* (Padua: Unipress, 1999).

Collection of previously published articles

Ando, C. (ed.), *Roman Religion*. Edinburgh Readings on the Ancient World (Edinburgh: Edinburgh University Press, 2003). Fairly advanced level.

Guides

Johnston, S. I. (ed.), *Religions of the Ancient World: A Guide* (Cambridge, MA: Belknap Press, 2004). Contains numerous short but worthwhile essays on many aspects of Roman religion.

Iconography

R. Turcan, *Religion romaine*. Iconography of Religions, 17.1–2 (Leyden: Brill, 1988).
I. Scott Ryberg, *Rites of the State Religion in Roman Art*. Memoirs of the American Academy in Rome, 22 (New York: American Academy in Rome, 1955).
J. C. Balty et al. (eds), *Thesaurus cultus et rituum antiquorum* (6 vols. so far) (Los Angeles: Getty Publications, 2004 [2005] –). An iconographical encyclopaedia of ancient religion, with extensive treatment of Etruscan and Roman materials.

Source materials in translation

For obvious reasons, there exists no full or complete collection of sources, in the original or in translation; the following however offer a good selection:
Beard, M., North, J. and Price, S. *Religions of Rome*, vol. 2 (see above under General accounts).
Lane, E. N. and MacMullen, R., *Paganism and Christianity, 100–425 C.E.: A sourcebook* (Minneapolis: Fortress Press, 1992).
Le Glay, M. *La religion romaine* (Paris: Colin, 1971).
Valantasis, R. *Religions of Late Antiquity in Practice* (Princeton: Princeton University Press, 2000).

No English translations yet exist even of such important sources as Festus' abridgement of Verrius Flaccus' *De verborum significatione* (although a team directed by M. H. Crawford in London is currently working on a new text, translation and commentary of both Festus and Paulus), or of the fragments of Varro's *Antiquitates rerum divinarum*. The same applies to most inscriptions. On the other hand, the historians and philosophical writers such as Livy or Cicero are easily available both in commented editions and in translation. A list of the best/most useful translations, other than those included in the Loeb series and in Penguin Classics, may be given here:

Aristides Aelius (P.), *The Complete Works*, trans. C. A. Behr (Leyden: Brill, 1981–86) [the Loeb version of 1973 no longer appears in the Loeb catalogue].

Apuleius, *The Metamorphoses*, trans. P. G. Walsh. Oxford World's Classics (Oxford: Oxford University Press, 1999).

Aurelius Victor, *De Caesaribus*, trans. H. W. Bird. Translated Texts for Historians, 17 (Liverpool: Liverpool University Press, 1994).

Cicero, *The Nature of the Gods*, trans. P. G. Walsh (Oxford: Clarendon Press, 1997).

The Republic and the Laws, trans. P. G. Walsh, introd. J. Powell. Oxford World's Classics (Oxford: Oxford University Press, 1998).

Codex Theodosianus and Novels and Sirmondian Constitutions, trans. C. Pharr et al. (Princeton: Princeton University Press, 1952; repr. 2001).

Eutropius, *Breviarium ab urbe condita*, trans. and comm. H. W. Bird. Translated Texts for Historians, 14 (Liverpool: Liverpool University Press, 1993).

Horace, *The Complete Odes and Epodes*, trans. D. West. Oxford World's Classics (Oxford: Oxford University Press, 2000).

Iamblichus, *On the Pythagorean Life*, trans. G. Clark. Translated Texts for Historians, 8 (Liverpool: Liverpool University Press, 1989).

The Emperor Julian: Panegyric and polemic, ed. S. N. C. Lieu. Translated Texts for Historians, 2 (Liverpool: Liverpool University Press, 1989 2nd edn).

Juvenal, *The Satires*, trans. N. Rudd. Oxford World's Classics (Oxford: Oxford University Press, 1991).

Lactantius, *Divine Institutes*, trans. A. Bowen, introd. P. Garnsey. Translated texts for Historians 40 (Liverpool: Liverpool University Press, 2003).

Antioch as a centre of Hellenic culture, as observed by Libanius, trans. and ed. A. F. Norman. Translated Texts for Historians, 24 (Liverpool: Liverpool University Press, 2000).

Livy, *The Dawn of the Roman Empire*, trans. J.C. Yardley, introd. W. Heckel. Oxford World's Classics (Oxford: Oxford University Press, 2000).

Hannibal's War, trans. J. C. Yardley, intro. D. Hoyos. Oxford World's Classics (Oxford: Oxford University Press, 2006).

The Rise of Rome, trans. J. C. Luce. Oxford World's Classics (Oxford: Oxford University Press, 1998).

Lucian, *Selected Dialogues* (including *Alexander the false prophet*), trans. C. D. N. Costa. Oxford World's Classics (Oxford: Oxford University Press, 2006).

Lucretius, *On the Nature of the Universe*, trans. R. Melville, intro. D. and P. Fowler. Oxford World's Classics (Oxford: Oxford University Press, 1999).

Macrobius, *Saturnalia*, trans. P. V. Davies. Records of Civilisation, 73 (New York: Columbia University Press, 1969).

Ovid, *Metamorphoses*, trans. A. D. Melville, ed. E. J. Kenny. Oxford World's Classics (Oxford: Oxford University Press, 1998).

In Praise of Later Roman Emperors: The Panegyrici Latini, trans. and comm. C. E. V. Nixon and B. S. Rodgers (Berkeley: University of California Press, 1994).

Pliny the Younger, *Complete Letters*, trans. P. G. Walsh. Oxford World's Classics (Oxford: Oxford University Press, 2006).

Neoplatonic Saints: The Lives of Plotinus and Proclus by their students, trans. and comm. M. Edwards. Translated Texts for Historians, 35 (Liverpool: Liverpool University Press, 2000).

Plutarch, *Roman Lives*, trans. R. Waterfield, ed. P. A. Stadter. Oxford World's Classics (Oxford: Oxford University Press, 1999).

Propertius, *The Poems*, trans. G. M. Lee, introd. R. O. A. M. Lyne. Oxford World's Classics (Oxford: Oxford University Press, 1999).
Suetonius, *Lives of the Caesars*, tr. C. Edwards. Oxford World's Classics (Oxford: Oxford University Press, 2000).
Tacitus, *The Histories*, trans. W. H. Fyfe, rev. D. S. Levene. Oxford World's Classics (Oxford: Oxford University Press, 1999).
Vergil, *The Aeneid*, trans. C. Day Lewis, introd. J. Griffin. Oxford World's Classics (Oxford: Oxford University Press, 1998).
The Georgics, trans. P. Fallon, introd. E. Fantham. Oxford World's Classics (Oxford: Oxford University Press, 2006).

SECONDARY LITERATURE CITED (SEE ALSO THE LIST OF ABBREVIATIONS)

It should be noted that, as the English translation of *Der Neue Pauly*, *Brill's New Pauly*, makes progress, the references here to German articles in that work will gradually become available in English. References to the Brill translation have been included here up to and including vol. 8 (2006).

AA. VV. 1981. *Die Göttin von Pyrgi. Akten des Kolloquiums zum Thema "Die Göttin von Pyrgi": Archäologische, linguistische und religionsgeschichtliche Aspekte* (Tübingen, 16.–17. Januar 1979). Istituto di Studi etruschi ed italici: Biblioteca di Studi etruschi 12 (Florence: Olschki).
1986. *L'association dionysiaque dans les sociétés anciennes: Actes de la table ronde, Rome 24–25 mai 1984*. CEFR, 89 (Rome: École Française).
1998. *La mémoire perdue: Recherches sur l'administration romaine*. CEFR, 243 (Rome: École française de Rome).
Aberson, M. 1994. *Temples votifs et butin de guerre dans la Rome républicaine*. Bibliotheca Helvetica Romana, 26 (Rome: Institut Suisse de Rome).
Abramenko, A. 1993. *Die munizipale Mittelschicht im kaiserzeitlichen Italien: Zu einem neuen Verständnis von Sevirat und Augustalität*. Europäische Hochschulschriften Reihe 3, 547 (Frankfurt a.M.: Lang).
Adams, D. and Apostolos-Cappadona, D. (eds) 1990. *Dance as Religious Studies* (New York: Crossroad).
Aghion, I., Barbillon, C. and Lissarrague, F. 1996. *Gods and Heroes of Classical Antiquity*. Flammarion Iconographic Guides (Paris: Flammarion). Transl. of *Héros et dieux de l'Antiquité* (Paris: Flammarion, 1994).
Ahn, G. 1993. ' "Monotheismus" – "Polytheismus": Grenzen und Möglichkeiten einer Klassifikation von Gottesvorstellungen', in M. Dietrich and O. Loretz (eds), *Mesopotamica – Ugaritica – Biblica: Festschrift für Kurt Bergerhof zur Vollendung seines 70. Lebensjahres am 7. Mai 1992* (Kevelaer/Neukirchen-Vluyn: Butzon and Bercker/Neukirchener Verlag) 1–24.
Aleshire, S. B. 1992. 'The economics of dedication at the Athenian Asklepieion', in Linders and Alroth 1992: 85–99.
Algra, K. 2003. 'Stoic theology', in B. Inwood (ed.), *The Cambridge Companion to the Stoics* (Cambridge: Cambridge University Press).
Algra, K., Barnes, J., Mansfeld J. and Schofield, M. (eds). 1999. *The Cambridge History of Hellenistic Philosophy* (Cambridge: Cambridge University Press).
Altheim, F. 1930. *Griechische Götter im alten Rom*. RGVV, 22.1 (Gießen: Töpelmann).

Alvar, J. 1985. 'Matériaux pour l'étude de la formule *sive deus, sive dea*', *Numen* 32: 236–73.

Alvino, G. 1995. 'Santuari, culti e paesaggio in un'area italica: il Cicolano', *Archeologia Laziale* 12: 475–86.

Ando, C. and Rüpke J. (eds) 2006. *Religion and Law in Classical and Christian Rome*. PAwB, 15 (Stuttgart: F. Steiner).

Angenendt, A. 1997. *Geschichte der Religiosität im Mittelalter* (Darmstadt: Wissenschaftliche Buchgesellschaft).

Anglo, S. 1977. 'The *Malleus maleficarum*', in S. Anglo (ed.), *The Damned Art: Essays in the literature of witchcraft* (London: Routledge and Kegan Paul), 1–31.

Anzidei, A. P. and Gioia, P. 1995. 'Rinvenimenti preistorici nell'area del Tempio della Vittoria al Palatino', *Archeologia Laziale* 12: 29–32.

Appel, G. 1909. *De Romanorum precationibus*. RGVV, 7 (Gießen: Töpelmann).

Arcella, L. 1986. 'Introduzione', in C. Koch, *Giove Romano* (trans. L. Arcella). Dalla Grande Città, 1 (Rome: Rari Nantes) 50–64.

Assmann, A. and Assmann, J. (eds) 1987. *Kanon und Zensur*. Archäologie der literarischen Kommunikation, 2 (Munich: Fink).

Assmann, A. and Assmann, J. 1998. s.v. 'Mythos', *HrwG* 4: 179–200.

Athanassiadi, P. and Frede, M. (eds) 1999. *Pagan Monotheism in Late Antiquity* (Oxford: Clarendon Press).

Attridge, H. W. 1978. 'The philosophical critique of religion under the Early Empire', *ANRW* II.16,1: 45–78.

Audollent, A. 1904. *Defixionum tabellae . . . praeter Atticas in Corpore Inscriptionum Atticarum editas* (Paris: Fontemoing; repr. Frankfurt a.M.: Minerva, 1967).

Aune, D. F. 1980. 'Magic in Early Christianity', in *ANRW* II.23,2: 1507–58.

Ausbüttel, F. M. 1982. *Untersuchungen zu den Vereinen im Westen des Römischen Reiches*. Frankfurter Althistorische Studien, 11 (Kallmünz: Laßleben).

Baggieri, G. (ed.) 1999. *'Speranza e sofferenza' nei votivi anatomici dell' antichità: complesso monumentale del S. Michele di Roma, Sala degli aranci, ott.-nov. 1996* (Rome: Ministero per i beni culturali e ambientali).

Bakker, J. T. 1994. *Living and Working with the Gods: studies of evidence for private religion and its material environment in the city of Ostia (100–500 AD)*. Dutch Monographs on Ancient History and Archaeology, 12 (Amsterdam: Gieben).

Balty J. C. et al. (eds) 2004–06. *Thesaurus cultus et rituum antiquorum* (6 vols. so far) (Los Angeles: Getty Publications).

Ball, L. F. 2003. *The Domus Aurea and the Roman Architectural Revolution* (Cambridge: Cambridge University Press).

Bang, P. F. 2002. 'Romans and Mughals: economic integration in a tributary empire', in L. de Blois and J. Rich (eds), *The Transformation of Economic Life under the Roman Empire: proceedings of the 2nd workshop of the International Network 'Impact of Empire', Nottingham July 4–7th 2001* (Amsterdam: Gieben) 1–27.

Barceló, P. 1999. 'Warum Christus? Überlegungen zu Constantins Entscheidung für das Christentum', in Batsch et al. 1999: 255–69.

Barchiesi, A., Rüpke, J., Stephens, S. (eds) 2004. *Rituals in Ink: a conference on Religion and Literary production in ancient Rome held at Stanford University, Feb. 2002*. PAwB, 10 (Stuttgart: F. Steiner).

Bargebuhr, F. P. 1991. *The Paintings of the 'New' Catacomb of the Via Latina and the Struggle of Christianity against Paganism.* AHAW 1991 no. 2 (Heidelberg: Winter).

Barocelli, P. 1932. *Inscriptiones Italiae,* XI.1: *Praetoria Augusta* (Rome: Libreria dello Stato).

Barton, S. C. and Horsley, G. H. R. 1981. 'A Hellenistic cult-group and the New Testament churches', *Jahrbuch für Antike und Christentum* 24: 7–41.

Barton, T. 1994. *Ancient Astrology* (London and New York: Routledge).

Basanoff, V. 1947. *Evocatio: Étude d'un rituel militaire romain.* Bibliothèque de l'École des Hautes Études, Sciences religieuses, 61 (Paris: Presses Universitaires de France).

Batsch, C., Egelhaaf-Gaiser, U. and Stepper, R. (eds) 1999. *Zwischen Krise und Alltag: Antike Religionen im Mittelmeerraum.* PAwB, 1 (Stuttgart: F. Steiner).

Baudy, D. 1998. *Römische Umgangsriten: Eine ethologische Untersuchung der Funktion von Wiederholung für religiöses Verhalten.* RGVV, 43 (Berlin: de Gruyter).

Baumgarten, R. 1998. *Heiliges Wort und Heilige Schrift bei den Griechen: Hieroi Logoi und verwandte Erscheinungen.* Script-Oralia, 110 (Tübingen: Narr).

Beard, M. 1986. 'Cicero and divination: the formation of a Latin discourse', *Journal of Roman Studies* 76: 33–46.

1987. 'A complex of times: no more sheep on Romulus' birthday', *PCPhS* 33: 1–15.

1990. 'Priesthood in the Roman Republic', in Beard and North 1990: 17–48.

1991. 'Writing and religion: *Ancient Literacy* and the function of the written word in Roman religion', in Humphrey 1991: 35–58.

1993. 'Looking (harder) for Roman myth: Dumézil, declamation and the problems of definition', in Graf 1993c: 44–64.

2007. *The Roman Triumph* (Cambridge, MA: Harvard University Press).

Beard, M. and North, J. (eds) 1990. *Pagan Priests: religion and power in the Ancient World* (London: Duckworth).

Beard, M., North, J. and Price, S. 1998. *Religions of Rome.* vol. 1: *A History*; vol. 2: *A Sourcebook* (Cambridge: Cambridge University Press).

Beck, R. L. 2004. *Beck on Mithraism: Collected works with new essays* (Aldershot and Burlington, VA: Ashgate).

2006. *The Religion of the Mithras Cult in the Roman Empire: mysteries of the Unconquered Sun.* (Oxford: Clarendon Press).

2007. *A Brief History of Ancient Astrology* (Oxford: Blackwell).

Becker, C. 1967. *Der Octavius des Minucius Felix: Heidnische Philosophie und frühchristliche Apologetik.* SBAW 1967 no. 2 (Munich: Bayerische Akademie der Wissenschaften).

Behr, C. A. 1968. *Aelius Aristides and the Sacred Tales* (Amsterdam: Hakkert).

Belayche, N. 2001. *Iudaea-Palaestina: The Pagan Cults in Roman Palestine (Second to Fourth Century).* Religionen der römischen Provinzen, 1 (Tübingen: Mohr Siebeck).

Bendlin, A. 1997. 'Peripheral centres – central peripheries: religious communication in the Roman Empire', in Cancik and Rüpke 1997: 35–68.

2000a. 'Looking beyond the civic compromise: religious pluralism in Late Republican Rome', in Bispham and Smith 2000: 114–35.

2000b. s.v. 'Mundus', *Der Neue Pauly* 8: 474f.

2000c. s.v. 'Pantheon, III', *Der Neue Pauly* 9: 265–8.

2000d. s.v. 'Phylakterion', *Der Neue Pauly* 9: 978–81.

2001a. s.v. 'Polytheismus, I' *Der Neue Pauly* 10: 80–3.

2001b. 'Rituals or beliefs? Religion and the religious life of Rome [review essay on M. Beard, J. North and S. Price, *Religions of Rome*]', *Scripta Classica Israelica* 20: 191–208.

2001c. s.v. 'Sünde', in *HrwG* 5: 125–34.

2002. 'Gemeinschaft, Öffentlichkeit und Identität: Forschungsgeschichtliche Anmerkungen zu den Mustern sozialer Ordnung in Rom', in Egelhaaf-Gaiser and Schäfer 2002: 83–121.

2005. ' "Eine Zusammenkunft um der *religio* willen ist erlaubt . . ."? Zu den politischen und rechtlichen Konstruktionen von (religiöser) Vergemeinschaftung in der römischen Kaiserzeit', in H. G. Kippenberg and G. Folke Schuppert (eds), *Die verrechtliche Religion: Der Öffentlichkeitsstatus von Religionsgemeinschaften* (Tübingen: Mohr Siebeck) 165–207.

Benoist, S. 1999. *La fête à Rome au premier siècle de l'Empire: Recheches sur l'univers festif sous les règnes d'Auguste et les Julio-Claudiens*. Collection Latomus, 248 (Brussels: Latomus).

Bergmann, M. 1998. *Die Strahlen der Herrscher. Theomorphes Herrscherbild und politische Symbolik im Hellenismus und der römischen Kaiserzeit* (Mainz: von Zabern).

Bernabé, A. and Jiménez San Cristóbal, A. I. 2001. *Instrucciones para el Más Allá: Las laminillas órficas de oro* (Madrid: Ediciones Clásicas).

Bernstein, F. 1998. *Ludi publici: Untersuchungen zur Entstehung und Entwicklung der öffentlichen Spiele im republikanischen Rom*. Historia Einzelschriften, 119 (Stuttgart: F. Steiner).

Berrens, S. 2004. *Sonnenkult und Kaisertum von den Severern bis zu Constantin I. (193–337 n. Chr.)*. Historia Einzelschriften, 185 (Stuttgart: F. Steiner).

Berschin, W. 2003. 'Autobiography §IV', *Brill's New Pauly* 2: 408–10.

Bettini, M. 1991. *Anthropology and Roman Culture: kinship, time, images of the soul*. Transl. by J. Van Sickle (Baltimore: Johns Hopkins University Press). Orig. ed.: *Antropologia e cultura romana: parentela, tempo, immagini dell'anima* (Rome: La Nuova Italia Scientifica, 1988).

Betz, H. -D. 1997. 'Jewish magic in the Greek Magical Papyri', in Schäfer and Kippenberg 1997: 45–63.

Bietti Sestieri, A. M. 1992. *The Iron Age Community of Osteria dell'Osa: A study of social-political development in central Tyrrhenian Italy* (Cambridge: Cambridge University Press).

Binder, G. 1997. 'Kommunikative Elemente im römischen Staatskult am Ende der Republik: Das Beispiel der Lupercalia des Jahres 44', in Binder and Ehlich 1997: 225–41.

Binder, G. and Ehlich, K. (eds) 1997. *Religiöse Kommunikation. Formen und Praxis vor der Neuzeit*. Stätten und Formen der Kommunikation im Altertum, 6 = Bochumer Altertumswissenschaftliches Colloquium, 26 (Trier: Wissenschaftlicher Verlag Trier).

Bispham, E. and Smith, C. (eds) 2000. *Religion in Archaic and Republican Rome and Italy: evidence and experience* (Edinburgh: Edinburgh University Press).

Blänsdorf, J. 1991. 'Ein System oraler Gebrauchspoesie: Die alt- (und spät) lateinischen Zaubersprüche und Gebete', in H. L. C. Tristram (ed.), *Metrik und Medienwechsel*. Script-Oralia, 35 (Tübingen: Narr) 33–52.

Blanc, N. 2004–6. 'Offrandes alimentaires, encens', in Balty et al. 2004–6: 2, 444–48.

Blech, M. 1982. *Studien zum Kranz bei den Griechen*. RGVV, 38 (Berlin: de Gruyter).

Bleicken, J. 1988. *Geschichte der römischen Republik*. Oldenbourg-Grundriß der Geschichte, 2 (Munich: Oldenbourg).

Bloch, R. 1958. 'Sur les danses armées des Saliens', *Annales ESC* 13: 706–15.

Blomart, A. 1997. 'Die *evocatio* und der Transfer fremder Götter von der Peripherie nach Rom', in Cancik and Rüpke 1997: 99–111.

Boatwright, M. T. 1987. *Hadrian and the City of Rome* (Princeton: Princeton University Press).

Bodei Giglioni, G. 1977. 'Pecunia fanatica: l'incidenza economica dei templi laziali', *Rivista storica italiana* 89: 33–76.

Bömer, F. 1952. s.v. 'Pompa, 1', *RE* 21.2: 1878–993.

Boethius, A. and J. B. Ward-Perkins. 1970. *Etruscan and Roman Architecture* (Harmondsworth: Penguin Books).

Bohak, G. 2002. 'Ethnic continuity in the Jewish Diaspora in antiquity', in J. R. Bartlett (ed.), *Jews in the Hellenistic and Roman Cities* (London and New York: Routledge) 175–92.

Bollmann, B. 1998. *Römische Vereinshäuser: Untersuchungen zu den Scholae der römischen Berufs-, Kult- und Augustalen-Kollegien in Italien* (Mainz: Zabern).

Bonfante Warren, L. 1973. 'Roman costumes: a glossary and some Etruscan derivations', *ANRW* I.4: 584–614.

Bonnefond-Coudry, M. 1989. *Le sénat de la république romaine de la guerre d'Hannibal à Auguste: Pratiques délibératives et prise de décision*. BEFAR, 273 (Rome: École Française).

Bonfioli, M. and Panciera, S. 1971/2. 'Della cristianità del collegium quod est in domo Sergiae Paullinae', *Rendiconti della Pontificia Accademia di Archeologia* 44: 185–201.

Bonner, C. 1932. 'Witchcraft in the lecture room of Libanius', *TAPhA* 63: 34–44.
   1950. *Studies in Magical Amulets, chiefly Graeco-Egyptian* (Ann Arbor: University of Michigan Press).

Borgeaud, W. A. 1982. *Fasti Umbrici: Études sur le vocabulaire et le rituel des Tables eugubines*. Collection d'études anciennes de l'Université d'Ottawa, 1 (Ottawa: Édition de l'Université).

Bosworth, B. 1999. 'Augustus, the *Res Gestae* and Hellenistic theories of apotheosis', *Journal of Roman Studies* 89: 1–18.

Botermann, H. 1996. *Das Judenedikt des Kaisers Claudius: Römischer Staat und Christiani im 1. Jahrhundert*. Hermes Einzelschriften, 71 (Stuttgart: F. Steiner).

Bouma, J. W. 1996. *Religio votiva: the archaeology of Latial votive religion. The 5th-3rd cent. BC votive deposit south-west of the main temple at 'Satrium' Borgo Le Ferriere*. 3 vols. (Groningen: University of Groningen diss.).

Bourdieu, P. 1977. *Outline of a Theory of Practice*. Transl. by Robin Nice. Cambridge Studies in Social Anthropology, 16 (Cambridge: Cambridge University Press). Original ed.: *Ésquisse d'une théorie de la pratique, précédé de trois études d'ethnologie Kabyle* (Geneva: Droz, 1972).

Bourdillon, M. F. C. and Fortes, M. (eds). 1980. *Sacrifice* (London: Academic Press).

Bowersock, G. W. 1969. *Greek Sophists in the Roman Empire* (Oxford: Clarendon Press).

Bravo, B. 1997. *Pannychis e simposio: feste private notturne di donne e uomini nei testi letterari e nel culto. Con uno studio iconografico di Françoise Frontisi-Ducroux.* Filologia e critica, 79 (Pisa: Istituti Editoriali e Poligrafici Internazionali).

Brelich, A. 1969. *Paides e parthenoi, 1.* Incunabula graeca, 36 (Rome: Ateneo).

Bremmer, J. N. 1983. 'Scapegoat rituals in Ancient Greece', *Harvard Studies in Classical Philology* 87: 299–320.

——— 1990. 'Adolescents, symposion and pederasty', in Murray 1990: 135–48.

——— 1993. 'Three Roman aetiological myths', in Graf 1993c: 158–74.

——— 1994. 'The soul, death and the afterlife in Early and Classical Greece', in J. M. Bremer, T. P. J. van den Hout, and R. Peters (eds), *Hidden Futures: Death and Immortality in Ancient Egypt, Anatolia and the Classical, Biblical and Arabic-Islamic Worlds* (Amsterdam: Amsterdam University Press) 91–106.

——— 1999. 'The birth of the term "magic"', *Zeitschrift für Papyrologie und Epigraphik* 126: 1–12; rev. and shortened in idem and J. R. Veenstra (eds), *The Metamorphosis of Magic from Late Antiquity to the Early Modern Period* (Leuven: Peeters, 2002) 267–71.

——— 2002. *The Rise and Fall of the After-Life.* Read-Tuckwell Lectures, University of Bristol, 1995 (London and New York: Routledge).

——— 2006. 'Atheism in antiquity', in M. Martin (ed.), *The Cambridge Companion to Atheism* (Cambridge: Cambridge University Press) 11–26.

Brenk, F. E. 1986. 'In the light of the moon: demonology in the Early Imperial Period', *ANRW* II.16,3: 2068–145.

Brennan, T. C. 2004. 'Power and process under the Republican "constitution"', in Flower 2004: 31–65.

Bricault, L. 2001. *Atlas de la diffusion des cultes isiaques (IVᵉ siècle av. J.C.- IVᵉ apr. J.C.).* Mémoires de l'Académie des Inscriptions et Belles-Lettres, 23 (Paris: Le Boccard).

Brisson, L. 2004. *How Philosophers saved Myths: allegorical interpretation and classical mythology.* Transl. by Catherine Tihanyi (Chicago: University of Chicago Press). Orig. editions: *Einführung in die Philosophie des Mythos, 1: Antike, Mittelalter und Renaissance* (Darmstadt: Wissenschaftliche Buchgesellschaft, 1996) and *Introduction à la philosophie du mythe, 1: Sauver les mythes* (Paris: J. Vrin, 1996).

Broise, H. and Scheid, J. 1987. *Recherches archéologiques à la Magliana: Le balneum des frères arvales.* Roma antica, 1 (Rome: École française de Rome).

Broise, H. and Thébert, Y. 1999. 'Élagabal et le complexe religieux de la Vigna Barberini: *Heliogabalum in Palatino monte iuxta aedes imperatorias consecravit eique templum fecit* (HA, *Ant. Heliog.*, III, 4)', *MEFR(A)* 111: 729–47.

Brown, F. E. 1974–1975. 'La protostoria della Regia', *RPAA* 47: 15–36.

Brown, P. R. L. 1971. *The World of Late Antiquity* (London: Thames and Hudson).

——— 1978. *The Making of Late Antiquity* (Cambridge, MA: Harvard University Press).

——— 1988. *The Body and Society: men, women and sexual renunciation in Early Christianity* (New York: Columbia University Press).

——— 1995. *Authority and the Sacred: aspects of the Christianization of the Roman World* (Cambridge: Cambridge University Press).

Brown, P. R. L. et al. 1997. 'The world of Late Antiquity revisited', *Symbolae Osloenses* 72: 5–90.

Bruce, S. 1999. *Choice and Religion: a critique of Rational Choice Theory* (Oxford: Oxford University Press).

Brulé, P. and Vendries, C. (eds) 2001. *Chanter les dieux: musique et religion dans l'Antiquité grecque et romaine. Actes du colloque, 16–18 déc. 1999 (Rennes et Lorient)* (Rennes: Presses Universitaires de Rennes).

Bruun, P. 1972. '*Evocatio deorum*: some notes on the Romanization of Etruria', in H. Biezais (ed.), *The Myth of the State: based on papers read at the Symposium on the Myth of the State hold at Åbo, 6th–8th September 1971.* Scripta Instituti Donneriani Aboensis, 6 (Stockholm: Almqvist and Wiksell) 109–120.

Bruun, C. (ed.) 2000. *The Roman Middle Republic: politics, religion and historiography c. 400–133 B.C.* Acta Instituti Finlandiae, 23 (Rome: Institutum Romanum).

Burckhardt, L. A. 1988. *Politische Strategien der Optimaten in der späten römischen Republik.* Historia Einzelschriften, 57 (Stuttgart: Steiner).

Burkert, W. 1972. *Lore and Science in Ancient Pythagoreanism.* Trans. by E. LeR. Minar, jr. (Cambridge, MA: Harvard University Press). Orig. ed. *Weisheit und Wissenschaft. Studien zu Pythagoras, Philolaos und Platon* (Nuremberg: Carl, 1962).

1979. *Structure and History in Greek Mythology and Ritual.* Sather Classical Lectures, 47 (Berkeley, CA: University of California Press).

1983. *Homo Necans: The Anthropology of Ancient Greek Sacrificial Ritual and Myth.* Trans. by P. Bing (Berkeley, CA: University of California Press). Orig. title: *Homo Necans: Interpretationen altgriechischer Opferriten und Mythen*, RGVV, 32 (Berlin: de Gruyter, 1972).

1984. *Die Anthropologie des religiösen Opfers: Die Sakralisierung der Gewalt.* C. F. von Siemens Stiftung, Themen 40 (Munich: Siemens-Stiftung, privately circulated).

1987. *Ancient Mystery Cults* (Cambridge, MA: Harvard University Press).

1996. *Creation of the Sacred: Tracks of biology in early religions* (Cambridge, MA: Harvard University Press).

Caballos Rufino, A. 2006. *El nuevo Bronce de Osuna y la politica colonizadora romana* (Universidad de Sevilla: Seville).

Calame, C. 2001. *Choruses of Young Women in Ancient Greece: their morphology, religious role and social functions.* Trans. by D. Collins and J. Orion (Lanham, MD and London: Rowman and Littlefield). Original edition: *Les choeurs de jeunes filles en Grèce archaïque 1: morphologie, fonction religieuse et sociale.* Filologia e critica, 20–1 (Rome: Ed. dell' Ateneo and Bizzarri, 1977).

Cameron, A. 1973. *Porphyrius the Charioteer* (Oxford: Clarendon Press).

1976. *Circus Factions: Blues and Greens at Rome and Byzantium* (Oxford: Clarendon Press).

Cancik, H. 1973. 'Römischer Religionsunterricht in apostolischer Zeit: Ein pastoralgeschichtlicher Versuch zu Statius, *Silvae* V.3, 176–84', in H. Feld and J. Nolte (eds), *Wort Gottes in der Zeit: Festschrift für K. H. Schelkle* (Düsseldorf: Patmos) 181–97.

1977. 'Reinheit und Enthaltsamkeit in der römischen Philosophie und Religion', in F. von Lilienfeld et al. (eds), *Aspekte frühchristlicher Heiligenverehrung.* Oikonomia, 6 (Erlangen: Lehrstuhl für Geschichte und Theologie des christlichen Ostens) 1–15.

1978. 'Die republikanische Tragödie', in E. Lefèvre (ed.), *Das römische Drama.* Geschichte der Literatur nach Gattungen (Darmstadt: Wissenschaftliche Buchgesellschaft) 308–47.

1985–1986. 'Rome as sacred landscape: Varro and the end of Republican religion in Rome', *Visible Religion* 4/5: 250–65.

1986. 'Nutzen, Schmuck und Aberglaube: Ende und Wandlungen der römischen Religion im 4. und 5. Jahrhundert', in H. Zinser (ed.), *Der Untergang von Religionen* (Berlin: Reimer) 65–90.

1991. 'La religione', in B. Andreae et al. (eds), *Princeps urbium: Cultura e vita sociale dell'Italia romana* (Milan: Scheiwiller) 337–416.

1995. 'M. Tullius Cicero als Kommentator: Zur Formgeschichte von Ciceros Schriften. *Über den Bescheid der haruspices* (56 v. Chr.) und *Über die Gesetze II* (ca. 52 v. Chr.)', in J. Assmann and B. Gladigow (eds), *Text und Kommentar.* Archäologie der literarischen Kommunikation, 4 (Munich: Fink) 292–310.

1996a. '*Carmen* und *sacrificium*: Das Saecularlied des Horaz in den Saecularakten des Jahres 17 v. Chr.', in R. Faber and B. Seidensticker (eds), *Worte, Bilder, Töne: Studien zur Antike und Antikerezeption. Bernhard Kytzler zu ehren* (Würzburg: Königshausen and Neumann) 99–113.

(ed.) 1996b. *Geschichte – Tradition – Reflexion: Festschrift für Martin Hengel zum 70. Geburtstag 2: Griechische und Römische Religion* (Tübingen: Mohr Siebeck).

Cancik, H. and Mohr, H. 1988. 'Religionsästhetik', *HrwG* 1: 121–56.

Cancik, H. and Rüpke, J. (eds) 1997. *Römische Reichsreligion und Provinzialreligion* (Tübingen: Mohr-Siebeck).

Cancik-Lindemaier, H. 1996. 'Der Diskurs Religion im Senatsbeschluß über die Bacchanalia von 186 v. Chr. und bei Livius (Buch XXXIX)', in Cancik 1996b: 77–96.

Carandini, A. 1997. *La nascita di Roma: Dèi, lari, eroi e uomini all' alba di una civiltà.* Biblioteca di cultura storica, 219 (Turin: Einaudi).

Carandini, A. and Cappelli, R. (eds). 2000. *Roma: Romolo, Remo e la fondazione della città* (Milan: Electa).

Castagnoli, F. 1979. *Il culto di Minerva a Lavinium: conferenza tenuta nella seduta del 13 gennaio 1979.* Problemi attuali di scienza e di cultura, 246 (Rome: Accademia Nazionale dei Lincei).

Cecamore, C. 1999. '*Faustinae aedemque decernerent* (SHA Marcus, 26): les fragments 69–70 de la Forma urbis et la première dédicace du temple de la vigna Barberini', *MEFR(A)* 111: 311–49.

Champeaux, J. 1989. ' "Pietas": piété personelle et piété collective à Rome', *Bulletin de l'Association G. Budé* 48: 263–79.

Chaniotis, A. 1997. 'Reinheit des Körpers – Reinheit des Sinnes in den griechischen Kultgesetzen', in J. Assmann and T. Sundermeier (eds), *Schuld, Gewissen und Person.* Studien zum Verstehen fremder Religionen, 9 (Gütersloh: Mohn) 142–79.

Charlesworth, M. P. 1936. 'Providentia and aeternitas', *Harvard Theological Review* 39: 107–21.

Christol, M. et al. (eds). 1992. *Institutions, société et vie politique dans l'empire romain au IVe siècle ap. J. -C. Actes de la table ronde autour de l'œuvre d'André Chastagnol (Paris, 20–21 janvier 1989).* CEFR, 159 (Rome: École française).

Chuvin, P. 1990. *Chronicle of the Last Pagans.* Trans. by B. A. Archer (Cambridge, MA: Harvard University Press). Simultaneously in French: *Chronique des derniers païens: la disparition du paganisme dans l'Empire romain, du règne de Constantin à celui de Justinien* (Paris: Belles Lettres,1990, 1991, 2nd edn).

Cichorius, C. 1922. *Römische Studien: Historisches Epigraphisches Literaturgeschichtliches aus vier Jahrhunderten Roms* (Berlin: Teubner).

Cipriano, P. 1983. *Templum*. Biblioteca ricerche linguistiche e filologiche, 13 (Rome: Università 'La Sapienza').

Claridge, A. 1998. *Rome* (Oxford: Oxford University Press).

Clark, S. 1997. *Thinking with Demons: the idea of witchcraft in Early Modern Europe* (Oxford: Oxford University Press).

Clarke, J. R. 1991. *The Houses of Roman Italy, 100 BC–AD 250: ritual, space and decoration* (Berkeley: University of California Press).

Clauss, M. 1994. 'Die Anhängerschaft des Silvanus-Kultes', *Klio* 76: 381–7.

1999. *Kaiser und Gott: Herrscherkult im römischen Reich* (Stuttgart: Teubner).

2000. *The Roman Cult of Mithras: the god and his mysteries*. Revised ed., trans. by Richard Gordon (Edinburgh: Edinburgh University Press). Orig. title: *Mithras: Kult und Mysterien* (Munich: Beck, 1990).

Claussen, M. A. 1995. 'Pagan rebellion and Christian apologetics in fourth-century Rome: the *Consultationes Zacchaei et Apollonii*', *Journal of Ecclesiastical History* 46: 589–614.

Coarelli, F. 1983a. *Il Foro Romano 1: Periodo arcaico* (Rome: Edizioni Quasar).

1983b. 'Architettura sacra e architettura privata nella tarda repubblica', in *Architecture et société. De l'archaïsme grec à la fin de la république romaine* (Rome: École Française) 191–217.

1985. *Il Foro Romano 2: Periodo repubblicano e augusteo* (Rome: Edizioni Quasar).

1987. *I santuari del Lazio in età repubblicana*. Studi NIS archeologia, 7 (Rome: Nuova Italia Scientifica).

1988. *Il Foro Boario: Dalle origine alla fine della repubblica* (Rome: Edizioni Quasar).

1997. *Il Campo Marzio: Dalle origini alla fine della repubblica* (Rome: Edizioni Quasar).

Cole, S. Guettel. 1995. 'Civic cult and civic identity', in M. H. Hansen (ed.), *Sources for the Ancient Greek City-State*. Acts of the Copenhagen Polis Centre, 2 = Det Kongelige Danske Videnskabernes Selskab, Hist.-filosof. Meddeleser, 72 (Copenhagen) 292–325.

Colini, A. M. et al. 1977. *Lazio arcaico e mondo greco = La Parola del Passato* 32: 9–128 (Naples: Macchiaroli).

Colpe, C. and Holzhausen, J. (trans. and introduction). 1997. *Das Corpus Hermeticum deutsch: Übersetzung, Darstellung und Kommentierung in drei Teilen. 1: Die griechischen Traktate und der lateinische 'Asclepius'*. Clavis Pansophiae, 7.1–2 (Stuttgart-Bad Cannstatt: Frommann-Holzboog).

Comella, A. 1981. 'Tipologia e diffusione dei complessi votivi in Italia in epoca medio- e tardo-repubblicana: contributo alla storia dell'artigianato antico', *MEFR(A)* 93: 717–803.

Connor, W. R. 1987. 'Tribes, festivals and processions: civic ceremonial and political manipulation in Archaic Greece', *Journal of Hellenic Studies* 107: 40–50.

Copenhaver, B. P. 1992. *Hermetica. The Greek Corpus Hermeticum and the Latin Asclepius in a new English translation with notes and introduction* (Cambridge: Cambridge University Press).

Cordischi, L. 1993. 'Nuove acquisizioni su un'area di culto al Colle Oppio', *Archeologia Laziale* 11: 39–44.

Cornell, T. J. 1975. 'Aeneas and the Twins: the development of the Roman foundation legend', *PCPhS* n.s. 21: 1–32.

1995. *The Beginnings of Rome: Italy and Rome from the Bronze Age to the Punic Wars (c. 1000–264 BC)* (London: Routledge).

Cotter, W. 1996. 'The *collegia* and Roman law: state restrictions on voluntary associations, 64 BCE-200 CE', in Kloppenborg and Wilson 1996: 74–89.

Courtney, E. (ed. and comm.) 1993. *The Fragmentary Latin Poets* (Oxford: Clarendon Press).

Cracco Ruggini, L. 1988. 'La lettera di Anna a Seneca nella Roma pagana e cristiana del IV secolo', *Augustinianum* 28: 301–25.

Cramer, F. H. 1954. *Astrology in Roman Law and Politics*. Memoirs of the American Philosophical Society, 37 (Philadelphia: American Philosophical Society).

Crawford, M. H. 1996. *Roman Statutes*. Bulletin of the Institute of Classical Studies, Supplement 64 (Institute of Classical Studies: London).

Cristofani, M. 1987. 'I santuari: tradizioni decorative', in idem (ed.), *Etruria e Lazio arcaico: Atti dell' incontro di studio (10–11 novembre 1986) = Quaderni del Centro di Studio per l' Archeologia Etrusco-Italica*, 15 (Rome: Consiglio Nazionale delle Ricerche) 95–120.

Croke, B. and Harries, J. (eds). 1982. *Religious Conflict in Fourth-Century Rome: A Documentary Study* (Sydney: Sydney University Press).

Csapo, E. 2005. *Theories of Mythology* (Oxford: Blackwell Publishing).

Curran, J. 2000. *Pagan City and Christian Capital: Rome in the Fourth Century* (Oxford: Oxford University Press).

D'Arms, J. H. 1984. 'Control, companionship and clientela: some social functions of the Roman communal meal', *Échos du monde classique* 3: 327–48.

1990. 'The Roman *convivium* and the idea of equality', in Murray 1990: 308–20.

2000. 'Memory, money and status at Misenum: Three new inscriptions from the *Collegium* of the Augustales', *Journal of Roman Studies* 90: 126–44.

Davies, J. P. 2004. *Rome's Religious History: Livy, Tacitus and Ammianus on their gods* (Cambridge: Cambridge University Press).

De Bomhard, A. S. 1999. *The Egyptian Calendar* (London: Periplus).

Debord, P. 1982. *Aspects sociaux et économiques de la vie religieuse dans l'Anatolie gréco-romaine*. EPROER, 88 (Leyden: Brill).

De Cazenove, O. 1991. 'Ex-voto de l'Italie républicaine: sur quelques aspects de leur mise au rebut', in J. -L. Brunaux (ed.), *Les sanctuaires celtiques et le monde méditerranéen: Actes du colloque de St-Riquier (8–11 nov. 1990) organisé par la Direction des Antiquités de Picardie et l'UMR 126 du CNRS* (Paris: Errance) 203–14.

1997. 'La plastique de terre-cuite: un indicateur des lieux du culte? L'exemple de la Lucanie', *Cahiers Gustave Glotz* 8: 151–69.

2000. 'Some thoughts on the "religious Romanisation" of Italy before the Social War', in Bispham and Smith 2000: 71–6.

De Fine Licht, K. 1968. *The Rotunda in Rome: a study of Hadrian's Pantheon*. Jutland Archaeological Society Publications, 7 (Copenhagen: Gyldendal).

De Libero, L. 1992. *Obstruktion: Politische Praktiken im Senat und in der Volksversammlung der ausgehenden römischen Republik (70–49 v. Chr.)*. Hermes Einzelschriften, 59 (Stuttgart: F. Steiner).

De Ligt; L. 2000. 'Governmental attitudes towards markets and collegia', in E. Lo Cascio (ed.), *Mercati permanenti e mercati periodici nel mondo romano. Atti degli Incontri capresi di storia dell'economia antica, Capri, 13–15 ott. 1997* (Bari: Edipuglia), 237–52.

De Marchi, A. 1903. *Il culto privato di Roma antica, 2: La religione gentilizia e collegiale* (Milan: Hoepli).

Deming, W. 2003. *Paul on Marriage and Celibacy* 2nd edn (Grand Rapids and Cambridge: W. J. Eeerdmans).

Derks, T. 1995. 'The ritual of the vow in Gallo-Roman religion', in Metzler, D. et al. (eds), *Integration in the early Roman West. The role of culture and ideology.* Dossiers d'Archéologie du Musée National d'Histoire et d'Art, 4 (Luxembourg) 111–27.

—— 1998. *Gods, Temples and Ritual Practices: the transformation of religious ideas and values in Roman Gaul.* Amsterdam Archaeological Studies, 2 (Amsterdam: Amsterdam University Press).

De Robertis, F. M. 1963. *Lavoro e lavoratori nel mondo romano* (Bari: Adriatica, repr. New York: Arno, 1979).

Deschler-Erb, S. 1998. *Römische Beinartefakte aus Augusta Raurica: Rohmaterial, Technologie, Typologie und Chronologie 1: Text und Tafel* (Augst: Römermuseum).

DeVoe, R. F. 1987. *The Christians and the Games: the relationship between Christianity and the Roman Games from the first through the fifth Centuries A.D.* Diss. Texas Tech. U., Lubbock, TX.

De Vos, A. and De Vos, M. 1982. *Pompei, Ercolano, Stabia.* Guide archeologiche Laterza (Rome and Bari: Laterza).

Devoto, G. 1974. *Le tavole di Gubbio* (= *Tabulae iguvinae* 4th edn) (Florence: Sansoni).

Dickie, M. W. 2001. *Magic and Magicians in the Graeco-Roman World* (London and New York: Routledge).

Digeser, E. de P. 2006. 'Religion, law and the Roman polity: the era of the Great Persecution', in Ando and Rüpke 2006: 68–84.

Dilke, O. A. W. 1971. *The Roman Land Surveyors: an introduction to the Agrimensores* (Newton Abbot: David and Charles).

Dodds, E. R. 1951. *The Greeks and the Irrational.* Sather Classical Lectures, 25 (Berkeley, CA: University of California Press).

Döpp, S. (ed.) 1993. *Karnevaleske Phänomene in antiken und nachantiken Kulturen und Literaturen.* Bochumer Altertums–wissenschaftliches Colloquium, 13 = Stätten und Formen der Kommunikation im Altertum, 1 (Trier: Wissenschaftlicher Verlag Trier).

Dorcey, P. F. 1992. *The Cult of Silvanus: a study in Roman folk religion* (Leyden: Brill).

Doren, M. van. 1954. 'Peregrina sacra: Offizielle Kultübertragungen im alten Rom', *Historia* 3: 488–97.

Douglas, J. D. 1997. *Death, Ritual and Belief: the rhetoric of funerary rites* (London: Cassell).

Douglas, M. (ed.) 1970. *Witchcraft Confessions and Accusations.* Papers mostly presented to the annual conference of the Association of Social Anthropologists of the Commonwealth, at King's College, Cambridge, 3–6 April 1968 (London: Tavistock).

Dräger, O. 1994. *Religionem significare: Studien zu reich verzierten römischen*

Altäre und Basen aus Marmor. Mitteilungen des Deutschen Archäologischen Instituts Rom, Ergänzungsheft 33 (Mainz: Zabern).

Draper, R. D. 1988. *The Role of the Pontifex Maximus and its Influences in Roman Religion and Politics* (Diss. Brigham Young University).

Dubourdieu, A. 1989. *Les origines et le développement du culte des Pénates à Rome.* CEFR, 118 (Rome: École française).

Dumézil, G. 1966. *La religion romaine archaïque avec un appendice sur La religion des Étrusques* (Paris: Payot). English ed.: *Archaic Roman Religion: with an Appendix on the Religion of the Etruscans.* 2 vols., trans. by P. Krapp (Chicago: Chicago University Press, 1970).

1975. *Fêtes romaines d'été et d'automne suivi de Dix questions romaines* (Paris: Gallimard).

1980. *Camillus: a study of Indo-European religion as Roman history.* Ed. with an introd. by U. Strutynski (Berkeley, CA: University of California Press).

Dunand, F. and Zivie-Coche, C. 2004. *Gods and Men in Egypt: 3000 BCE to 395 CE* (Ithaca: Cornell University Press).

Dunbabin, K. M. D. 2003. *The Roman Banquet: images of conviviality* (Cambridge: Cambridge University Press).

Duncan-Jones, R. P. 1982. *The Economy of the Roman Empire: quantitative studies* 2nd edn (Cambridge: Cambridge University Press).

1994. *Money and Government in the Roman Empire* (Cambridge: Cambridge University Press).

Dunn, J. 2007. 'Boundary markers in Early Christianity', in J. Rüpke (ed.), *Gruppenreligionen im römischen Reich: Sozialformen, Grenzziehungen, Leistungen.* Studien und Texte zu Antike und Christentum (Tübingen: Mohr Siebeck) 55–74.

Durand, J. -L. 1979. 'Bêtes grecques: propositions pour une topologique des corps à manger', in M. Detienne and J. -P. Vernant (eds), *La cuisine du sacrifice en pays grec* (Paris: Gallimard) 137–65.

Durand, J. -L. and Scheid, J. 1994. ' "Rites" et "religion": Remarques sur certains préjugés des historiens de la religion des grecs et des romains', *Archives de sciences sociales des religions* 85: 23–43.

Duthoy, R. 1976. *Recherches sur la répartition géographique et chronologique des termes sevir Augustalis, Augustalis et sevir dans l'Empire romain.* Epigraphische Studien, 11 (Köln: Rheinland Verlag).

Duval, P. -M. and Pinault, G. 1986. *Recueil des inscriptions gauloises, 3: Les calendriers (Coligny; Villards d'Héria).* Gallia Supplement, 45 (Paris: Éditions du Centre National de la Recherche Scientifique).

Duval, Y. -M. 1977. 'Des Lupercales de Constantinople aux Lupercales de Rome', *Revue des Études Latines* 55: 222–70.

Dzielska, M. 1986. *Apollonius of Tyana in Legend and History.* Trans. by Piotr Pienkowski. Problemi e ricerche di storia antica, 10 (Rome: 'L'Erma' di Bretschneider).

Eck, W. 1997. 'Die religiösen und kultischen Aufgaben der römischen Statthalter in der hohen Kaiserzeit', in M. Mayer (ed.), *Religio deorum. Actas del Coloquio internacional de epigrafía: Culto y sociedad en occidente* (Sabadell, Barcelona: Editorial AUSA) 151–60.

Edlund, I. E. M. 1987. *The Gods and the Place. The location and function of the sanctuaries in the countryside of Etruria and Magna Graecia, 700 – 400 BC.* Acta Instituti Romani Regni Suecae, 43 (Stockholm: Almqvist and Wiksell).

Edlund-Berry, I. E. M. 1992. 'Etruscans at work and play. Evidence for an Etruscan calendar', in H. Froning et al. (eds), *Kotinos: Festschrift für E. Simon* (Mainz: Philip Zabern) 330–38.

Edwards, M., Goodman, M., and Price, S. (eds) 1999. *Apologetics in the Roman Empire: pagans, Jews and Christians* (Oxford: Oxford University Press).

Egelhaaf-Gaiser, U. 2000. *Kulträume im römischen Alltag: das Isisbuch des Apuleius und der Ort von Religion im kaiserlichen Rom*. PAwB, 2 (Stuttgart: F. Steiner).

2001. 'Träger und Transportwege von Religion am Beispiel des Totenkultes in den Germaniae', in Spickermann 2001: 225–57.

Egelhaaf-Gaiser, U. and Rüpke, J. 2000. 'Orte des Erscheinens – Orte des Verbergens: Höhlen in Kult und Theologie', *Orbis Terrarum* 6: 155–76.

Egelhaaf-Gaiser, U. and Schäfer, A. (eds) 2002. *Religiöse Vereine in der römischen Antike: Untersuchungen zu Organisation, Ritual und Raumordnung*. Studien und Texte zu Antike und Christentum, 13 (Tübingen: Mohr-Siebeck).

Elsner, J. 1998. *Imperial Rome and Christian Triumph: the art of the Roman Empire AD 100–450* (Oxford: Oxford University Press).

Engemann, J. 1975. 'Zur Verbreitung magischer Übelabwehr in der nichtchristlichen und christlichen Spätantike', *JfAC* 18: 22–48.

2000. 'Anmerkungen zu philologischen und archäologischen Studien über spätantike Magie', *JfAC* 43: 55–70.

Eriksson, S. 1956. *Wochentagsgötter, Mond und Tierkreis: Laienastrologie in der römischen Kaiserzeit*. Studia Graeca et Latina Gothoburgensia, 3 (Stockholm: Almquist and Wiksell).

Erler, M. et al. 1994. *Die Philosophie der Antike 4: Die hellenistische Philosophie*. Grundriss der Geschichte der Philosophie, ed. H. Flashar (Basle: Schwabe).

Erskine, A. 2001. *Troy between Greece and Rome: local tradition and imperial Rome* (Oxford: Oxford University Press).

Estienne, S. et al. 2004–6. 'Personnel de culte: monde romain', in Balty et al. 2004–6: 5, 66–146.

Étienne, R. 1959. *Le culte impérial dans la péninsule ibérique d'Auguste à Dioclétien*. BEFAR, 191 (Paris: De Boccard).

1984. 'Aeternitas Augusti – Aeternitas Imperii: quelques aperçus', in *Les grandes figures religieuses: Fonctionnement pratique et symboliques dans l'antiquité (Besançon 25–26 avril 1984)*. Centre de recherches d'histoire ancienne, 68 = Lire les polythéismes, 1 (Paris: Belles-Lettres) 445–54.

Fantham, E. 1996. *Roman Literary Culture: from Cicero to Apuleius* (Baltimore and London: Johns Hopkins University Press). The German edition is in many respects a considerable improvement on the original: *Literarisches Leben im antiken Rom: Sozialgeschichte der römischen Literatur von Cicero bis Apuleius* (Stuttgart: Metzler, 1998).

Faraone, C. A., and Obbink, D. (eds) 1997. *Magika Hiera: ancient Greek magic and religion* (New York: Oxford University Press).

Fears, J. R. 1981a. 'The cult of Jupiter and Roman imperial ideology', *ANRW* II. 17,1: 3–141.

1981b. 'The theology of victory at Rome: approaches and problems', *ANRW* II. 17,2: 736–826.

Feeney, D. 1998. *Literature and Religion at Rome: cultures, contexts and beliefs* (Cambridge: Cambridge University Press).

Fellmeth, U. 1987. *Die römischen Vereine und die Politik: Untersuchungen zur sozialen Schichtung und zum politischen Bewußtsein in den Vereinen der städtischen Volksmassen in Rom und Italien* (Stuttgart: Historisches Institut der Universität Stuttgart).

Fenelli, M. 1984. 'Lavinium', *Archeologia Laziale* 6: 325–44.

Ferrary, J.-L. 1988. *Philhellénisme et impérialisme: aspects idéologiques de la conquête romaine du monde hellénistique, de la seconde guerre de Macédoine à la guerre contre Mithridate*. BEFAR, 271 (Rome: École française).

Ferrua, A. 1991. *The Unknown Catacomb: a unique discovery of Early Christian art*. Transl. by I. Inglis (New Lanark: Geddes and Grosset). Orig. ed.: *Catacombe sconosciute, una pinacoteca del IV secolo sotto la Via Latina* (Florence: Nardini, 1990).

Festinger, L., Riecken, H. W., and Schachter, S. 1964. *When Prophecy Fails: a social and psychological study of a modern group that predicted the end of the world* (New York: Harper Torchbooks). Orig. ed.: Minneapolis: University of Minnesota Press, 1956.

Février, P.-A. 1992. 'Un plaidoyer pour Damase: les inscriptions des nécropoles romaines', in Christol et al. 1992: 497–506.

Fiedrowicz, M. 2000. *Apologie im frühen Christentum: Die Kontroverse um den christlichen Wahrheitsanspruch in den ersten Jahrhunderten* (Paderborn: Schöningh).

Fink, J. 1978. 'Vorstellungen und Bräuche an Gräbern bei Griechen, Römern und frühen Christen', in S. Şahin, E. Schwertheim, and J. Wagner (eds), *Studien zur Religion und Kultur Kleinasiens: Festschrift für Friedrich Karl Dörner zum 65. Geburtstag am 28. Februar 1976*. EPROER, 66 (Leyden: Brill) 1, 295–323.

Finley, M. I. 1962. *The World of Odysseus* 2nd edn (Harmondsworth: Penguin). Orig. ed.: New York: Viking, 1954; London: Chatto and Windus, 1956.

Fischer, W. and Marhold, W. 1983. 'Das Konzept des Symbolischen Interaktionismus in der deutschen Religionssoziologie', in K.-F. Daiber and T. Luckmann (eds), *Religion in den Gegenwartsströmungen der deutschen Soziologie* (Munich: Kaiser) 157–81.

Fishwick, D. 1987–2005. *The Imperial Cult in the Latin West: studies in the ruler cult of the western provinces of the Roman Empire*. 3 vols. in 8. EPROER, 108.1–4 and RGRW, 145–8 (Leyden: Brill).

Flaig, E. 1991. 'Amnestie und Amnesie in der griechischen Kultur: Das vergessene Selbstopfer für den Sieg im athenischen Bürgerkrieg 403 v. Chr.', *Saeculum* 42: 129–49.

1992. *Den Kaiser herausfordern: Die Usurpation im römischen Reich*. Historische Studien, 7 (Frankfurt a.M.: Campus).

1995a. 'Die Pompa Funebris: Adlige Konkurrenz und annalistische Erinnerung in der Römischen Republik', in O. G. Oexle (ed.), *Memoria als Kultur* (Göttingen: Vandenhoeck and Ruprecht) 115–48.

1995b. 'Entscheidung und Konsens: Zu den Feldern der politischen Kommunikation zwischen Aristokratie und Plebs', in M. Jehne (ed.), *Demokratie in Rom? Die Rolle des Volkes in der Politik der römischen Republik*. Historia Einzelschriften, 96 (Stuttgart: F. Steiner) 77–127.

Fleischhauer, G. 1964. *Etrurien und Rom*. Musikgeschichte in Bildern, II.5 (Leipzig: Deutscher Verlag für Musik).

Fless, F. 1995. *Opferdiener und Kultmusiker auf stadtrömischen historischen Reliefs: Untersuchungen zur Ikonographie, Funktion und Benennung* (Mainz: Zabern).

301

Flint, V., Gordon, R. L., Luck, G. and Ogden, D. 1999. *Witchcraft and Magic in Europe, 2: Ancient Greece and Rome.* The Athlone History of Witchcraft and Magic in Europe, B. Ankarloo and S. Clark (eds) (London: The Athlone Press; now Continuum).

Flower, H. I. 1996. *Ancestor Masks and Aristocratic Power in Roman Culture* (Oxford: Clarendon Press).

2004. *The Cambridge Companion to the Roman Republic* (Cambridge: Cambridge University Press).

Fögen, M. -T. 1993. *Die Enteignung der Wahrsager: Studien zum kaiserlichen Wissensmonopol in der Spätantike* (Frankfurt a.M.: Suhrkamp).

Forsythe, G. 2005. *A Critical History of Early Rome* (Berkeley: University of California Press).

Fowden, G. 1986. *The Egyptian Hermes: a historical approach to the late pagan mind* (Cambridge: Cambridge University Press; corr. repr.: Princeton: Princeton University Press, 1993).

Fowler, R. and Graf, F. 2004–06. 'Magische Rituale', in J. C. Balty et al. (eds) 2004–06: 3: 283–301.

Frankfurter, D. 1998. *Religion in Roman Egypt: assimilation and resistance* (Princeton: University Press).

Fraschetti, A. 1990. *Roma e il principe: Ricerche di storia urbana nell'età di Augusto e di Tiberio* (Bari: Laterza).

Fridh, A. 1990. 'Sacellum, sacrarium, fanum, and related terms', in *Greek and Latin Studies in Memory of C. Fabricius.* Studia Graeca et Latina Gothoburgensia, 54 (Gothenburg: Acta Univ. Gothoburgensis) 173–87.

Fridh-Haneson, B. M. 1987. 'Votive terracottas from Italy: types and problems', in Linders and Nordquist 1987: 66–75.

Frier, B. W. 1977. 'The rental market in early imperial Rome', *Journal of Roman Studies* 67: 27–37.

1979. Libri annales pontificum maximorum: *the origins of the annalistic tradition.* Monographs of the American Academy in Rome, 27 (Rome: American Academy).

1980. *Landlords and Tenants in Imperial Rome* (Princeton: Princeton University Press).

Friesen, S. J. 1993. *Twice neokoros: Ephesus, Asia and the cult of the Flavian imperial family.* RGRW 116 (Leyden: Brill).

Frischer, B. et al. 2006. 'A new digital model of the Roman Forum', in Haselberger and Humphrey 2006: 163–82.

Furley, W. D. and Bremer, J. M. 2001. *Greek Hymns.* 2 vols. Studien und Texte zu Antike und Christentum, 9 (Tübingen: Mohr Siebeck).

Gabba, E. 1984. 'The *collegia* of Numa: problems of method and political ideas', *Journal of Roman Studies* 74: 81–6.

1991. *Dionysius and the History of Archaic Rome.* Sather Classical Lectures, 56 (Berkeley: University of California Press).

Gager, J. G. (ed.) 1992. *Curse Tablets and Binding Spells from the Ancient World* (New York: Oxford University Press).

Galsterer, H. 1976. *Herrschaft und Verwaltung im republikanischen Italien: Die Beziehungen Roms zu den italischen Gemeinden vom Latinerfrieden 338 v. Chr. bis zum Bundesgenossenkrieg 91 v.Chr.* Münchener Beiträge zur Papyrusforschung und antiken Rechtsgeschichte, 68 (Munich: Beck).

Gargola, J. D. 1995. *Lands, Laws and Gods: magistrates and ceremony in the reg-*

ulation of public lands in Republican Rome (Chapel Hill and London: University of North Carolina Press).

Garnsey, P. D. A. and Saller, R. P. 1987. *The Roman Empire: economy, society and culture* (London: Duckworth).

Gatti Lo Guzzo, L. 1978. *Il deposito votivo dall' Esquilino detto di 'Minerva Medica'* (Florence: Sanzoni).

Gebhard, V. 1925. *Die Pharmakoi in Ionien und die Sybakchoi in Athen* (Diss. Munich).

Gehlen, R. 1995. *Welt und Ordnung: Zur soziokulturellen Dimension von Raum in frühen Gesellschaften* (Marburg: diagonal).

Gell, A. 1992. *The Anthropology of Time: cultural constructions of temporal maps and images* (Providence, RI and Oxford: Berg).

Gelzer, T., Lurje, M. and Schäublin, C. (eds) 1999. *Lamella Bernensis: ein spätantikes Goldamulett mit christlichem Exorzismus und verwandte Texte.* Beiträge zur Altertumskunde, 124 (Stuttgart and Leipzig: Teubner).

Georgoudi, S., Koch Piettre, R. and Schmidt, F. (eds) 2005. *La cuisine et l'autel: les sacrifices en question dans les sociétés de la Méditerranée ancienne.* Bibliothèque de l'École Pratique des Hautes Études, Sciences Religieuses, 124 (Turnhout: Brepol).

Gerson, L. P. 1990. *God and Greek Philosophy: studies in the early history of Natural Philosophy* (London: Routledge).

Ghinatti, F. 1983. 'Manifestazioni votive, iscrizioni e vita economica nei santuari della Magna Grecia', *Studia Patavina* 30: 241–322.

Gill, D. H. 1974. 'Trapezomata: a neglected aspect of Greek sacrifice', *Harvard Theological Review* 67: 117–37.

—— 1991. *Greek Cult Tables.* Harvard Dissertations in the Classics (New York: Garland).

Ginestet, P. 1991. *Les organisations de la jeunesse dans l'occident romain.* Collection Latomus, 213 (Brussels: Latomus).

Giuliani, C. F. and Verduchi, P. 1987. *L'area centrale del Foro Romano.* Il Linguaggio dell' Architectura Romana, 1 (Florence: Olschki).

Gladigow, B. 1971. 'Ovids Rechtfertigung der blutigen Opfer: Interpretationen zu Ovid, *Fasti* I 335–456', *Der altsprachliche Unterricht* 14.3: 5–23.

—— 1979. 'Der Sinn der Götter: Zum kognitiven Potential der persönlichen Gottesvorstellung', in P. Eicher (ed.), *Gottesvorstellung und Gesellschaftsentwicklung.* Forum Religionswissenschaft, 1 (Munich: Kösel) 41–62.

—— 1980. '*Naturae deus humanae mortalis*: Zur sozialen Konstruktion des Todes in römischer Zeit', in G. Stephenson (ed.), *Leben und Tod in den Religionen: Symbol und Wirklichkeit* (Darmstadt: Wissenschaftliche Buchgesellschaft) 119–33.

—— 1981. 'Gottesnamen (Gottesepitheta) I (allgemein)', *RfAC* 11: 1202–38.

—— 1983. 'Strukturprobleme polytheistischer Religionen', *Saeculum* 34: 292–304.

—— 1986. 'Mythologie und Theologie: Aussagestufen im griechischen Mythos', in H. von Stietencron (ed.), *Theologen und Theologien in verschiedenen Kulturkreisen* (Düsseldorf: Patmos) 70–88.

—— 1988. 'Gegenstände und wissenschaftlicher Kontext von Religionswissenschaft', *HrwG* 1: 26–40.

—— 1990a. 'Epiphanie, Statuette, Kultbild: Griechische Gottesvorstellungen im Wechsel von Kontext und Medium', *Visible Religion* 7: 98–121.

303

1990b. 'Divination', *HrwG* 2: 226–68.
1992. 'Audi Juppiter, Audite Fines', in O. Behrends and L. Capogrossi Colognesi (eds), *Die römische Feldmeßkunst: Interdisziplinäre Beiträge zu ihrer Bedeutung für die Zivilisationsgeschichte Roms* (Göttingen: Vandenhoeck and Ruprecht) 172–91.
1994. 'Zur Ikonographie und Pragmatik römischer Kultbilder', in H. Keller and N. Staubach (eds), *Iconologia sacra: Mythos, Bildkunst und Dichtung in der Religions- und Sozialgeschichte Alteuropas*. Arbeiten zur Frühmittelalterforschung, 23 (Berlin: de Gruyter) 9–24.
1995. 'Anatomia sacra: Religiös motivierte Eingriffe in menschliche oder tierische Körper', in van der Eijk et al. 1995: 2, 345–61.
1997. 'Erwerb religiöser Kompetenz: Kult und Öffentlichkeit in den klassischen Religionen', in Binder and Ehlich 1997: 103–18.
1998. 'Polytheismus', *HrwG* 4: 321–30.
2005. *Religionswissenschaft als Kulturwissenschaft*. Religionswissenschaft, 1 (Stuttgart: Kohlhammer).
Glinister, F. 2000. 'Sacred rubbish', in Bispham and Smith 2000: 54–70.
Glucker, J. 1995. '*Probabile, Veri simile*, and related terms', in Powell 1995b: 115–43.
Goar, R. J. 1972. *Cicero and the State Religion* (Amsterdam: Hakkert).
Görgemanns, H. 2003. 'Autobiography §§ II–III, V', *Brill's New Pauly* 2: 406–8; 410.
Goldberg, S. 1998. 'Plautus on the Palatine', *Journal of Roman Studies* 88: 1–20.
Gordon, R. L. 1979. 'The real and the imaginary: production and religion in the Graeco – Roman world', *Art History* 2: 5–34. [Repr. in idem, *Image and Value in the Graeco-Roman World: studies in Mithraism and religious art* (Aldershot: Variorum, 1996) no. I.]
1990. 'The veil of power: emperors, sacrificers and benefactors', in Beard and North 1990: 201–31.
1995. 'The healing event in Graeco-Roman folk-medicine', in van der Eijk et al. 1995: 2, 363–76.
1997. '*Quaedam veritatis umbrae*: Hellenistic magic and astrology', in P. Bilde et al. (eds), *Conventional Values of the Hellenistic Greeks*. Studies in Hellenistic Civilization, 8 (Aarhus: Aarhus University Press) 128–58.
1999. 'Imagining Greek and Roman magic', in Flint et al. 1999: 159–275.
2007. 'Institutionalized religious options: Mithraism', in Rüpke 2007.
Gordon, R. L. and Marco Simón, F. (eds) 2008. *Magical Practice in the Latin West: Papers from the international conference at Zaragoza, Sept. 30th–Oct. 1st 2005*. RGRW (Leyden: Brill).
Gould, J. 2001. '*Hiketeia*', with 'Addendum 2000', in idem, *Myth, Ritual, Memory and Exchange: essays in Greek literature and culture* (Oxford: Oxford University Press) 22–77. Orig. published in *Journal of Hellenic Studies* 93 (1973) 74–103.
Gradel, I. 2002. *Emperor Worship and Roman Religion* (Oxford: Clarendon Press).
Graepler, D. 1997. *Tonfiguren im Grab: Fundkontexte hellenistischer Terrakotten aus der Nekropole von Tarent* (Munich: Biering and Brinkmann).
Graf, F. 1991. 'Textes orphiques et rituel bacchique. À propos des lamelles de Pélinna', in P. Borgeaud (ed.), *Orphisme et Orphée: en l'honneur de J. Rudhardt*. Recherches et rencontres, 3 (Geneva: Droz) 87–102.
1993a. *Greek Mythology: An Introduction*. Trans. by T. Marier (Baltimore and

London: Johns Hopkins University Press). Original ed.: *Griechische Mythologie: Eine Einführung* (Munich: Artemis, 1987).

1993b. 'Der Mythos bei den Römern. Forschungs- und Problemgeschichte', in Graf 1993c: 25–43.

(ed.) 1993c. *Mythos in mythenloser Gesellschaft: Das Paradigma Roms.* Colloquium Rauricum, 3 (Stuttgart: Teubner).

1997. *Magic in the Ancient World.* Trans. F. Philip. Revealing Antiquity, 10 (Cambridge, MA: Harvard University Press). Original ed. *La magie dans l'antiquité gréco-romaine* (Paris: PUF, 1994).

Grafton, A. T. and Swerdlow, N. M. 1988. 'Calendar dates and ominous days in ancient historiography', *Journal of the Warburg and Courtauld Institutes* 51: 14–42.

Grandazzi, A. 1997. *The Foundation of Rome: myth and history* (Ithaca, NY: Cornell University Press).

Green, C. 2006. *Roman Religion and the Cult of Diana at Aricia* (Cambridge: Cambridge University Press).

Gregori, G. L. 1999. *Brescia Romana, 2: Analisi dei documenti.* Vetera, 13 (Rome: Edizioni Quasar).

Gregory, J. A. 1994. 'Powerful images: responses to portraits and the political uses of images in Rome', *Journal of Roman Archaeology* 7: 80–99.

Griffin, J. 1997. 'Cult and personality in Horace', *Journal of Roman Studies* 87: 54–69.

Grig, L. 2004 [2005]. *Making Martyrs in Late Antiquity* (London: Duckworth).

Gros, P. 1976. *Aurea Templa: Recherches sur l'architecture religieuse de Rome à l'époque d'Auguste.* BEFAR, 231 (Rome: École française).

Gruen, E. S. 1984. *The Hellenistic World and the Coming of Rome.* 2 vols. (Berkeley: University of California Press).

1990. *Studies in Greek Culture and Roman Policy.* Cincinnati Classical Studies, n.s. 7 (Leyden: Brill).

1992. *Culture and National Identity in Republican Rome.* Cornell Studies in Classical Philology, 52 (Ithaca, NY: Cornell University Press).

Gustafsson, G. 1999. *Evocatio deorum: Historical and mythical interpretations of ritualised conquests in the expansion of ancient Rome* (Uppsala: Dept. of Theology).

Haase, M. and Rüpke, J. 2001. 'Saeculum', *Der Neue Pauly* 10: 1207f.

Hack, A. 1997. 'Zur römischen Doppelapostolizität: Überlegungen ausgehend von einem Epigramm Papst Damasus' I. (366–84)', *Hagiographica* 4: 9–33.

Haehling, R. von. 1989. *Zeitbezüge des T. Livius in der ersten Dekade seines Geschichtswerkes:* Nec vitia nostra nec remedia pati possumus. Historia Einzelschriften, 61 (Stuttgart: F. Steiner).

Hall, E. T. 1966. *The Hidden Dimension: man's use of space in public and private* (London: The Bodley Head/Garden City, NY: Doubleday).

Hallett, C. H. 2005. *The Roman Nude: heroic portrait statuary, 200 BC – AD 300* (Oxford: Oxford University Press).

Hallpike, C. R. 1979. *The Foundations of Primitive Thought* (Oxford: Clarendon Press).

Hannah, R. 2005. *Greek and Roman Calendars: Constructions of time in the Classical World* (London: Duckworth).

Hantos, T. 1983. *Das römische Bundesgenossensystem in Italien.* Vestigia, 34 (Munich: Beck).

Harland, P. A. 2003. *Associations, Synagogues and Congregations: claiming a place in ancient Mediterranean society* (Minneapolis: Fortress Press).

Harmon, D. P. 1988. 'The religious significance of games in the Roman age', in W. J. Raschke (ed.), *The Archaeology of the Olympics: the Olympics and other festivals in Antiquity* (Madison: University of Wisconsin Press) 236–55.

Harris, B. F. 1961. *Cicero as an Academic: a study of the* De natura deorum. University of Auckland Bulletin, 52: Classics series, 2 (Auckland: University of Auckland).

Harris, W. V. (ed.) 1984. *The Imperialism of Mid-Republican Rome.* Papers and Monograophs of the American Academy in Rome, 21 (Rome: American Academy).

1989. *Ancient Literacy* (Cambridge, MA: Harvard University Press).

Hartmann, M. 2005. *Die frühlateinischen Inschriften und ihre Datierung. Eine linguistisch-archäologisch-paläographische Untersuchung.* Münchener Forschungen zur historischen Sprachwissenschaft, 3 (Bremen: Hempen Verlag).

Haselberger, L. and Humphrey, J. (eds) 2006. *Imaging Ancient Rome: Documentation – Visualization – Imagination: Proceedings of the Third Williams Symposium on Classical Archictecture, Rome May 20–23, 2004.* Journal of Roman Archaeology, Supplement 61 (Portsmouth, RI: Journal of Roman Archaeology).

Häuber, C. and Schütz, F. X. 2006. 'Das Archäologische Informationssystem AIS ROMA: Antike Straßen und Gebäude aus Nollis Romkarte im modernen Stadtgrundriß', in Haselberger and Humphrey 2006: 253–69.

Heilmann, W. 1982. *Ethische Reflexion und römische Lebenswirklichkeit in Ciceros Schrift* De officiis: *Ein literatursoziologischer Versuch.* Palingenesia, 17 (Wiesbaden: F. Steiner).

Heim, F. 1991. *Virtus: Idéologie politique et croyances religieuses au IVe siècle.* Europäische Hochschulschriften, Reihe 15, 49 (Bern: Lang).

1992. *La théologie de la victoire, de Constantin à Théodose.* Théologie historique, 89 (Paris: Beauchesne).

Heim, R. L. M. 1892. 'Incantamenta magica graeca latina', *Jahrbuch für classische Philologie,* Supplementband 19: 465–575.

Hengel, M. and Deines, R. 1994. 'Die Septuaginta als "christliche Schriftensammlung", ihre Vorgeschichte und das Problem ihres Kanons', in M. Hengel and A. M. Schwemer (eds), *Die Septuaginta zwischen Judentum und Christentum* (Tübingen: Mohr Siebeck) 182–284.

Herman, G. 1987. *Ritualised Friendship and the Greek City* (Cambridge: Cambridge University Press).

Herz, P. 1975. *Untersuchungen zum Festkalender der römischen Kaiserzeit nach datierten Weih- und Ehreninschriften* (Diss. Mainz).

1978. 'Kaiserfeste der Prinzipatszeit', ANRW II.16,2: 1135–200.

Heurgon, J. (préf.). 1981. *Gli Etruschi e Roma: Atti dell' incontro di studio in onore di Massimo Pallottino, Roma, 11–13 dicembre 1979.* Istituto di Etruscologia e Antichità Italiche, Rome (Rome: G. Bretschneider).

Heyob, S. K. 1975. *The Cult of Isis Among Women in the Graeco-Roman World.* EPROER, 51 (Leyden: Brill).

Hickson, E. V. 1993. *Roman Prayer Language: Livy and the Aeneid of Vergil.* Beiträge zur Altertumskunde, 30 (Stuttgart: Teubner).

Hinard, F. and Dumont, J. -C. (eds) 2003. *Libitina: Pompes funèbres et supplices en Campanie à l'époque d'Auguste* (Paris: Le Boccard).

Hinnells, J. R. (ed.) 1994. *Studies in Mithraism* (Rome: 'L'Erma' di Bretschneider).

Hoffmann, P. 1993. *Der Isis-Tempel in Pompeji.* Charybolis, 7 (Münster: Lit).

Hölkeskamp, K. -J. 1987. *Die Entstehung der Nobilität: Studien zur sozialen und politischen Geschichte der Römischen Republik im 4. Jhdt. v. Chr.* (Stuttgart: F. Steiner).

—— 1988. 'Das plebiscitum Ogulnium de sacerdotibus: Überlegungen zu Authentizität und Interpretation der livianischen Überlieferung', *Rheinisches Museum* 131: 51–67.

—— 2000. '*Fides-deditio in fidem* – *dextra data et accepta*: Recht, Religion und Ritual in Rom', in Bruun 2000: 223–50.

—— 2001. 'Capitol, Comitium und Forum: Öffentliche Räume, sakrale Topographie und Erinnerungslandschaften der römischen Republik', in S. Faller (ed.), *Studien zu antiken Identitäten.* Identitäten und Alteritäten, 9 (Würzburg: Ergon) 97–132.

Holleman, A. J. W. 1976. *Pope Gelasius I and the Lupercalia* (Amsterdam: Hakkert).

Hölscher, T. et al. 2004–6. 'Kultinstrumente', in Balty et al. 2004–6: 5, 147 420.

Hörig, M. and Schwertheim, E. 1987. *Corpus cultus Iovis Dolicheni.* EPROER, 106 (Leyden: Brill).

Hopkins, K. 1983. *Death and Renewal: sociological studies in Roman history, 2* (Cambridge: Cambridge University Press).

Hopkins, K. and Burton, G. 1983. 'Political succession in the Late Republic (249–50 BC)', in Hopkins 1983: 31–119.

Horsfall, N. 1991. 'Statistics or states of mind?' in Humphrey 1991: 59–76.

Hossenfelder, M. 1995. *Die Philosophie der Antike 3: Stoa, Epikureismus und Skepsis.* 2nd edn. Geschichte der Philosophie, 3 (Munich: Beck).

Huet, V. et al. 2004–6a. 'Les sacrifices dans le monde romain', in Balty et al. 2004–06: 1, 183–235.

—— 2004–6b. 'Le banquet à Rome', in Balty et al. 2004–6: 2, 268–97.

Humbert, M. 1978. *Municipium et civitas sine suffragio: L'organisation de la conquête jusqu'à la guerre sociale.* CEFR, 36 (Rome: École Française).

Humm, M. 1996–97. 'Les origines du pythagorisme romain: problèmes historiques et philosophiques, 1', *Les Études Classiques* 64: 339–53; -, 2: ibid. 65: 25–42.

Humphrey, J. A. (ed.) 1991. *Literacy in the Roman World.* Journal of Roman Archaeology, Supplement 3 (Ann Arbor: Journal of Roman Archaeology).

Hunink, V. 1997. *Apuleius of Madaura*, Pro se de magia (Apologia). 2 vols. (Amsterdam: J. C. Gieben).

Højte, J. M. (ed.) 2002. *Images of Ancestors*, Aarhus Studies in Mediterranean Autiquity, 5 (Aarhus: Aarhus University Press).

Jackson, R. 1988. *Doctors and Diseases in the Roman Empire* (London: British Museum Publications).

James, W. 2003. *The Ceremonial Animal: a new portrait of anthropology* (Oxford: Oxford University Press).

Jameson, M. H. 1988. 'Sacrifice and animal husbandry in Classical Greece', in C. R. Whittaker (ed.), *Pastoral Economies in Classical Antiquity.* PCPhS, Supplement 14 (Cambridge: Cambridge Philological Society), 87–119.

Jocelyn, H. D. 1976. 'The ruling class of the Roman Republic and Greek philosophers', *Bulletin of the John Rylands Library* 59: 323–64.

1980. 'On editing the remains of Varro's "Antiquitates rerum divinarum"', *Rivista di Filologia Italiana Classica* 108: 100–22.

1982. 'Varro's *Antiquitates rerum divinarum* and religious affairs in the Late Roman Republic', *Bulletin of the John Rylands Library* 65: 148–205.

Johns, C. 1982. *Sex or Symbol: erotic images of Greece and Rome* (London: British Museum Publications).

Johnston, S. I. 1999. *Restless Dead: encounters between the living and the dead in Ancient Greece* (Berkeley: University of California Press).

Jolivet, V. and Marchand, F. 2003. 'L'affaire du Bacanal: Nouvelles réflexions sur le sanctuaire bacchique du Poggio Moscini à Bolsena', in L. Quilici and S. Quilici-Gigli (eds), *Santuari e luoghi di culto nell' Italia antica* ('L'Erma' di Bretschneider: Rome) 35–51.

Jongman, W. 1988. *The Economy and Society of Pompeii*. 2nd edn. Dutch Monographs on Ancient History and Archaeology, 4 (Amsterdam: Gieben).

2002. 'The Roman economy: from cities to empire', in L. de Blois and J. W. Rich (eds), *The Transformation of Economic Life under the Roman Empire. Proceedings of the second Workshop if the international network 'Impact of Empire (Roman Empire, c. 200 BC – AD 476)', Nottingham July 4–7, 2001* (Amsterdam: J. C. Gieben) 28–47.

Junginger, H. 1999. *Von der philologischen zur völkischen Religionswissenschaft*. Tübinger Beiträge zur Universitäts- und Wissenschaftsgeschichte, 51 (Stuttgart: F. Steiner).

Kähler, H. 1970. *Der römische Tempel* (Berlin: Mann).

Kehrer, G. 1982. *Organisierte Religion* (Stuttgart: Kohlhammer).

Keresztes, P. 1970. 'The *Constitutio Antoniniana* and the persecutions under Caracalla', *American Journal of Philology* 91: 446–59.

Kierdorf, W. 1980. Laudatio funebris: *Interpretationen und Untersuchungen zur Entwicklung der römischen Leichenrede*. Beiträge zur Klassischen Philologie, 106 (Meisenheim am Glan: Hain).

Kiley, M. et al. (eds) 1997. *Prayer from Alexander to Constantine: A Critical Anthology* (London: Routledge).

King, A. 1999. 'Diet in the Roman world: a regional inter-site comparison of the mammal bones', *Journal of Roman Archaeology* 12: 168–202.

King, H. 2004. 'Illnesses and other crises: Greece and Rome', in Johnston 2004: 464–67 (see under Guides, p. 286).

Kippenberg, H. G. 1995. 'Lokale Religionsgeschichte von Schriftreligionen: Beispiele für ein nützliches Konzept', in idem and Luchesi 1995: 11–20.

1997. 'Magic in Roman civil discourse: why rituals could be illegal', in Schäfer and Kippenberg 1997.

Kippenberg, H. G. and Luchesi, B. (eds) 1978. *Magie: Die sozialwissenschaftliche Kontroverse über das Verstehen fremden Denkens* (Frankfurt a. M.: Suhrkamp).

(eds). 1995. *Lokale Religionsgeschichte* (Marburg: diagonal).

Kirk, G. S., Raven, J. E., and Schofield, M. 1983. *The Presocratic Philosophers* 2nd edn (Cambridge: Cambridge University Press).

Klein, R. 1972. *Der Streit um den Victoria-Altar und die dritte Relatio des Symmachos und die Briefe 17, 18 und 57 des Mailänder Bischofs Ambrosius* (Darmstadt: Wissenschaftliche Buchgesellschaft).

Klinghardt, M. 1999. 'Prayer formularies for public recitation: their use and function in ancient religion', *Numen* 46: 1–52.

308

Kloppenborg, J. S. 1996. '*Collegia* and *thiasoi*: issues in function, taxonomy and membership', in idem. and Wilson 1996: 16–30.

Kloppenborg, J. S. and Wilson, S. G. (eds) 1996. *Voluntary Associations in the Graeco-Roman World* (London: Routledge).

Koch, C. 1933. *Gestirnverehrung im alten Italien: Sol Indiges und der Kreis der Di Indigetes.* Frankfurter Studien zur Religion und Kultur der Antike, 3 (Frankfurt a. M.: Klostermann).

—— 1937. *Der römische Juppiter.* Frankfurter Studien zur Religion und Kultur der Antike, 14 (Frankfurt a. M.: Klostermann).

—— 1960. *Religio: Studien zu Kult und Glauben der Römer* (O. Seel, ed.). Erlanger Beiträge zur Sprach- und Kunstwissenschaft, 7 (Nuremberg: Carl).

Kötzsche-Breitenbruch, E. 1976. *Die neue Katakombe an der Via Latina in Rom.* JfAC, Ergänzungsband 4 (Münster, Westphalia: Aschendorffsche Verlagsbuchhandlung).

Köves-Zulauf, T. 1970. 'Die *Epoptides* des Valerius Soranus', *Rheinisches Museum* 113: 323–58.

—— 1972. *Reden und Schweigen: Römische Religion bei Plinius Maior.* Studia et Testimonia antiqua, 12 (Munich: Fink).

—— 1990. *Römische Geburtsriten.* Zetemata, 87 (Munich: Beck).

Kolb, F. 1981. *Agora und Theater, Volks- und Festversammlung.* Deutsches Archäologisches Institut: Archäologische Forschungen, 9 (Berlin: Mann).

—— 1995. *Rom: Die Geschichte der Stadt in der Antike* (Munich: Beck).

Kotansky, R. 1991. 'Incantations and prayers for salvation on inscribed Greek amulets', in Faraone and Obbink 1991: 107–37.

—— 1995. 'Greek exorcistic amulets', in Meyer and Mirecki 1995: 243–77.

Krämer, H. J. 1965. 'Die Sage von Romulus und Remus in der lateinischen Literatur', in H. Flashar and K. Gaiser (eds), *Synusia: Festschrift Wolfgang Schadewaldt* (Pfullingen: Neske) 355–402.

Kroll, W. 1928. 'Manalis lapis', *RE* 14: 969–71.

Kron, U. 1996. 'Priesthoods, dedications and euergetism: what part did religion play in the political and social status of Greek women?', in P. Hellström and B. Alroth (eds), *Religion and Power in the Ancient Greek World: Proceedings of the Fourth Uppsala Symposium, 1993.* Boreas, 24 (Uppsala: Acta Universitatis Upsaliensis) 139–82.

Krug, A. 1993. *Heilkunst und Heilkult: Medizin in der Antike.* 2nd edn (Munich: Beck).

Kümmel, H. M. 1968. 'Ersatzkönig und Sündenbock', *Zeitschrift für die alttestamentliche Wissenschaft* 80: 289–318.

Kuttner, A. L. 2004. 'Roman art during the Republic', in Flower 2004: 294–321.

Lampe, P. 1989. *Die stadtrömischen Christen in den ersten beiden Jahrhunderten: Untersuchungen zur Sozialgeschichte.* 2nd edn. Wissenschaftliche Untersuchungen zum Neuen Testament, Reihe 2. 18 (Tübingen: Mohr-Siebeck).

Lanciani, R. 1892. *Ancient Rome in the Light of Recent Exavations* (Boston and New York: Houghton, Mifflin and Co.).

Lane Fox, R. 1986. *Pagans and Christians in the Mediterranean world from the second century AD to the conversion of Constantine* (Harmondsworth and New York: Viking / Viking Penguin).

Lapatin, K. D. S. 2002. *Chryselephantine Statuary in the Ancient Mediterranean World* (Oxford: Oxford University Press / Clarendon Press).

Latte, K. 1960. *Römische Religionsgeschichte*. 2nd edn. Handbuch der Altertumswissenschaft 5. 4 (Munich: Beck).

Lattke, M. 1991. *Hymnus: Materialien zu einer Geschichte der antiken Hymnologie*. Novum Testamentum et Orbis Antiquus, 19 (Fribourg/Freiburg i.U. and Göttingen: Universitätsverlag/Vandenhoeck and Ruprecht).

Laum, B. 1960. *Schenkende Wirtschaft: Nichtmarktmäßiger Güterverkehr und seine soziale Funktion* (Frankfurt a. M.: Klostermann).

Laurence, R. 1994. *Roman Pompeii: Space and Society* (London: Routledge).

Lawson, E. Th. 2000. 'Towards a cognitive science of religion', *Numen* 47: 338–49.

Leach, E. 1976. *Culture and Communication: the logic by which symbols are connected* (Cambridge: Cambridge University Press).

Le Blois, L., Funke, P. and Hahn, J. (eds) 2006. *The Impact of Imperial Rome on Religions, Ritual and Religious Life in the Roman Empire: Proceedings of the Fifth Workshop of the International Network 'Impact of Empire' (Roman Empire, 200 BC – AD 476), Münster June 30th–July 4th 2004* (Leyden: Brill).

Le Bohec, Y. 2003. *Inscriptions de la cité des Lingons: Inscriptions sur pierre*. Inscriptiones latinae Galliae Belgicae, 1 = Archéologie et l'histoire de l'art, 17 (Paris: Comité des travaux historiques et scientifiques).

Le Bonniec, H. 1958. *Le culte de Cérès à Rome des origines à la fin de la République*. Études et Commentaires, 27 (Paris: Klincksieck).

Le Glay, M. 1971. *La religion romaine* (Paris: Colin).

Le Guen, B. 2001. *Les associations des technites dionysiaques à l'époque hellénistique* (Nancy: Le Boccard).

Lehmann, Y. 1997. *Varron théologien et philosophe romain*. Collection Latomus, 237 (Brussels: Latomus).

Lembke, K. 1994. *Das Iseum Campense in Rom: Studie über den Isiskult unter Domitian*. Archäologie und Geschichte, 3 (Heidelberg: Verlag Archäologie und Geschichte).

Lenaghan, J. O. 1969. *A Commentary on Cicero's Oration* De Haruspicum Responso. Studies in Classical Literature, 5 (The Hague: Mouton).

Leonhardt, J. 1999. *Ciceros Kritik der Philosophenschulen*. Zetemata, 103 (Munich: Beck).

Levack, B. P. 1987. *The Witch Hunt in Early Modern Europe* (London: Longman).

Levene, D. S. 1993. *Religion in Livy*. Mnemosyne Supplement 127 (Leyden: Brill).

Lévi-Strauss, C. 1966. *The Savage Mind*. Anonymous trans. (London: Weidenfeld and Nicholson). Orig, ed.: *La pensée sauvage* (Paris: Plon, 1962).

Ley, A. and Struß, R. 1982. 'Gegenarchitektur: Das Heiligtum der Fortuna Primigenia als Symbol der politischen Selbstbehauptung Praenestes', *Hephaistos* 4: 117–38.

Liebenam, W. 1890. *Zur Geschichte und Organisation des römischen Vereinswesens: Drei Untersuchungen* (Leipzig: Teubner, repr. Aalen: Scientia, 1964).

Lieberg, G. 1982. 'Die *theologia tripartita* als Formprinzip antiken Denkens', *Rheinisches Museum* 125: 25–53.

Liebeschuetz, J. H. W. G. 1979. *Continuity and Change in Roman Religion* (Oxford: Clarendon Press).

Liertz, U.-M. 1998. *Kult und Kaiser: Studien zur Kaiserkult und Kaiserverehrung in den germanischen Provinzen und in Gallia Belgica zur römischen Kaiserzeit.* Acta Instituti Romani Finlandiae, 20 (Rome: Institutum Romanum Finlandiae).

Lieu, J. M. 2004. *Christian Identity in the Jewish and Graeco-Roman World* (Oxford: Oxford University Press).

Linders, T. and Nordquist, G. (eds) 1987. *Gifts to the Gods. Proceedings of the Uppsala Symposium, 1985.* Boreas, 15 (Uppsala: Acta Universitatis Upsaliensis).

Linders, T. and Alroth, B. (eds) 1992. *Economics of Cult in the Ancient Greek World: Proceedings of the Uppsala Symposium, 1990.* Boreas, 21 (Uppsala: Acta Universitatis Upsaliensis).

Linderski, J. 1968. 'Der Senat und die Vereine' in M. N. Andreev and J. Irmscher (eds), *Gesellschaft und Recht im griechisch-römischen Altertum,* 1 (Berlin: Akademie-Verlag) 94–132 (= Linderski 1995: 165–203).

—— 1982 [1983]. 'Cicero and divination', *Parola del Passato* 37: 12–38 (= Linderski 1995: 458–84).

—— 1986. 'The augural law', *ANRW* II.16, 3: 2146–312.

—— 1995. *Roman Questions: Selected papers.* HABES 20 (Stuttgart: F. Steiner).

Linke, B. 1995. *Von der Verwandtschaft zum Staat: Die Entstehung staatlicher Organisationsformen in der römischen Frühgeschichte* (Stuttgart: F. Steiner).

—— 1998. 'Die *agnatio*: Ein römischer Sonderweg in der sozialen Organisation', *Historische Anthropologie* 6: 104–31.

Lintott, A. W. 1968. '*Nundinae* and the chronology of the late Roman Republic', *Classical Quarterly* 62: 189–94.

Liou-Gille, B. 1993. 'Le pomerium', *Museum Helveticum* 50: 94–106.

Lissi Caronna, E. 1986. *Il mitreo dei* Castra Peregrinorum (*S. Stefano Rotondo*). EPROER, 104 (Leyden: Brill).

Löw, M. 2001. *Raumsoziologie.* Wissenschaft, 1506 (Frankfurt/Main: Suhrkamp).

Long, A. and Sedley, D. N. 1987. *The Hellenistic Philosophers.* 2 vols. (Cambridge: Cambridge University Press).

Lonsdale, S. H. 1993. *Dance and Ritual Play in Greek Religion* (Baltimore: Johns Hopkins University Press).

Lorsch Wildfang, R. 2006. *Rome's Vestal Virgins: A study of Rome's vestal priestesses in the late Republic and early Empire* (London: Routledge).

Losemann, V. 1999. 'The Nazi concept of Rome', in C. Edwards (ed.), *Roman Presences: Receptions of Rome in European culture, 1789–1945* (Cambridge: Cambridge University Press) 221–35.

Lott, J. B. 2004. *The Neighbourhoods of Augustan Rome* (Cambridge: Cambridge University Press).

Lucas, H. 1938. 'Martial's *kalendae nataliciae*', *Classical Quarterly* 32: 5f.

Luce, T. J. 1977. *Livy: the composition of his history* (Princeton: Princeton University Press).

MacBain, B. 1982. *Prodigy and Expiation: a study in religion and politics in Republican Rome.* Collection Latomus, 177 (Brussels: Latomus).

MacDonald, W. L. 1982. *The Architecture of the Roman Empire.* 2nd edn. 2 vols. Yale Publications in the History of Art, 17 (New Haven: Yale University Press).

McKay, H. A. 1994. *Sabbath and Synagogue: The Question of Sabbath Worship in Ancient Judaism.* RGRW, 122 (Leyden: Brill).

MacKinnon, M. 2004. *Production and Consumption of Animals in Roman Italy: integrating the zooarchaeological and textual evidence.* JRA, Supplement 54 (Portsmouth, RI: Journal of Roman Archaeology).

311

MacMullen, R. 1981. *Paganism in the Roman Empire* (New Haven: Yale University Press).

Magdelain, A. 1976. 'Le pomerium archaïque et le mundus', *Revue des Études Latines* 54: 71–109.

Malaise, M. 1972. *Les conditions de pénétration et de diffusion des cultes égyptiens en Italie*. EPROER, 22 (Leyden: Brill).

Maltby, R. 1991. *A Lexicon of Ancient Latin Etymologies*. Arca, 25 (Leeds: Francis Cairns).

Mansfeld, J. 1999. 'Theology', in Algra et al. 1999: 452–78.

Marchand, S. 1996. *Down from Olympus: archaeology and philhellenism in Germany, 1750–1970* (Princeton: Princeton University Press).

Marco Simón, F. 1996. *Flamen Dialis: El sacerdote de Júpiter en el religión romana* (Madrid: Ediciones Clásicas).

Markschies, C. 1992. *Valentinus Gnosticus? Untersuchungen zur valentinianischen Gnosis mit einem Kommentar zu den Fragmenten Valentins*. Wissenschaftliche Untersuchungen zum Neuen Testament, 65 (Tübingen: Mohr-Siebeck).

— 1997. *Zwischen den Welten wandern: Strukturen des antiken Christentums* (Frankfurt a.M.: Fischer-Taschenbuch-Verlag).

— 2007. Kaiserzeitliche christliche Theologie und ihre Institutionem: Prolegomena zu einer Geschichte der antiken christlichen Theologie (Tübungen: Mohr Siebeck).

Martin, D. B. 2004. *Inventing Superstition: from the Hippocratics to the Christians* (Cambridge, MA: Harvard University Press).

Martin, H. G. 1987. *Römische Tempelkultbilder: eine archäologische Untersuchung zur späten Republik*. Studi e Materiali del Museo della Civiltà Romana, 12 (Rome: 'L'Erma' di Bretschneider).

Martin, J. 1990. 'Aspekte antiker Staatlichkeit', in W. Eder (ed.), *Staat und Staatlichkeit in der frühen römischen Republik. Akten eines Symposiums 12.–15. Juli 1988, Freie Universität Berlin* (Stuttgart: F. Steiner) 220–32.

Martin, J. -P. 1982. *Providentia deorum: Recherches sur certains aspects religieux du pouvoir impérial romain*. CEFR, 61 (Rome: École Française).

Martin, R. 1988. 'Agriculture et religion: le témoignage des Agronomes latines', in D. Porte and J. -P. Néraudau (eds), *Hommages à Henri Le Bonniec: Res Sacrae*. Collection Latomus, 201 (Brussels: Latomus) 294–305.

Marwick, M. (ed.) 1970. *Witchcraft and Sorcery: selected readings* (Harmondsworth: Penguin Education).

Masaracchia, A. (ed.) 1993. *Orfeo e l'orfismo. Atti del Seminario Nazionale, tenuto a Roma e Perugia, 1985–1991* (Rome: Gruppo Ed. Internazionale).

Mason, S. 1996. 'Philosophiai: Graeco-Roman, Judaean and Christian', in Kloppenborg and Wilson 1996: 31–58.

Matthews, J. 1992. 'The poetess Proba and fourth-century Rome: questions of interpretation', in Christol et al. 1992: 277–304.

Mattingly, H. 1950–1. 'The imperial *Vota*', *Proceedings of the British Academy* 36: 155–95; 37: 219–68.

Mauss, M. 1954. *The Gift: forms and functions of exchange in ancient societies*. Trans. by I. Cunnison (London: Cohen and West). Original ed. as 'Essai sur le don', *L'Année sociologique* n.s. 1 (1923/24 [1925]) 130–86.

Meiggs, R. 1973. *Roman Ostia*. 2nd edn (Oxford: Clarendon Press).

Mellor, R. 1975. *THEA ROME: The worship of the Goddess Roma in the Greek world*. Hypomnemata, 42 (Göttingen: Vandenhoeck and Ruprecht).

Mengarelli, R. 1935. 'Il tempio del Manganello a Caere', *Studi Etruschi* 9: 83–94.
Merkelbach, R. 1984. *Mithras* (Königstein: Hain).
1995. *Isis Regina – Zeus Sarapis* (Stuttgart and Leipzig: Teubner).
Merlat, P. 1960. *Jupiter Dolichenus. Essai d'interprétation et de synthèse.* Institut d'Art et d'Archéologie de l'Université de Paris V (Paris: Presses Universitaires de France).
Merz, J. M. 2001. *Das Heiligtum der Fortuna in Palestrina und die Architektur der Neuzeit.* Römische Forschungen der Bibliotheca Hertziana, 29 (Munich: Hirmer).
Meslin, M. 1970. *La fête des kalendes de janvier dans l'empire romain: Étude d'un rituel de Nouvel An.* Collection Latomus, 115 (Brussels: Latomus).
Metzger, B. M. 1987. *The Canon of the New Testament: its origin, development, and significance* (Oxford: Clarendon Press).
Metzler, D. 1981. 'Ökonomische Aspekte des Religionswandels in der Spätantike: Die Enteignung der heidnischen Tempel seit Konstantin', *Hephaistos* 3: 327–40.
Meyboom, P. G. P. 1995. *The Nile-Mosaic of Palestrina: early evidence of Egyptian religion in Italy.* RGRW, 121 (Leyden: Brill).
Meyer, J. Ch. 1983. *Pre-Republican Rome: an analysis of the cultural and chrono-logical relations 1000–500 BC.* Analecta Romana Instituti Danici, Suppl. 11 (Odense: Odense University Press).
Meyer, M. and Mirecki, P. (eds) 1995. *Ancient Magic and Ritual Power.* RGRW, 129 (Leyden: Brill).
2002. *Magic and Ritual in the Ancient World.* RGRW, 141 (Leyden: Brill).
Meyer, M. and Smith, R. 1994. *Ancient Christian Magic: Coptic texts of ritual power* (New York: Harper San Francisco).
Michel, S. 2001. *Magische Gemmen im British Museum* (London: British Museum Press).
2004. *Die magischen Gemmen: Zu Bildern und Zauberformeln auf geschnittenen Steinen der Antike und Neuzeit.* Studien aus dem Warburg-Haus, 7 (Berlin: Akademie-Verlag).
Michels, A. K. 1967. *The Calendar of the Roman Republic* (Princeton: Princeton University Press, repr. Westport, Conn.: Greenwood, 1978).
Miles, G. B. 1995. *Livy: reconstructing early Rome* (Ithaca and London: Cornell University Press).
Misch, G. 1950. *A History of Autobiography in Antiquity.* 2 vols. Trans. by E. W. Dickes (London: Routledge and Kegan Paul). Original ed.: *Geschichte der Autobiographie* I.1–2. 3rd edn (Bern: Franke, 1949–50, first edition 1907, Leipzig and Berlin: Teubner).
Mitchell, S. 1993. *Anatolia: land, men and gods in Asia Minor* (Oxford: Clarendon Press).
Mitchell, T. J. 1991. *Cicero: the senior statesman* (New Haven and London: Yale University Press).
Mörth, I. 1986. *Lebenswelt und religiöse Sinnstiftung: Ein Beitrag zur Theorie des Alltagslebens.* Tuduv-Studien: Reihe Sozialwissenschaften, 39 (Munich: Tuduv).
1993. 'Kommunikation', *HrwG* 3: 392–414.
Mol, H. 1976. *Identity and the Sacred: a sketch for a new social-scientific theory of religion* (New York: The Free Press).
Momigliano, A. 1967. 'Osservazioni sulla distinzione fra patrizi e plebei', in *Les Origines de la république romaine.* Entretiens sur l'antiquité classique, 13 (Vandoeuvres: Fondation Hardt) 197–221.

1975. *Alien Wisdom: the limits of Hellenization* (Cambridge: Cambridge University Press).

1984. 'The theological efforts of the Roman upper classes in the first century BC', *Classical Philology* 79: 199–211.

1986. 'The disadvantages of monotheism for a universal state', *Classical Philology* 81: 285–97. (Repr. *Ottavo contributo alla storia degli studi classici* Rome 1987: 313–28).

Monaca, M. 2005. *La Sibilla a Roma: I libri sibillini fra religione e politica.* Collana di studi storico-religiosi, 8 (Edizioni Lionello Giordano).

Montanari, E. 1986. 'Premessa', in C. Koch, *Giove Romano.* Trans. by L. Arcella. Dalla Grande Città, 1 (Rome: Rari Nantes) 11–49.

Mora, F. 1990. *Prosopografia Isiaca.* 2 vols. EPROER, 113 (Leyden: Brill).

1995a. *Il pensiero storico-religioso antico: Autori greci e Roma, 1: Dionigi d'Alicarnasso* (Rome: 'L'Erma' di Bretschneider).

1995b. 'Per una tipologia del politeismo', in U. Bianchi (ed.), *The Notion of 'Religion' in Comparative Research: Selected Proceedings of the XVI IAHR Congress, held at La Sapienza, Rome, Sept. 1990* (Rome: 'L'Erma' di Bretschneider) 823–30.

Morandi, A. 1982. *Epigrafia italica* (Rome: 'L'Erma' di Bretschneider).

Morley, N. 1996. *Metropolis and Hinterland: the city of Rome and the Italian economy, 200 BC – AD 200* (Cambridge: Cambridge University Press).

Morris, I. 1992. *Death-Ritual and Social Structure in Classical Antiquity* (Cambridge: Cambridge University Press).

Moscati, S. 1997. *Così nacque l'Italia: Profili di antichi popoli riscoperti* (Turin: SEI).

Mouritsen, H. 1997. 'Mobility and social change in Italian towns during the Principate', in H. M. Parkins (ed.), *Roman Urbanism: beyond the Consumer City* (London: Routledge) 59–82.

Müller, R. J. 1993. 'Überlegungen zur *Hiera Anagraphē* des Euhemeros von Messene', *Hermes* 121: 276–300.

Murray, O. (ed.) 1990. *Sympotica. A symposium on the symposion* (Oxford: Oxford University Press).

Mustakallio, K. 1994. *Death and Disgrace: capital penalties with post-mortem sanctions in early Roman historiography.* Annales Academiae Scientiarum Fennicae, Dissertationes humanarum litterarum, 72 (Helsinki: Suomalainen Tiedeakatemia).

Muth, S. 1998. *Erleben von Raum-Leben im Raum: Zur Funktion mythologischer Mosaikbilder in der römisch-kaiserzeitlichen Wohnarchitektur.* Archäologie und Geschichte, 10 (Heidelberg: Archäologie und Geschichte).

Nagy, B. 1985. 'The Argei Puzzle', *American Journal of Ancient History* 10: 1–27.

Naiden, F. S. 2006. *Ancient Supplication* (New York: Oxford University Press).

Newman, J. K. 1969. *The Concept of* vates *in Augustan Poetry.* Collection Latomus, 89 (Brussels: Latomus).

Neymeyr, U. 1989. *Die christlichen Lehrer im zweiten Jahrhundert: Ihre Lehrtätigkeit, ihr Selbstverständnis und ihre Geschichte.* Vigiliae Christianae, Supplement 40 (Leyden: Brill).

Nilsson, M. P. 1945. 'Pagan divine service in Late Antiquity', *Harvard Theological Review* 38: 63–70.

Nimtz, P. 1925. *Die Haltung und Zucht des Schweines und dessen Bedeutung für*

Volkswirtschaft und Kultus im griechisch-römischen Altertum (Diss.vet. med. Berlin).

Noethlichs, K. L. 1986. 'Heidenverfolgung', *RfAC* 13: 1149–90.

Norden, E. 1995. *Aus altrömischen Priesterbüchern*. 2nd edn. With an afterword by John Scheid (Stuttgart and Leipzig: Teubner). Original ed. in Acta Reg. Societatis Humaniorum Litterarum Lundensis, 1939 (Lund: Gleerup).

North, J. A. 1975. '*Praesens Divus*' (Review of S. Weinstock, *Divus Iulius*), *Journal of Roman Studies* 65: 171–7.

1979. 'Religious toleration in Republican Rome', *PCPhS* 25: 85–103.

1990a. 'Family strategy and priesthood in the Late Republic', in J. Andreau and H. Bruhns (eds), *Parenté et stratégies familiales dans l'antiquité romaine*. CEFR, 129 (Rome: École française) 527–43.

1990b. 'Diviners and divination at Rome', in Beard and North 1990: 51–71.

1995. 'Religion and rusticity', in T. J. Cornell and K. Lomas (eds), *Urban Society in Roman Italy* (London: University College Press) 135–50.

1998. 'The books of the pontifices', in AA.VV. 1998: 45–63.

2000. 'Prophet and text in the third century BC', in Bispham and Smith 2000: 92–107.

Noy, D. 2000. *Foreigners at Rome: citizens and strangers* (London: Duckworth).

Oakley, S. H. 1997–98. *A Commentary on Livy, Books VI-X*. 2 vols. (Oxford: Clarendon Press).

Obbink, D. 1989. 'The atheism of Epicurus', *Greek, Roman and Byzantine Studies* 30: 187–223.

Oberhelman, S. M. 1987. 'The diagnostic dream in ancient medical theory and practice', *Bulletin of the History of Medicine* 61: 47–60.

Önnerfors, A. 1985. 'Iatromagische Beschwörungen in der *Physica Plinii Sangallensis*', *Eranos* 83: 235–52.

1988. 'Zaubersprüche in Texten der römischen und frühmitteralterlichen Medizin', in Centre Jean Palerne, *Mémoires, 8: Études de médecine romaine* (G. Sabbah, ed.) (St-Étienne: Centre Jean Palerne) 113–56.

1993. 'Magische Formeln im Dienst römischer Medizin', *ANRW* II. 37,1: 157–224.

Ogden, D. 1999. 'Binding spells: curse tablets and voodoo dolls in the Greek and Roman worlds', in Flint et al. 1999: 3–90.

Ogilvie, R. M. 1965. *A Commentary on Livy Books 1-5* (Oxford: Clarendon Press).

Orlin, E. M. 1997. *Temples, Religion and Politics in the Roman Republic*. Mnemosyne Supplement 164 (Leyden: Brill).

Orr, D. G. 1978. 'Roman domestic religion: the evidence of the household shrines', *ANRW* II.16, 2: 1557–91 [based on a Bryn Mawr dissertation of the same title, 1972].

Pack, E. 1989. 'Sozialgeschichtliche Aspekte des Fehlens einer christlichen Schule in der römischen Kaiserzeit', in W. Eck (ed.), *Religion und Gesellschaft in der römischen Kaiserzeit: Kolloqium zu Ehren von Friedrich Vittinghoff*. Kölner historische Abhandlungen, 35 (Köln: Böhlau) 185–263.

Paglieri, S. 1960. 'Una stipe votiva vulcente', *Rivista dell' Istituto Nazionale di Archeologia e Storia dell'Arte* n.s. 9: 74–96.

Pailler, J. -M. 1988. *Bacchanalia. La répression de 186 av. J.-C. à Rome et en Italie: vestiges, images, tradition*. BEFAR, 270 (Rome: École française).

Pallottino, M. 1991. *A History of Earliest Italy* (London: Radius). Orig. title: *Storia della prima Italia*. 3rd edn (Milan: Rusconi, 1985).

Palmer, R. E. A. 1965. 'The censors of 312 B.C. and the state religion', *Historia* 14: 293–324.

1974. *Roman Religion and Roman Empire: five essays* (Philadelphia: Pennsylvania University Press).

Panella, C. 1996. *Meta Sudans* (Rome: Istituto Poligrafico e Zecca dello Stato).

Pape, M. 1975. *Griechische Kunstwerke aus Kriegsbeute und ihre öffentliche Aufstellung in Rom: Von der Eroberung von Syrakus bis in augusteische Zeit*. (Diss. Hamburg: Fachbereich Kulturgeschichte und Kulturkunde).

Parke, H. W. 1988. *Sibyls and Sibylline Prophecy in Classical Antiquity*. Ed. B. C. McGing (London and New York: Routledge).

Parker, R. C. T. 2005. *Polytheism and Society at Athens* (Oxford: Oxford University Press).

Parkins, H. M. (ed.) 1997. *Roman Urbanism: beyond the Consumer City* (London: Routledge).

Pascal, C. B. 1981. 'October horse', *Harvard Studies in Classical Philology* 85: 261–91.

Patterson, J. R. 1994. 'The *collegia* and the transformation of the towns of Italy in the second century AD', in [M. Lenoir (ed.)], *L'Italie d'Auguste à Dioclétien. Actes du colloque international organisé par l' École française de Rome, l' École des Hautes Études en Sciences sociales, le Dipartimento di scienze storiche, archeologiche, antropologiche dell' Antichità dell' Università di Roma La Sapienza et le Dipartimento di scienze dell' Antichità dell' Università di Trieste (Rome, 25–28 mars 1992)*. CEFR, 198 (Rome: École française) 227–38.

Pautasso, A. 1994. *Il deposito votivo presso la porta Nord a Vulci*. CStipiVot. 7, Regio VII, 3 (Rome: G. Bretschneider).

Pavolini, C. 1983. *Ostia*. Guide archeologiche Laterza (Rome and Bari: Laterza).

Peacock, D. and Williams, D. (eds) 2006. *Food for the Gods: new light on the ancient incense trade* (Oxford: Oxbow Books).

Pease, A. S. (ed.) 1920–3. *M. Tullius Cicero, De Divinatione*. 2 vols. University of Illinois Studies in Language and Literature, 6 and 8 (Illinois: Illinois University Press; repr. Darmstadt: Wissenschaftliche Buchgesellschaft, 1977).

Pease, A. S. (ed.) 1955–8. *M. Tullionis Ciceronis De natura deorum*. 2 vols. (Cambridge, MA: Harvard University Press).

Péché, V. 2001. '*Collegium tibicinum romanorum*, une association de musiciens au service de la religion romaine', in Brulé and Vendries 2001: 307–38.

Pensabene, P. et al. 1980. *Terracotte votive dal Tevere*. Seminario di Archeologia e storia dell'arte greca e romana dell'Università di Roma: Studi miscellanei, 25 (Rome: 'L'Erma' di Bretschneider).

Pernice, A. 1885. 'Zum römischen Sakralrechte 1', *Sitzungsberichte der Königlich Preussischen Akademie der Wissenschaften zu Berlin* 1885, 2 (Berlin: Akademie der Wissenschaften) 1143–59.

Perry, J. S. 2006. *The Roman collegia: the modern evolution of an ancient concept*. Mnemosyne, Supplement 277 (Leyden: Brill).

Petersmann, H. 1973. 'Zu einem altrömischen Opferritual (Cato, *de agr.* 141)', *Rheinisches Museum* 96: 238–55.

1991. 'Springende und tanzende Götter beim antiken Fest', in J. Assmann (ed.), *Das Fest und das Heilige: Religiöse Kontrapunkte zur Alltagswelt*. Studien zum Verstehen fremder Religionen, 1 (Gütersloh: Mohn) 69–87.

Pezzella, S. 1972. *Cristianesimo e paganesimo romano: Minucio Felice* (Bari: Adriatica).

Phillips, C. R. 1986. 'The sociology of religious knowledge in the Roman Empire to A.D. 284', *ANRW* II.16,3: 2677–773.

——— 1991. 'Nullum crimen sine lege: socio-religious sanctions on magic', in Faraone and Obbink 1991: 260–76.

——— 1997. 'Cato the Elder', in Kiley et al. 1997: 128–32.

——— 1998a. 'Walter Burkert *in partibus infidelium*: a classicist's appraisal of the creation of the sacred', *Method and Theory in the Study of Religion* 10: 92–105.

——— 1998b. Review of F. Graf, Magic in the Ancient World, *Bryn Mawr Classical Review* 15 March 1998 [98.3.15] (electronic) = 9.6: 519–24 (printed).

Pietilä-Castrén, L. 1987. *Magnificentia publica: the victory monuments of the Roman generals in the era of the Punic Wars*. Commentationes Humanarum Litterarum, 84 (Helsinki: Societas Scientiarum Fennica).

Pietri, C. 1976. *Roma christiana: Recherches sur l'Église de Rome, son organisation, sa politique, son idéologie, de Miltiade à Sixte III (311–440)*. 2 vols. BEFAR, 224 (Rome: École française).

——— 1978. 'Évergétisme et richesses ecclésiastiques dans l'Italie du IVe à la fin du Ve siècle: l'exemple romain', *Ktema* 3: 317–37.

——— 1983. 'Liturgie, Kultur und Gesellschaft: Das Beispiel Roms in der ausgehenden Antike (4.–5. Jhdt.)', *Concilium* 19: 116–24.

Pietri, C. and Markschies, C. 1996. 'Theologische Diskussionen zur Zeit Konstantins: Arius, der 'arianische Streit' und das Konzil von Nizäa, die nachnizänischen Auseinandersetzungen bis 337', in C. Pietri (ed.), *Das Entstehen der einen Christenheit (250–430)*. [Eds. Th. Böhm et al.] (Freiburg: Herder) 271–344.

Pighi, G. B. 1941. *De ludis saecularibus populi Romani Quiritium: Libri sex*. 2nd edn. Pubblicazioni dell' Università Cattolica del S. Cuore, ser. 5. 35 (Milan: Società Ed. Vita e Pensiero, repr. Amsterdam: Schippers, 1965).

Piranomonte, M. 2008. 'Religion and magic at Rome: new discoveries in the *Fons Annae Perennae*', in Gordon and Marco Simón 2008.

Polignac, F. de. 1995a. *Cults, Territory and the Origins of the Greek City-State*. Trans. by Janet Lloyd (Chicago: University of Chicago Press). Original title: *La naissance de la cité grecque: cultes, espaces et société, VIIIe – VIIe siècles*. 2nd edn (Paris: La Découverte, 1984).

——— 1995b. 'Repenser la cité? Rituels et société en Grèce archaïque', in M. H. Hansen and K. Raaflaub (eds), *Studies in the Ancient Greek Polis*. Historia Einzelschriften, 95 (Stuttgart: F. Steiner) 7–19.

Porte, D. 1984. 'La noyade rituelle des hommes de jonc', in R. Altheim-Stiehl and M. Rosenbach (eds), *Beiträge zur altitalischen Geistesgeschichte: Festschrift Gerhard Radke zum 18. Februar 1984*. Fontes et Commentationes Suppl., 2 (Münster, Westphalia: Aschendorff) 193–211.

——— 1989. *Les donneurs de sacré: le prêtre à Rome* (Paris: Les Belles Lettres).

Potter, T. W. 1989. *Una stipe votiva da Ponte di Nona*. Lavori e studi di archeologia, 13 (Rome: De Luca).

Potter, T. W. and Wells, C. 1985. 'A Republican healing-sanctuary at Ponte di Nona near Rome and the classical tradition of votive medicine', *Journal of the British Archaeological Association* 138: 23–47.

Poucet, J. 1985. *Les origines de Rome: tradition et histoire*. Publications des Facultés univ. Saint-Louis, 38 (Brussels: Facultés universitaires Saint-Louis).

Poultney, J. W. 1959. *The Bronze Tablets of Iguvium* (Baltimore: Johns Hopkins University Press).

Powell, J. G. F. 1995a. 'Cicero's philosophical works and their background', in Powell 1995b: 1–35.

(ed.) 1995b. *Cicero the Philosopher* (Oxford: Clarendon Press).

Prayon, F. 1988. 'Zur Baupolitik im archaischen Rom', in H. Büsing and F. Hiller (eds), *Bathron: Beiträge zur Architektur und verwandten Künsten für Heinrich Drerup zu seinem 80. Geburtstag von seinen Schülern und Freunden.* Saarbrücker Studien zur Archäologie und alten Geschichte, 3 (Saarbrücken: Saarbrücker Verlag) 331–42.

Preller, L. 1858. *Römische Mythologie* (Berlin: Weidmannsche Buchhandlung). Repr. Essen: Phaidon, n.d..

Preus, J. S. 1987. *Explaining Religion: criticism and theory from Bodin to Freud* (New Haven: Yale University Press).

Price, S. R. F. 1984. *Rituals and Power: the Roman imperial cult in Asia Minor* (Cambridge: Cambridge University Press).

Pulleyn, S. 1997. *Prayer in Greek Religion* (Oxford: Clarendon Press).

Putnam, M. C. J. 2000. *Horace's* Carmen Saeculare: *ritual magic and the poet's art* (New Haven and London: Yale University Press).

Quasten, J. 1973. *Musik und Gesang in den Kulten der heidnischen Antike und christlichen Frühzeit.* 2nd edn. Liturgiegeschichtliche Quellen und Forschungen, 25 (Münster, Westphalia: Aschendorff).

Quilici, L. and Quilici Gigli S. 1995. 'Un grande santuario fuori la porta occidentale di Tusculum', *Archeologia Laziale* 12: 509–34.

Quispel, G. 1996. 'The original doctrine of Valentinus', *Vigiliae Christianae* 50: 327–52.

Raaflaub, K. A. (ed.) 1986. *Social Struggles in Archaic Rome: new perspectives on the conflict of the Orders* (Berkeley, CA: California University Press).

Radke, G. 1936. *Die Bedeutung der weißen und der schwarzen Farbe in Kult und Brauch der Griechen und Römer* (Diss. Berlin).

1970. 'Das Wirken der römischen Götter', *Gymnasium* 77: 23–46.

1979. *Die Götter Altitaliens* 2nd edn. Fontes et Commentationes, 3 (Münster, Westphalia: Aschendorff).

1987. *Zur Entwicklung der Gottesvorstellung und der Gottesverehrung in Rom.* Impulse der Forschung, 50 (Darmstadt: Wissenschaftliche Buchgesellschaft).

1989. ' "Wolfsabwehrer" oder "Wachstumsbitter": Überlegungen zum römischen Lupercalienfest', *Würzburger Jahrbücher für die Altertumswissenschaft* 15: 125–38.

1990. 'Gibt es Antworten auf die "Argeerfrage"?' *Latomus* 49: 5–19.

Rajak, T. 2002. *The Jewish Dialogue with Greece and Rome: studies in cultural and social interaction* (Leyden: Brill).

Ramage, E. S. 1991. 'Sulla's propaganda', *Klio* 73: 93–121.

Rawson, E. 1975. *Cicero: a portrait* (London: Allen Lane; repr.: Ithaca: Cornell University Press, 1983; corr. repr.: London: Bristol Classical Press, 1994).

1978. 'Caesar, Etruria and the *disciplina Etrusca*', *Journal of Roman Studies* 68: 132–52.

1985. *Intellectual Life in the Late Roman Republic* (London: Duckworth).

1991. 'Religion and politics in the late second century BC at Rome', *Phoenix* 28: 193–212.

Rea, J. R. 1988. 'On the Greek Calends', in B. G. Mandilaras et al. (eds), *Proceedings of the XVIIIth International Congress of Papyrology, Athens 25–31 May 1986* (Athens: Greek Papyrological Society) 203–8.

Reale, G. 1990. *A History of Ancient Philosophy 4: The Schools of the Imperial Age* (Albany: State University of New York Press).

Rebenich, S. 1992. *Hieronymus und sein Kreis: Prosopographische und sozialgeschichtliche Untersuchungen*. Historia Einzelschriften, 72 (Stuttgart: F. Steiner).

Reitzenstein, R. 1927. *Die hellenistischen Mysterienreligionen nach ihren Grundgedanken und Wirkungen*. 3rd edn (Stuttgart: Teubner, repr. Darmstadt: Wissenschaftliche Buchgesellschaft, 1966, 1980).

Remus, H. 1996. 'Voluntary association and networks: Aelius Aristides at the Asclepieion in Pergamon', in Kloppenborg and Wilson 1996: 146–75.

Rich, J. W. 1976. *Declaring War in the Roman Republic in the Period of Transmarine Expansion*. Collection Latomus, 149 (Brussels: Latomus).

Richard, J. -C. 1978. *Les origines de la plèbe romaine: Essai sur la formation du dualisme patricio-plébéien*. BEFAR, 132 (Rome: École française).

——— 1994. '*Kalendis Ianuariis*: sur deux épisodes de la carrière de C. Marius', *Museum Helveticum* 51: 73–87.

Richardson, L. 1992. *A New Topographical Dictionary of Ancient Rome* (Baltimore: Johns Hopkins University Press).

Rilinger, R. 1976. *Der Einfluß des Wahlleiters bei den römischen Konsulwahlen von 366 bis 50 v. Chr.* Vestigia, 24 (Munich: Beck).

Rives, J. 1995. 'Human sacrifice among pagans and christians', *Journal of Roman Studies* 85: 65–85.

——— 1999. 'The decree of Decius and the religion of empire', *Journal of Roman Studies* 89: 135–54.

——— 2002. 'Magic in the XII Tables revisited', *Classical Quarterly* 52: 270–90.

——— 2006. 'Magic, religion and the law: the case of the *Lex Cornelia de sicariis et veneficiis*', in Ando and Rüpke 2006: 47–67.

——— 2008. '*Magus* and its cognates in Classical Latin', in Gordon and Marco Simón 2008.

Robinson, O. F. 1992. *Ancient Rome: city planning and administration* (London and New York: Routledge).

Roller, M. B. 2006. *Dining Posture in Ancient Rome: bodies, values, status* (Princeton: Princeton University Press).

Rose, H. J. 1913. 'Italian "Sondergötter" ', *Journal of Roman Studies* 3: 233–41.

——— 1948. *Roman Religion* (London: Hutchinson).

Rosen, K. 1985. 'Die falschen Numabücher: Politik, Religion und Literatur in Rom 181 v. Chr.', *Chiron* 15: 65–90.

Rosenberger, V. 1998. *Gezähmte Götter: Das Prodigienwesen der römischen Republik*. HABES 27 (Stuttgart: F. Steiner).

——— 2006. 'Der verschwundene Leichnam', in B. Kranemann and J. Rüpke (eds), *Text und Ritual*. Europäische Religionsgeschichte, 3 (Marburg: diagonal).

Ross Holloway, R. 1994. *The Archaeology of Early Rome and Latium* (London: Routledge).

Roullet, A. H. 1972. *The Egyptian and Egyptianizing Monuments of Imperial Rome*. EPROER 20 (Leyden: Brill).

Royden, H. L. 1988. *The Magistrates of the Roman Professional Collegia in Italy from the first century to the third century AD* (Pisa: Giardini).

Rüpke, J. 1990. *Domi militiae: Die religiöse Konstruktion des Krieges in Rom* (Stuttgart: F. Steiner).

1993a. *Römische Religion bei Eduard Norden: Die "Altrömischen Priesterbücher" im wissenschaftlichen Kontext der dreißiger Jahre.* Religionswissenschaftliche Reihe, 7 (Marburg: diagonal).

1993b. 'Vexillum caeruleum', *Rheinisches Museum* 136: 374–6.

1993c. 'Livius, Priesternamen und die *annales maximi*', *Klio* 74: 155–79.

1995a. *Kalender und Öffentlichkeit: Die Geschichte der Repräsentation und religiösen Qualifikation von Zeit in Rom.* RGVV, 40 (Berlin: de Gruyter).

1995b. 'Wege zum Töten, Wege zum Ruhm: Krieg in der römischen Republik', in H. von Stietencron and J. Rüpke (eds), *Töten im Krieg*. Schriften des Instituts für Historische Anthropologie, 6 (Freiburg: Alber) 213–40.

1995c. 'Heilung/Heilungen I. Religionswissenschaftlich', *Lexikon für Theologie und Kirche* 4: 1357–8.

1996a. 'Controllers and professionals: analyzing religious specialists', *Numen* 43: 241–62.

1996b. 'Innovationsmechanismen kultischer Religionen: Sakralrecht im Rom der Republik', in Cancik 1996b: 265–85.

1997a. 'Römische Religion und "Reichsreligion": Begriffsgeschichtliche und methodische Bemerkungen', in Cancik and Rüpke 1997: 3–23.

1997b. 'Kognitive Einheit ritueller Sequenzen? Zur kommunikativen Funktion kalendarischer Gattungen in Rom', in Binder and Ehlich 1997: 191–223.

1997c. *Römische Geschichtsschreibung: Zur Geschichte des geschichtlichen Bewußtseins und seiner Verschriftlichungsformen in der Antike* (Potsdam: AVZ/Universitätsbibliothek).

1998a. 'Merkur am Ende: Horaz, *carm.* 1.30', *Hermes* 126: 435–53.

1998b. 'Kommensalität und Gesellschaftsstruktur: Tafelfreu(n)de im alten Rom', *Saeculum* 49: 193–215.

1998c. 'Les archives des petits collèges: le cas des vicomagistri', in AA.VV. 1998: 27–44.

1999. 'Apokalyptische Salzberge: Zum sozialen Ort und zur literarischen Strategie des Hirten des Hermas', *Archiv für Religionsgeschichte* 1: 148–60.

2001a. 'Pluralismus und Polytheismus', in A. Gotzmann, V. N. Makrides, J. Malik, and J. Rüpke (eds), *Pluralismus in der europäischen Religionsgeschichte: Religionswissenschaftliche Antrittsvorlesungen.* Europäische Religionsgeschichte, 1 (Marburg: diagonal) 17–34.

2001b. 'Kulturtransfer als Rekodierung: Überlegungen zum literaturgeschichtlichen und sozialen Ort der frühen römischen Epik', in idem (ed.), *Von Menschen und Göttern erzählen: Formkonstanzen und Funktionswandel vormoderner Epik.* PAwB, 4 (Stuttgart: F. Steiner) 42–64.

2001c. 'Antike Religion als Kommunikation', in K. Brodersen (ed.), *Gebet und Fluch, Zeichen und Traum: Aspekte religiöser Kommunikation in antiken Gesellschaften.* Studien zur Alten Geschichte, 2 (Münster, Westphalia: Lit) 13–30.

2001d. 'Religion X: Rom', *Der Neue Pauly* 10: 910–17.

2002. '*Collegia sacerdotum* – religiöse Vereine in der Oberschicht', in Egelhaaf-Gaiser and Schäfer 2002: 41–67.

2003. 'Calendar', in *Brill's New Pauly* 2: 938–51.

2004. 'Religion und Gruppe: Ein religionssoziologischer Versuch zur römischen Antike', in B. Luchesi and K. von Stuckrad (eds), *Religion im kulturellen*

Diskurs: Festschrift für Hans G. Kippenberg zu seinem 65. Geburtstag. RGVV, 52 (Berlin: de Gruyter) 235–58.

2005a. *Fasti sacerdotum: Die Mitglieder der Priesterschaften und das sakrale Funktionspersonal römischer, griechischer, orientalischer und jüdisch-christlicher Kulte in der Stadt Rom von 300 v.Chr. bis 499 n.Chr.* 3 vols. PAwB, 12.1–3 (Stuttgart: F. Steiner).

2005b. 'Gäste der Götter – Götter als Gäste: zur Konstruktion des römischen Opferbanketts', in Georgoudi et al., 2005: 227–39.

2005c. 'Varro's *tria genera theologiae*: Religious thinking in the late Republic', *Ordia Prima* 4: 107–29

2006a. 'Religion in the *lex Ursonensis*', in Ando and Rüpke 2006: 34–46.

2006b. 'Urban religion and imperial expansion: priesthoods in the *Lex Ursonensis*', in Le Blois et al. 2006: 11–23.

2006c. 'Roman imperial and provincial religion', *Archiv für Religionsgeschichte* 8: 327–43.

2006d. 'Triumphator and ancestor rituals between symbolic anthropology and magic', *Numen* 53: 251–89.

2006e. 'The rational choice approach towards religion: Theoriegeschichte als Religionsgeschichte', in W. Reinhard, and J. Stagl (eds), *Wirtschaftsanthropologie: Geschichte und Diskurse.* Veröffentlichungen des Instituts für Historische Anthropologie, 9 (Vienna: Böhlau) 435–49.

2006f. 'Organisationsmuster religiöser Spezialisten im kultischen Spektrum Roms', in C. Bonnet, J. Rüpke, and P. Scarpi (eds), *Religions orientales – culti misterici: Neue Perspektiven – nouvelles perspectives – prospettive nuove.* PAwB, 16 (Stuttgart: F. Steiner) 13–26.

2006g. Zeit und Fest: Kulturgeschichte es Kalenders (Munich: Beck).

(ed.) 2007. *The Blackwell Companion to Roman Religion* (Oxford: Blackwell).

forthcoming. 'Transferring religious structure: observations on Judaism, Iuppiter Dolichenus and other oriental cults in Rome', in A. Bendlin (ed.), *Religion and Culture in the Eastern Parts of the Roman Empire* (Tübingen: Mohr-Siebeck).

Rutgers, L. V. 1995. *The Jews in Late Ancient Rome: evidence of cultural interaction in the Roman Diaspora.* RGRW, 126 (Leyden: Brill).

Rutgers, L. V. et al. (eds). 1998. *The Use of Sacred Books in the Ancient World* (Leuven: Peeters).

Sælid Gilhus, I. 2006. *Animals, Gods and Humans: changing attitudes to animals in Greek, Roman and early Christian ideas* (London and New York: Routledge).

Sahlins, M. 1972. *Stone Age Economics* (Chicago: Aldine-Atherton).

1976a. 'Colors and cultures', *Semiotica* 16: 1–22.

1976b. *Culture and Practical Reason* (Chicago: University of Chicago Press).

Salama, P. 1992. 'Anniversaires impériaux constantino-liciniens à Djemila', in Christol et al. 1992: 137–59.

Salamito, J. -M. 1987. 'Les dendrophores dans l'empire chrétien: à propos de Code Théodosien, XIV.8.1 et XVI.10.20.2', *MEFR(A)* 99: 991–1018.

Saller, R. P. 1984. '*Familia, domus* and the Roman concept of the family', *Phoenix* 38: 336–55. Another version in id., *Patriarchy, Property and Death in the Roman Family* (Cambridge: Cambridge University Press, 1994) 74–101.

Salway, B. 1994. 'What's in a name? A survey of Roman onomastic practice from c. 700 BC – AD 700', *Journal of Roman Studies* 84: 124–45.

Salzman, M. R. 1990. *On Roman Time: The Codex-Calendar of 354 and the Rhythms of Urban Life in Late Antiquity*. The Transformation of the Classical Heritage, 17 (Berkeley: University of California Press).

2002. *The Making of a Christian Aristocracy: social and religious change in the western Roman Empire* (Cambridge, MA: Harvard University Press).

Sauron, G. 1994. *Quis deum? L'expression plastique des idéologies politiques et religieuses à Rome à la fin de la république et au début du principat*. BEFAR, 285 (Rome: École française).

2001. 'La musique dionysiaque sur la grande fresque de la villa des Mystères de Pompéi', in Brulé and Vendries 2001: 291–321.

Scardigli, B. 1991. *I Trattati romano-cartaginesi* (Pisa: Scuola Normale Superiore).

Scarpi, P. 1979. 'La pyrrhíche o le armi della persuasione: appunti per una semiologia storico-religiosa e antropologica', *Dialoghi di Archeologia* n.s. 1.1: 78–97.

Schäfer, P. 1990. 'Jewish magic literature in Late Antiquity and Early Middle Ages', *Journal of Jewish Studies* 41: 75–91.

1997. 'Magic and religion in Ancient Judaism', in Schäfer and Kippenberg 1997: 19–43.

Schäfer, P. and Kippenberg, H. G. (eds) 1997. *Envisioning Magic: a Princeton seminar and symposium*. Studies in the History of Religions, 75 (Leyden: Brill).

Scheer, T. S. 2000. *Die Gottheit und ihr Bild: Untersuchungen zur Funktion griechischer Kultbilder in Religion und Politik*. Zetemata, 105 (Munich: Beck).

Scheid, J. 1984. 'Le prêtre et le magistrat: réflexions sur les sacerdoces et le droit public à la fin de la République', in C. Nicolet (ed.), *Des ordres à Rome*. Histoire Ancienne et Médiévale, 13 (Paris: Publications de la Sorbonne) 243–80.

1985a. *Religion et piété à Rome*. (Paris: Découverte).

1985b. 'Sacrifice et banquet à Rome: quelques problèmes', *MEFR(A)* 97: 193–206.

1986. 'Le thiase du Metropolitan Museum (*IGUR* I, 160)', in AA.VV. 1986: 275–90.

1987. 'Polytheism impossible, or the empty gods: reasons behind a void in the history of Roman religion', *History and Anthropology* 3: 303–25.

1988. 'La spartizione sacrificiale a Roma', in C. Grottanelli (ed.), *Sacrificio e società nel mondo antico* (Bari: Laterza) 267–92.

1990a. *Romulus et ses frères: Le collège des frères arvales, modèle du culte public dans la Rome des empereurs*. BEFAR, 275 (Rome: École française).

1990b. *Le collège des frères arvales: Étude prosopographique du recrutement (69–304)*. Saggi di storia antica, 1 (Rome: 'L'Erma' di Bretschneider).

1990c. 'Rituel et écriture à Rome.' in A.-M. Blondeau and K. Schipper (eds), *Essais sur le rituel 2*. Bibliothèque de l'École des Hautes Études, Sciences religieuses, 95 (Louvain: Peeters) 1–15.

1990d. '*Hoc anno immolatum non est*: les aléas de la *voti sponsio*', *Scienze dell'antichità* 3–4 (1989–1990) 773–84.

1993. 'La vita religiosa a Roma alla fine della repubblica e durante l'impero', in G. De Rosa, T. Gregory, and A. Vauchez (eds), *Storia dell'Italia religiosa 1: L'antichità e il medioevo* (Bari: Laterza) 41–77.

1994. 'Les archives de la piété: réflexions sur les livres sacerdotaux', in C. Nicolet (ed.), *La mémoire perdue. À la recherche des archives oubliées, publiques et privées de la Rome antique*. Histoire Ancienne et Médiévale, 30 (Paris: Publications de la Sorbonne) 173–85.

BIBLIOGRAPHY

1995. '*Graeco ritu*: a typically Roman way of honouring the gods', *Harvard Studies in Classical Philology* 97: 15–31.

1997. 'La religion romaine à la fin de la république et au début de l'empire: un problème généralement mal posé', in H. Bruhns, J.-M. David, and W. Nippel (eds), *Die späte römische Republik – la fin de la république romaine: un débat franco-allemand d'histoire et d'historiographie*. CEFR, 235 (Rome: École française) 127–39.

1998a. *Commentarii fratrum Arvalium qui supersunt: les copies épigraphiques des protocoles annuels de la confrérie arvale (21 av.-304 ap. J.-C.)*. Avec la collaboration de Paola Tassini et Jörg Rüpke. Roma antica, 4 – Recherches archéologiques à La Magliana (Rome: École française/Soprintendenza archeologica di Roma).

1998b. 'Les annales des pontifes: une hypothèse de plus', *Convegno per Santo Mazzarino. Roma 9–11 maggio 1991*. Saggi di Storia Antica, 13 (Rome: 'L'Erma' di Bretschneider), 199–220.

1999. 'Aspects religieux de la municipalisation: quelques réflexions générales,' in M. Dondin-Payre and M.-Th. Raepsaet-Charlier (eds), *Cités, municipes, colonies: les processus de municipalisation en Gaule et en Germanie sous le Haut-Empire romain*. Histoire ancienne et médiévale, 53 (Paris: Publications de la Sorbonne) 381–423.

2003. *An Introduction to Roman Religion*. Transl. by Janet Lloyd, ed. Mary Beard (Edinburgh: Edinburgh University Press). Original title: *La religion des Romains* (Paris: Armand Colin, 1998).

2005. 'Manger avec les dieux. Partage sacrificiel et et commensalité dans la Rome antique', in Georgoudi et al. 2005.

Scheid, J. and Granino Cecere, M. G. 1999. 'Les sacerdoces publics équestres', in S. Demougin, H. Devijver, and M. -Th. Raepsaet-Charlier (eds), *L'ordre équestre: histoire d'une aristocratie (IIe siècle av. J.-C.-IIe siècle ap. J.-C.)*. CEFR, 257 (Paris: École française) 79–189.

Scheidel, W. (ed.) 2001. *Debating Roman Demography* (Leyden: Brill).

Schilling, R. 1980. 'La déification à Rome: tradition latine et interférence grecque', *Revue des Études Latines* 58: 137–52.

Schluchter, W. 1998. 'Handlungs- und Strukturtheorie nach Max Weber', in W. Schluchter (ed.), *Kolloquien des Max Weber-Kollegs I-V* (Erfurt: Universität Erfurt) 109–34.

Schmidt, P. L. 1989. '*Postquam ludus in artem paulatim verterat*: Varro und die Frühgeschichte des römischen Theaters', in G. Vogt-Spira (ed.), *Studien zur vorliterarischen Periode im frühen Rom* (Tübingen: Narr) 77–134.

Schnegg-Köhler, B. 2002. *Die augusteischen Säkularspiele*. Archiv für Religionsgeschichte, Monogr. 4 (Munich: K. Saur).

Schofield, M. 1986. 'Cicero for and against divination', *Journal of Roman Studies* 76: 47–65.

Scholtissek, K. (ed.) 2000. *Christologie in der Paulus-Schule : zur Rezeptionsgeschichte des paulinischen Evangeliums: Neutestamentliches Kolloquium, Münster, Westfalen, 24–25.04.1998*. Stuttgarter Bibelstudien, 181 (Stuttgart: Verlag Kath. Bibelwerk).

Scholz, U. W. 1970. *Studien zum altitalischen und altrömischen Marskult und Marsmythos* (Heidelberg: Winter).

Schott, R. 1990. 'Die Macht des Überlieferungswissens in schriftlosen Gesellschaften', *Saeculum* 41: 273–316.

Schraudolph, E. 1993. *Römische Götterweihungen mit Reliefschmuck aus Italien: Altäre, Basen und Reliefs* (Heidelberg: Verlag Archäologie und Geschichte).

Schröter, R. 1963. 'Die varronische Etymologie', in C. O. Brink (ed.), *Varron. Entretiens sur l'antiquité classique*, 9 (Vandoeuvres: Fondation Hardt) 79–100.

Schultz, C. E. 2006. *Women's Religious Activity in the Roman Republic* (Chapel Hill: University of North Carolina Press).

Schulze-Oben, H. 1989. *Freigelassene in den Städten des römischen Hispanien: Juristische, wirtschaftliche und soziale Stellung nach dem Zeugnis der Inschriften* (Bonn: Habelt).

Schumacher, L. 1978. 'Die vier hohen römischen Priesterkollegien unter den Flaviern, den Antoninen und den Severern (69–235 n. Chr.)', *ANRW* II.16,1: 655–819.

Schwarte, K.-H. 1994. 'Diokletians Christengesetz', in R. Günther and S. Rebenich (eds), *E fontibus haurire: Beiträge zur römischen Geschichte und zu ihren Hilfswissenschaften*. Studien zur Geschichte und Kultur des Altertums, NF 1. 8 (Paderborn: Schöningh) 203–40.

Schwartz, B. 1967. 'The social psychology of the gift', *American Journal of Sociology* 73: 1–11.

Scott Ryberg, I. 1955. *Rites of the State Religion in Roman Art.* Memoirs and Papers of the American Academy at Rome, 22 (New Haven and Rome).

Scullard, H. H. 1981. *Festivals and Ceremonies of the Roman Republic* (London: Thames and Hudson).

Sedley, D. 1999. 'Hellenistic physics and metaphysics', in Algra et al. (eds) 1999: 355–411.

Segal, R. A. 1999. *Theorizing about Myth* (Amhurst, MA: University of Massachusetts Press).

Selinger, R. 2002. *The Mid-Third Century Persecution of Decius and Valerius* (Bern and Frankurt a.M.: Lang).

Sharples, R. W. 1996. *Stoics, Epicureans and Sceptics: An Introduction to Hellenistic Philosophy* (London: Routledge).

Simon, E. et al. 2004–6. 'Weihgeschenke: Altitalien und Imperium Romanum', in Balty et al. 2004–06: 1, 327–450.

Sini, F. 1983. *Documenti sacerdotali di Roma antica 1: Libri e commentarii.* Università di Sassari, Facoltà di Giurisprudenza, Seminario di Diritto Romano, 2 (Sassari: Dessi).

Small, A. (ed.) 1996. *Subject and Ruler: the cult of the ruling power in Classical Antiquity. Papers presented at a conference held in The University of Alberta on April 13–15, 1994 to celebrate the 65th anniversary of Duncan Fishwick.* Journal of Roman Archaeology, Supplement 17 (Ann Arbor: Journal of Roman Archaeology).

Smith, C. J. 1996a. *Early Rome and Latium: economy and society c. 1000 to 500 BC.* (Oxford: Clarendon Press).

—— 1996b. 'Dead dogs and rattles: time, space and ritual sacrifice in Iron Age Latium', in J. B. Wilkins (ed.), *Approaches to the Study of Ritual: Italy and the Ancient Mediterranean.* Accordia Specialist Studies on the Mediterranean, 2 (London: Accordia) 73–89.

—— 2006. *The Roman Clan: the gens from ancient ideology to modern anthropology* (Cambridge: Cambridge University Press).

Smith, J. Z. 1978. 'Towards interpreting demonic powers in Hellenistic and Roman antiquity', *ANRW* II.16,1: 425–39.

1998. 'Religion, religions, religious', in M. C. Taylor (ed.), *Critical Terms for Religious Studies* (Chicago: University of Chicago Press) 269–84.

Smith, M. 1979. 'Relations between magical papyri and magical gems', *Paapyrologica Bruxellensia* 18: 129–36.

Smith, M. 1993. *The Liturgy of Opening the Mouth for Breathing* (Oxford: Griffith Institute – Ashmolean Museum).

Smith, R. R. R. 2000. 'Nero and the Sun-god: divine accessories and political symbols in Roman imperial images', *Journal of Roman Archaeology* 13: 532–42.

Solin, H. 1999. 'Epigrafia repubblicana: bilanco, novità, prospettive', in AA.VV., *Atti del XI Congresso Internazionale di Epigrafia Greca e Latina, Roma, 18–24 sett. 1997* (Rome: Edizioni Quasar) 1: 379–404.

Sommella Mura, A. 1977. 'La decorazione architettonica del tempio arcaico', in Colini et al. 1977: 62–128.

Sordi, M. 1979. 'Sergia Paulina e il suo collegium', *Istituto Lombardo: Rendiconti, Classe di Lettere* 113: 14–20.

Sordi, M. and Cavigiolo, M. L. 1971. 'Un' antica chiesa domestica di Roma? (Il *collegium quod est in domo Sergiae L. f. Paulinae*)', *Rivista di storia della chiesa in Italia* 25: 369–74.

Sourvinou-Inwood, C. 1995. *'Reading' Greek Death: to the end of the Classical period* (Oxford: Clarendon Press).

Spaeth, B. S. 1996. *The Roman Goddess Ceres* (Austin: University of Texas Press).

Spickermann, W. (ed.) 2001. *Religion in den germanischen Provinzen Roms.* Hrsg. in Verbindung mit H. Cancik und J. Rüpke (Tübingen: Mohr Siebeck).

2003. *Religionsgeschichte des römischen Germanien, 1: Germania Superior.* Religion der römischen Provinzen, 2 (Tübingen: Mohr Siebeck).

Spurr, M. S. 1986. *Arable Cultivation in Roman Italy, c. 200 BC – c. AD 100.* Journal of Roman Studies, Monograph 3 (London: Society for the Promotion of Roman Studies).

Stambaugh, J. E. 1978. 'The functions of Roman temples', *ANRW* II.16,1 : 554–628.

Stamper, J. W. 2005. *The Architecture of Roman Temples: the Republic to the Middle Empire* (Cambridge: Cambridge University Press).

Stark, R. 1996. *The Rise of Christianity: how the obscure, marginal Jesus Movement became the dominant religious force in the Western World in a few centuries* (Princeton: Princeton University Press).

Steiner, D. T. 2001. *Images in Mind: statues in Archaic and Classical Greek literature and thought* (Princeton: Princeton University Press).

Stepper, R. 1999. 'Der Oberpontifikat von Caesar bis Nerva: Zwischen Tradition und Innovation', in Batsch et al. 1999: 171–85.

2003. *Augustus et sacerdos: Untersuchungen zum römischen Kaiser als Priester.* PAwB, 9 (Stuttgart: F. Steiner).

Stern, H. 1953. *Le calendrier de 354: étude sur son texte et ses illustrations.* Institut français d'Archéologie de Beyrouth: Bibliothèque archéologique et historique, 55 (Paris: Imprimerie Nationale: Librérie P. Geuthner).

Stern, S. 2001. *Calendar and Community: a history of the Jewish calendar, second century BCE – tenth century CE* (Oxford: Oxford University Press).

Steuernagel, D. 1999. ' "Corporate identity": über Vereins-, Stadt- und Staatskulte im kaiserzeitlichen Puteoli', *MDAI(R)* 106: 149–87.

2001. 'Kult und Community: Sacella in den Insulae von Ostia', *MDAI(R)* 116: 41–56.

2004. *Kult und Alltag in römischen Hafenstädten: Soziale Prozesse in archäologischer Perspektive.* PAwB, 11 (Stuttgart: F. Steiner).

Stewart, P. C. N. 2003. *Statues in Roman Society: representation and response* (Oxford: Oxford University Press).

Stroumsa, G. 1998. 'The Christian hermeneutical revolution and its double helix', in Rutgers et al. 1998: 9–28.

2005. *La fin du sacrifice: les mutations religieuses de l'Antiquité tardive* (Paris: Odile Jacob).

Struck, M. 2001. 'The *Heilige Römische Reich Deutscher Nation* and Hermann the German', in R. Hingley (ed.), *Images of Rome: perceptions of ancient Rome in Europe and the United States in the modern age.* Journal of Roman Archaeology, Supplement 44 (Portsmouth, RI: Journal of Roman Archaeology) 91–112.

Stuckrad, K. von. 2000. *Das Ringen um die Astrologie: Jüdische und christliche Beiträge zum antiken Zeitverständnis.* RGVV, 49 (Berlin: de Gruyter).

2002. ' "Christen" und "Nichtchristen" in der Antike: von religiös konstruierten Grenzen zur diskursorientierten Religionswissenschaft', in M. Hutter et al. (eds), *Hairesis. Festschrift für Karl Hoheisel.* Jahrbuch für Antike und Christentum, Ergänzungsband 34 (Münster, Westphalia: Aschendorff).

Stübler, G. 1941. *Die Religiösität des Livius.* Tübinger Beiträge zur Altertumswissenschaft, 35 (Stuttgart: Kohlhammer, repr. Amsterdam: Hakkert, 1964).

Sullivan, T. A. 1983. 'Family morality and family mortality: speculations on the demographic transition', in W. V. d'Antonio and J. Aldous (eds), *Families and Religions: conflict and change in modern society* (Beverley Hills, CA and London: Sage Publications) 49–66.

Swerdlow, N. M. (ed.) 1999. *Ancient Astronomy and Celestial Divination* (Cambridge, MA: MIT Press).

Syme, R. 1975–76 [1978]. 'The pomerium in the Historia Augusta', in *Bonner Historia-Augusta-Colloquium,* 8 = Antiquitas, 4 (Beiträge zur Historia-Augusta-Forschung, 13) (Bonn: Habelt) 217–31.

Szemler, G. J. 1972. *The Priests of the Roman Republic: a study of interactions between priesthoods and magistracies.* Collection Latomus, 127 (Brussels: Latomus).

Takács, S. A. 1990. *Isis and Sarapis in the Roman World.* RGRW, 124 (Leyden: Brill).

Tambiah, S. J. 1990. *Magic, Science, Religion, and the Scope of Rationality* (Cambridge: Cambridge University Press).

Taylor, D. J. 1974 [1975]. *Declinatio. A study of the linguistic theory of M. Terentius Varro* (Amsterdam: Benjamin).

Taylor, L. R. 1942. 'The election of the Pontifex Maximus in the Late Republic', *Classical Philology* 37: 421–4.

Tenbruck, F. H. 1993. 'Die Religion im Maelstrom der Reflexion', in J. Bergmann, A. Hahn, and T. Luckmann (eds), *Religion und Kultur.* Kölner Zeitschrift für Soziologie und Sozialpsychologie, Sonderheft 33 (Opladen: Westdeutscher Verlag) 31–67.

Thom, J. C. 2005. *Cleanthes' Hymn to Zeus.* Studien und Texte zu Antike und Christentum, 33 (Tübingen: Mohr Siebeck).

Thomas, K. 1971. *Religion and the Decline of Magic: studies in popular beliefs in sixteenth- and seventeenth-century England* (London: Weidenfeld and Nicholson).

Thomas, Y. 1990. 'L'institution de l'origine: *Sacra principiorum populi Romani*', in M. Detienne (ed.), *Tracés de fondation*. Bibliothèque de l'École des Hautes Études, Section des sciences religieuses, 113 (Louvain: Peeters) 143–70.

Timpe, D. 'Was ist Kirchengeschichte? Zum Gattungscharakter der *Historia Ecclesiastica* des Eusebius', in W. Dahlheim, W. Schuler, and J. von Ungern-Sternberg (eds), *Festschrift Robert Werner*. Xenia, 22 (Constance: Universitätsverlag) 171–204.

Todd, M. 1975. *The Northern Barbarians, 100 BC – AD 300* (London: Hutchinson).

Toner, J. P. 1995. *Leisure and Ancient Rome* (Cambridge: Polity).

Torelli, M. 1984. *Lavinio e Roma: Riti iniziatici e matrimonio tra archeologia e storia* (Rome: Edizioni Quasar).

Torelli, M. et al. 2004–06. 'Luoghi di culto: mondo etrusco, italico e romano', in Balty et al. 2004–06: 4, 128–361.

Towler, R. 1974. *Homo Religiosus: sociological problems in the study of religion* (London: Constable).

Toynbee, J. M. C. 1971. *Death and Burial in the Roman World* (London: Thames and Hudson).

Tran tam Tinh, V. 1964. *Essai sur le culte d'Isis à Pompéi* (Paris: Le Boccard).

—— 1971. *Les cultes des divinités orientales à Herculanum*. EPROER, 17 (Leyden: Brill).

Treggiari, S. 1991. *Roman Marriage: Iusti coniuges from the time of Cicero to the time of Ulpian* (Oxford: Clarendon Press).

Trombley, F. R. 1995. *Hellenic Religion and Hellenism, c. 370–529.* 2nd edn. RGRW 115 (Leyden: Brill).

Turcan, R. 1978. 'Le culte impérial au IIIe siècle', in *ANRW* II.16,2: 827–948.

—— 1983. 'Enée, Lavinium et les treize autels: en marge d'un livre récent', *Revue de l'Histoire des Religions* 200: 41–66.

—— 1988. *Religion romaine*. Iconography of Religions, 17.1–2 (Leyden: Brill).

—— 1996. *The Cults of the Roman Empire*. Trans. by Antonia Nevil (Oxford: Blackwell). Orig. title: *Les cultes orientaux dans le monde romain* 2nd edn (Paris: Les Belles Lettres, 1992; 1st edn 1989).

—— 2003. *Liturgies de l'initiation bacchique à l'époque romaine: documentation littéraire, inscrite et figuré*. Mémoires de l'Académie et Belles-Lettres, 27 (Paris: Diffusion De Boccard).

Turner, V., and Vallier, I. A. 1968. 'Religious specialists', in D. L. Sills (ed.), *International Encyclopedia of the Social Sciences* (New York: Macmillan and Free Press) 13: 437–53.

Ulf, Ch. 1982. *Das römische Lupercalienfest: Ein Modellfall für Methodenprobleme in der Altertumswissenschaft*. Impulse der Forschung, 38 (Darmstadt: Wissenschaftliche Buchgesellschaft).

Usener, H. 1896/2000. *Götternamen: Versuch einer Lehre von der religiösen Begriffsbildung* (Bonn: Cohen; 4th edn, Frankfurt a.M.: Klostermann).

Vaahtera, J. E. 2000. 'Roman religion and the Polybian politeia', in Bruun 2000: 251–64.

Van der Eijk, Ph. J., Horstmanshoff, H. F. J., and Schrijvers, P. H. (eds). 1995. *Ancient Medicine in its Socio-Cultural Context* (Amsterdam: Rodopi).

Van der Horst, P. W. 1994. 'Silent prayer in antiquity', *Numen* 41: 1–25.

Vanggaard, J. H. 1979. 'The October horse', *Temenos* 15: 81–95.

1988. *The Flamen: a study in the history and sociology of Roman religion* (Copenhagen: Museum Tusculanum Press).

Van Haeperen, F. 2002. *Le collège pontifical, IIIe av.J-C.–IVe ap. J-C.: Contribution à l'étude de la religion publique romaine.* Études de philologie, d'archéologie et d'histoire anciennes, 39 (Brussels and Rome).

Van Hooff, A. J. L. 1977. 'Polybius' reason and religion: the relations between Polybius' casual thinking and his attitude towards religion in the studies of history', *Klio* 59: 101–28.

Van Nijf, O. 1997. *The Civic World of Professional Associations in the Greek East* (Amsterdam: Gieben).

Van Straten, F. T. 1981. 'Gifts for the gods', in H. S. Versnel (ed.), *Faith, Hope and Worship: aspects of religious mentality in the Ancient World.* Studies in Greek and Roman Religion, 2 (Leyden: Brill) 65–151.

1993. 'Images of gods and men in a changing society: self-identity in Hellenistic religion', in A. W. Bulloch et al. (eds) *Image and Ideologies* (Berkeley: University of California Press) 248–64.

1995. *Hierà kalá: images of animal sacrifice in Archaic and Classical Greece.* RGRW, 127 (Leyden: Brill).

Vendries, C. 2001. 'Pour les oreilles de Cybèle: images plurielles de la musique sur les autels tauroboliques de la Gaule romaine', in Brulé and Vendries 2001: 197–218

Vermaseren, M. J. 1956–60. *Corpus inscriptionum et monumentorum religionis Mithriacae (CIMRM).* 2 vols. (The Hague: Martinus Nijhoff).

Vermaseren, M. J. and Van Essen, C. C. 1965. *The Excavations in the Mithraeum of the Church of Santa Prisca in Rome* (Leyden: Brill).

Vermeule, C. C. 1987. *The Cult Images of Imperial Rome.* Archaeologica, 71 (Rome: 'L'Erma' di Bretschneider).

Versnel, H. S. 1970. *Triumphus: an inquiry into the origin, development and meaning of the Roman triumph* (Leyden: Brill).

1976. 'Two types of Roman devotio', *Mnemosyne*[4]. 29: 365–410.

1985. ' "May he not be able to sacrifice." Concerning a curious formula in Greek and Latin curses', *Zeitschrift für Papyrologie und Epigraphik* 58: 247–69.

1990. *Inconsistencies in Greek and Roman Religion 1: Ter unus. Isis, Dionysos, Hermes. Three Studies in Henotheism.* Studies in Greek and Roman Religion, 6 (Leyden: Brill).

1991. 'Beyond cursing: the appeal to justice in judicial prayers', in Faraone and Obbink 1991: 60–106.

2002. 'The poetics of the magical charm: an essay on the magical power of words', in Meyer and Mirecki 2002: 105–58. Original version of 'Die Poetik der Zaubersprüche', in T. Schabert and R. Brague (eds), *Die Macht des Wortes* (Munich: Wilhelm Fink, 1996) 233–97.

2004. 'Making sense of Jesus' death: the pagan contribution', in J. Frey and J. Schröter (eds), *Deutungen des Todes Jesu im Neuen Testament* (Tübingen: Mohr-Siebeck) 213–94.

2008. 'Prayers for justice East and West: new finds and publications since 1990', in Gordon and Marco 2008.

Veyne, P. 1983. *Les grecs ont-ils cru à leurs mythes? Essai sur l'imagination con- stituante* (Paris: Éditions du Seuil). Transl. by Paula Wissing as *Did the Greeks believe their Myths? An essay on the constitutive imagination* (Chicago: University of Chicago Press, 1988).

Veyne, P. 2000. 'Inviter les dieux, sacrifier, banqueter. Quelques nuances de la religiosité gréco-romaine', *Annales ESC* 55: 3–42.

Victor, U. 1997. *Lukian von Samosata: Alexandros oder der Lügenprophet.* RGRW, 132 (Leyden: Brill).

Ville, G. 1981. *La gladiature en Occident des origines à la mort de Domitien* (Rome: École française).

Wachsmuth, D. 1967. Pompinos ho daimon: *Untersuchung zu den antiken Sakralhandlungen bei Seereisen* (Diss. Freie Universität, Berlin, presented 1960).

Wachter, R. 1987. *Altlateinische Inschriften: Sprachliche und epigraphische Untersuchungen zu den Dokumenten bis etwa 150 v. Chr.* Europäische Hochschulschriften, Reihe XV, 38 (Bern: Peter Lang).

Waegemann, M. 1987. *Amulet and Alphabet: magical amulets in the first Book of Cyranides* (Amsterdam: Gieben).

Wagenvoort, H. 1947. *Roman Dynamism: studies in ancient Roman thought, language and custom* (Oxford: Oxford University Press). Repr. Westport, CON: Greenwood, 1976. Orig. ed. *Imperium: studien over het 'mana' begrip in zede en taal der Romeinen* (Amsterdam: H.J. Paris, 1941).

Walbank, F. W. 1957–79. *A Historical Commentary on Polybius.* 3 vols. (Oxford: Clarendon Press).

Wallace-Hadrill, A. 1993. *Augustan Rome* (London: Bristol Classical Press).

Walser, G. 1984. *Summus Poeninus: Beiträge zur Geschichte des Großen Sf. Bernhard Passes in römischer Zeit.* Historia Einzelschriften, 46 (Stuttgart: F. Steiner).

1994. *Studien zu Alpengeschichte in antiker Zeit.* Historia Einzelschriften, 86 (Stuttgart: F. Steiner).

Warde Fowler, W. 1911. *The Religious Experience of the Roman People, from the earliest times to the death of Augustus* (London: Macmillan). Repr. New York: Cooper Square, 1971.

Ward-Perkins, J. B. 1970. 'From Republic to Empire: reflections on the early provincial architecture of the Roman West', *Journal of Roman Studies* 60: 1–19.

1981. *Roman Imperial Architecture* 2nd edn (New Haven: Yale University Press).

Warmington, E. H. 1935. *Remains of Old Latin*, 1 (Loeb vol. 294) (Cambridge and London: Harvard University Press and W. Heinemann).

Watson, A. 1971. *Roman Private Law around 200 BC* (Edinburgh: Edinburgh University Press).

Weinreich, O. 1929. 'Gebet und Wunder', *Genethliakon Wilhelm Schmid.* Tübinger Beiträge zur Altertumswissenschaft, 5 (Stuttgart: Kohlhammer) 167–464.

Weinstock, S. 1964. 'Saturnalien und Neujahrsfest in den Märtyrerakten', in A. Stuiber (ed.), *Mullus: Festschrift Theodor Klauser.* Jahrbuch für Antike und Christentum, Ergänzungsband 1 (Münster: Aschendorff) 391–406.

1971. *Divus Julius* (Oxford: Clarendon Press).

West, M. L. 1983. *The Orphic Poems* (Oxford: Clarendon Press). Repr. Oxford: Sandpiper, 1998.

White, L. M. 1990. *Building God's House in the Roman World: architectural adaptation among pagans, Jews, and Christians* (Baltimore: Johns Hopkins University Press).

Whittaker, C. R. 1993. 'The poor in the city of Rome', in idem, *Land, City and Trade in the Roman Empire* (Aldershot: Variorum) no. VII. Orig. published in Italian, 'Il povero', in A. Giardina (ed.), *L'uomo romano* (Rome and Bari: Laterza, 1989) 301–33.

Wille, G. 1967. *Musica Romana: Die Bedeutung der Musik im Leben der Römer* (Amsterdam: Schippers).

Williams, M. A. 1996. *Rethinking 'Gnosticism': an argument for dismantling a dubious category* (Princeton: Princeton University Press).

Williams, J. 2007. 'Religion and Roman coins', in Rüpke 2007.

Winiarczyk, M. 1984. 'Wer galt im Altertum als Atheist?' *Philologus* 128: 157–83.

——— 1990. 'Methodisches zum antiken Atheismus', *Rheinisches Museum* 133: 1–15.

——— 1991. *Euhemeri Messenii Reliquiae* (Stuttgart and Leipzig: Teubner).

——— 1992. 'Antike Bezeichnungen der Gottlosigkeit und des Atheismus', *Rheinisches Museum* 135: 216–25.

——— 1994. 'Ennius' *Euhemerus* sive *Sacra historia*', *Rheinisches Museum* 137: 274–91.

Winkler, L. 1995. *Salus: Vom Staatskult zur politischen Idee.* Archäologie und Geschichte, 4 (Heidelberg: Archäologie und Geschichte).

Wischmeyer, W. 1990. 'Die Epistula Anne ad Senecam: Eine jüdische Missionsschrift des lateinischen Bereichs', in J. van Amersfoort and J. van Oort (eds), *Juden und Christen in der Antike* (Kampen: Kok) 72–93.

Wiseman, T. P. 1994. *Historiography and Imagination: eight essays on Roman culture.* Exeter Studies in History (Exeter: Exeter University Press).

——— 1995a. *Remus: A roman myth* (Cambridge: Cambridge University Press).

——— 1995b. 'The god of the Lupercal', *Journal of Roman Studies* 85: 1–22.

——— 2000. 'Liber: myth, drama and ideology in Republican Rome', in Bruun 2000: 265–99.

Wissowa, G. 1912. *Religion und Kultus der Römer.* 2nd edn. Handbuch der Altertumswissenschaft 5.4 (Munich: Beck).

Wolf, G. 1990. *Salus populi Romani: Die Geschichte römischer Kultbilder im Mittelalter* (Weinheim: VCH, Acta Humaniora).

Wrede, H. 1981. Consecratio in formam deorum: *Vergöttlichte Privatpersonen in der römischen Kaiserzeit* (Mainz: Zabern).

——— 1983. 'Statuae Lupercorum habitu', *Mitteilungen des Deutschen Archäologischen Instituts (Römische Abteilung)* 90: 187–200.

Wright, D. P. 1987. *The Disposal of Impurity: elimination rites in the Bible and in Hittite and Mesopotamian Literature.* Society of Biblical Literature, Diss. Series 101 (Atlanta, GA: Scholars Press).

Wytzes, J. 1977. *Der letzte Kampf des Heidentums in Rom.* EPROER, 56 (Leyden: Brill).

Yakobson, A. 1999. *Elections and Electioneering in Rome: a study in the political system of the Late Republic.* Historia-Einzelschriften, 128 (Stuttgart: F. Steiner).

Zanker, P. 1988. *The Power of Images in the Age of Augustus.* Transl. by Alan Shapiro (Ann Arbor: University of Michigan Press). Orig. title: *Augustus und die Macht der Bilder* (Munich: Beck, 1987).

——— 1998. *Pompeii: public and private life.* Trans. by D. L. Schneider (Cambridge,

MA: Harvard University Press. Orig. title: *Pompeji: Stadtbild und Wohngeschmack* (Mainz: von Zabern, 1995).

Zappata, E. 1996. 'Les divinités dolichéniennes et les sources épigraphiques latines', in G. M. Bellelli and U. Bianchi (eds), '*Orientalia sacra urbis Romae: Dolichena et Heliopolitana*', *Recueil d'études archéologiques et historico-religieuses sur les cultes cosmopolites d'origine commagénienne et syrienne.* Studia Archaeologica, 84 (Rome: 'L'Erma' di Bretschneider) 87–255.

Zetzel, J. 2003. 'Plato with pillows: Cicero on the uses of Greek culture', in D. Braund and C. Gill (eds), *Myth, History and Culture in Republican Rome: Studies in honour of T. P. Wiseman* (Exeter: University of Exeter Press) 119–38.

Ziehen, L. 1929. 'Sphágia', *RE* 3A, 2: 1669–79.

Ziolkowski, A. 1992. *The Temples of Mid-Republican Rome and their Historical and Topographical Context.* Saggi di Storia antica, 4 (Rome: 'L'Erma' di Bretschneider).

INDEXES

General

Academics, 58, 122, 124

Acta Arvalia (records of the Arval
    Brothers), 40, 151, 163, 219,
    249

action, religious, 6f, 10, 13, 31, 37,
    75f, 85–116, 205, 238

adaptation, 165

adoption, 29f

aedile: see magistrates

aediles, in colonies, 222

agriculture, 16, 79, 137

altar, 6, 7, 27, 28, 37, 71, 88, 95, 97,
    102, 107, 141f, 145, 148, 177,
    180, 239, 253

amulets, 167, 173

anatomicals, 155f, 158f, 161

ancestor cult; see funerary cult

ancestors, 15, 27, 132, 143

antica, 183

antiquarians, Roman, 41, 59, 134,
    181, 190, 251f

apex: see *galerus*

apokatastasis, 66

archaeology, 44, 46, 47–50, 154–61

architecture
    imperial, 244–48
    Republican, 51f, 175–81

Argei (dolls or puppets), 178

aristocracy, religio-political roles
    of, 25f, 53–61, 143, 200,
    255

art
    appropriation of, 58
    divine images, 69–74

Arvals, see *fratres Arvales*

assemblies, popular, 25, 51, 111, 187,
    198

associations, 15, 20f, 30, 34, 57, 193,
    205–14

astrology, astrologers, 229f, 254
    expulsion of ~ , 33
    popular (Laienastrologie) ~, 196

attributes, of gods, statues, 72, 75, 84,
    98, 126, 167

auguraculum, 177

augurium salutis, 228

Augurs, 28, 40, 54–6, 59, 71, 98,
    124, 175, 177, 215f, 217, 225,
    228, 248f, 274 n 1, 276 n 33
    Cicero as, 119, 124, 125
    equestrian, 226
    in colonies, 36, 223
    ius augurale, 130f
    and *templum*, 182f
    as word for 'diviner', 230, 253

(sodales) Augustales etc: see specialists

auspicium (see also bird-flight,
    obnuntiatio), 7, 175, 177, 223,
    228f

axe, 23, 147, 148

Bacchanals, 31–33, 57, 206

banquet, 26, 46, 51, 103, 142–7,
    208f, 219

purity, 103, 268 n 30
Pythagoreanism, 125, 126, 269 n 14

reading, 104f, 126, 132–4
reciprocity, 102, 149
Regal period of Rome, 21f, 41–44,
    59, 111, 129, 176
religion
  religiones, 9, 218, 280 n 2
  'licita', 35
religion
  city ~ , 17–21
  classification of foreign ~ , 35,
    212–4
  costs of ~ , 21f, 152f, 216f
  criticism of ~ , 58, 103, 122f, 125,
    128f, 241f
  diffuse, 10
  embedded, 5–12
  intellectual ~ , 126, 134f
  learning about ~ , 10f
  legitimacy of ~ , 6
  'local' ~ , 20f
  of the book, 15, 252
  organized ~ , 10, 29
  polis ~ , 18–21, 113
  private ~ , 19, 24–6, 29f
  public ~ , 7f, 11, 18, 20, 26–9, 122,
    130
  terms for ~ , 6–9, 130f
religiosus, 9, 59, 241
religious
  instruction, 10f
  policy, 248, 253f
res publica, 24f, 76
rhetors (expulsion of), 125
ritual (see also cults; *sacra*)
  basic forms, 97–106
  cleansing ~ , 92, 114f, 142, 149,
    231, 267 n 18
  complex ~ , 93, 106–14
  crisis ~ , 68, 103, 163f
  and drama, 139, 149f, 212
  fictive ~ , 111f
  funerary ~ , 30, 51, 69, 235
  initiation ~ , 11, 91–3, 99, 211,
    213, 239f
  interpretation of, 12, 86f, 88f, 95,
    98, 107–10, 114, 115, 127
  as marker, 93, 95

protective or apotropaic ~ , 231
repression of foreign ~ , 33f, 206
routine ~ , 40, 163, 193f, 218
semantics of ~ , 107f, 115, 168
special ~ , 120, 145, 163, 165
'syntax' of, 110–13, 115
terms for, 8f
ritus graecus, 34, 95
ritus patrius (romanus), 34, 95
ruler-cult: see cult

sacellum (cult site), 59, 176f, 179,
    183f, 185, 259 n 37
sacer, 8, 21, 181ff
sacerdotes publici; see specialists
sacra
  familiaria, 30
  gentilicia, 26f, 52, 250f
  peregrina, 35
  privata (see also cult, private), 24,
    29
  publica (see also cult, public), 22,
    24, 29, 35f, 259 n 37
  of colonies, 221–3
sacrarium, 179
Sacred Record (Euhemerus), 58, 123
sacred, the, 5
sacrifice (see also *daps*, offering)
  animal~ , 7, 88, 93, 97, 102f, 123,
    137–53
  cookery, 88, 142, 145f, 150, 266 n
    1
  caviares, 145
  criticism of, 103, 122f
  expiatory ~, 80f
  at dedication, 28
  functions of ~, 107ff, 145ff
  holocaust, 102
  horse ~ : see October Horse
  human ~ , 34
  magmenta, 145
  non-animal, 97, 140, 155
  not a test of loyalty, 29, 200f
  participation at, 10f, 23, 99, 103,
    110, 147, 190, 191
  porca praecidanea, 138f
  preliminaries to ~ , 141f
  private/domestic, 15
  role of divination in, 106, 139, 228,
    231

Gods and cults

Names of Persons

(This list is not intended to serve as an index locorum)

Aemilius Scaurus, M. (c. 163–88 BC), 22

Aeneas, 129, 154

Alexander of Macedon (356–323 BC), 123

Alexander Severus (emperor, BC 222–35), 250, 251

Ambrose of Milan (c. AD 340–397, bishop), 7, 11, 237

Antonius, M. (82–30 BC: here, Mark Antony), 111, 223, 226

Apelles (pupil of Marcion), 243

Apollonius (2nd century AD, Christian Philosopher in Rome), 118

Apollonius (pagan interlocutor), 243

Apollonius of Tyana (1st century AD), 123, 299

Apuleius of Madaura (c. 125–170 AD), 90–95, 99, 169

Aristeides (1st half 2nd century AD, Christian apologist), 117

Aristides, P. Aelius (AD 117–180, Greek rhetor), 166

Athanasius (c. AD 295–373, bishop of Alexandria), 118

Athenagoras of Athens (2nd century AD, Christian apologist), 117

Augustine (AD 354–430, of Hippo), 14, 20, 60, 86, 121f

Augustus (emperor 29 BC–AD 14), 26f, 81, 95, 151, 163, 193, 195, 217, 244, 245, 251

Aulus Gellius (2nd century AD), 134, 197

Aurelian (emperor AD 270–75), 208, 225, 251

Aurelius Victor Augentius (late-Roman senator), 240

Balbillus, Tib. Claudius (1st cent. AD equestrian and astrologer), 230

Caesar, C. Iulius (100–44 BC), 209, 219, 223, 226, 236, 244, 248, 250

Cassius Dio (c. AD 155–235), 41, 109

Cato the Elder (234–149 BC), 11, 39, 81, 137, 139, 149, 166, 172, 192, 230

Catullus (86–55 BC), 40

Celsus (Greek philosopher, mid-second cent. AD), 252

Chrysippus (c. 280–206 BC, Stoic philosopher at Athens), 66

Cicero, M. Tullius (106–43 BC), 39f, 58, 119, 124f, 194, 216

Claudius Caecus, Appius (censor 312 BC), 26, 28, 31, 55

Cleanthes of Assos (c. 330–230 BC, Greek Stoic), 66

Cleopatra, 111

Clodius Pulcher, P. (late-Republican popularis), 133

Columella, Lucius Iunius Moderatus (1st century AD), 192

Commodus (sole emperor ad 180–92), 247, 250, 276 n 27

Constantine I (emperor, AD 306–337), 22, 200, 237, 244, 248, 252

Constantius I Chlorus (Caesar, AD 293–306), 140

Cornutus, L. Annaeus (1st century AD, grammarian), 124

Damasus I (episkopos of Rome AD 366–84), 244

Democritus (c. 460–370 BC, Greek atomist philosopher), 65

Diagoras of Melos (late 5th century BC, poet and 'atheist'), 164

Diocletian, C. Aurelius Valerius Diocletianus (emperor AD 284–305), 140, 248 (see also Tetrarchs)

Diogenes (Cynic), 281 n 17

Dionysius of Halicarnassus (c. 60 BC–AD 7, Greek writer in Rome), 43, 232

Domitian (emperor AD 81–96), 244, 245, 247, 250, 252, 265 n 12

Ennius (239–169 BC, Latin poet), 58, 123, 269 n 9

Valentinus (mid-2nd century AD, Christian theologian in Rome), 118, 242
Valerius Soranus, L. (c. 130–82 BC, antiquarian), 133
Varro, M. Terentius (116–27 BC), 59f, 69, 79, 119–22, 125, 132, 251f, 270 n 32
Vergil (70–19 BC), 132, 252
Verrius Flaccus, M. (1st century BC/AD, Latin antiquarian), 109, 133, 184, 286

Vespasian (emperor, AD 69–79), 163, 230, 245, 247, 250, 273 n 19
Vitellius (failed emperor, AD 69), 273 n 19
Vitruvius Pollio, M. (late 1st cent. architect), 70, 100, 177, 286 n 32

Zacchaeus (Christian interlocutor), 243
Zeno of Citium (c. 333–262 BC, founder of Stoicism), 66

SHERLOCK HOLMES
MYSTERY MAGAZINE

VOL. 6, NO. 5   Issue #20

FEATURES

NON FICTION

FICTION

CLASSIC REPRINT

ART & CARTOONS

Publisher: John Betancourt
Editor: Marvin Kaye
Non-fiction Editor: Carla Coupe
Assistant Editor: Steve Coupe

Sherlock Holmes Mystery Magazine is published by Wildside Press, LLC. Single copies: $10.00 + $3.00 postage. U.S. subscriptions: $59.95 (postage paid) for the next 6 issues in the U.S.A., from: Wildside Press LLC, Subscription Dept. 9710 Traville Gateway Dr., #234; Rockville MD 20850. International subscriptions: see our web site at www.wildsidepress.com. Available as an ebook through all major ebook etailers, or our web site, www.wildsidepress.com.